The Culture of Love

Victorians to Moderns

Stephen Kern

HARVARD UNIVERSITY PRESS
Cambridge, Massachusetts
London, England

First Harvard University Press paperback edition, 1994

Library of Congress Cataloging-in-Publication Data

Kern, Stephen.
  The culture of love: Victorians to moderns / Stephen Kern.
    p.   cm.
  Includes bibliographical references and index.
  ISBN 0–674–17958–7 (cloth)
  ISBN 0–674–17959–5 (pbk.)
  1. Love in literature. 2. Love in art. 3. Literature,
  Modern—19th century—History and criticism. 4. Literature,
  Modern—20th century—History and criticism. I. Title.
PN56.L6K47 1992
809.3'9354—dc20
92–1391
CIP

To Mary

Acknowledgments

Research for this book was assisted by a National Endowment for the Humanities Summer Stipend (1988) and a Northern Illinois University Presidential Research Professorship (1988–1992).

My first acknowledgment is long overdue, because Robert Brenner has been talking about history with me since we first met in a high school history class almost thirty-five years ago. I am particularly grateful for his sharp reading of the theoretical issues I address in the Introduction. Early on Levi Smith evaluated my selection of paintings and then critiqued my final interpretation, as did Maria Makela, who generously shared her expertise on the modern period. Susan Casteras helped with the maddening job of finding archival photographs, and her reading of my interpretation of Victorian and modern art was indispensable. Frank Court read most expertly the pages on literature, Paul Heyer made some crucial corrections, and John Toews asked the right question at the right time. Thanks once again to Rudolph Binion for his many substantive tips and exacting marginalia. Michael Gelven made a special effort to come across disciplinary dividers and help me adapt Heidegger's philosophy for the theoretical foundation of this study. Sean Shesgreen looked at hundreds of slides with me, suggested numerous interpretations of them, and read a first draft of each chapter. My work has benefited enormously from the breadth of his knowledge and the depth of his friendship.

Although this book ends in 1934, it is, of course, also based on the way I understand love to this day. That understanding has been enriched immeasurably by my wife, Mary Damer, who took a happy interest in this work from the beginning, which coincided with our meeting a decade ago. She has been a sounding board for my thinking since then and read the final draft with intelligence and good sense. Sharing a marriage and the birth of two children with her has been an endless discovery of love. My words here are brief, because no full expression of my gratitude would be appropriate in a formal dedication. Suffice it to say, her influence is on every page.

Contents

THE CULTURE OF LOVE

Introduction

ONE OF LIFE'S deepest mysteries and most powerful emotions has remained one of the darkest corners of history. Most historians dismiss love as an irrational distraction from rational behavior or an interruption in the course of important events that makes one bow out of history, as when a king abdicated for the woman he loved. Virginia Woolf's complaint about the critic applies equally to the historian: "This is an important book, the critic assumes, because it deals with war. This is an insignificant book, because it deals with the feelings of women in a drawing room." [1] My book underscores her objection and redresses historians' preference for noisy public events over the private stirrings of emotion. It is an attempt at writing a convincing history of love as well as a call to reconsider what really matters. Its argument draws from an improbable theoretical pairing—Woolf's argument on behalf of women writers and Heidegger's philosophy of human existence—for I will argue that between the Victorian and the modern periods love became more authentic as men and women came to reflect more profoundly about what it means *to be* in love.

This introduction deals with four aspects of my approach—periodization, sources, thematization, and interpretation.

At first I intended to identify what was distinctive about love in the early twentieth century, but it soon became clear that for this purpose I ought to contrast that period with the preceding one. I settled on a span of eighty-seven years, with 1847–1880 the starting period, 1880–1900 the transitional period, and 1900–1934 the final period. Often I refer to the years up to 1900 as "Victorian" and those after as "modern," but these terms are used solely for periodization. "Victorian" is not intended to suggest England, a queen, or any particular sexual morality. "Modern" is also merely a period marker. For the beginning and ending years of my study I use the publication dates of novels in order to emphasize the evidence upon which it is based. The word "culture" in my title does not refer to an aspect of experience but to my sources: philosophy, literature, and art. That selection raises questions about other kinds of sources not used, about my reliance on the literary canon, and about the evidentiary value of my sources.

I originally intended to use a broader variety of sources, but I came to see that an interpretation of change based on a novel for the Victorians and an exchange of love letters or a questionnaire survey for the moderns, for example, would lose persuasiveness from the different kind of sources. To sharpen the distinctively historical differences between Victorian and modern ways of loving I therefore used the same kind of source for each contrast between them.

The decision to limit sources was not merely to sharpen contrasts; it was also made because novels offered the most direct source for past ways of loving. More than poetry or drama, novels render the social world and historical context of the relationships that sustain their plots. As a rule, love letters are more fragmentary and tend to contain more censorship, embellishment, fantasy, and clichés than do novels. There are similar problems with most autobiographies and diaries. Advice books are repetitive and mired in formulaic morality or religious rhetoric. Philosophy analyzes and interprets love in the abstract, and I used it primarily to define basic elements and suggest ways of interpreting.

After reading novels of greater and lesser reputation, I concluded that the classics are the preferred source.[2] First, their canonical status means that readers are more likely to have read them, which reduces the confusion that occurs when small parts are excerpted from the story, as my detailed thematic approach entails. Love in classics also tends to be more profound, nuanced, and complex than it is in lesser novels. Classics often have the greater historical impact on subsequent writers and critics as well as the wider reading public, since they are frequently valorized in their own time and thereafter. In those cases they are more historically representative than popular novels.

Classics survive the oblivion that buries popular novels precisely because they capture the actual sights and sounds of an age. Their descriptions enable us to see lovers in years past, and their dialogues enable us to hear them. Their plots and characters may be made up, but that creativity allows perceptive authors to come closer to the truth, not stray from it. *Jane Eyre,* for example, is indeed a subjective response to life in a small English town in the

1830s and 1840s, but it also presents the actual circumstances of that time. Brontë did not dream up boarding schools, governesses, primogeniture, inheritance, marriage proposals, dowries, dueling, postal service, missionary service, fortune-tellers, or fear of "fog-bred pestilence." These features of her world shaped the ways of love in her time and made up the setting for her novel, and I have therefore concluded that the novel is representative of her time.

Using art along with literature created some special problems. Art critics object to the way historians sometimes first work out an argument and then look for visual material to go with it. Sympathetic with the art critics' insistence that art be used as evidence rather than as illustration, for some time I tried to maintain for art an equal role in the thematization of basic elements. But for a number of reasons I was obliged to rely on novels for that crucial analysis. The most pressing reason was that the history of love is embodied in stories that take place in time and hence are the more fully rendered in novels. In the art all across my period there is no single painting, no series of paintings, that offers as vivid and detailed a record of loving as do novels in which we can hear and see complex modes of loving.

Nevertheless, art proved to be an invaluable source. A pair of paintings on the same theme from different periods offers a vivid and concise image of change. To be sure, many factors caused the differences between any single pair of paintings other than the simple passage of time, but the pair reveals something about that passage. And while no single pair of contrasts by itself makes a convincing historical argument, the accumulation of such contrasts does.

The abundance and richness of my evidence and the complexity of my main theme created special analytical difficulties. The crucial importance of thematization can be indicated by considering some problems that result when it is not carried out rigorously. In a two-volume history of Victorian love, Peter Gay offers a bewildering array of themes. The chapter titles of both volumes include a class, a doctrine, a lesson, a legacy, a struggle, a book title, a painting title, a neurosis, metaphors, puns, quotations, and dual biographical sketches. This all makes up a richly documented but thematically disjointed cultural history. Irving Singer traces massive themes such as "courtly love" and "romantic love" through their transformations in the philosophy and literature of Western civilization, focusing on major figures one after the other and generating vast interpretive coagulations for each that defy precise subthematization and hence make sharp historical arguments impossible. Other writers abandon thematic analysis altogether and offer dual biographies of famous couples. Phyllis Rose suggests that the "parallel lives" of five Victorian marriages reveal a "paradigm" at the heart of Victorian love.[3]

My own search for fundamental elements alternated between reading philosophy for systematic typologies and immersing myself in the empirical data of novels and paintings. I had no *a priori* master list of elements—there is no such list. I began with a provisional list adapted from Sartre's analysis of love in *Being and Nothingness:* the gaze, desire, expansion of self, caress, opening of self, fusion, possession, withdrawal, and reconstitution of self. Reading novels suggested other elements and new terms for interpreting them, and so I returned to philosophy to sharpen my understanding of their fundamental nature. My final list of elements came from repeated alternations between philosophy, literature, and art.

I tried to find elements that were fundamental, comprehensive, mutually exclusive, and ordered according to a compelling sequence, but the complexity of love made satisfaction of those criteria impossible. My final list includes elements that ground all loves fundamentally, such as encounter, desire, and power, as well as elements that occur only in particular loves contingently, such as kissing, wedding, and marriage. Although the elements treat numerous aspects of love, they are neither comprehensive nor mutually exclusive. The ordering is also a compromise. I tried to follow a "typical" love scenario beginning with waiting and meeting, followed by language and disclosure, then elements that concern the way lovers are influenced by others, elements that are formally regulated by custom such as the proposal, wedding, and marriage, and finally the ways love ends. The physical aspect is interspersed throughout this sequence in chapters on embodiment, desire, kissing, gender, and sex. Chapters on encounter, power, and selfhood could go almost anywhere, and I have positioned them where they clarify what precedes or follows. Thus my Table of Contents contains elements of differing degrees of fundamentality, comprehensiveness, mutual exclusivity, and sequential specificity.

My interpretation also changed. At first I intended to interpret changing modes of loving for each element without trying to make them conform to a single interpretation. I was determined to do justice to the richness of the sources, but that richness got out of hand. As the elements and their changing modes proliferated, I was obliged to find a way of unifying their meaning so as to make this history comprehensible. I found such an approach in phenomenology, especially in Heidegger's *Being and Time* (1927), which, for all its jarring terminology, suggested a way of unifying my interpretation.

To investigate the meaning of human existence, which Heidegger calls *Dasein*,[4] he focuses on the ways we exist, which he calls "existentials." Examples of these include being-in-the-world, being-with, talk, care, guilt, and death. Each existential is either authentic or inauthentic; that is, in each way that we exist we can either reveal to ourselves what it means to be in that way or conceal from ourselves what it means to be in that way. He generally begins with the way the existentials are lived inauthentically, without reflecting on their meaning. We normally do that when we are interested in something or excited or ready for pleasure. When we begin to think about the meaning of existing we become more authentic *(eigentlich)*. Existence is always located along a gradation between these two fundamental ways of being.

Just as Heidegger interpreted the existentials of Dasein according to his authentic-inauthentic distinction, so have I interpreted the elements of loving according to the same distinction, suitably modified for my historical argument. Heidegger stresses that he is using these terms in a "strict sense." That strictness refers to the German root, *eigen*, which means "own." In popular usage *eigentlich* means real, essential, or intrinsic, but these meanings obscure its root. A similar set of meanings define its standard English translation, which is "authentic." Heidegger's strict use of *eigentlich* calls attention to the sense of "ownness" underlying these meanings, and he urges his readers to keep that restoration in mind throughout his study. I make the same request for my use of "authentic." Compared with the Victorians, the moderns reflected more about the meaning of their experience of each of the elements, and therefore experienced them more authentically, more as their very own.

One example of this change concerns the meaning of choice. An important condition for authentic existence is that we understand possibility—that is, who we are in terms of what we can be. The history of choosing in love, which comes to an especially dramatic focus when the woman responds to a marriage proposal, reveals movement toward greater reflection on the meaning of possibility. While Victorian women were limited to "yes" or "no," or mere *consent,* some modern women could exercise more genuine *choice.* In theory, both groups were equally capable of (authentically) becoming aware of their response as their own or of (inauthentically) allowing it to be made in accord with what "they" (people in general) do. But in practice, changing circumstances made it easier for modern women to come to understand and question their limited possibilities.

Heidegger is careful to emphasize how human existence is always poised between accepting life as governed by external circumstances over which we have no control, and the possibility of acting resolutely in the face of those circumstances. His philosophy is incompatible with the notion that any fundamental aspect of human existence such as choice could become more authentic in history. My study shows why the emphasis on fundamentality must be relaxed in order to write a history of love, which I interpret as moving in the direction of greater authenticity as modern men and women become increasingly able to think about and experience the meaning of these new possibilities. For even though their authenticity was facilitated by changes that came about through no effort of their own, these changing circumstances enabled modern lovers, more than Victorian lovers, to act resolutely in the face of circumstance, reflect on the meaning of their love, and hence make it more their own.

One problem with this approach is the ethic that it seems to imply. Heidegger repeatedly denied that the authentic-inauthentic distinction was ethical. His warnings are necessary because the distinction does sound like an ethical distinction, since in everyday speech it is better to be authentic than inauthentic. He insisted, however, that the crucial reason for introducing his distinction was to provide a way of interpreting the meaning of existence, not to inform his readers how to behave. Whether he entirely succeeded is debatable. Many sympathetic commentators have found it impossible to follow Heidegger in this aspect of his philosophy and have seen this distinction as entailing ethical implications. Hans-Georg Gadamer recalled how, in a lecture he attended in the 1920s, "the pointedness of [Heidegger's] invective made it appear simply incredible when [he] described the world of the 'they' and 'idle chatter' with bitter acrimony and then added, 'this is intended without any negative meaning.' The existential seriousness that characterized Heidegger in his lectures seemed to suggest that the rejection of inauthenticity and the embracing of authenticity was the meaning of his doctrine." [5]

As I began the research for this book I thought I would be able to interpret differences between the Victorians and the moderns, element by element, without any unifying interpretation and certainly without any ethical judgments. But the need for interpretive unity became apparent as the differences proliferated; and as I wrote, my determination to avoid ethical judgment gave way, for I realized that I had been consistently judging the Victorians as deficient compared with the moderns, even though I had tried to restrain such judgment. The simple act of focusing on degrees of authenticity attaches value to reflecting on the meaning of existence. I realized that I was using Heidegger not to eliminate all ethical evaluation, which is impossible, but to keep it clearly defined and under control.

This altering of Heidegger's purpose is partly a consequence of trying to use philosophy to ground history. Philosophers carefully select their simple examples and aim at universal truths; historians are confronted with masses of disparate data and aim to understand change. The difference between these undertakings creates a strain when one tries to combine them in practice. That strain forced my compromise with Heidegger's philosophy, but it also helped keep my study from lapsing into an abstract philosophical tract without any evidentiary flesh and blood or into a meandering historical essay without any rigorous thematic spine.

Although I abandoned Heidegger's commitment to ethical neutrality, I adapted his method for several reasons. His existentials provide a compelling example of a framework for analyzing the elements of love. His authentic-inauthentic distinction bases interpretation of those elements on what is most fundamental—being aware of what it means to be a human being. That distinction, since it applies to all the existentials, suggested a way of solving the problem of unifying my varying interpretations of the ever-increasing elements of love. Although I have allowed myself more ethical evaluation than is consistent with a close reading of his philosophy, I have followed him and other twentieth-century phenomenologists in shifting the grounds for my interpretation from ethics (the foundation for Victorian philosophizing about human relatedness) to phenomenology. Finally, his approach to thinking about human existence profoundly influenced a generation of intellectuals, including Sartre, Merleau-Ponty, and Simone de Beauvoir, whose philosophies also contributed to my theoretical framework.

I treat the novels which are my sources primarily as a reflection of what was happening at the time when they were being written, although on occasion I emphasize the authors' interpretive distance from their characters' ways of loving. For example, in *Madame Bovary* Flaubert was acutely aware of the problem of communication, which he shared with his reader in his narration. That awareness is not entirely shared by his characters. Rodolphe frets over the tediousness of Emma's clichés but is not as troubled by them as was Flaubert. In showing his Victorian readers the deficiencies of language Flaubert was thus more modern than the characters in his novel. That modernist insight, however, does not undermine my argument or periodization. It merely shows that Flaubert was in that respect ahead of his time. There is a logic to the history of love, but not all authors experienced it or recreated it at the same historical moment.

My study is an interpretation of change—not an explanation. I treat a span of time when developments in biology, sexual theory, gynecology, obstetrics, medicine, psychiatry, education, labor, law, feminism, transportation, communication, warfare, politics, and religion made possible new modes of loving. Although I briefly survey such causal factors where they pertain to my interpretation, I do not attempt to explain systematically how they may have influenced particular novelists or artists or the actual historical circumstances that their novels or paintings were intended to portray.

The historical specificity of my argument is threatened by other factors that no doubt shaped the works I draw on as evidence; for these novelists and artists were also influenced by regional customs, class circumstances, gender roles, prevailing artistic conventions, and their personal experiences. This last influence was an especially tempting avenue of research but one fraught with difficulties. Consider, for example, the interpretive problems I would create by exploring the biographical sources for *Jane Eyre*. Personal experience undoubtedly shaped Charlotte Brontë's writing, especially an erotic tie to her brother Branwell, with whom she co-authored stories about an imaginary kingdom, ruled by a dashing Byronic hero. There is evidence that Branwell was recast into Rochester, the hero of the novel, and her feelings for Branwell clearly shaped the love between Jane and Rochester. Were I to explicate such influences of life on work for all my sources, I would also have to treat the influence of Flaubert's mistress, Proust's chauffeur, Meredith's dead wife, Musil's dead sister, and Hemingway's wartime nurse. Among artists there is the influence of Magritte's suicidal mother, Schiele's mistress-model, and several of Picasso's wives. I would also have to assess the influence of Virginia Woolf's possible sexual molestation as a child as well as D. H. Lawrence's sexual impotence in early middle age. Such influences make fascinating challenges for biographers who have the time and the page space to do justice to them, but the cultural historian pursuing broad generalizations does not. Personal experiences (along with regional, class, gender and artistic influences) no doubt shaped all my sources, but I believe that it is possible to control for them in determining the distinctively historical significance of these works by finding shared attitudes among a large enough number of writers and artists in a single historical period so that they can be factored out. I do occasionally include biographical facts to enliven my text, but not as evidence for a systematic argument.

Victorian love was more patient, more polite, more self-sacrificing, and more Christian than modern love. It conformed more to parental influence and was structured more in deference to public rituals. It may have been more explosive, but it was not as authentic as modern love, and that is my argument.

In addition to this substantive argument, I also make a formal argument about love in novels and works of art. A distinctive feature of modernism was the increasing effort to render the creative process itself. This development is evident in modern painting and sculpture and is highlighted in the writings of Rilke, Proust, Gide, Ford, Joyce, and Woolf, all of whom strove to make their art more their very own.[6] Across this period there was thus a formal transformation from rendering love *in* art to rendering love *as* art. Because this involved a more careful reflection on the meaning of the creative process, I interpret it as moving in the direction of authenticity.

1 Waiting

ONE OF THE most important contributions of phenomenology to twentieth-century thought was its exploration of the way people actually experience time, in contrast to the way it is objectively divided into parts and precisely measured by clocks. By 1927 Heidegger established that lived time or "temporality" is the foundation of human existence, hence his arresting title, *Being and Time*. Among the three major temporal orientations—past, present, and future—Heidegger emphasized the importance of the last because it includes the forward, purposeful dynamic of what we will be as well as what we are. The future is not merely some happening down the road of time that we will come upon in due course; rather, it is experienced immediately and directly in the present. Although individuals have many possible concrete futures, these are all structured by a fundamental distinction. Inauthentically, we *wait for* a future that will happen to us by force of circumstances over which we have no control. Such a future is not our own. Authentically, we *anticipate* a future resolutely as our own responsibility in the face of circumstance.

As a title for this chapter I have used the term Heidegger uses for inauthentic futurity, because it captures the predominant mode at the start of my history. Around 1850 waiting for love was focused on a supreme "now-or-never" moment when the "one-and-only" would appear and make love happen. Waiting for love to begin was particularly characteristic of women, but men also experienced future love as something that would come at them, however commanding their role upon first meetings.

Although Jessica Hayllar's *A Coming Event* (Figure 1, 1886) depicts a couple who have already met and are awaiting a wedding, it is an icon of passive waiting, for at that time a wedding was the ultimate goal of waiting for love. The importance of that goal is indicated by the position, size, detail,

1. Jessica Hayllar, *A Coming Event*, 1886.

and elegance of the wedding paraphernalia. The gown spills over the chair the way it will overwhelm the body of the bride to be, who will not so much march resolutely as teeter down the aisle under its weight. The whiteness of her dress, flowers, shoes, and fan symbolize her innocence and hence inability to shape the coming events. On the chair is a fan, a courtship prop for flirting while waiting for a man to act. The seated woman and standing man, barely visible in the second room (literally an aside), are subordinate in volume, centrality, perspective, and hence importance. They are positioned between the overpowering foreground and the barely visible woman in the center background, who is either the matchmaker, permission granter, or witness to their union. As the representative of tradition, she stands like a sentinel observing the result of her efforts which, in this highly regulated society, are about to be fulfilled according to a logic as rigorous as the perspective that radiates from her and structures this still-life of the couple's immediate future. Time is calendric and public. It is determined by a preordained scenario that dictates a transfer of power over the woman from one man to another and runs straight through events like the gaze of the background figure, down the center line of the carpet to the viewer. Although the painting emphasizes the woman's lack of control, the man as well as the woman is swept up by the coming event.

The value of protracted waiting is satirized in Charles Dickens's *Great Expectations* (1861) with the character of Miss Havisham, that macabre caricature of the Victorian bride-to-be. Jilted on her wedding day, Miss Havisham secluded herself in her home for twenty-five years, while raising beautiful Estella to jilt men and take revenge on them. During that time Miss Havisham's virginal white dress turned yellow. "The bride within the bridal dress had withered like the dress, and like the flowers, and had no brightness left but the brightness of her sunken eyes" (87). As a bitter parody of the bride-to-be she shows how passive, helpless waiting can turn passionate love into venomous hate. Dickens's portrayal and Hayllar's image belong to the same era when protracted waiting for love withered the processes of self-reflection that living toward the future makes possible.

Contrasting paintings from 1856 and 1912 reveal change toward a more authentic futurity for women, especially prior to meeting a lover. In Abraham Solomon's *Doubtful Fortune* (Figure 2, 1856) the woman hanging on the shoulder of a friend is the antithesis of resoluteness. She leans on her friend for support, relies on the cards and the fortune-teller for hope, and depends on the long-awaited man for her destiny as a human being, if only he will show up. Passivity and activity are further signified by the hands. The nervous supplicant entwines her fingers with those of her friend in contrast to the practiced hands of the fortune-teller that deviously manipulate her client's future in the cards. The supplicant is seeking happiness through love, symbolized by the vine that connects the carved bluebird (happiness) and the cupid statue (love) under the table. She does not actively anticipate

2. Abraham Solomon, *Doubtful Fortune,* 1856.

but passively awaits, and her passivity implies futility: the fortune-teller, with sinister pleasure, is pointing to a joker.

Suzanne Valadon's *The Future Unveiled* (Figure 3, 1912) treats a similar theme differently. Solomon's passive and tightly corseted innocent is here replaced by a daring full-body nude.[1] In contrast to Solomon's monument of dependency, Valadon shows a powerful recumbent woman, full of self-confidence, propped up on a squared elbow, with both hands in soothing composure. Her body is solidly flexed or gracefully relaxed where it needs to be. Valadon repudiates the passivity of centuries of female eroticism, which is suggested here not for titillation but to emphasize the rich erotic potential of a woman in and for herself. In addition to unveiling the woman's future, she also unveils her body. Although this is not a self-portrait, the

3. Suzanne Valadon, *The Future Unveiled*, 1912.

artist did nude self-portraits around this time, and in this painting there is a sense of the artist revealing herself through her model.[2]

Valadon's fortune-telling is for amusement, not for divining the future. Whereas Solomon's woman looks heavenward in breathless expectation, Valadon's woman, in a more secular age, looks down calmly and reads her own fortune along with the fortune-teller. The card in the fortune-teller's hand is a Queen of Diamonds, signifying a woman of power and value. The four Kings have been "dropped" and lie flat on their backs, passively awaiting the play of the active Queen, looking up at her in supine helplessness.

Valadon shows us anticipatory resoluteness in the model's physical strength, self-reliance, camaraderie, and love, which if it comes will be enlivened with a flowing eroticism suggested by her calm nude pose and cascading red hair. She hears her fortune with an air of queenly serenity rather than helpless passivity: hers is a bemused inquiry. She is vulnerable like any nude, but she is clearly in control. Her future may include love but is not exclusively focused on it.

Authentic futurity also involves a reappropriation of the past as one's own, continuously projected ahead. Valadon's most important unveiling was that of her art. She was also the mother of Maurice Utrillo (b.1883) and taught him to paint. But even without this information, we can see that she is a woman with a past that is her own, manifest in her talent. Valadon seized her past, present, and future by taking up the brush. In contrast, the past of Solomon's woman has been consumed by anxious expectation of a dubious goal for which she is unprepared.

The preparation for love of nineteenth-century men is a myth. Their carousing cultivated few skills for mature loving. In *Jane Eyre* (1847) Rochester boasted to Jane: "I have battled through a varied experience with many men of many nations and roamed over half the globe, while you have lived quietly with one set of people in one house" (165). Actually he had had a disastrous affair in Paris that landed him with a child whom he hires Jane to educate, and he caroused about the Caribbean only to be bamboozled into marrying an insane woman he knew nothing about. In *Middlemarch* (1872) Will Ladislaw had a "thirst for travelling" (54) but was no more worldly than Dorothea for all his travels.

Victorian art reveals the limits of women's preparation for anything but love. In the popular fairy tale "The Sleeping Beauty," the Princess waits for one hundred years in a death trance until revived by Prince Charming's kiss. A trifle less passive are the sleeping women depicted all over Victorian art—under trees, at the edge of lakes, and on hammocks, beds, sofas, benches, and grass.[3] John Fitzgerald envisioned sleeping women surrounded by goblins in various wish-fulfilling activities. In *The Captive Dreamer* (1856) they are being rescued by a knight. In *The Stuff That Dreams Are Made of* (1850s) aspects of courtship are acted out by diminutive weirdos such as the masturbatory cellist, avidly bowing just below the dreamer's hand. In the misty background a man and a woman, symbolizing the ultimate goal, stand intently face to face.[4]

Women also daydream. Frederick Burton's *Dreams* (1861) shows a prepubescent girl lounging in melancholy contemplation of a sprig of pink flowers. Her sexuality is suspended in passive waiting as suggested by the color of the flowers between virgin-white and passion-red. In Lord Leighton's *The Garden of the Hesperides* (1892) one woman sleepily fingers a bowl, a second is too groggy to pluck her harp, while a third strokes a monstrous python coiled snugly around her abdomen and up into the apple tree under which they lie. Hercules' eleventh labor was to save all three from a dragon, but they seem to be content in their somnolent captivity, unconcerned about rescue. The implied message is that these women have waited so long in idle helplessness that this has become their defining activity.

John Millais arranged eight girls in various postures of waiting across his *Spring* (1859). Like the apple blossoms that fill the trees under which they picnic, these girls are just beginning to be. Three are minimally active preparing porridge. Another sits next to a basket of flowers, dreamily fingering her waist-length hair. The other four are in stages of decline: two sit, another props her head in hand, and on the far right one fully reclining girl on her back, with a stem in her mouth, regards the viewer coyly. Behind her a scythe is stuck in the ground as a deadly portent of the future of their waiting.[5]

John Ruskin's essay "Of Queens' Gardens" (1865) defined the proper location of women as in the home, a domestic substitute for the earlier place of peace (the enclosed garden or *hortus conclusus* of the medieval Virgin) protected from the active and actual world of men. J. Atkinson Grimshaw's painting *The Rector's Garden: Queen of the Lilies* (1887) depicts the essentials of this typical nineteenth-century theme. Standing in a walled garden full of multi-colored flowers a woman in a laced white dress grasps a stalk of virginal white lilies. She is but one more flower waiting to be plucked. At the center of the garden is a ring of passional red flowers, symbolizing her own protected sexuality. Leading to this prized inner circle is a path just wide enough for one man. The garden's massive wall is covered with ivy—a long-growing, tenacious, and tangled protective cover. Her passive orientation toward the future is symbolized by a minute door in the wall, because the door's small size, the surrounding ivy, and its remoteness from her reduce the odds of any man finding it or her.[6]

The high walls of these gardens prevented men from seeing in, but, more important, they prevented women from seeing and going outside into their own future. We first encounter Jane Eyre at a window seat, looking out. Later at Lowood School, Jane tells us that "the garden was a wide enclosure, surrounded with walls so high as to exclude every glimpse of prospect" (80). Her dramatic breakthroughs all involve seeing or traveling beyond barriers. Victorian artists portrayed many women looking out of windows or down from balconies upon the active world of men.[7]

Even outside or downstairs women engage in varieties of passive waiting. In Edward Poynter's *Water Babies* (1900) naked maidens splash in a fountain, open to the sky but placed inside a Roman villa. Outside, generally in some enclosed garden, women pick flowers for nosegays; those who have already met a man wistfully fondle some forget-me-nots. Others are shown with pets, generally dogs, which symbolize fidelity or hope (for love in a far future). In Walter Deverell's *A Pet* (1853) there is some ambiguity about just who is the pet—the woman or the caged bird—since both are enclosed in a walled garden.

Needlework is a busy form of passivity. It took about thirty minutes to trace, embroider, and cut a single one of the hundreds of eyelets in a petticoat, which might have taken two months to complete. From around the age of twelve, young girls occupied their hands with embroidery and crochet, filling up their futures materially (literally) with hope chests containing napkins, towels, sheets, quilts, table cloths, runners, doily antimacassars, drawers, chemises, nightgowns, corset-covers, and petticoats.[8] Many women were read to by their fathers. Women shown reading to themselves were only marginally more active, and the texts were presumed to inspire religious devotion, good morals, or correct etiquette, all in the service of self-control. An occasional novel, invariably a wicked "French novel," signified amatory crisis and its inevitable consequence of family breakdown. Some women are shown playing an instrument, but their talent was for performance and was worn like a bauble to play up to men and instruct or amuse children.[9]

Endlessly waiting women in voluptuous preparations were depicted in Roman baths or Middle Eastern marriage markets, slave auctions, and harems. These exotics, shown as if far away and long ago, were removed from real contexts and hence from the possibility of real activity. In Ingres's *Turkish Bath* (1856) a roomful of women are being fed, perfumed, and massaged in preparation to service a man. The women bathing between puffs on a hookah in Gérôme's *The Grand Bath at Bursa* (1885), those who are being auctioned off in Edwin Long's *The Babylonian Marriage Market* (1875), and those wearing Dionysian regalia after a wild celebration in Alma-Tadema's *The Women of Amphissa* (1880) are also having their sex expropriated. These paintings deny the productive function of sex in love, marriage, or child bearing. They emphasize rather circumstances in which women's sexuality is not their own. Even the odalisques of nineteenth-century art have an innocence linking them to the virgins with whom they share a life of inauthentic waiting.

This brief sketch of the iconography of waiting has drawn from popular and illustrative art, which, though not formally daring, was nevertheless skillfully produced, prominently displayed, and reflective of current values. Novels also explored the inner realities and consequences of years of passive waiting.

The poignancy of Jane Eyre's girlhood came from the oppressive limitations that set up her ultimate release in love.[10] In *Madame Bovary* (1857) Emma believed that love was "something that comes suddenly, like a blinding flash of lightning—a heaven-sent story hurled into life, uprooting it, sweeping every will before it like a leaf" (114). In *Daniel Deronda* (1876), Gwendolen sensed the need to make a life of her own before and after marriage, but did not know how to go about it. "Her horizon was that of the genteel romance where the heroine's soul poured out in her journal is full of vague power, originality, and general rebellion, while her life moves strictly in the sphere of fashion." She did not wish "to lead the same sort of life as ordinary young ladies," but did not know "how she should set about leading any other" (83). Projects of anticipatory resoluteness were beyond Gwendolen's reach, because a horizon of steamy fantasy had left her ill-equipped to resist Grandcourt's courtship and get on with a life of her own.

Although most of the art and literature of waiting focuses on women, it must not be assumed that men drew authentic capital from women's passivity, because authenticity is incompatible with either side of passivity or oppression. As the novels clearly show, men were also swept up by the public expectations that governed the courtship scenario. They may have acted outside the confines of garden and home, but these conventions worked on them with equal force.

In *Les Misérables* (1862), Victor Hugo celebrates the climactic goal of waiting for love: "Cosette in her solitude, like Marius in his, was ready to be set alight. Fate, with its mysterious and inexorable patience, was slowly bringing together these two beings charged, like thunder-clouds, with electricity, with the latent forces of passion, and destined to meet and mingle in a look as clouds do in a lightning-flash" (773). This conventional metaphor evokes the couple's passive waiting: there is isolation of each from the other during stretches of inactive waiting, polar attraction of gender opposites, a climactic meeting caused by powerful external agents, and the inexorable governance of fate. Their intense climactic love at first sight is a consequence of protracted waiting and lack of communication. They have never spoken and for six months have not seen one another. Hugo concedes that meeting with the eyes alone was already deemed passé, but he still celebrates its value. "We scarcely dare say in these days that two persons fell in love because their eyes met. Yet this is how one falls in love and in no other way" (773). As the story proceeds, Cosette and Marius will need the mediation of Jean Valjean both to protect them from others and to enable them to communicate. They are both passive, ready "to be set alight," because they do not know how to talk to one another.

By the twentieth century novelists disparage waiting for affirmation by others. Before breaking away, the heroine of Wells's *Ann Veronica* (1909) rages against her limited activities—calls, tennis, walks, selected novels, and dusting her father's house. She tells her father that she wants "to learn about things and know about things, and not to be protected as something too precious for life, cooped up in one narrow little corner." Her father's rejoinder—"Cooped up! ... You've got a bicycle!"—separates two eras, two views of the value of time and productive activity (30). Ann wants to go into the future resolutely. In that same spirit Vera Brittain recalled how after reading Olive Schriner's manifesto *Woman and Labour* (1911), she and other women felt that "there is no closed door we do not intend to force open; and there is no fruit in the garden of knowledge it is not our determination to eat." [11]

The three men who land in Charlotte Gilman's utopian *Herland* (1915) are astonished to find there women who have not spent their lives waiting for love, because there are no men. The pressure tactics that work on less experienced women back home do not work in Herland, as the sympathetic narrator explains. "You see, if a man loves a girl who is in the first place young and inexperienced; who in the second place is educated with a background of caveman tradition, a middle-ground of poetry and romance, and a foreground of unspoken hope and interest all centering upon the one Event; and who has, furthermore, absolutely no other hope or interest worthy of the name—why, it is a comparatively easy matter to sweep her off her feet" (93). The women of Herland are not sweepable. Gilman rejects circumstances such as the one depicted in Hayllar's *A Coming Event*, which does show precisely "a foreground of unspoken hope and interest all centering upon one Event." Gilman envisions a world in which there is no iconic wedding gown and no climactic love "Event" with a capital "E" to center women's lives.

Proust treats the painful anticipation of love as a suffering which inspires art. His narrator Marcel spends two summers in the heat of Combray "sick with longing" for an imaginary "woman who would enrich [him] with her love" (I, 92). But such waiting for love makes him abjectly dependent. It is also futile. Love may come along in the future but can only be experienced as a past recaptured. Marcel's anticipation becomes productive but not of its intended object, for it yields art instead of love when he crafts that experience of longing into a novel.

In Joyce's *Ulysses* (1922) Gerty MacDowell is "waiting, always waiting to be asked." She dreams about a "manly man" who will "take her in his sheltering arms, strain her to him in all the strength of his nature and comfort her with a long long kiss" (351). Her love fantasies come from contemporary sources of inauthentic love—wedding liturgy, pulp magazines, movies, and local gossip. Her fantasies are like Emma Bovary's and, were it not for Gerty's modern function in *Ulysses,* would not document historical change. But sitting on the rocks at the shore Gerty snaps out of her fantasizing about her manly man when she notices unmanly Leopold Bloom staring at her avidly. She then raises her dress to help him masturbate—an unthinkable act for any nineteenth-century heroine. Joyce shows us her active cooperation with a loving gesture that would have scandalized the most freethinking nineteenth-century critic. This historically unique cooperation is a creative act that reworks the significance of her passive waiting. She has taken charge in a way that is daringly her own.

As a young girl in D. H. Lawrence's *The Rainbow* (1915) Ursula read about Elaine, high in her tower, guarding Launcelot's shield. "How she loved it! How she leaned in her bedroom window with her black, rough hair on her shoulders." She "would remain the lonely maid high up and isolated in the tower, polishing the terrible shield . . . and waiting, waiting, always remote and high" (263). Ursula also resembles Emma Bovary, but she gets down from her imaginary tower and stops waiting. She goes to college, becomes a schoolmistress, and is able to reject one man's proposal on the strength of a distinctively anti-Romantic and anti-Victorian philosophy, for she believes "that love was a way, a means, not an end in itself." And, she tells a woman friend, "I believe there are many men in the world one might love—there is not only one man" (411). The one-and-only must be awaited, but if there are to be two or more, one can go get them.

These shifting emphases are not to be taken as radical disjuncts. The history of waiting is not, of course, a movement from total passivity to resolute activity, from inauthentic expectation to authentic anticipatory resolve. And against any sweeping historical generalization there is always counterevidence. George Eliot understood the ruinous consequences that helpless waiting would have for Gwendolen, and the Gerty MacDowells continued their devotional waiting into the twentieth century. Nevertheless there is a gradual historical shift toward a fuller appreciation of the importance of openness to the future and a realization that, however formidable the obstacles, some part of the future may be made into one's own. In painting and literature the victimizing passivity of waiting for love, especially among women, is identified as an intolerable condition, sometimes the focus of explicit polemic. Valadon positions herself above her own future. The theme of the woman waiting for a tryst, so pervasive in Victorian art, entirely disappears in modern art. Wells preached autonomy through Ann Veronica, Gilman exposed the existential devastation of waiting on one love Event, and Proust salvaged creative resolve from futile and unfulfillable expectations.

The urgent waiting period of the Victorian world expanded in the twentieth century, allowing men and women *more time* to wait for love and a *larger pool* from which to choose.

I

There is no more graphic reminder of the passage of public time than one's age. The novels I read show considerable change in the relative ages of the lovers, especially the women (see the Appendix). For the nineteenth-century group, the mean age of all the women was 19.7 years; for the twentieth-century group, it was 28.6 years. In the nineteenth-century group there was only one female lover over the age of 23, and that was in a novel from 1893 about "odd women." In the twentieth-century group 15 women were over the age of 23. The ages of the men remained similar, averaging around 30 years for the nineteenth-century group and 32 years for the twentieth-century group.

These calculations are of course statistically insignificant but of interest nevertheless. To make these literary relationships believable to readers the ages of the lovers had to be credible. The average increase of nine years for women at the inception of the relationship suggests that in the twentieth century they could wait longer and focus less intensely on the big Event. Twentieth-century women had more educational and professional opportunities which gave them more to do. They also had more latitude about the age of eligibility, so their waiting was less urgent.

II

One consequence of more time for love is an increase in the number of prospective lovers. Numerous historical developments increased that pool:

greater travel and communication opportunities from new technology, more dynamic social life in the cities to which populations moved, increasing access to co-educational and co-professional settings, erosion of class barriers, new recreational possibilities and the leisure time to explore them, relaxation of sexual morality and chaperonage, and the extensive dislocations of World War I.

Around 1850 women in particular faced a short period of eligibility and a small pool of potential lovers. The Brontës were the epitome of an isolated rustic family of mid Victorian England. In the 1850 Introduction to *Wuthering Heights* Charlotte described their world. "Resident in a remote district where education had made little progress, and where, consequently, there was no inducement to seek social intercourse beyond our own domestic circle, we were wholly dependent on ourselves and each other" (30). In a biography of Charlotte, Elizabeth Gaskell explained that the three sons of the neighboring Yorkes family "were almost the only young men [Charlotte] knew intimately, besides her brother." [12] In *Jane Eyre* Charlotte projected that limited experience onto Jane, who explained the reason for her shock upon first meeting Rochester: "I had hardly ever seen a handsome youth; never in my life spoken to one" (145).

The love relationships dramatized by the Brontës and other novelists of that time reveal the limited opportunity of a small love pool. In *Wuthering Heights* (1847) Catherine loves her foster brother Heathcliff and marries a neighbor, Edgar Linton. Heathcliff marries Edgar's sister, Isabella. Cathy II marries Heathcliff's son, her cousin Linton, and after he dies, marries another cousin, Hareton. The romantic hero of George Lewes's *Ranthorpe* (1847) falls in love with a foster sister. In *Villette* (1853) Lucy Snowe's first love is her godmother's son, John Bretton. In Tolstoy's "Family Happiness" (1859) Masha marries her guardian, a neighbor and friend of her father. George Eliot explains that there had been much intermarrying over three generations of Vincys, a typical old manufacturing family in *Middlemarch,* and the close atmosphere of Dorothea's endogamous first marriage to Casaubon is underscored by her second marriage, after Casaubon's death, to his cousin Will.

The pattern continues into the next generation of novels. In Hardy's *A Pair of Blue Eyes* (1873) Elfride falls in love with a cousin by her father's second marriage. The aristocratic families of Levin and Kitty in Tolstoy's *Anna Karenina* (1873) had been intimate for generations. Hardy's Tess, like many country girls of the 1890s, was "unaccustomed to many eyes." Hardy compounds an incestuous love-obsession over three generations in *The Well-*

Beloved (1892) as Pierston falls in love first with Avice Caro, then with Avice's daughter, and finally with her granddaughter. In Fontane's *Effi Briest* (1894) we learn that before proposing to Effi, Innstetten had proposed to Effi's mother twenty years earlier. In Hardy's *Jude the Obscure* (1895) Sue Bridehead is Jude's cousin; the hero of Ward's *Helbeck of Bannisdale* (1898) falls in love with his niece; and the hero of Rostand's *Cyrano de Bergerac* (1898) loves his cousin Roxanne.

In the twentieth century we find men and women gaining access to a larger variety of potential lovers over a longer stretch of time and able to explore serious involvements of considerable importance before meeting their major love interest. Ann Veronica had four relationships prior to Jonathan Capes. In *Howards End* (1910), by way of criticizing how girls "enter on the process known as throwing themselves away," Forster lists the exotic types of men whom contemporary young women were able to meet—"unshaven musicians," "some German cousins," and "acquaintances picked up at continental hotels" (14)—types not likely to be found in the love pool of mid-Victorian women. Around 1875, according to Lawrence's dating in *The Rainbow,* Tom Brangwen was desperate to get away from home and meet foreign women. He half-fulfilled his fantasy by marrying a local Polish widow, Lydia Lensky, whose daughter Anna also grew up restless with minimal opportunities for love. Until the age of ten, Lawrence explains, "the only man she knew was her father." Eventually she married her cousin Will. Their daughter Ursula struggled out of a conventional relationship with a man who was a friend of the family—Anton Skrebensky. Ursula eventually met Rupert on her own, at her own workplace.[13]

In *The Age of Innocence* (1920) Wharton reconstructed a fictionalized history of love between the 1870s and the early twentieth century. Archer and May are matched by upper New York society of the 1870s according to all its conventions (such as those of Sillerton Jackson, who "knew all the ramifications of New York's cousinships"). The romance of Archer and Ellen looks ahead, as she broadens the vista of his narrowly circumscribed world with her past travels and unorthodox education. Wharton presses the historical argument by concluding the story thirty years later with the marriage of Archer's son Dallas to Fanny, who embodies a number of concrete historical changes that expanded the variety and number of love opportunities, for Fanny is "lower class" and has traveled to exotic Constantinople, Russia, and Buenos Aires.

The urgency of time running out was in some ways intensified by the First

World War, when many couples rushed to marry after short courtships. But the war also expanded the love pool by breaking down conventional barriers of locale, class, race, custom, and morality. In *The Happy Foreigner* (1920) Enid Bagnold recalled her own experiences as a nurse in a story about Fanny who has volunteered to drive an ambulance for the French army. "The smiles of strange men upon the road whom she would never see again became her social intercourse. The lost smiles of kind Americans, the lost, mocking whistles of Frenchmen, the scream of a nigger, the twittering surprise of a Chinese scavenger . . . The country around her was a vast tract of men sick with longing for the four corners of the earth" (20). Even though the war drastically reduced the number of men available, it permanently reworked conventional courtship scenarios and expanded modes of access between the sexes. After centuries of waiting for men to return from battle, women went into or at least near the front lines and became actively involved. Those who remained at home engaged for the first time in exclusive male activities and professions.

The war also improved transportation and communications technologies that brought men and women together in ever more varied ways. The Ziegfield Follies of 1922 included one song about a man who hoped his love might be "listening on the radio." [14] In Fitzgerald's *This Side of Paradise* (1920) sixteen-year-old Isabelle's "capacity for love-affairs was limited only by the number of the susceptible within telephone distance" (63). In *The Great Gatsby* (1925) eighteen-year-old Daisy had a little white roadster, and the telephone rang in her house all day long as young officers asked her out (75).

Although ideas about future love continued to focus on climactic moments that would transform the lives of men and women, there was change. In the twentieth century we find far fewer "teenage" heroines, and the younger age of consent gives way to a more mature age of decision. These changes did not intensify the sense of expectation of some big Event but rather allowed more time for reflection about the meaning and possibilities of love. More time to wait for love also increased the varieties of love and its quality. For as the conventional limitations gave way, there was a growing consciousness of the devastating consequences for men and women when the vital resources of anticipatory resoluteness are shut off and the future of love is left in the hands of match-makers and fortune-tellers.

2 Meeting

FOUR DEVELOPMENTS can be identified in the history of meeting: there is a greater variety of places where lovers could meet; these places acquire new meanings; the mediation of others diminishes; and the moment of meeting becomes less climactic.

I

Between 1847 and 1934 a revolution in transportation technologies expanded the distances men and women were able to travel in comfort and safety. Enormous populations used these technologies for a variety of purposes other than love. Tens of millions of persecuted, impoverished, or adventurous people flocked out of Europe between 1820 and 1920. Increasing numbers visited the resorts that sprang up in the later decades of the nineteenth century. As one expert noted, "Until recently no one left his native town . . . Today no one stays put. Until recently we stayed in Paris all year round. Now, in 1880 . . . how can we stay in Paris during summer?"[1] Mass tourism gave the middle and even the working classes access to places that in years past could only be reached by means of expensive, uncomfortable, and dangerous exploration, and for the purpose of meeting lovers there were new skating rinks, dance halls, fairs, expositions, cabarets, and movie houses.

In keeping with all this activity, the older practice of women waiting at home for love to arrive at the doorstep gave way to traveling in search of love. The change may be clarified by juxtaposing it with Jane Eyre's constraint and struggle to comprehend the larger world. She realized "that the real world was wide, and that a varied field of hopes and fears . . . awaited those who had courage . . . to seek real knowledge of life amidst its perils."

But she had to strain to think how to get out. For "nearly an hour" her brain "worked in chaos" until "a kind fairy . . . dropped the suggestion on [her] pillow." As she lay down it came to her—"you must advertise in the—*shire Herald*" (118). Even after securing a new position, the old sense of confinement remained, as she reflected: "Women feel just as men feel; they need . . . a field for their efforts as much as their brothers do; they suffer from too rigid a restraint, too absolute a stagnation, precisely as men would suffer" (141).

In *The Mill on the Floss* (1860) Eliot criticizes the "emmet-like Dodsons and Tullivers" who imposed their "oppressive narrowness" on Tom and Maggie, and she theorizes that "every historical advance" was a result of the "onward tendency of human beings" to get beyond such provincialism. In *Middlemarch* Eliot notes that "women both old and young regarded traveling by steam as presumptuous and dangerous." The hero of Meredith's *The Egoist* (1879) recovers from a jilt as no woman of his time could—by traveling around the world for three years. Hardy sketches the small world of his heroine in *Tess of the d'Urbervilles* (1891) as "the Vale in which she had been born, and in which her life had been blindfolded" (29). She travels twenty miles to her eventual seduction at Tantridge, which seems to her a "far-away spot." [2]

In *The Education of Henry Adams* (1903) we learn that "one had but to pass a week in Florida, or on any of a hundred huge ocean steamers, or walk through the Place Vendôme, or join a party of Cook's tourists to Jerusalem, to see that the woman had been set free." [3] For men accustomed to their privileges, women's freedom to travel made for some startling reversals. By the time of James's *The Portrait of a Lady* (1881) transatlantic travel was safe and accessible enough for fourteen-year-old Isabel Archer to have made the crossing three times. In one such reversal of gender roles the dutiful Caspar Goodwood follows adventurous Isabel across the Atlantic in vain pursuit of love. In Ward's *Helbeck of Bannisdale* young Laura could tell Helbeck that she and a Cambridge girl "are to travel a great deal and work at music." Helbeck replies: "That is what young ladies do nowadays, I understand" (145). In James's *The Golden Bowl* (1904) Maggie Verver is more traveled than her Italian fiancé. After Maggie describes her love as "water tight . . . the best cabin and the main deck and the engine-room and the steward's pantry," James explains that her imagery was "drawn from steamers and trains, from a familiarity with 'lines', a command of 'own' cars, from an experience of continents and seas" (37).

The sense of distance was not merely a matter of mileage. Ann Veronica has a "vast unexampled release" when she gets out of her small town and first breathes London air, and in Forster's *A Room with a View* (1908) Lucy Honeychurch feels her social constraints let loose in Florence. Both women eventually find a lover in these new and exotic settings, although they do so in pursuit of other objectives, not as the sole purpose of their journey. In *Summer* (1918), Wharton shows woman's confinement with one revealing detail. Charity Royall is from a small town, and when her lover leaves for a couple of months, she is intimidated by the return address on his letter. "The address frightened her. It was in New York . . . She had the feeling that her letter would never reach its destination. She had never written to anyone farther away than Hepburn" (213).

In *The Age of Innocence* contrasting senses of distance are expressed by characters from different historical periods. Before his wedding, Archer's conservative in-laws-to-be had already selected the house that he and his bride would occupy upon return from their honeymoon, a house located at a "remote" address on East Thirty-Ninth Street. Archer's feeling of being cramped by their pushiness and by the prospect of living so close to his in-laws is accentuated by the contrasting expansiveness of his fiancée's cousin, Ellen Olenska, who toured the world as a young girl, married a Polish nobleman, and then left him to travel on her own. Heating up to Ellen's exotic allure, Archer is overwhelmed by her apartment, with its strange artifacts and its "scent of some far-off bazaar" (72). Ellen offers Archer a love that incorporates those distant places, but he can only respond with an occasional romantic outburst. Wharton is sensitive to the instability and difficulty of her heroine's changing values. Ellen did not spend her life waiting passively for love to come along, but her sense of independence is shaky, and she aspires to be accepted back into the narrow world of New York society from which she had struggled to escape. She is as self-possessed as she can manage, but the disapproval of others takes its toll. Archer's fits of rebelliousness produce but moments of hope in the face of her own tenuous rebellion. Wharton draws a compelling historical contrast between Archer's conventional wife and his adventuresome lover that dramatizes the new opportunities as well as the new perils for women who dared to go somewhere new.

Ellen shares the historical stage with the heroine of Roger Martin du Gard's *The Thibaults* (1922), Rachel Goepfert, who speaks four languages and whose past travels in Africa and nonchalant disclosure about "love making in those parts" prove to be too much for Antoine Thibault to handle. Like Wharton, Du Gard reverses the conventional gender travel roles. "Rachel was an uncharted land for him . . . He felt so alien from her, rooted to the soil of France by his middle-class upbringing" (455). But unlike Ellen, Rachel has no regrets, much to Antoine's dismay. The disappointment of Archer and Antoine comes from seeking love with women who have actually traveled; in their presence they feel themselves to be in passive roles, as if each had been waiting in a humdrum setting for his woman to return from abroad.

II

Human beings do not meet the way two lines intersect at some precise point on a grid. They meet one another in a specific place that is unlike any other and invested with meaning. The history of lovers' first meetings reveals a dramatic shift in the meaning of those places—especially for women, who became increasingly able to travel more widely on their own.

Ellen Rothman has described the cramped courting ground of the early nineteenth century. "Girls and boys met on the lanes and commons of the village and in the houses of their neighbors and kinfolk; they encountered each other in church, schoolroom, and shop . . . Even when going about their separate tasks, men and women moved within the same small world." [4] The fact that many nineteenth-century lovers met in the woman's home under close supervision is a matter of record. [5] When they met on the road, it was generally near the woman's home, such as the spot where Gabriel met Bathsheba in *Far from the Madding Crowd* (1874). The courting ground is expanded in Conrad's *Victory* (1915), in which Heyst meets Lena on an island in the East Indies where she is touring with a woman's band. His solitary life had been a "system of restless wanderings," and "she really had no definite idea where she was on the surface of the globe." The primitive setting and common danger force them to reconstitute love. "The girl he had come across . . . so near and still so strange, gave him a greater sense of his own reality than he had ever known in all his life" (164). The remoteness of their meeting place allows them both to discover a fuller sense of their own reality.

Outside the home Victorian lovers often met in romantic spots such as "Red Deeps" in *The Mill on the Floss*. This was Maggie and Philip's first post-childhood meeting place, a "fleckered shade of the hollows, away from all that was harsh and unlovely" (424). The meeting of Victorian lovers in large cities was often spiked with melodrama. Daniel Deronda meets Mirah while he is rowing on the Thames and he sees her about to jump in and drown herself. Their first meeting is a rescue.

Twentieth-century novelists resisted romantic spots and melodramatic action. Mann's title *The Magic Mountain* (1924) is ironic, for although the location is high in the Swiss Alps, the setting for love has none of the wondrous beauty the title suggests. Hans Castorp first sees his beloved, the tubercular Russian patient Clavdia Chauchat, when she is sitting at the Russian table in a sanatorium atop the mountain. He first meets her outside the x-ray room, where they are both awaiting treatment. He is unable to perform any magic or rescue Clavdia from death. In Musil's *The Man Without Qualities* (1930–1943) Ulrich meets his sister Agatha again at their father's funeral after a long separation. These deathly places are the settings for two of the steamiest loves of twentieth-century literature, as if their remoteness from clichéd romantic spots forced these doom-tinged relationships to be inventive.

The classic nineteenth-century meeting of lovers in a railroad station is that of Anna Karenina and Vronsky, but the station signifies not freedom and transcendence but retribution and death. Anna leaves her husband to visit her sister in Moscow. When she arrives there, Vronsky is at the station to meet his mother. Anna and Vronsky exchange telling glances, but the setting also portends her death, because, shortly after her arrival, a brakeman is crushed under a car. Retribution for her adulterous surrender comes at the end, when Anna throws herself under a train and fulfills the epigraph to the novel, "Vengeance is mine; I will repay." In the nineteenth century, a married woman, especially a mother, traveling by train alone to an exciting city was courting the corruption of her marriage and love.

Far different is the significance of a first meeting on a train in Musil's "The Perfecting of a Love" (1911). Claudine, like Anna, is traveling on a train without her husband or child and becomes intrigued by a stranger sitting opposite, but he is no dashing cavalry officer like Vronsky: "he might have been anyone; he was no more than a sombre bulk of alien being" (141). The contrast between the fortuitousness of Claudine's relationship with this stranger and the necessity of her relationship with her husband becomes clear in a moment of exhilaration, when she grasps her own responsibility in both relationships. The ineluctability of her marriage is the source of its oppressiveness. Musil focuses on the overpowering sense of presence in any place, under any circumstances, with any man. When the train becomes snowbound, Claudine has an affair with the stranger and discovers a power and terror in her own sexuality, which leads ironically to the "perfecting" of her love for her husband. Although the setting where Anna and Claudine first meet their respective lovers is similar, the significance attached to such places in the twentieth century is without the nineteenth-century's sense of evil and doom.

In *The Mill on the Floss* Maggie first meets Philip in a school, but it is her brother Tom's school, not Maggie's. Eliot avoids polemicizing, but her account of the different educations available to Maggie and Tom does not hide her outrage at the trivialization of the education of girls in her time. By the early twentieth century there was progress toward more equitable education for women, and in a number of modern novels fathers are obliged to confront daughters requesting permission to attend college. The title of Grant Allen's novel *The Woman Who Did* (1895) refers to a number of doings, including going to Cambridge, where the heroine first meets her lover. In *Ann Veronica* the heroine's most mature relationship is with a professor of comparative anatomy at the Central Imperial College.[6]

The entry of women in new professions in the twentieth century increased the variety and number of contact points for men and women to meet on the job. In contrast, the few professional opportunities of Victorian women limited their range of travel and access to men. Jane first sees Rochester riding a horse. They meet as he falls from it and their first words deal with his resulting sprain, when he concedes grudgingly, "Necessity compels me to make you useful." Rochester topples repeatedly until he and Jane are on more equal footing. Her work for him thus begins with the most basic assistance, and she is sensitive to its meaning. "My help had been needed and claimed: I had given it: I was pleased to have done something; trivial, transitory though the deed was, it was yet an active thing, and I was weary of an existence all passive" (146).

As Heidegger noted, people do not actually meet at some point; rather, they clear away space and make room for one another. To do that they must first have some space, and that is what Jane had for but one moment. When Jane next meets Rochester it is in his mansion (his space) and in his employ (his time and space). She must work to comprehend that space, command it, and make it her own. To make that possible Brontë must resort to an improbably tragic event—a fire that burns down his place and creates a new place where Jane can once again work for Rochester but in equality, a modest cottage where they can rearrange the furniture and make room for one another.

Most unmarried Victorian women worked either in their parents' homes or in the conventional professions outside the home—as governess, servant, clerk, teacher, or seamstress. In *Daniel Deronda* Gwendolen does not work at all. Her first meeting with Grandcourt takes place in an Archery Hall, which Eliot describes as if it were the setting for a flower show. She concludes her account of the young girls on display with triple irony: "They prompt attitudes full of grace and power, where that fine concentration of energy seen in all marksmanship, is freed from associations of bloodshed" (134). In fact Gwendolen has no real power, she is rather Grandcourt's target, and her marriage to him will be her own bloodletting.

Hardy's attack on courtship and marriage in *Jude the Obscure* begins with an unforgettable first meeting of Jude with Arabella at her place of work. He is walking along a country lane, reflecting on the progress he has made studying the classics, when something smacks him in the ear—"a piece of flesh, the characteristic part of a barrow-pig, which country gentlemen used for greasing their boots" (33). Jude looks over the hedge from where it came and sees three women at work washing heaps of pigs' chitterlings. One of the three is Arabella, who had initiated their first meeting by intentionally throwing a pig's penis at him. The crude sensuality of their subsequent relationship is anticipated by the crudity of their first meeting.

In the twentieth century lovers meet ever more frequently where the woman works. In *Women in Love* (1920) Ursula meets Rupert at a school where she is a teacher and he is an inspector. In Colette's *The Vagabond* (1910) the meeting place is where Renée works as a dancer in a music-hall review. After one exhausting performance someone knocks at her dressing-room. A stranger presents himself and tells her that he has seen her every night for a week. Renée narrates: "I do not answer this imbecile. Damp with sweat and still out of breath, with my dress half undone, I look at him, while I wipe my hands with such evident ferocity that his fine phrases falter and die suddenly on his lips." She contemplates slapping his face or cursing him, and then instead firmly tells him to leave: "Well then, Monsieur, I will say to you politely what a moment ago I would have said harshly: please go!" (21). Colette reverses the conventional settings, roles, and circumstances of first meetings. Here they meet at the woman's place of work. She has hardly been passively waiting for the active man to come courting. She responds to his knock mechanically, not with breathless expectation. Her partial undress is no coquettish décolletage but a routine transition away from her necessary professional exposure. She is at first reluctant to make room for this intruder and keeps him standing. His is the active role only in the superficial sense of his entering her dressing-room; Renée is in control of the place and defines its meaning.

In *The Thibaults* Antoine and Rachel meet during an emergency operation. The respected and self-possessed Dr. Antoine Thibault is called to treat a young girl who was run over by a delivery car and has a broken leg and ruptured femoral artery. In the girl's apartment Antoine makes a tourniquet with his suspenders and piles up plates to support a lamp to light an emergency surgery. He is assisted by a woman who slowly emerges from the shadows and, upon his request, applies chloroform with surprising composure. "She obeys orders, he mused, like a soldier under fire. Women!" When the patient begins to fail, Antoine asks the woman to go to the pharmacy. "She stood before him, waiting; her tentative gesture—to wrap the dressing-gown more closely round her body—told him of her reluctance at going thus, half dressed, into the streets, and for the fraction of a second a picture of the opulent form under the garment held his imagination." She eventually runs the errand and returns with the prescription, enabling the injured girl to survive.

Rachel and Antoine make room for one another in a place that is invested with the meaning of their shared project of saving a life. In the afterglow of that success and in the tantalizing half-light of a cramped and steamy apartment, Antoine becomes aroused by repeated glimpses of her body. "Outlined as in a shadow-play under the flimsy dressing-gown, the young woman's body was silhouetted, frankly provocative as if she stood naked before him." Sexual desire begins to displace work as the meaning of their meeting place. They both fall asleep in exhaustion and he awakens to discover that their thighs are touching (321–329). Du Gard romanticizes the solidity of this untrained woman, to be sure, and the basis for her appeal, at least in this first meeting, is a frank sexuality that, while not common in the nineteenth century, was not unthinkable. But her strong presence during this first meeting is a long way from the feigned, if not fainting, delicacy of earlier heroines. Her unusual performance "under fire" in this pre-war episode became a way of life for many women after 1914.

World War I relocated and redefined the courting ground of Western literature as it transformed European topography.[7] Many soldiers were obliged to find love close to the trenches, largely with prostitutes or other men or with local women in liaisons that were invariably short on time, space, and safety. The invasions across established frontiers and the remapping of Europe after the armistice were also metaphors for the changing spatiality of love.

The most memorable wartime meeting places were the hospitals and relief stations where soldiers met nurses and ambulance drivers. The heroine of Bagnold's *The Happy Foreigner* is indeed happy to get away from home even though the circumstances are tragic. The romantic focus of this autobiographical novel about an Englishwoman who volunteers for ambulance duty is an affair with a French officer, whom she meets at a dance in Metz. They continue to meet now and then between ambulance runs along the Metz to Chantilly road.

Love in Hemingway's *A Farewell to Arms* (1929) is emphatically international: an American ambulance driver meets an English nurse at a German villa in Milan, converted into a British hospital treating soldiers from all over Europe. In Radclyffe Hall's *The Well of Loneliness* (1928) another powerful war romance begins when Stephen Gordon meets a new recruit to The London Ambulance Column, Mary Llewellyn, who is taken on as a driver to replace a woman suffering from shell-shock. Mary had made her way from the quiet seclusion of Wales to war-ravaged France, where these volunteers became "pawns in the ruthless and complicated game of existence, moved hither and thither on the board by an unseen hand, yet moved side by side, so that they grew to respect each other" (285). Working at the front enabled Stephen and Mary to break new ground, especially because Stephen Gordon was a woman, the protagonist of the most important novel about lesbian love in its time.

Although my study focuses on heterosexual love, I have included novels that treat homosexual love because they document the cultural reinterpretation of gender that was underway during these years. Homosexual love emerges in literature from the disguised gender reversals of Proust and early Gide, the exploration of bisexuality in Lawrence and Woolf, the more explicit treatment of homosexuality in Forster's *Maurice* (published posthumously in 1971), the later Gide, and finally Hall's bold novel. Aside from the last, none is set near the fighting, but the dislocation of love brought about by the war displaced many of the conventions that governed love. Stephen's struggle to be herself as a lesbian was facilitated by that dislocation and the opportunity to work side by side with Mary under fire.

III

War also allowed relationships to develop far from match-makers or chaperons who may have attempted to initiate first meetings. In *A Farewell to Arms* Lieutenant Rinaldi takes Frederic along to meet his new love and is quick to concede, as they leave, "Miss Barkley prefers you to me"—hardly a conventional introduction. Rinaldi's directness perhaps involves some Italian *insouciance*, but the war swept away the patience to wait for formal introductions, reduced the timidity that necessitated match-making, and demolished the protective sexual morality that required chaperonage.

In the nineteenth century match-making and chaperonage were respectable and viable mediations in love even if they were not everywhere the rule. *Middlemarch*'s town gossip Mrs. Cadwallader explains to her husband what must be done to get Dorothea a new husband. "How are matches made, except by bringing men and women together?" In response to her husband's suggestion that Dorothea pick her own husband, she replies that with young women strictly isolated and protected from men the assistance of others is necessary: "How can she choose if she has no variety to choose from? A woman's choice usually means taking the only man she can get" (371). And a young woman could only get that one if she was introduced.

In *The Egoist* Meredith uses the passive voice to suggest the universality and publicness of two would-be lovers, as if their meeting, decreed from on high and viewed by royalty and the gods, had to be what "one does." "The great meeting of Sir Willoughby Patterne and Miss Middleton had taken place at Cherriton Grange, the seat of a county grandee, where this young lady of eighteen was first seen rising above the horizon . . . He was one of a pack; many were ahead of him, the whole of them were eager." The effect of this mating ritual was "to hurry him with all his might into the heat of the chase, while yet he knew no more of her than that he was competing for a prize" (71). Matched up by Miss Middleton's conniving father and swept up by a swarm of contending rivals, Willoughby's genuine vitality is drained from the outset. Miss Middleton is not so much a sex object as a social prize. This ironically titled novel is essentially about the failure of selfhood in a match that is thoroughly mediated by others.

Forster's chaperon, Miss Bartlett, was delightfully ineffective at keeping her younger cousin Lucy from meeting George, who offered the two "a room with a view" at the Pension Bertolini where all were vacationing. Miss Bartlett refused George's offer, she explained, in order not to put Lucy "under an obligation to people of whom we know nothing." As Forster understood, everyone knows nothing about everyone else before they meet. With this modernist caricature of the chaperon, Forster recorded the passing of its usefulness. He took sharper aim in *Howards End*. Even before Helen met Paul Wilcox, her infatuation with him had been stimulated by his entire family. "Helen had fallen in love, not with an individual, but with a family." As a result she lost hold of her own identity. "The energy of the Wilcoxes had fascinated her . . . and had led to that abandonment of personality that is a possible prelude to love" (24). Forster creates a number of lovers, like Helen, who belong to the historical past and share a common loss of selfhood. Authentic love is not asocial but, he would insist, must be based on a measure of autonomy.

Left more on their own, twentieth-century men and women had to go to great lengths to cross the terrifying expanse separating them from one another. The hero of *The Great Gatsby* (1925) arranges his reunion with Daisy by spending millions on a mansion to be across the bay from her in the hope that his next-door neighbor might by chance invite the two of them over at the same time. Jordan Baker recalls her reaction to Gatsby's plan. "The modesty of the demand shook me. He had waited five years and bought a mansion where he dispensed starlight to casual moths—so that he could 'come over' some afternoon to a stranger's garden" (80). In *Lady Chatterley's Lover* (1928), Connie, in the company of her husband, has a few casual encounters with the gamekeeper Mellors. She then ventures into the woods alone to find Mellors washing himself, naked to the hips. This first private meeting is for Connie a "visionary experience," which "hit her in the middle of the body" (62). The class lines that Connie crosses to love Mellors are also in place in Aldous Huxley's *Point Counter Point* (1928), which includes an account of the first meeting of Mark and Mary Rampion, a fictionalized married couple based on the real D. H. and Frieda Lawrence. Mary and her brother George are standing in a park owned by their father when a poor young man walks up in "earnest defiance" and says, "I'm trespassing here . . . Do you mind?" (101). He continues to trespass on the formalities and class prejudices that separate him from Mary, just as D. H. Lawrence had bypassed the obstacles to first meetings which he believed kept apart the men and women of his age.

One of the most unforgettable first meetings in twentieth-century literature was that of a young boy and girl, described from the boy's inner consciousness. In *Remembrance of Things Past* (1913–1927) Proust sets the scene for the girl's first appearance—a hedge of jasmine, a long green hose coiling across the gravel and spraying a fan of prismatic droplets. The boy sees a red-haired, freckled little girl holding a trowel in her hand. As she returns his look he is terrified that his father or grandfather will call him away. Suddenly a lady in white he had not seen until that moment calls out, "Gilberte, come along; what are you doing?" Proust sums up the experience. "So it came to me, uttered across the heads of the stocks and jasmines, pungent and cool as the drops which fell from the green watering-pipe; impregnating and irradiating the zone of pure air through which it had passed—and which it set apart and isolated—with the mystery of the life of her whom its syllables designated to the happy beings who lived and walked and traveled in her company; unfolding beneath the arch of the pink hawthorn, at the height of my shoulder, the quintessence of their familiarity— so exquisitely painful to myself—with her and with the unknown world of her existence into which I should never penetrate" (153–155). He assigns equal significance to the riveting first exchange of glances and the seemingly accidental sights and smells of the setting. The sound of Gilberte's name begins "to impregnate, to overlay, to perfume everything with which it had any association." The heat of the sun and season of the year, the odor of flowers and the sound of a name, the pink freckles and a girl's trowel all shape this first meeting, which is distinctively modern, because it is not mediated by another person but by his entire ambient universe.

IV

A fourth subelement of meeting bears distinctive historical markings—the intensity of the climactic moment. I have treated this theme in the context of waiting for a "now-or-never" moment but must reconsider the way it actually occurs in meetings.

It is hard to imagine any historical period in which climactic moments of love and understanding do not break into the long stretches of lovelessness and misunderstanding that every human being experiences. I therefore view such peak moments as universal. What does change is the meaning of those moments and the value attached to them in literature. Victorians tended to view "falling in love" as a dangerous but valuable foundation for the everyday routine of love that follows, while moderns seriously questioned its value.

In Les Misérables Hugo stretches out the time before the first actual meet-

ing of Marius and Cosette for several years in order to heighten its climacticality. During the first year Marius noticed from afar a thirteen-year-old girl
with her father in the Luxembourg Garden. Two years later he finally caught
her eye. "She looked steadily at him with a soft pensive glance that caused
him to tremble from head to foot," and Marius "was head over heels in love
. . . A single look had done it. When the charge is prepared and the fuse is
laid nothing can be simpler. A glance is all the spark that is needed." In an
age when meeting places were limited and carefully regulated by others,
such climactic responses to a single glance from across a romantic garden
were routine. Hugo is quick to add that a gaze like Cosette's is "deadly," for
it causes "a momentary absence of mind and we are lost." This warning,
however, reads like an invitation to such reckless daring. Hugo does list the
deficiencies that make romantic impulsiveness possible: "Solitude and detachment, pride, independence, a love of nature, the absence of regular employment, life lived for its own sake, the secret struggles of chastity and an
overflowing goodwill towards all created things—all this had paved the way
in Marius for the advent of what is known as passion" (611–613). But Hugo
does not construct his story to show the devastating consequences of such
impulsive and unreflective passion.

Although Marcel was struck as intensely and even more rapidly than
Marius, the two first impressions are markedly different. Cosette's face is
marbleized perfection; Gilberte has freckles. Cosette returns a "soft pensive
glance," while Gilberte settles upon Marcel a look of "infinite contempt."
Proust fills out the ambience with simple objects and ordinary people who
are distracted, caught off guard, or confused; while Hugo throws an aura of
holiness around Cosette with attentive angels and statuesque models classically posed to inspire the masters of literature and art. The trigger mechanisms are similar, but their respective outcomes and hence meanings are
worlds apart. Marius will live with Cosette happily ever after; Marcel will
suffer alone.

While few Victorian novelists indulged in romantic fancy as unabashedly
as Hugo, most of them did include climatic first meetings or sightings. In
Sentimental Education (1869) Flaubert springs Frédéric Moreau into love at
first sight with Madame Arnoux, who is sitting across the deck from him on
a river boat. "It was like a vision . . . He had never seen anything to compare
with her splendid dark skin, her ravishing figure, or the delicate, translucent
fingers" (18). Vision is the preferred sense for communication between lovers in Hardy's *A Pair of Blue Eyes*. But blue eyes are only blue when looked

at. "Stephen fell in love with Elfride by looking at her; Knight by ceasing to do so." While Stephen manifests a positive mode of the climactic first meeting, Knight repudiates it. "Knight's experience," Hardy explains, "was a complete disproof of the assumption that love always comes by glances of the eye and sympathetic touches of the fingers: that, like flame, it makes itself palpable at the moment of generation. Not till they were parted, and she had become sublimated in his memory, could he be said to have even attentively regarded her" (244–245). If Knight cannot think straight until he has stopped looking, his example provides a tenuous disproof of the notion that an exchange of glances can be decisive.

The history of the four subelements of meeting shifted in the direction of more places to meet, a greater variety of meanings attached to those places, a reduction of the mediation of meetings by others, and a lessening of their terrifying climacticality. These changes gave lovers more opportunity to reflect on the meaning and purpose of their meetings and to work out consequences that would suit their real needs. New transportation and communication technologies made it cheaper, easier, and safer to go farther. The courting ground also expanded as conventions about proper or romantic courting spots gave way to a wider range of meeting places and of meanings attached to them. Hugo's Luxembourg Garden is an unforgettable romantic spot, but it has far less to do with what took place in it than the ordinary spot near Tansonville where Marcel discovered myriad meanings that attended his first meeting with Gilberte and that subsequently colored his love. Most significant is the increasing number of novels in which couples meet where the woman works. A man and a woman could make room for one another more authentically when they each had some room of his or her own.

Victorians typically had long engagements, but the initial courtship was often rushed and hence the first meeting had an overwhelming climactic aspect. "Solitude and detachment" as well as "the secret struggles of chastity" are part of Hugo's explanation for Marius' short fuse, and women were kept even more unprepared. The joy of "love at first sight" draws its intensity from the "firstness" but also from the sense that it's "now or never." Pressed for time, men and women were less able to reflect on past experience and approach first meetings in their own way. The authenticity of meetings could also be diminished by the mediation of chaperons and match-makers, and, most important, by the internalization of society's impersonal sense of how things are done—what "they" do. Heidegger defined inauthenticity as precisely that—an impersonal way of being as if one had no say in the matter. In the modern novels chaperons become comical figures and cease to determine where, when, how, or with whom love is found. Instead of romantic spots we find quirky, sometimes unromantic settings where men and women meet a bit farther from the madding crowd.

3 Encounter

IN HEIDEGGER'S philosophy encounter is the existential that grounds human relatedness. It does not refer to the actual meeting of two people, which was my preceding subject. It is thus not chronologically prior to a love but ontologically prior—that which makes such a relationship possible. It belongs among such terms as "intersubjectivity," "empathy," "communication," and the "I-Thou relation," which several phenomenologists of the early twentieth century introduced to challenge a long philosophical tradition that affirmed the primacy of the individual.

In the course of the seventeenth century the emergence of political absolutism, capitalism, and Protestantism engendered a new sense of the importance of the individual, which was elaborated to different ends in the philosophies of Hobbes, Locke, and Descartes. Hobbes envisioned human relatedness as emerging out of a primary isolation of men, who exist "as if sprung out of the earth, and suddenly, like mushrooms, come to full maturity, without all kind of engagement to each other." [1] The logical origin of society is a pleasure-seeking solitary individual, who, out of self-interest, contracts with other solitary individuals to renounce some of his own powers and create a single, all-powerful individual, the Leviathan, who will protect them all from each other.

Locke founded political authority on the individual's natural rights, which he derived from an epistemology based on the individual's sensations. He rejected the theory of innate ideas and argued rather that the mind is initially an "empty cabinet" that lets in particular ideas through the senses. He discussed human relations in the *Second Treatise on Government,* which assumed a connection between selfhood and possessiveness: "Every man has a property in his own person." [2] He justified property rights by analogy with the way an individual relates to his body. An individual's body and labor are unquestionably his own, as is anything he mixes with his labor. If he picks up an acorn or encloses a farm, they become his legitimate property. The individual would remain in possession of his self at all times were it not for others; but farmland, unlike acorns, runs out, and scarcity necessitates enforcement of property rights against others. Selfhood is also dependent on protection from others: we become aware of our own selves only after a government protects our natural rights and private property against others.

The cornerstone of seventeenth-century metaphysics of the self is Descartes' *Cogito, ergo sum* ("I think, therefore I am"). His search for certain knowledge began with what he believed he knew indubitably—his own self—which he defined as "a thing which thinks." Knowledge of it remains privileged: "I see clearly that there is nothing which is easier for me to know than my mind." His body is another kind of thing altogether, tenuously related to his mind. One analogy he offers to illustrate the connection between mind and body is that of a pilot in a ship. In addition to the mind-body dualism Descartes added another dualism of subject and object that intruded a second separation between the self and others. He comes to know that other human beings exist only by inference: "when looking from a window and saying I see men who pass in the street, I really do not see them, but infer that what I see is men . . . and yet what do I see from the window but hats and coats which may cover automatic machines? Yet I judge these to be men."[3] His uncertainty about the existence of those men would presumably not be reduced even if the men were to come upstairs and take off their hats and coats. This backhanded introduction of human relations is one reason Cartesian philosophy became associated with a fundamental separation between the self and others.

John Stuart Mill's *On Liberty* (1859) presumed the individual to be the source of all knowledge, the point of departure for human relations, and the "ultimate sanction" for morality and political liberty. Two definitions emphasized the self-sufficiency and moral primacy of the individual. "Human nature," Mill suggested, is like "a tree, which requires to grow . . . according to the tendency of the inward forces which make it a living thing." This was a typical nineteenth-century conception of the individual, sufficient unto himself, fully realizable from the "tendency of inward forces." The second definition affirmed the individual's moral primacy: "Over himself, over his own body and mind, the individual is sovereign."[4] Mill's sovereign individual, like Locke's proprietary self, is sacrosanct. Others are largely pests who interfere with the individual's inner forces and disrupt the moral harmony of sovereign individuality.

In opposition to the philosophies of Hobbes, Locke, Descartes, and Mill, the phenomenology of encounter rejected both a philosophy of self-sufficient individuals relating externally to one another and a morality based on maximizing the individual's security, property rights, or pleasure.

In 1913 Max Scheler published the first phenomenology of love, which took on previous theories that began with a primary self and had to "build up a picture of other people's experiences from the immediately given data furnished by [its] own." For Scheler what occurs is rather "an immediate flow of experience, *undifferentiated as between mine and thine,* which actually contains both our own and others' experiences intermingled and without distinction from one another." Out of this primal flow begins a gradual identification of the self as separate from the other. Scheler emphasized the primacy of relatedness, pointing out that we tend to err not by imputing our own experience on to others but by confusing the two. "A man tends to live more in *others* than in himself; more in the community than in his own individual self." Scheler bolstered that argument with speculation about the child's earliest experience of fusion with all that is external to it before self-definition.[5]

In contrast to philosophies that started with the individual and then sought to bridge the gap between the individual and the other, Martin Buber began with the bridge itself, "the between" or "the interhuman."[6] In *I and Thou* (1923) he viewed experience in the two ways a man relates to the world, "in accordance with the two basic words he can speak." The first basic word, the primordial *a priori* of relation, is "I-Thou." That primacy is chronological and ontological: it grounds prenatal life and early infancy as well as all human relatedness. "The genesis of the thing [or the "It"] is a late product that develops out of the split of the primal encounters ... In the beginning is the relation." The I-Thou relation is prelinguistic, undifferentiated, and unmediated; it "teaches you to encounter others and to stand on your own in such encounters." In contrast, the second basic word, "I-It," dominates everyday life of prediction and control. I-It relations lack the spontaneity, intimacy, and genuineness of I-Thou relations.

Love relations may be I-It or I-Thou. The former refers to a superficial love in which others are used as objects; the latter refers to a loving relatedness that transcends the limited tactile sensations of mere sexual relating in the sphere of the I-It. Buber emphasizes *the between.* Love is a reciprocal encounter between responsible equals in a direct relation. Such an encounter is difficult to achieve and maintain, because in every genuine encounter the Thou is doomed to collapse into the It of "thinghood."[7] He insists on the fullness of commitment and yet resistance to fusion with the other, and he urges that I-It relationships be replaced by I-Thou relationships. Buber thus presents an ontology, developmental psychology, epistemology, theology, and ethics of encounter.

Heidegger had a different approach. Rather than asking what kind of thing a human being is and then asking how two human beings relate, he asked, what does it mean to be human? Rather than define what we are, he interpreted the ways we are. This approach also challenged philosophies grounded on self-sufficient individuals. Heidegger rejected Descartes's primary insular realm of pure knowing, both of Descartes's dualisms, and the roundabout access to others by a self-certainly existing ego. He thus rejected the idea that a thinking thing *possesses* another kind of extended thing, a body, which it uses instrumentally to *perceive* other bodies and then *infer* that those other bodies are *analogously* piloted by another thinking thing. Instead, he argued that human existence is fundamentally a direct and immediate sharing with others. He also scrapped the metaphor that Locke used for the instrument which relates to the external world by acquiring knowledge through sensations. "The perceiving of what is known is not a process of returning with one's booty to the 'cabinet' of consciousness after one has gone out and grasped it" (89). Getting out of a purified inner realm, crossing the big divide to others by receiving sensations, and then returning to the self are not real human projects; they are rather artificial projects of philosophers who interpret human relatedness erroneously with such fictitious entities as a thinking thing purified of all doubt or an empty cabinet of the mind. Locke's theory of possessive individualism is also inadequate from the perspective of the phenomenology of encounter, because, like one's farm, even one's own person, body, or labor cannot be entirely one's own, independent of others. When selfhood is conceived in terms of possession or ownership, conflict arising from scarcity is inevitable, and human relations must be fundamentally competitive. Human existence is necessarily a being with others in a variety of ways that include conflict, but not merely a being pitted against all others.

In contrast to the "purity" of traditional philosophical reflection about life removed from the everyday world, Heidegger began in the world with the "everydayness" of human existence, precisely as it is "fascinated with" and "absorbed by" the world. His approach did not solve the traditional problem of "other minds"—it eliminated it. He was concerned not with how we "know" other minds, the traditional epistemological approach, but rather with how we live with others and interpret the meaning of being with them.

In encountering others one does not start out by "isolating the 'I' so that one must seek some way of getting over to the others from this isolated subject." To correct this misconception Heidegger clarified what he meant by "the others." They are not everyone else except me, they are rather those from whom one does not distinguish oneself. Human existence is *with* others *in* the world *already.* Each emphasized word requires clarification. We are "with" others as we live together, not as two isolated physical objects externally related to one another. Human existence is a process of disentangling one's self from inauthentic immersion in impersonal otherness. We are "in" the world not as a marble may be in a jar but as we may be in a community or in love. Finally, there is no sequence of existing and then experiencing others. We do not open the visor, peer out, and lo!—discover others. We are primordially and necessarily with others "already." We are always in the world with others, but there are different ways of understanding the meaning of such "being-with." Inauthentically we may conceal from ourselves its meaning, whereas authentically we may reflect on its meaning.

We encounter others directly with *solicitude,* an existential that is a form of the most fundamental existential—*care.*[8] Being for, against, or without one another, passing one another by or even having nothing to do with one another are ways of caring, although these latter are deficient modes. This is not doubletalk. Heidegger is elaborating those existentials that make all modes possible. We may consider others more or less, but both options are grounded equally in solicitude.

Solicitude has inauthentic and authentic modes that govern love relations. We may *leap in* for the other inauthentically in order to take away the other's "care," but in so doing the other becomes "dominated and dependent." Or we may *leap ahead* of the other "not in order to take away his 'care' but rather to give it back to him authentically." In an authentic loving encounter solicitude "frees the other in his freedom for himself." Love is a combination of authentic and inauthentic modes of being-with which has a history. "Being-with . . . brings numerous mixed forms to maturity," but, Heidegger adds, "to describe and classify them would take us beyond the limits of this investigation" (158–161). My study undertakes such a description and classification of the mixed forms of being-with that constitute the history of love, interpreted as authentic and inauthentic ways of encountering others.

I

Developments in literature and art paralleled the emergence of a phenome-nology of encounter. The rise of the English novel in the century following that of Locke and Hobbes produced a literary form ideally suited to explore the experience of an individual, for it galvanized in dramatic encounters those experiences that defined someone as an individual. Defoe's prototypi-cal novel, *Robinson Crusoe* (1719), has been interpreted by Ian Watt as a "defiant assertion of the primacy of individual experience" analogous to Descartes's *Cogito, ergo sum*.[9] Crusoe's story is indeed a literary analog to Descartes's "proof" of his own existence, as it forced the representative man to reconstitute the process of socialization. For Crusoe, human contact be-gins in panic when, after fifteen years alone on the island, he sees a man's footprint in the sand and spends the next ten years frantically planting rows of trees and building a second wall around his cave for protection against this unseen other. After they meet, he and Friday struggle to overcome dif-ferences in language, nationality, class, and education. Although the rela-tionship remains one of master and servant, Defoe never questions the pos-sibility of human relationship itself.

Heidegger's criticism of philosophies that approach human relations "by marking out and isolating the 'I' so that one must then seek some way of getting over to the others from this isolated subject" is a gloss on the consti-tution of relationship in most novels from *Robinson Crusoe* through the nineteenth century. Characters start out as self-contained (though perhaps lonely and longing) individuals who seek some way of getting through to the other. The way may be strewn with obstacles, but authors seldom question the possibility of ever getting across. Nor do they explicitly thematize hu-man relatedness. Even when exploring impossible relationships such as that between Charles and Emma Bovary, who were never able to understand one another, Flaubert did not question the possibility of human relatedness it-self. He constructed his novel, like so many novels from his period, as a struggle to surmount differences and misunderstandings. In contrast, mod-ern novelists often interrogated the foundations of relatedness even as they explored them. Modernists shared with phenomenologists of encounter an interest in those foundations, which were highlighted in the epigraph to *Howards End:* "Only connect . . ."

This motto refers to all sorts of connections—between the working and middle classes, between the beast and the monk, and, most important, be-tween lovers. In the novel Henry and Margaret try and only partially succeed in connecting. Henry is a stuffed shirt. "I am not a fellow who bothers about my own inside," he boasts. Outwardly he is "cheerful, reliable, and brave," but inwardly he is "a little ashamed of loving a wife." Margaret tries to love him nevertheless. "She would only point out the salvation that was latent in his own soul . . . Only connect! That was the whole of her sermon. Only connect the prose and the passion, and both will be exalted, and human love will be seen at its height." Her message need not even take the form of talking. "By quiet indications the bridge would be built and span their lives with beauty. But she failed. For there was one quality in Henry for which she was never prepared, however much she reminded herself of it: his obtuseness. He simply did not notice things, and there was no more to be said" (186–187). Charles and Emma Bovary both failed to notice things, and so Emma had adulterous affairs and committed suicide; but Henry and Margaret remain alive and together, although their emotional circuitry is intermittent and incomplete. After a climactic argument in which Margaret chastises him for hypocrisy, he still fails to comprehend. "He had refused to connect, on the clearest issue that can be laid before a man, and their love must take the consequences." Forster, by focusing on a love that struggles to find meaning without the breakthroughs of understanding that resolve nineteenth-century novels, is able to explore the compromises, lulls, and dead spots of love that are distinctive to the modernist novel. He makes visible "the between" that had been the invisible ether for the love relationships of nineteenth-century novels.

In a history of love, why dwell on a "love that failed?" [10] That question applies to all other deficient modes of love such as jealousy, conflict, and finitude, which I will consider in subsequent chapters. Heidegger's explanation of the function of existentials offers an answer. Existentials ground both positive and deficient modes of being, as in the example of solicitude. Its positive mode is considerate being for the sake of another; its deficient mode is being without or passing by one another. Henry and Margaret manifest both positive and deficient modes of encounter. They focus on some aspects of one another with intensity and care, deeply cognizant of the bond that connects them, but they also fail to understand and care about many other aspects of their relationship. To show what their love failed to achieve Forster had to bring to life something that failed to be and yet was. He effectively crafted a love between two people who never quite connected and never would. This dramatization of the possibilities of relatedness that ground the success and failure of love parallels the phenomenology of encounter.

Forster's *A Passage to India* (1924) turns on conflicts between nations, religions, castes, and sexes. It also dramatizes the deficient and positive modes of relatedness. Tension mounts as the skittish Englishwoman Adela Quested contemplates Ronny's recent proposal while she hikes toward the Marabar Caves, led by her Indian guide Dr. Aziz. Her exertion triggers a revelation—"Not to love the man one's going to marry! Not to find out till this moment! Not even to have asked oneself the question until now!" But she decides not to break off her engagement because "it would cause too much trouble to others." When Aziz tells her about his wife, whom he adores, she offends him by asking if he has more than one wife, although she was "quite unconscious that she had said the wrong thing." When she gets into the caves she imagines that Aziz tries to rape her. She flees in panic and brings charges against him. Much later, after realizing the falseness of her accusation, she sees her difficulties as part of a more fundamental problem. "What is the use of personal relationships when everyone brings less and less to them?" (197). Forster symbolizes the central difficulty of personal relationship with the echoes of the Marabar caves. When Adela cannot be found, a guide explains that to shout is useless, "because a Marabar cave can hear no sound but its own" (154).

On the positive side, Forster constructs the novel as a search for love, as articulated by the Hindu philosopher Dr. Godbole who says that all things are their opposite, that everything in the universe has its echo and is also an echo of the echo. But the novel is not merely about how people fail to connect; failure is only conceivable when viewed against its opposite, the possibility of success. Forster dramatizes the miraculous connection of love by taking it away from characters who desperately want it but cannot quite bring it off. He thus shows the dialectic of the positive modes of encounter emerging out of the ever-present deficient modes.

In *Women in Love* (1920) Lawrence probes the foundations of relatedness through his hero Rupert. "Even when he said, whispering with truth, 'I love you, I love you,' it was not the real truth . . . How could he say 'I' when he was something new and unknown, not himself at all? This I, this old formula of the age, was a dead letter." This historical claim sounds more like Buber than Heidegger, as Lawrence continues. "In the new, superfine bliss . . . there was no I and you, there was only the third, unrealised wonder, the wonder of existing not as oneself but in a consummation of my being and of her being in a new one, a new, paradisal unit regained from the duality" (361). This gush would align with the older romantic ideal of fusion between lovers were it not for Rupert's chronic self-questioning. For Rupert the deficient mode of love is "the degradation" of a love that is "dictated from outside." He insists that man approach "his own self" with deep respect out of which the "old idea" will perish and people will be able to "speak out to one another" (viii).

In *Mrs. Dalloway* (1925) Virginia Woolf takes us through a day leading up to a climax of deficient encounter—Clarissa Dalloway's cocktail party. Along the way, Woolf explores several strained relationships, beginning with Clarissa's sexually remote and yet vibrant marriage to Richard. Then there is Peter Walsh, who in years past failed with Clarissa. Recently returned from India, Peter thinks how much of his life "she knew nothing whatever about," and she recalls that it was his "lack of a ghost of a notion what anyone else was feeling that annoyed her" (69). But traces of the old attachment flash in their memories. In contrast to these important but deficient loves with two men is the intense sense of connection Clarissa has with a complete stranger, a lady in a passing cab. Clarissa continues to think that somehow "on the ebb and flow of things, here, there, she survived, Peter survived, lived in each other, she being part, she was positive, of the trees at home . . . of people she had never met; being laid out like a mist between the people she knew best" (12). Woolf thus gives substance to the mist of encounter.

In another book I surveyed how technologies distinctive to this period—telephone, wireless, automobile, airplane, high-speed rotary press, and cinema—transformed the older sense of the present moment as a sequence of single local events into an interconnected simultaneity of multiple distant events. That new sense of connectedness was identified at that time with the concept of "simultaneity," and it was manifested culturally with simultaneous poetry, montage editing in cinema, and those literary techniques which Joyce used in *Ulysses* to render the experience of Dublin in a single day.[11] In *Mrs. Dalloway* people from all over London are linked visually and spatially as they view a skywriting airplane from different perspectives all at the same time, and linked auditorily and temporally by hearing Big Ben strike the hour. Clarissa senses that one ring of Big Ben has "forced" her neighbor, an old lady, to move away from the window. Following the woman out of sight, Clarissa reflects on the problem of encounter, "the supreme mystery which . . . was simply this: here was one room; there another. Did religion solve that, or love?" (193). She realizes that the passionate love that Peter offered her was no simple solution to the mystery of her connection with the old lady. Toward the end of the novel, after all the gos-

sip, snobbery, hypocrisy, insensitivity, and failure to understand what anyone else is saying, Clarissa intuits a solution to the mystery of relatedness-
in-separation while she observes the old lady quietly preparing to go to bed,
unaware of Clarissa at her window and of everyone else at her party noisily
failing to communicate. In celebrating Clarissa's bond with this stranger
Woolf gives dramatic substance to the protean nature of encounter.

The "without" in the title *The Man Without Qualities* refers to the literary reduction that Musil performs on his protagonist, Ulrich, to disclose his
fundamental humanity beneath the accumulated "qualities" of Western civilization. Ulrich ponders the nature of his reunion with his sister Agatha
when, after a long absence, she returns to live with him. The chapter title—
"Agatha Is Really There"—is phenomenologically direct and points to the
immediacy of the presence to be explored. Ulrich had been alone all his life.
Now he feels "an utterly incomprehensible plenitude of presence, and all in
all it kept on coming back to the little statement: 'Now Agatha is here.'"
Ulrich and Agatha will have a unique opportunity to explore their relatedness because while they are brother and sister, they were raised apart and do
not have that "sterilised brother-and-sister relationship which prevails in
European families." This accidental reduction leaves them without the qualities that oblige most brothers and sisters to relate in prescribed ways. Their
relationship is theirs to make, as Musil explains. "For finding something
beautiful doubtless means above all *finding* it: whether it is a landscape or a
woman one falls in love with, there it is, gazing back on its complacent
finder and appearing to have been waiting simply and solely for him." The
force of her "being there for him to discover" fills him with a sense of the
plenitude of being, his vulnerability to her otherness, and their responsibility
for constituting a relationship. He marvels at seemingly insignificant details
of her person. How her fragrance fills his air. How the movement of her
body beguiles: "now as knee, now as delicate finger, now as the stubbornness of a stray curl. The only thing that could be said about it was: that
it was there. It was here, where up to now there had been nothing" (III,
272–273).

Forster, Lawrence, Woolf, and Musil dramatize the phenomenology of
encounter. Each novelist attempts to isolate the nature of relatedness itself
by looking beyond or through the magnetic bonding of the conventional
romantic pair in order to explore the remaining foundation that constitutes
being-with.

II

The phenomenology, literature, and art of encounter are linked by a common focus on "the between." Phenomenologists defined that experiential terrain, novelists brought it to life in exchanges between characters, and artists painted it. A shift of focus in the subject matter of painting during this period also transformed the depiction of love. Artists stopped trying to depict some pivotal moment in a story of particular lovers and instead sought to paint conceptual aspects of human relatedness, which included deficient aspects of love as well as the constitutive function of the space between lovers.

These related changes can be seen most sharply in contrast with the nineteenth-century background, which is palpably manifest in John Millais's painting of the parting of two lovers. His full title is packed with narrative: *A Huguenot, on St. Bartholomew's Day, Refusing to Shield Himself from Danger by Wearing the Roman Catholic Badge* (Figure 4, 1857). The painting was exhibited accompanied by a quotation from an edict warning that when the bell sounds at daybreak all Catholics must have a strip of white linen bound around their arm; the woman is attempting to tie one on the Huguenot's sleeve to save his life, while he, who holds integrity and religious loyalty above life (and love), gently refuses. The dominance of narrative conventions in art is evident in Holman Hunt's objection to a sketch of an earlier version of this painting, which showed an unidentifiable couple saying farewell. Hunt told Millais that "a simple pair of lovers without any powerful story, dramatic or historical, attaching to the meeting was not sufficiently important." Millais complied. In addition to relocating the couple in a precise historical moment, he clarified the significance of the moment by using conventional symbols. The clinging ivy symbolizes the fidelity and longevity of their love; the yellow nasturtiums symbolize the sorrow of departure and unfulfilled love; the bells on the picture's original frame (not shown) symbolize the tolling at daybreak, the imminence of the disruptive, external forces of history; and the wall symbolizes the solidity of their love.[12]

Most mid-nineteenth-century artists inspired to paint something "about" love would do so in a narrative context inspired by a significant literary source, usually the Bible, mythology, fiction, or, as in *A Huguenot*, history. They would select some pivotal moment to indicate the past and future of

4. John Millais, *A Huguenot, on St. Bartholomew's Day, Refusing to Shield
Himself from Danger by Wearing the Roman Catholic Badge,* 1857.

the story, one that a viewer could readily comprehend but which might also
be clarified by a narrative title or accompanying quotation, both used by
Millais. The setting would correspond to the narrative source and might be
painted before the couple was placed in it (Millais painted his ivy-covered
wall first). The artist would select beautiful, young models posed to accent
a peak moment of longing. One reviewer wrote in 1878 that *A Huguenot*
depicted "the love of a man and a woman when they love [at] their closest and their best." [13] The artistic technique would obscure the paint, the picture surface, and the artistic process to make viewers believe that they were

actually observing a moment of elevated morality such as this reviewer implied.

A *Huguenot* exhibits three stereotypical characteristics of love in mid-nineteenth-century art. First, it is emphatically narrative. Its exquisite lovers exchanging intense gazes are posed to emphasize the poignancy of this particular moment on the eve of a massacre which actually took place in Paris on August 24, 1572, and which promises to end the man's life. Secondly, the danger to love comes from without, as Millais literally explains with his title. It is caused by the confrontation of pure and conflicting virtues—love of another person and love of God—not from any limitations in or conflict between the lovers themselves. The implied moral is that love would reign supreme if only the external obstacles of history, religion, or society could be surmounted. There is no hint of the deficient modes of love emanating from within that deepen the critical moments as interpreted by later painters. Thirdly, there is no pictorial significance attaching to "the between," the space between the lovers. It is, in the language of art criticism, "negative space," incidental to the relationship between the lovers.

The thematization of deficient modes, the decline of narrative, and an affirmation of the positive function of the space between lovers begin to appear in art of the 1890s, as, for example, in the painting of Gustav Klimt. His *Love* (Figure 5, 1895) shows a man and a woman exchanging gazes in rapt mutuality, very much like those in *A Huguenot,* except that the source of danger (or deficiency) is not entirely clear. A gallery of female faces representing various threatening others—baby, virgin, whore, mother, witch, and death—look down on the couple in judgment. But in contrast to Millais, who showed (and told) precisely what the danger was and identified its location as external to the lovers, Klimt preserves ambiguity. Do these faces represent a haunting past or a lurking future? Are they obstacles overcome or temptations ahead? Are they actual memories and projections or fantasies? Do they pertain to the man or to the woman?

The different ages of the female faces suggest a narrative, but one that is ambiguous and generalized. The lovers are captured not in a moment of a specific story but in a tension that structures all loves, torn between the desire for privacy and the divisiveness generated by the gaze of others. The narrative specificity of Millais is here replaced by a timeless moment. The space between the lovers is not a bit of architecture covered by nature, as it was in Millais, but a distinctively artistic space that has no measurable vol-

5. Gustav Klimt, *Love*, 1895.

ume or specific location. It is not even a shadow or fog but a dusky area on a picture surface, the murky protective aura of lovers' self-absorption. Klimt's positive and deficient love set in a minimally narrative time frame and more exclusively aesthetic space marks a transition between nineteenth-century story-telling and later, more explicit, renderings of encounter.

Another transitional painting of encounter is Edvard Munch's *Eye in Eye* (Figure 6, 1894). The narrative content of this image is negligible, although

6. Edvard Munch, *Eye in Eye*, 1894.

it was exhibited as the second of fifteen works in a series of "moods" of art triumphing over death through love. Its position in that series might imply that it shows a first meeting, but it is a generalized image of encounter. It contrasts sharply with conventional "love-at-first-sight" images popular in the nineteenth century. There is, however, a suggestion of a story line with the house and the magnetic force-lines of the woman's hair—both of which symbolize entanglements of home, sex, and reproduction—drawing the man to her. To accentuate the couple's reciprocal gaze Munch has exaggerated the size and fixed openness of their eyes while muting other features of their faces. Deficiency is internal to this pair, isolated from the pressures of history and from observation by others and yet apparently unable to see each other even though staring directly at one another. Far from Millais's couple who, his painting seems to cry out, "could love so wonderfully if only

. . . ," Munch suggests that even if all external obstacles were removed, the man and woman would confront one another across vast stretches of lived space which compromise understanding and love.

Munch's rendering of "the between" by a tree must be interpreted in the context of a distinctive feature of modern art: the replacement of narrative themes by creative process, a replacement that signifies a shift from love *in* art to love *as* art. The tree is an updating of the Edenic tree of knowledge, but it is more importantly a symbol of the art that grows out of death through love. In a number of Munch's works images of erotic desire, sexual intercourse, loneliness, jealousy, sexual reproduction, metabolism, and growth out of death (especially plants growing out of dead lovers) refer to the creative struggle that is art; and these images are metaphorical references to the artist himself.[14] In a drawing of Munch's explicitly titled *Art* (1893), the plant (of art) grows directly out of the bodies of an entombed man and woman. His *Flower of Pain* (1897) shows the lily of art nourished by a stream of blood flowing out of the man/artist's broken heart. The tree that separates the couple in *Eye in Eye* is one more symbol of love and art, which energize each other. Munch expresses the deficiency of both with the severed lowest branch. As an early offshoot, it may represent primal separation, castration, self-denial, or the intrusion of the creative artist into untrammelled nature. Art is a series of first cuts.

Wassily Kandinsky provides the most explicit theorizing about the artistic rendering of encounter. In 1911 he published *On the Spiritual in Art,* which proposed that artists replace representation with a combination of abstract and semi-abstract forms to render as directly as possible the spiritual nature of human existence. Only by moving away from the particularity of material objects could artists get away from a deadly mechanical imitation of the material world. The dynamic, constitutive function of space must also be given expression, and he depicted, among many other spaces, the space between lovers.

In the book *Point and Line to Plane* (1926) he theorized about how different forms relate to one another on the picture surface. By 1932 he was painting geometric and biomorphic forms to which he gave titles that conjured up all manner of relatedness, such as *Connection* and *Cool Distance.* The following year he painted *From Here to There* and *Lightly Together.* In 1934 he painted *Relations, Two Surroundings,* and *Between Two* (Figure 7, 1934). The helmeted male form on the left of *Between Two* faces a female whose "face" is actually a black fetus in an enlarged crescent-shaped

7. Wassily Kandinsky, *Between Two*, 1934.

uterus.[15] *Point and Line to Plane* suggests how he may have intended this painting to capture male-female relatedness. "A composition," he wrote, is an "organization of the vital forces which, in the form of tensions, are shut up within the elements." Such compositions are made of forms created by lines, each of which has a specific meaning. A curved line is a straight line that has come to "maturity" by outward pressure from within; the more complex the curvature the more "self-conscious" these maturing processes of tension and release. The shapes created by such curved lines suggest the inner characteristics of individual forms as well as the relationships between them. Complex curves indicate an "especially temperamental struggle between the two forces," which in *Between Two* takes place between the male

and female forms. "Approaching-of-the-boundary" indicates intense interaction. In this painting the protruding curves of the male and female forms
closely approach one another's boundaries, indicating the powerful attractive and repulsive forces between them.

In Kandinsky's scheme vertical lines evoke height and warmth, while horizontal lines evoke flatness and coldness. In this painting the square of half-
vertical and half-horizontal lines at the top announces contrasting sexual
temperaments below on either side. Left and right locations are also significant. Left, he theorized, "produces the effect of great looseness, a feeling of
lightness, of emancipation and, finally, of freedom." Right creates the effect
of "a resistance which is greater, compacter and harder than the resistance
of 'left.'" Movement to the right is in the "right direction." It is safe and
predictable and moves toward home and rest. "The tensions of the forms
moving to the right become ever weaker, and the possibility of movement
becomes increasingly limited." This male (on the left) has delivered his sexual product, indicated by the presence of a fetus, and his movement is toward rest. Movement from right to left is an "adventure." The movement of
the relationship that this painting shows will be completed by the woman's
movement to the left, a continuing sexual adventure toward birth.

With the title of the painting Kandinsky drew attention to what is happening *between* the two forms. On the picture surface he evoked the substan-
tiality of that relatedness with a space that is filled with variously colored
dots. This most dynamic space of the picture is red, a color which, he theorized, creates "an intensive inner seething—a tension within it." [16] Most of
the dots are white and empty, suggesting abundant male sperm, while a few
have variously colored centers indicating unfertilized eggs. Together these
sexual products swim in semen, itself a bubbly fluid that is the medium of
sexual reproduction. These bubble-dots fill the space in which the male and
female forms themselves also seem to be swimming or at least suspended.
The bubble-dots may also suggest the uterine fluid in which floats *the* "between" of love—the fetus. Kandinsky limited his theory to the spirit evoked
by lines, forms, and colors. My interpretation goes beyond that by including
some other possible and more specific meanings which span the scenario of
the relatedness of sexual loving from desire and attraction to conception and
birth.

The contrast between Millais's particular persons and Kandinsky's semi-
abstract forms embodies the emergence of modern art. Millais illustrates

what one man and one woman did and how they felt about one another under specific historical circumstances. Kandinsky shows how two artistic forms relate on the picture surface in a timeless moment. The difference also appears in the space between the two couples. Millais presents it as a skillfully executed but clichéd patch of ivy on a brick wall, peeking through the negative and meaningless air space between the two lovers. Kandinsky gives it a vibrant color filled with dynamic activity of several possible interpretations, which imply that it is equally significant as the forms it separates. His space provides an emphatically non-literary and distinctively artistic vision of ways men and women relate. With line, form, and color and with a minimal narrative suggested by barely identifiable male and female forms, he creates a historically unprecedented artistic rendering of encounter.

Whether or not Kandinsky's aquatic in-between was directly influenced by Freud's theory of the "oceanic feeling," elaborated in 1930, it is strongly suggestive of it. Freud argued that the sense of the self as a separate "I" emerges out of a primal immersion in the world. Although Freud's reconstruction of this process begins with the infant at the breast who cannot "distinguish his ego from the external world as the source of the sensations flowing in upon him," it may well begin even before, during the intrauterine period.[17] Normal traces of that sense of limitlessness and bonding with the entire universe persist into adulthood as normal romantic love or religious ecstasy, while pathological traces of it appear in psychosis. For Freud adult ways of relating are a palimpsest of ever more primitive ways of relating going back ultimately to the primordial oceanic feeling. Kandinsky would reject the tag of illustrator, but his *Between Two* is a striking artistic evocation of Freud's famous concept.

In the first decades of the twentieth century major works in philosophy, literature, art, and psychoanalysis viewed human relatedness in new ways. In contrast to earlier philosophers who began with the isolated self and derived human relations from it, phenomenologists of encounter began with modes of being with others and viewed the concept of the individual as derivative and secondary. That development in the history of philosophy established the primacy of being with others over being an isolated self. At the same time novelists and painters gave artistic substance to the foundations of love, which competed with the actions and feelings of isolated individuals around which their narratives and images were structured. Heidegger's elucidation of the deficient modes of being-with, Forster's exploration of the succinct command, "only connect . . .," Kandinsky's bubbly "between," and Freud's oceanic feeling constitute four aspects of a historically distinctive approach to the foundations of love. Together they thematized and valorized the foundations of human relatedness and expanded the experiential terrain of love.

4 Embodiment

FOR ANYONE who has dieted or broken an ankle, no term seems more apt than "my body." Why then are philosophers so determined to question its use? Because the possessive pronoun "my" is not quite right. It implies that I can possess my body as I would a car. But my body is not like my car, since even when I look at it objectively, as for example when looking in a mirror, that looking has a subjective aspect. That paradox lies at the center of philosophical inquiry into human existence.

Phenomenology inherited the concept of the body embedded in the traditional "mind-body problem," which included three major subproblems: (1) whether the distinction between the mind and the body was valid; (2) if the distinction was valid, whether any things in fact existed that corresponded to either term; and (3) if there were such things, what was the relation between them. Phenomenology did not solve these problems. It avoided them by shifting the focus of metaphysics away from relations between entities to ways of being in the world. And for that purpose phenomenology replaced the terms "mind" and "body" with terms that expressed a copresence of the mental and the physical, such as Gabriel Marcel's "incarnate being" and Merleau-Ponty's "living body." "Embodiment" is another phenomenological coinage that attempts to avoid the reification of human existence and express rather a way of being human.[1]

In a journal entry of October 23, 1920, thirty-five years after Nietzsche first called upon philosophers to listen to the "wisdom of the body," Marcel posed the problem: "What is the relation between myself and the instrument that I make use of—i.e. my body? Obviously I do not restrict myself to *making use* of my body. There is a sense in which I *am* my body, whatever that may mean." For the next thirty years he continued this self-correcting style of meditation on the incarnate mystery of the relation between "my-self" and "my body."

The source of the mystery is the relation between the mental and the cor-poreal. My body is mine, but I do not possess it as I do anything else, since in order to be able to possess or have, I must first be. I am my body before I become aware of it; my body is an absolute priority that mediates my atten-tion to anything at all. At times I seem to use it, but not like any other instru-ment, for it is not an object or a thing. As soon as I treat my body as a thing, I exile myself from it. Descartes's image of the mind piloting the body was unacceptable to Marcel, because, as Marcel argued, "I am not the master or the proprietor of the content of my body." No matter how diligently I search, I will never find the pilot in the ship. At the center of my incarnate being is an opacity that is also, mysteriously, the source of all illumination. The relation between me and all of existence is the same as the relation that unites me to my body, which he defined as a "sympathetic mediation." The entire universe is thus my universe and centered in my body.[2]

The most extensive phenomenology of embodiment was that of Merleau-Ponty. His title *Phenomenology of Perception* emphasizes the role of percep-tion, but not as some bodiless Cartesian act. "Consciousness is in the first place not a matter of 'I think that' but of 'I can'." And I *can*, not because I *have* a body that collects knowledge for my mind or carries out orders from it, but because I *am* my body. My body is my point of view upon the world as well as an object in it. My body has a unique spatiality. Its "inner" parts are not spread out side by side but "enveloped in each other."[3] I know where each limb is through a body image. I live my body not as an assemblage of organs but as a unified, meaningful whole. Its outline is a frontier which ordinary spatial relations do not cross. I experience my body as a subject in projects which I understand only because I can perform them. Embodied existence is a stable core that organizes sensory experience, perpetually rein-terpreting exchanges between the self and the external world.

In 1951 Merleau-Ponty summed up the accomplishment of the phenome-nology of embodiment. "Our century has wiped out the dividing line be-tween 'body' and 'mind,' and sees human life as through and through mental and corporeal, always based upon the body and always (even in its most carnal modes) interested in relationships between persons. For many think-ers at the close of the nineteenth century, the body was a bit of matter, a network of mechanisms. The twentieth century has restored and deepened the notion of flesh, that is, of animate body."[4] Phenomenology never quite succeeded in wiping out the dividing line between mind and body, although it offered a compelling alternative to the dualistic theory that viewed them as different kinds of things. Its ongoing struggle against a substance metaphysics unquestionably deepened our understanding of the animate body. Phenomenology did not question the necessary objectivization of the body in anatomy or physiology but did oppose the reduction of human existence to material terms alone.[5]

Victorians not only viewed mind and body as different kinds of things, but most assigned a lower status to the body. Darwin jolted the lofty Victorian conception of human nature by arguing that sexual appeal played a fundamental role in human selection and by implying that man was not divinely conceived because his origins were in the animal world. Darwin's evidence for evolution included useless "remnants" of animal forbears, such as men's nipples and the appendix, which mocked the theory that man was created in God's image. For anyone who missed the existential degradation implied by evolution, Darwin ended *The Descent of Man* with this unambiguous phrase: "with all these exalted powers—Man still bears in his bodily frame the indelible stamp of his lowly origins."[6] In subsequent years the exalted powers got lost in the outrage over the lowly origins. Nineteenth-century culture was thus caught in two basic dilemmas: whether evolution meant that humans had ascended from the animal world or were still mired in it, and whether natural science offered a solution to the riddle of existence or a reduction of it to "a bit of matter, a network of mechanisms."

In the 1880s and 1890s evolutionary theory and the methods of experimental science captured the cultural imagination. Novels reflected this growing emphasis on the corporeal underpinnings of love. At the mid-century they would typically focus on the face with only veiled reference to the rest of the body; by the twentieth century authors were increasingly willing to disclose the details and interpret the meaning of the entire visible surface of the body as well as its inner processes: face, hair, limbs, figure, movement (swimming), nakedness, external sex organs, and smell.

I

The Victorian face stuck out of its heavily clothed body like the head of a turtle. In *On the Eve* (1859) Turgenev describes Elena with large gray eyes, arched eyebrows, firmly closed mouth, pointed chin, and pink hands. In *Sentimental Education* (1869) Flaubert describes Frédéric viewing Mme.

Arnoux's black hair, thick eyebrows, straight nose, dark skin, and "delicate, translucent fingers." Description of the lower body remains cloaked by euphemism and metaphor: Elena had "slender feet," and Mme. Arnoux a "ravishing figure." In *Far from the Madding Crowd* Hardy speculates about Bathsheba: "From the contours of her figure in its upper part she must have had a beautiful neck and shoulders, but since her infancy nobody had ever seen them." Under such circumstances, "rays of male vision seem to have a tickling effect upon virgin faces in rural districts" (67).

The focus on men's faces was even more exclusive than on women's, because their clothing was more uniform and drab, their figures commanded less interest, and their amorous appeal centered more on character. There was another critical gender difference: women's faces were to be looked at, while men's were to do the looking. In *North and South* (1855) Thornton possessed all the body that was required: "the straight brows fell over the clear, deep-set earnest eyes, which, without being unpleasantly sharp, seemed intent enough to penetrate into the very heart and core of what he was looking at" (121). The true test of a man's character was his ability to penetrate a woman's heart. The hero of *Ranthorpe* (1847) had a delicately cut forehead, deep blue eyes, a voluptuous yet refined mouth, but a "weak and faltering" chin. Lewes emphasizes the visibility of Ranthorpe's limitations. "A physiognomist would at once have pronounced him to be a remarkable person; but somewhat deficient in strength of will" (4).

Physiognomy is an ancient practice of reading character from the face. It won renewed attention around the mid-nineteenth century, when readers of novels could be counted on to know what specific facial features signified. As Jeanne Fahnestock points out: "From 1830 to 1860 more and more detail gradually replaces vague description until finally in the 1860s the reader is often given a virtual inventory of the heroine's features."[7] But these features remain facial, and their characteristics are easy to grasp. The simplicity of physiognomy could be simplistic, however, as Charlotte Brontë implied in *Villette* when Madame Beck directs Paul to read Lucy's character: "We know your skill in physiognomy; use it now. Read that countenance" (128). Victorian physiognomy was a serious discipline, although many practiced it as a stunt.

Even though Brontë was suspicious of it, she found physiognomy indispensable. Rochester, disguised as a gypsy fortune-teller, reads Jane Eyre's face, and in *Villette* Paul eventually tells Lucy what he sees in her forehead and eyes. Eliot had a similar conflict. In *Adam Bede* (1859), where the beautiful heroine kills her own baby, Eliot attacks physiognomy but concedes its appeal. "I find it impossible not to expect some depth of soul behind a deep grey eye with a long dark eyelash, in spite of an experience which has shown me that they may go along with deceit, peculation, and stupidity" (199). Her novel generates dramatic interest by challenging that tempting expectation.

Why did these novelists find physiognomy so appealing? Perhaps it reflects the spirit of an age that in fact conformed with zeal to uniform and public codes of behavior. Victorian readers attuned to physiognomy might then be particularly intrigued by the "exception" of a beautiful but evil heroine. Twentieth-century readers would be less persuaded that character was evident in the look of a face and more likely to expect vices in heroines who were as "exquisitely beautiful" as it was routine for them to be in the nineteenth century. Perhaps Victorians were preoccupied with the face as a way of not looking below it. Or maybe novelists needed to make good or evil characters readily identifiable to a new and growing reading public, which might take offense at descriptions of the "lower" parts of the body. Jane Eyre's repeated emphasis on her plainness is a call to arms against the typically beautiful Romantic heroine, but it still focuses attention on facial appearance. After Rochester leaves her to court the exquisite Blanche Ingram, Jane paints two portraits—one of herself, the "plain" governess, and one of her beautiful rival—and congratulates herself on the "wholesome discipline" to which she had bent her feelings. Jane's subsequent battle for Rochester's love turns on the different meanings of those two faces.

George Eliot opens *Daniel Deronda* with two questions that must make contemporary feminists recoil: "Was she beautiful or not beautiful? and what was the secret of form or expression which gave the dynamic quality to her glance?" Eliot attributes those questions to Daniel, but their stunning objectification of womanhood resounds throughout the novel as it did throughout the Victorian world. The follow-up inquiry about the expression behind Gwendolen's "dynamic quality" takes it beyond mere surface and situates the drama to unfold in her "inner" resources, but the sequence of Daniel's questions identifies a basic fact about nineteenth-century heroines—if they are not beautiful, they must have deep compensatory resources of character. Jane Eyre's face is "pale" and its features "irregular," but she is intelligent, kind, and loving.[8]

Far different is Virginia Woolf's interrogation of these contrasting polarities about physical beauty in *Mrs. Dalloway*. Clarissa has a "narrow pea-stick figure: a ridiculous little face, beaked like a bird's." This heroine is no classic beauty but nevertheless fills the "ugly, clumsy" Doris Kilman with resentment: "If only she could make her weep; could ruin her; humiliate her; bring her to her knees crying, You are right!" And yet Doris has a special affection for Clarissa's beautiful daughter Elizabeth, who is not so much vain as youthfully confident. Doris's resentment has taken refuge in religious fanaticism and a hatred for the world of the flesh. But the hatred of Doris is ambiguous, for she idolizes Elizabeth even as she seeks to replace the young woman's natural sensuousness with a religious asceticism. Clarissa's feelings are similarly complex. She sympathizes with Doris's fate but does not romanticize its effect. While Brontë implied that being "plain" helped make and keep Jane good, Woolf allows that being ugly filled Doris with resentment and filled Clarissa with regret: "Oh if she could have had her life over again! [she] could have looked even differently!" (14, 189). Elizabeth's easy beauty may be a temptation to laziness and vanity but need not be, and, more important, it spares her from Doris's resentment and Clarissa's regret.

Wilkie Collins structures the love interest of *The Woman in White* (1860) around a violation of a law of "natural" physical beauty. "Never was the old conventional maxim, that Nature cannot err, more flatly contradicted— never was the fair promise of a lovely figure more strangely and startlingly belied by the face and head that crowned it. [Marian's] complexion was almost swarthy, and the dark down on her upper lip was almost a moustache." The law of nature violated is not that beautiful bodies go with beautiful minds, but that beautiful bodies go with beautiful faces. Collins's exception may not establish the rule, but his hero's astonishment over its violation is distinctly nineteenth-century. That astonishment is further clarified as Collins elaborates its cause, which is "to be charmed by the modest graces of action through which the symmetrical limbs betrayed their beauty when they moved, and then to be almost repelled by the masculine form and masculine look of the features in which the perfectly-shaped figure ended" (25). The presumption of gender polarity as the ground for beauty, the idea that a face could "belie" a body, the primacy of facial beauty, and the response of Collins's hero all date these sensibilities about embodied beauty. In the twentieth century a woman with a perfect figure and graces of action would not be as likely to repel a man with her "masculine look."

The "finest thing" about Emma Bovary, Flaubert tells us, "was her eyes" (17). Like the eyes of many a beautiful Victorian heroine, hers excelled at being seen. In *Lady Audley's Secret* (1862), Mary Braddon proclaims a universal truth: "It was impossible, of course, that these young men could come within the radius of Clara's brown eyes without falling wildly in love with her" (436). When so much on hinged the face, character and plot could turn on the beauty of eyes. Hardy announces that focus with his title *A Pair of Blue Eyes*. He introduces its tragic heroine Elfride as a frame for her eyes. "One point in her, however, you did notice: that was her eyes. In them was seen a sublimation of all of her; it was not necessary to look further: there she lived" (51). Her first love with Stephen Smith begins and ends with her eyes.

> "What did you love me for?" she said, . . .
> "I don't know," he replied idly.
> "O yes, you do," insisted Elfride.
> "Perhaps for your eyes."
> "What of them?—now, don't vex me by a light answer. What of my eyes?"
> "Oh, nothing to be mentioned. They are indifferently good."
> "Come, Stephen, I won't have that. What did you love me for?"
> "It might have been for your mouth."
> "Well, what about my mouth?"
> "I thought it was a passable mouth enough—"
> "That's not very comforting."
> "With a pretty pout and sweet lips; but actually, nothing more than what everybody has."
> "Don't make up things out of your head as you go on, there's a dear Stephen. Now—what—did—you—love—me—for?"
> "Perhaps, 'twas for your neck and hair; though I am not sure: or for . . . your hands and arms, that they eclipsed all other hands and arms; or your feet, that they played about under your dress like little mice; or your tongue, that it was of a dear delicate tone. But I am not altogether sure."

Elfride complains about this "flat picture" and Stephen speaks plainly. "It comes to this sole simple thing: that at one time I had never seen you, and I didn't love you; that then I saw you, and I did love you. Is that enough?" Hardy interprets this ocular obsession—Stephen fell in love with Elfride

simply "by looking at her" (111–112). This summing up of a love in terms
of the eyes captures the externality of embodied love in the mid-nineteenth-
century novel.

Inauthentic eyes are seen; authentic eyes see. Flaubert, Braddon, and
Hardy critique the values of their age with tragic heroines whose major resource is a pair of beautiful eyes. Victorian women were obliged to present
themselves as an object under view, and in the novels of that period we are
less likely to find women with dynamic, authentic eyes like those of the modern woman Ellen in *The Age of Innocence* from 1920.

Archer begins to realize that all the women he knows are "curiously im-
mature" compared with Ellen. "It frightened him to think what must have
gone into the making of her eyes" (63). He is afraid of what she had seen in
the past as well as of what she now sees or does not see in him. There is a
supportive side to her vision, as he explains: "It's you who are . . . opening
my eyes to things I'd looked at so long that I'd ceased to see them" (76). But
he also becomes anxious when he contrasts her eyes with those of his fiancée. In exploring Archer's thoughts, Wharton writes a chapter in the history
of love. "It would presently be his task to take the bandage from this young
woman's eyes [those of his fiancée, May Wellend], and bid her look forth on
the world. But how many generations of the women who had gone into her
making had descended bandaged to the family vault? . . . What if, when he
had bidden May Wellend to open hers, they could only look out blankly at
blankness?" (83). This passage is a key to the tragedy that follows. The generations that produced May's blank stare included men (like Archer himself)
who demanded that women not see, men who were also the blankness at
which those women looked.

According to a standard Victorian treatise on physiognomy, the mouth is
the seat of "animal passion and propensity." "The horizontal width of the
lips indicates the permanence of these functions; their vertical extent, the
intensity."[9] Unless a man had exceptionally thin lips or crooked teeth, his
mouth was of little interest. The beautiful woman was supposed to have a
small and delicate rosebud. Although the mouth was defined as an index of
animal passion in a woman, it was generally viewed as a pair of to-be-
kissed-lips the way Hardy described Tess: "To a young man with the least
fire in him that little upward lift in the middle of her red top lip was distract-
ing, infatuating, maddening" (127). Fitzgerald's Rosalind in *This Side of
Paradise* may well have been speaking against the history of such idolatry
when she rebuked Amory's tiresome praise. "Please don't fall in love with

my mouth—hair, eyes, shoulders, slippers—but *not* my mouth. Everybody falls in love with my mouth" (176). This daring fetishistic displacement is unthinkable in Victorian heroines, who only let dogs kiss their slippers.

II

Victorian and modern descriptions of hair contrast sharply. In *The Egoist* Willoughby inventories the cascades of Clara's hair. He dotes on "the softly dusky nape of her neck, where this way and that the little lighter-colored irreclaimable curls running truant from the comb and the knot—curls, half-curls, root-curls, vine-ringlets, wedding-rings, fledgling feathers, tufts of down, blown wisps—waved or fell, waved over or up or involutedly, or strayed, loose and downward, in the form of small silken paws, hardly any of them much thicker than a crayon shading, cunninger than long round locks of gold to trick the heart" (125). This coiffure is literally full of meaning.[10] It reveals that Clara does not do demanding physical labor and that someone else does her hair. It will obviously take some time to "let it down"—a stock phrase for sexual intimacy. Her hair and by implication her mind is as cluttered and eclectic as a Victorian middle-class interior with its drapes, ornate picture frames, inlaid furniture, knickknacks, needlepoint, photos, mementos, potted plants, and bird cages. The exhaustiveness of the hair-styles is accented by their cramped site, as if, in an age when it was unthinkable to dwell on the varieties of body hair, she was forced to crowd every filament of her being on top of her head. No wonder twentieth-century feminists celebrated cutting those tresses off. The women of Gilman's *Herland* (1915) cut their hair short, leaving "some few inches at most" to get on with the cultivation of a land of their own.

In *The Portrait of a Lady* James portrayed Lord Warburton as a model Victorian gentleman, "with firm, straight features, a lively grey eye and the rich adornment of a chestnut beard." Although beard hair and head hair are often of a different texture and color, Victorian novelists dared not mention the difference. Warburton's full beard and Clara's abundant tresses are localized, for they do not lead to or derive from hair anywhere else. Aside from an occasional downy forearm and Zola's atypical description of Nana's "golden hairs in her armpits . . . observable in the glare of the footlights," Victorian novelists refrained from describing, and their readers did not therefore see, any other body hair than that of the face and head.[11] That restraint disappeared by the time of *Lady Chatterley's Lover*. There Connie, in a relaxed post-coital moment, comments on Mellors's "four kinds of hair," explaining frankly: "On your chest it's nearly black, and your hair isn't dark on your head: but your mustache is hard and dark red, and your hair here, your love-hair, is like a little bush of bright red-gold mistletoe. It's the loveliest of all!" (206).

These contrasting interpretations of hair seem at first to imply contradictory historical developments, because women's hair gets shorter and simpler, while men's hair textures become more diverse. But these contrasts do indicate historical change in the direction of greater authenticity. All hair stylings are for show, but Clara's coiffure was done spectacularly by and for others. Connie's revelation is about the nature of hair. The "four kinds" she observes are not fashions. They refer to the growth and texture of hair, all associated with different functions, meanings, and values of the body. Connie's exclamation at the end of her brief analysis reverberates against the preceding century's silence.

III

Aside from the face and hair, the only other unclothed and visible area of the body in nineteenth-century literature was the hands. And once again it is the woman's experience that underwent the most dynamic change.

In the vocabulary of courtship the hand stands for the heart and is a euphemism for sexual parts. A Victorian gentleman took a woman's hand or asked for it in marriage as prelude to greater intimacy and his greater control.[12] One remarkable observation of hands in Gaskell's *North and South* discloses a number of dynamics of mid-century love. Thornton observes Margaret engaged "with the tea-cups, among which her round ivory hands moved with noiseless daintiness." While she performs this ritual, a bracelet repeatedly falls down on her wrist. It "fascinated him to see her push it up impatiently, until it tightened her soft flesh." Thornton's desire heightens with every new tightening of the bracelet and reaches a peak with this extraordinary image: "He almost longed to ask her to do for him what he saw her compelled to do for her father, who took her little finger and thumb in his masculine hand, and made them serve as sugar-tongs" (120). Hands are a symbol of labor—what one does. A common gesture of helplessness is to open one's hands towards another person. Gaskell intensifies the meaning of Margaret's hands with three contrasts: the daintiness of the tea service with the overpowering humiliation of her father's grasp, the sweetness of the sugar with the bite of sugar-tongs, and the erotic desire of Thornton with the incestuous motives of her father. Inauthenticity cannot be forcibly imposed on an individual, because it involves an internalization of the will of others, but with this gesture Margaret's hands are forcibly taken from her. In a marriage the woman's hands are literally handed over from the grip of the father to the groom. Thornton's observation anticipates that element of the wedding ritual as a rivalry with Margaret's father for sole possession of her hands. This scene is a compelling historical marker, since it would be most unlikely, if not unthinkable, in a twentieth-century novel, except perhaps as parody.

Victorian women were not supposed to show their joints. The ideal female wrists were supposed to be round and dainty, although they generally went unmentioned. By the end of the century novelists began to direct attention to them. In Gissing's *The Odd Women* (1893) Everard notices Rhoda's "strong wrists, with exquisite vein-tracings on the pure white" (102). In *The Golden Bowl* Amerigo observes the "perfect working" of Charlotte's "main attachments." In Huxley's *Point Counter Point* Lucy asks Walter, "Where's your pulse? . . . I can't feel it anywhere . . . I don't believe you've got a pulse" (94). Nineteenth-century women did not know where to find the pulse. The narrator of Ford's *The Good Soldier* (1915) recalls: "Certain women's lines guide your eyes to their necks, their eyelashes, their lips, their breasts. But Leonora's seemed to conduct your gaze always to her wrist" (32). Disclosure of stronger, more flexible, and active wrists parallels the emergence of arms.

In *North and South* the description of Margaret's "noble figure" includes her "round white arms." In *The Mill on the Floss* Maggie's arms are "large," "round," and "pretty." Over the next seventy years novelists transform such marbleized perfection into living flesh. Max tells the heroine of *The Vagabond* that her arms taste salty when he bites them. Such an exploration of surface is matched by an even more daring revelation of what lies beneath. In 1891 Angel Clare kisses "the inside vein" of Tess's arm. In *Sons and Lovers* (1913) Paul is "obsessed by the desire to kiss the tiny blue vein that nestled in the bend of [Clara's] arm." In *The Magic Mountain* Hans dotes on the beauty of Clavdia's arms under a light gauze blouse. Years later, after tuberculosis has invaded her lungs, he becomes more infatuated when he sees as if under her skin and into her arm. Mann explains: "Folly! The utter, accentuated, blinding nudity of these arms, these splendid members of an infected organism, was an experience so intoxicating, compared with that earlier one, as to leave our young man no other recourse than again, with drooping head, to whisper, soundlessly: 'O my God!'" (325).

One of the most worn-out instances of early Victorian prudery is that of an Englishman traveling in the United States in the 1830s, who reported seeing trousers on the carved wooden legs of a pianoforte in a seminary for women, put there to protect the women from any impropriety that bare "legs" might stimulate.[13] But in novels as well, descriptions of legs are clothed in metaphor. In *Wuthering Heights* Nelly describes Catherine as having the "lightest foot in the parish." In *The Egoist,* when Mrs. Mountstuart says that Willoughby "has a leg," she means that he is well-behaved and courtly rather than muscular or sexually appealing. Modest revelations generate intense desire. In *Les Misérables* Marius tells Cosette: "My senses reel even at the sight of your slipper beneath the hem of your skirt" (847).

In sharp contrast Lawrence holds forth on the sensuous meaning of legs. Sitting next to her father, Connie Chatterley begins an interior monologue on his "stout thighs." They are, she reflects, "still strong and well-knit, the thighs of a healthy man who had taken his pleasure in life." They embody his "good-humored selfishness" and "unrepenting sensuality." Connie is able to think imaginatively about such forbidden anatomical terrain as her father's thighs because she is discovering her own body as flesh, including her own legs. "How few people had live, alert legs!" she thinks, as she views other men with "great puddingy thighs" or "well-shaped young legs without any meaning whatever." Connie is equally critical of women and their "millions of meaningless legs prancing meaninglessly around!" (237). The notion of meaningless legs is distinctly modern.

IV

The Victorian female figure is vague. Cathy II had an "admirable form," Margaret's way of carrying her head was "full of a soft feminine defiance," and Anna Karenina's figure was "supple." These descriptions promise a vague vitality. They belong in the picture gallery of nineteenth-century heroines who are healthy, stately, and "full-figured." Short and plain Jane Eyre is an exception, although even she is light-footed, strong, and healthy. With Clavdia, Mann scraps the requirements of health and vitality. Hans' passion intensifies as he looks at her and thinks, "How badly she held herself!" She sat "with drooping shoulders and round back; she even thrust her head forward until the vertebra at the base of the neck showed prominently above the rounded *décolletage* of her white blouse" (125). X-ray imagery in *The Magic Mountain* is a metaphor for the penetrating vision with which Mann probes the deeper recesses of embodied love.

Modern literature is also more likely to treat the body as a whole. At the shore in "Death in Venice" (1911) Aschenbach observed "every line and pose" of Tadzio's body, the outline of his ribs, the blue network of veins in the hollows of his knees. In *Women in Love,* after being cracked on the head with a paperweight by Hermione, Rupert dashed through the woods to cleanse himself of his sterile, cerebral relationship with her. "He took off his clothes and sat down among the primroses, moving his feet softly among the primroses, his leg, his knees, his arms right up to the arm-pits, lying down and letting them touch his belly, his breasts" (100). He clasped the trunk of a birch tree, rolled in the wet grass among the hyacinths, and scraped by the fir branches in a ceremonial resurrection of the body as flesh. In *Tender is the Night* the body was for pleasure. "It was fun spending money in the sunlight of the foreign city, with healthy bodies . . . that sent streams of color up to their faces; with arms and hands, legs and ankles that they stretched out confidently, reading or stepping with the confidence of women lovely to men" (97). Fitzgerald celebrates bodily pleasure with a simple word—"fun."

V

New opportunities for women to exercise and do sports developed with the introduction of Swedish gymnastics in the 1880s, the growing popularity of the bicycle in the 1890s, and the clothing reforms that accelerated in the 1900s with the campaign to eliminate the corset. One novelty in literature is women running. In Austen's *Pride and Prejudice* (1813), when Elizabeth walked alone three miles to Netherfield (far field), she made her hostess all agog over such "conceited independence." The nineteenth-century heroine rarely walked anywhere, and never ran. Twentieth-century heroines raced. The women of Herland teased their male visitors by letting them chase and get close but never quite catch up. In *Sons and Lovers* Lawrence contrasts two eras with the different running ability of Paul's lovers. Miriam did not care for his game of "jumping over," while Clara loved it and "could run like an Amazon." In *The Age of Innocence* Ellen suggests to Archer what is perhaps the first foot race between lovers in modern literature.

Nineteenth-century women rarely knew how to swim, and several of them drowned. Zenobia, like her real-life model Margaret Fuller, drowned in Hawthorne's *The Blithedale Romance* (1852), as did Maggie in *The Mill on the Floss*. There are also the many suicides by drowning—Ophelia, The Lady of Shallot, and numerous damned prostitutes. By the 1890s there is evidence of change. In *The Odd Women* Everard presumes that Rhoda cannot swim because, he explains, "it's so rare for any girl to learn swimming . . . As in everything else, women are trammeled by their clothes: to be able to get rid of them, and to move about with free and brave exertion of all the body, must tend to every kind of health" (256). In Chopin's *The Awakening* (1899) Edna spends the summer learning to swim, which becomes a symbol of her awakening and a means of escape from her confining life. "She wanted to swim far out, where no woman had swum before" (28). And she does. She leaves her husband and children for a lover, but, after witnessing a childbirth and then returning to find her lover gone, she goes for a final swim. At the shore "she cast the unpleasant, pricking garments from her, and for the first time in her life she stood naked in the open air." In the end she is able to swim to her suicide "with a long, sweeping stroke." Her lover's parting words pound in her ears as she goes down thinking, "he did not understand."

In Hardy's *The Return of the Native* (1878) Eustacia Vye also commits suicide by drowning, but her death is pathetic. Unlike Edna who actively swims out to drown herself, Eustacia, driven to despair by misunderstandings about love, jumps into a millpond and is immediately sucked under. Whereas Edna's suicide is described directly from the point of view of her own consciousness, Eustacia's is described indirectly as a "dull sound" of a body falling into water, barely heard above the noise of a storm. Her unsuccessful rescuers rush to the millpond where they see "a dark body . . . slowly borne by one of the backward currents." Edna takes charge of her suicide with the skill of a swimmer and thinks about the possibilities and difficulties of love in her last conscious moments, while Eustacia jumps into the frothy water in a state of tormenting confusion and drowns like a helpless cat. Hardy describes her recovered body as "an armful of wet drapery enclosing a woman's cold form" (374–377). In contrast Edna's drowned body is never found, and the abiding image of her suicide transcends the morbid actuality of a cold wet corpse.

The heroine of Rebecca West's "Indissoluble Matrimony" (1914), Evadne, has learned to swim well. She not only does not commit suicide by drowning but successfully resists her husband's effort to drown her. After a heated argument she storms away from her jealous husband. He follows, expecting to be led to her lover, but instead finds her at the lake taking a solo night swim. Her bathing suit, which reveals her "arms and legs and the broad streak of flesh laid bare by a rent down the back," gives her the appearance of a "grotesquely patterned wild animal." Her powerful stroke is "full of brisk delight." When she emerges he hits her in the stomach, she grabs him by the waist, and they fall together into the water, where he tries to push her under. He thinks he has succeeded in drowning her, but she has swum away under water. Later when he discovers her peacefully sleeping in bed at home, he realizes that he is incapable of killing her. This is, of course, not a love story. It is a story of deficient love in conflict, fought out in the water, and in the fight, for perhaps the first time in literature, a woman possesses superior skill and outmaneuvers a man.

For Lawrence swimming supplies a distinctly modern opportunity for full-bodied sensuousness. In *Sons and Lovers* Paul feels the most intense desire for Clara while they rub their bodies dry after a nighttime swim. In *The Rainbow* Ursula admires the body of her swimming teacher Winifred Inger: "how straight and fine was her back, how strong her loins, how calm and free her limbs!" As Winifred swims Ursula notices "the water flickering upon the white shoulder, the strong legs kicking" (337). In *Women in Love* Gudrun watches Gerald swim and envies the privileges of men: "God, what it is to be a man! . . . The freedom, the liberty, the mobility" (40). Her outburst contrasts sharply with Anna Karenina's jealousy upon hearing about a female Swedish swimmer.

Tender is the Night (1933) opens at a hotel on the French Riviera in 1925. The first activity is swimming. Before eight a man with "much grunting and loud breathing, floundered a minute in the sea." Later an eighteen-year-old girl, Rosemary, came on to the beach and went for a swim. She "laid her face on the water and swam a choppy little four-beat crawl out to the raft. The water reached up for her . . . seeped in her hair and ran into the corners of her body." The intimacy of water contacting the body is intensified by her being observed by an elderly monocled man. Edna's long stroke, Evadne's brisk delight, Winifred's white shoulders and powerful kick, and Rosemary's four-beat crawl and soaked hair create a composite image of the newly embodied woman: swimming alone or with another woman out to, away from, alongside, or under the gaze of men.[14]

The striking modernity of swimming women in literature becomes evident when contrasted with the "bathing" women in art. Two traditions governed the meaning of the nude female bather. The classical tradition includes mythical Diana, the athletic goddess of the hunt and protector of chastity, often shown beside a pool in a shady glade; or Venus, the goddess of fertility and love, stepping out of her bath or rising from the sea on a scallop shell. Biblical art represents the nude female bather as a cause of temptation and sin. Both chaste Susannah at her bath and even innocent Bathsheba at her watery toilette unwittingly arouse and corrupt the men who observe them.

Mid-century French art moves away from the protective cover of these approved subjects toward the *baigneuse*, a nude "bathing" in a landscape, one who may be only preparing to bathe or resting afterwards. Chassériau's *Nymph Sleeping by a Spring* (Figure 8, 1850) shows a sleeping bather whose sensuous torso is open to view, while her pubic area is partly obscured by a raised thigh. She is temptingly viewable, while her eyes are closed to diminish any shame that exposure might create for the viewer. The drapery mediates between nature and culture by partially cushioning her body from the prickly grass. It subtly conceals an innocuous portion of her leg but also guides our eye toward her feet at the edge of the pool, which suggest a quiescence that permeates everything: the title of the painting tells us that she is asleep, we can see that her eyes are closed, her feet seem to refrain from touching the pool, and its mirror-like surface is a metaphor for undisturbed nature. The way her feet barely touch the water contrasts with modern images that show ever deeper, active, and sensuous immersion of women in water.[15]

In *Turkish Women Bathing* (1854) Delacroix shows one woman lying extended up to her neck in a shallow pool and another emerging from it with dripping wet hair. But these are Turkish women. Artistic conventions dictated that nudity and even explicit eroticism were acceptable provided that they were displaced from contemporary life to distant places, ancient history, mythical characters, or mythical places. Throughout the nineteenth century nereids, sirens, undines, naiads, and mermaids are shown romping in the waves. These mythological creatures displaced the erotic from contemporary women, or at least suggested it within the guidelines of reigning aesthetic sensibilities and, in the case of mermaids, denied the possibility of genital arousal altogether.[16]

Manet began to bring the erotic *baignade* home to contemporary France in 1863 with *Le Bain (The Bath)*, subsequently retitled *Le Déjeuner sur l'herbe (Luncheon on the Grass)*. It shows two pairs of lovers who have rowed to a remote watery spot and brought along peaches, cherries, rolls,

8. Théodore Chasseriau, *Nymph Sleeping by a Spring,* 1850.

and a flask. One woman has disrobed and left a disorderly pile of clothes nearby. A twentieth-century viewer of this painting cannot at first see the reason for the scandal it created, even though that reason is literally staring him in the face. The naked woman in the foreground, looking directly at the viewer, was readily identifiable in her own time as a real person, Victorine Meurent.[17] That here-and-now actuality broke the mid-nineteenth-century convention of displacing explicit depictions of erotic bodies to distant places, persons, or ages. Her bold gaze engages the viewer's attention, and her casual nakedness engages her two male viewers, all of which distracts attention from the other woman in the background, who has modestly lifted the hem of her shift to bathe in a stream. The man's gesture almost crosses the viewer's sight line to her bath *(Bain)* in waters just purified by a gentle waterfall upstream. For all the painting's boldness, the relation of woman to water remains subdued.

The same year Manet exhibited *Déjeuner* at the first Salon des Refusés, Cabanel exhibited in the official Salon one of the most emphatic separations of woman and water in the history of art, *Birth of Venus.* As the goddess of love, Venus was born out of the sea from the foam released by the castration of Uranus. Cabanel shows Venus lying *on* the water in a tantalizing combination of mythical eroticism and contemporary reserve. Her voluptuous body is open and visible, but her half-bent knee conceals her pubis, and her right hand half-covers her half-closed eyes. Uranus's sperm is symbolized by the foam of a wavelet couching her head, cushioned on abundant red hair. Two putti toot on conch shells to celebrate the birth of this waterproofed goddess of love. She may be born out of the sea but is depicted impossibly separated from it, while her hair remains dry.

The first down-to-earth modern women to be depicted with wet hair are Degas's prostitutes—*Woman Combing Her Hair* (1879), *After the Bath* (1885), and *Having Her Hair Combed* (1886). Degas was fascinated by the female body and frequented two places where he could see its varieties of development and movement—the ballet and the brothel. He veiled his models' profession with titles suggesting that they were "bathing" or at "their toilette," but as Eunice Lipton has demonstrated, they were prostitutes.[18] Degas moved his "bathers" from the traditional Arcadian setting of innocent country landscapes to private rooms which accented the casual exposure of intimate details of the body and its care—washing and drying feet, buttocks, back, and hair. The water in these tubs is dirty and soapy, for unlike the spotless bathers of centuries past, these bathers are actually trying to get clean. In one exceptional early Degas, *Young Peasant Girls Bathing* (1876), several naked girls (who are not prostitutes) are standing in surf just above their ankles, and one of them is fixing her hair, presumably after a plunge. Gauguin painted a similar group of full-suited women wading out to meet the waves in water around the middle of their thighs. In 1889, shortly before departing for Tahiti, he painted *In the Waves*, showing a nude woman with soaking wet red hair about to dive into a foamy breaker. She anticipates the unencumbered women of Tahiti he had been reading about in travel literature and was soon to immortalize in Western art. As one art historian concluded, this "red-headed, snub-nosed Breton woman . . . who throws herself into the green wave, represents the earliest icon of joyous, primitive animality in Gauguin's universe: the myth of Tahiti born in an aging Europe."[19] These women in Degas and Gauguin are transitional: they are fully wet and out in a lively surf for their own pleasure, but they are not suited and not swimming.

Between 1912 and 1916 the German expressionists Otto Mueller and Ernst Kirchner depicted lovers and friends frolicking near water, striding hand-in-hand into the water, wading up to their necks, or jumping in the waves. But these figures are naked (not in swimming suits), their heads are always out of the water, and they are identified as bathers, not swimmers. Expressionists called for a resurrection of the flesh and a sensuous contact of body and water, but for all their celebratory athleticism, they probably did not know how to swim very well.

Futurists rejected the nude in art and championed modern fashions including swimwear. Carlo Carrà realized those objectives in *The Swimmers* (1910)—one of the earliest paintings of suited swimmers in Western art.[20] Its four fashionably suited women are swept along with aquatic force-lines of the swift current, but they manage to keep their heads afloat by *swimming*. Thomas Hart Benton's *Bathers* (1916–19) and Max Beckmann's *Lido* (1924) show suited male and female swimmers.[21] These paintings suggest a transformation of the body in art from a looked-at object to a functioning, embodied subject, immersed in nature and at the same time skillfully maneuvering against its powerful forces.

VI

The striking shift in the depiction of the body in art across this period is from the classical nude to the naked woman. Victorine Meurent's pile of clothes in *Le Déjeuner sur l'herbe* outraged sensibilities, because it signified that she had undressed in the presence of men and was therefore not acceptably nude but rather unacceptably naked. In literature the code was even stricter. As Hugo proclaimed in *Les Misérables:* "The reader may at a pinch be introduced into a marital bed-chamber, but not into a young girl's bedroom. This is something that verse scarcely dares; to prose it is utterly forbidden . . . A virgin girl is a vision in a dream, not yet become a thing to be looked at. Her alcove is buried in the depths of the ideal. An indiscreet caress of the eyes is a ravishment of this intangible veil. Even a glance is a profanation" (1017). Hugo's prudery is excessive even for the Victorians, but the rule of not describing undressed women did prevail.

In *A Pair of Blue Eyes,* as Elfride sits on a cliff and watches the boat carrying Stephen home, she is joined by Knight. Somehow they manage to fall over the cliff onto a ledge. In helping her up he slips further and saves himself by clinging to a root. She runs off, removes all her clothes, reclothes herself with outer garments, makes a rope of her underclothing, lowers it to him, and raises him to safety, during which time pelting rain soaks her clothing and reveals her body's contours. Hardy shows the reader as much as was permissible: "There is nothing like a thorough drenching for reducing the

protuberances of clothes, but Elfride's seemed to cling to her like a glove"
(276). This is Victorian salaciousness, with life and death heroics slipped out
from under outer clothing like a modest wife hurriedly preparing for her
marital duties behind a screen or under a sheet.

One unmistakable cause of the shift away from such fear of undressing
was World War I, when the proximity of men and nurses as well as the filth,
pain, and danger of trench warfare made such modesty impossible. Until
Vera Brittain entered the nursing service, she recalled, she had "never looked
upon the nude body of an adult male." Nursing released her from the "Victorian tradition which up to 1914 dictated that a young woman should
know nothing of men but their faces and their clothes until marriage pitch-
forked her into an incompletely visualised and highly disconcerting intimacy." Her war purified as much as it clarified: "from the constant handling
of their lean, muscular bodies, I came to understand the essential cleanliness,
the innate nobility, of sexual love on its physical side." Her autobiography,
Testament of Youth (1933), is an important document in the history of love.
"Since it was always Roland [her lover] whom I was nursing by proxy, my
attitude towards him imperceptibly changed; it became less romantic and
more realistic, and thus a new depth was added to my love" (165–166).
That new depth was also in the direction of making her love more authentic,
more about what it means *to be* in love.

In *The Man Without Qualities* Musil recalled that women in the prewar
period "were as chaste as they were shy, had to wear clothes covering them
from their ears down to the ground, but at the same time had to display a
swelling bosom and voluptuous posterior." Their clothing was designed to
enlarge the sheer volume of their being. "In the enormous dress, with all its
ruches, puffs, bell-skirts, cascading draperies, lace and pleatings, they had
created a surface five times as large as the original one, forming a many-
petalled, almost impenetrable chalice loaded with an erotic charge and concealing at its core the slim white animal that made itself fearfully desirable,
letting itself be searched for" (I, 58, 332). In private Agatha undresses and
examines her own body, "as though she were looking at herself properly for
the first time." That self-discovery is repeated before the desiring gaze of a
man after she moves in with Ulrich. Musil reconstructs Agatha's first bath in
Ulrich's home as a step-by-step reconstitution of the body-as-seen. Emerging
from her bath she hesitates and then decides to wrap herself in his robe. "It
was suitable to behave so much like an average young lady and ask Ulrich
to withdraw; so she decided not to acknowledge any sort of equivocal femi-

ninity, but simply to appear before him as the natural and familiar companion that she must be for him even when scantily clad." Later she is obliged to ask him to undo the fastenings at the back of her dress and is shocked that he is so adept with women's clothes (III, 221, 273). The man and his sister are "without qualities," at least the conventional ones, and must constitute their erotic embodiment before one another in their own way without historic precedent or public sanction.

VII

Literary accounts of women's breasts shift from oblique reference to graphic description, and the breasts themselves shift from adequate to deficient sizes, from regular to irregular shapes, and from rigid to malleable forms. The most notorious nineteenth-century breast is covered by an elaborately embroidered scarlet letter which screens any gaze on it without any reference to the underlying flesh that gives it shape. It is held firmly in place and in turn galvanizes the moral framework of Hester Prynne's entire social world. Beautiful Isola of *Ranthorpe* is "somewhat amply moulded, with a waist in perfect proportion" (11). The breast of Cathy II is described with similar euphemism, as we are told that "her figure was both plump and slender"— presumably in the "right" places (250). Jane Eyre desires to be "finely developed in figure" (130). Flaubert guides our vision through that of Frédéric to observe the swelling of Mme. Arnoux's "bosom" (59). In *A Modern Instance* (1892) Howells refers to the "outline of [Marcia's] bust and shoulders" that become visible as she opens the door for Bartley (6). In *Nana* (1880) the heroine has an "Amazonian bosom," and in another scene she squeezes her breasts as she admires and caresses her entire body before a mirror. Hardy's animal-like Arabella has "a round and prominent bosom" (33).

By the twentieth century breasts are described with greater detail, tolerance for irregularity, and irony. In *Sons and Lovers* Paul watches Clara's breasts swing provocatively in her blouse. Wharton implies a historical shift in *The Age of Innocence* with the contrasting figures of May, who was "tall, round-bosomed and willowy," and her daughter Mary, who was "large-waisted, flat-chested, and slightly slouching" (348). Early in *Ulysses* Joyce records Leopold's view of Molly's "large soft bubs, sloping within her nightdress like a shegoat's udder" (63). In the concluding interior monologue Joyce reconstructs Molly's image of her own breasts:

yes I think he [Leopold] made them a bit firmer sucking them like that so long he made me thirsty titties he calls them I had to laugh yes this one anyhow stiff the nipple gets for the least thing Ill get him to keep that up and Ill take those eggs beaten up with marsala fatten them out for him what are all those veins and things curious the way its made 2 the same in case of twins theyre supposed to represent beauty placed up there like those statues in the museum one of them pretending to hide it with her hand are they so beautiful . . . (753)

Molly thinks about her "curious" breasts as if she had just discovered "all those veins." She views her breasts not as the hallowed springs of nourishment eulogized by romantic poets but as "titties" to be fattened for her sex-hungry husband who, as he sucked them firm, made one nipple more erect than the other.

A clue to Victorian reserve about describing the genitals is the obstetrical practice of examining a patient without looking at her vagina (Figure 9, 1822).[22] A prevalent attitude in the United States at the mid-century was that of a distinguished professor of midwifery and the diseases of women at the Jefferson Medical College in Philadelphia, who was proud that "there are women who prefer to suffer the extremity of danger and pain rather than waive those scruples of delicacy which prevent their maladies from being fully explored. I say it is an evidence of the dominion of a fine morality in our society."[23] Violating that morality could be costly. In 1850 James White, a professor of obstetrics at the Buffalo Medical College, allowed his students to observe a delivery, and they praised this training in a newspaper article. In a subsequent article Dr. Horatio Loomis criticized White for exposing the woman to the salacious stare of his students and committing a "gross outrage upon public decency." White brought libel charges against Loomis, and during the trial Loomis's attorney further asserted that exposing the woman was a "bestial innovation."[24]

These obstetricians were, of course, not in love with their patients. I refer to this practice to show to what extent Victorian prudery proscribed, if it did not outlaw, literary descriptions of how or under what circumstances a man could look at a woman's sex organs, let alone describe what he might see if he did. That there should be such a heated debate over this practice, which common sense and sound medical thinking ought to require, suggests how knotted up the Victorians were. And when they did not have the moral

9. From Jacques P. Maygrier, *Midwifery Illustrated:* "Touching, the
female erect" (unsighted digital examination of women). 1834.

cover of medical education or the urgencies of an actual delivery when the
woman's life was at stake, the code that required not looking was all the
more firmly in place. In literature that code was scrupulously observed.

It is impossible to compare twentieth-century descriptions of the genitals
in literature with those of the nineteenth century, because aside from pornography there were none in the earlier period, not even veiled references to
forms underlying clothing. Historians rightly question whether this omission signifies an accurate reflection of the high levels of public suppression
of sexuality, novelists' reluctant capitulation before the threat of official censorship, a condition for publication set by editors who may or may not have
accepted the need for censorship, novelists' grudging acquiescence to the
reading public's hypocrisy, or novelists' genuine literary sensibilities about
good taste. Whatever the reason, neither the nineteenth-century readers of
serious novels nor the characters in them were shown male or female genitals, however passionate the love that stimulated them. Much of the explicit
detail of the body undressed and ready for sexual pleasure will be included

in my subsequent chapters on desire and sex, but some descriptions of the way the external genitalia appeared belongs here.

The body of the Victorian romantic hero, generally described as dark and muscular, implied how his genitals may have looked and performed. In contrast Leopold Bloom's body is pale and pudgy, and when he observes his genitals while bathing, they seem equally unmasculine: "the dark tangled curls of his bush floating, floating hair of the stream around the limp father of thousands, a languid floating flower" (86). Although we never are shown the penises of Victorian heroes, we may presume that they were not thought of as languid floating flowers and certainly not as "limp." After a century of mandatory tumescence, the twentieth-century hero could relax a bit. In *The Captive* (1923) Proust describes the man's penis as an oversight in creation. Man "is disfigured as though by an iron clamp left sticking in a statue that has been taken down from its niche" (74). Although this corresponds roughly to conventional images of male hardness, it is far more explicit, irreverent, and comical than was typical of Victorian assessments of masculine anatomy.

In *The Sun Also Rises* (1926) the love between Jake and Brett cannot be fulfilled because he has lost his penis in the war.[25] The novel includes no explicit description of the genitals as seen but focuses attention and incites interest by Jake's deficiency. Hemingway inquires into what it means to have a penis through a character who cannot forget that he has lost his own.

These descriptions of detumescent, comical, and deficient modes in literature parallel the striking fragmentations, dislocations, and ironic juxtapositions of the genitals and other body parts by Expressionist, Cubist, and Surrealist painters. In one of Egon Schiele's portraits of himself masturbating, *Eros* (1911), his index finger points to the tip of his blood-red erection as if to show viewers what they must learn to see. His *Red-Haired Girl with Spread Legs* (1910) exposes her pink vulva framed by white underclothes and a dark dress. Her black boots further accent the shock of visible genitals. In *Dark-Haired Girl with Raised Skirt* (1911) the model's limbs are omitted to narrow the focus to her exposed dark red vulva and pubic musculature.

In *The Bride* (1912) Duchamp attached to the bride's head a "sex cylinder," which is a symbol for the female genitals. In *The Bride Stripped Bare by Her Bachelors, Even* (1915–1923) he represented the male genitals playfully with the three cylinders of a chocolate grinder, which presumably can grind on endlessly all by themselves, while the bride's sex cylinder is attended by nine "Malic Moulds" patterned after the uniforms of various professions, strung on a line in front of her like so many spare phallic parts for her insatiable sexual appetite. In the mid-1920s Miró exaggerated the sex organs by confounding them with the entire body, sometimes in androgynous mixtures. The most famous such transposition was Magritte's *The Rape* (1934), which replaced a woman's eyes by her breasts, her nose by her navel, and her mouth by her pubic triangle.

Beginning in 1924 Picasso began to interchange sexual organs with other body parts, creating visual metaphors for the pansexualism that the Surrealists took from their reading of Freud.[26] Noses turn into penises, mouths into vaginas, tongues into phallic spikes, and jawbones into terrifying mandibular visions of the *vagina dentata*. Heads shrink to a pinpoint as genitals swell into elephantine globules; the lock of a dressing cabin symbolizes a vagina, and its key, a penis. In 1933 Picasso drew a set of thirty images of women titled *An Anatomy*—a lexicon of sexual-anatomical transpositions that seems to have been created by some sex-crazed gadgeteer. The seam of a massive peach-like torso or a wedge-shaped trough represent a woman's vagina; a chair becomes a woman's lap. One woman totes her breasts that look like two balls on a string attached to the tip of her nose, one carries them like a purse with the string attached at her shoulder, and another rests them on a pillow. Other breasts are represented by tea-cups or yarn spools. A number of drawings from 1933 show couples in the sex act. A cyclopean male plunges his massive horse phallus into the body of a biomorphic female whose head is an ambiguous combination of heart, peach, and vagina. Another child-like drawing of the sex act diagrams a tubular erection attached to two round balls at right angles to a square box of a torso, like some hurried how-to-do-it sketch.

VIII

There is also a history of what was happening underneath the skin, as evinced by the sense of smell. Body hygiene, laundering, clothing, and perfumes are used to mask this transcendent function of olfaction which can reveal the health, cleanliness, age, activity level, and mood of others. Around the mid-century references are generally to subtle, if intensely provocative, odors in women.[27] Baudelaire reveled in the perfume of women's hair. In *On the Eve* Insarov is aroused by the persistence of the faint odor of mignonette which Elena leaves in a room. In *Sentimental Education* Frédéric sneaks a tantalizing whiff of Mme. Arnoux's perfumed handkerchief as she passes. By the mid-1870s Zola made body odor an essential element of character description. In *The Sin of Father Mouret* (1875) each character has a distinctive odor. The heroine of *Nana* has her own haunting smell, a composite of "the odor of gas, the glue used in scenery, the dirt in dark corners, the underwear of the chorus-girls ... the acidity of the toilet waters, the perfumes of soaps, the putrid smells of exhalations ... an odor of womanhood—a musky scent of make-up mixed with the primitive smell of human hair" (123).

In the twentieth century, novelists followed Zola's lead in exploring the funky disclosures and dark corners of olfaction. A passing whiff turns Leopold's thoughts to Molly's odor which clings to everything she takes off—stockings, shoes, underclothing. "Wonder where it is really. There or the armpits or under the neck. Because you get it out of all holes and corners ... Dogs at each other behind. Good evening. Evening. How do you sniff? Hm. Hm. Very well, thank you. Animals go by that ... We're the same. Some women for instance warn you off when they have their period. Come near. Then get a hogo you could hang your hat on." Molly also responds to Leopold's "celery sauce" smell that "diffuses itself all through the body" (375).

In Musil's "The Perfecting of a Love," the perfecting is triggered by the powerful associations of primitive smell. In anticipation of having sex with the stranger she has met on a train, Claudine undresses in her hotel room. She imagines that the scent from her clothes mingles with the smells from persons who occupied the room before her, stepped on the rug in their bare feet, and permeated it with odors that in turn "entered into other people's being." She is seized "by a wild urge to throw herself down on this rug and kiss the repulsive traces of all those feet, exciting herself with their smell like a bitch in heat." Claudine realizes that her marriage had been made for her and that she had lived it mechanically as something external to herself. As she kneels on the rug she sees "her own heavy thighs, a mature woman's thighs, hideously arched and without meaning" (170). This moment of self-degradation becomes a moment of self-constitution. Indulging the most primitive sex instincts associated with olfaction momentarily undoes the lofty pretence of her marriage and enables her to reconstruct love with this stranger and "perfect" it by making it more her own.

If Victorian characters had only a vague understanding of the bodily processes indicated by smell, their knowledge of the actual subcutaneous workings of love were even more limited. *Middlemarch*'s Lydgate is typical. "A liberal education had of course left him free to read the indecent passages in the school classics, but beyond a general sense of secrecy and obscenity in connection with his internal structure, had left his imagination quite unbiassed, so that for anything he knew his brains lay in small bags at his temples" (98).

In the twentieth century Ann Veronica tackles such ignorance directly by enrolling in a course on comparative anatomy, and her instructor eventually becomes her lover. In *The Magic Mountain* x-rays show the inner workings of diseased bodies in love. The chief physician Behrens has painted a portrait of Hans's beloved Clavdia which renders her inner essence, as he tells Hans. "Well, I know her under her skin—subcutaneously, you see: blood pressure, tissue tension, lymphatic circulation." Behrens elaborates on the anatomical structures and physiological processes that underlie her dazzling eyes, slinking walk, "tender, though not emaciated, bosom," and skin which he has painted so insightfully that it seems to show the "perspiration, the invisible vapour which the life beneath threw off" (257–258). Hans asks for and gets a lecture on the human skin that surveys blushing, shivering, goose bumps, oil secretion, and perspiration. The revelations of Behrens' painting and commentary augment Hans's knowledge of his beloved's body inside and out, supplementing the keepsake image he keeps framed beside his bed—an x-ray of Clavdia's tubercular lungs.

While Wells and Mann sacrificed some conventional delicacy to undo generations of silence about the inner workings of the body in love, Joyce, Huxley, and Lawrence profaned that delicacy with reference to *the* forbidden bodily process. In Joyce's *Exiles* Robert maintains that the most attractive qualities of even the most beautiful woman are not her exceptional features but what she has in common with other women. "I mean . . . the commonest . . . I mean how her body develops heat when it is pressed, the movement of her blood, how quickly she changes by digestion what she eats into—what shall be nameless" (42). In *Point Counter Point* Huxley's stand-in for Lawrence, Mark Rampion, rails against the disembodiment of love in Shelley, who allowed for "no blood, no real bones and bowels." Mark is particularly incensed by Shelley's "To a Skylark," especially the lines, "Hail to thee, blithe spirit! Bird thou never wert!" He questions why the lark "couldn't be allowed to be a mere bird, with blood and feathers and a nest and an appetite for caterpillars. Oh no! that wasn't nearly poetical enough, that was much too coarse. It had to be a disembodied spirit. Bloodless, boneless . . . I

wish to God the bird had . . . dropped a good large mess in his eye. It would
have served him damned well right for saying it wasn't a bird. Blithe spirit,
indeed!" (123–124).

Lawrence attempted to end the "excursion into bodilessness" which, as
he saw it, characterized the last three thousand years of mankind. Love
would only be possible when the final dark secret of the body had been
accepted. In *Women in Love* Rupert and Ursula engage in digital anal erotism, and in *Lady Chatterley's Lover* Mellors sodomizes Connie. Lawrence
did not intend these practices to become routine, but they needed to be explored at least once to dispel the fear of any part of the body so intimately
associated with sexual arousal. In "A Propos of *Lady Chatterley's Lover*" he
argued that past generations have been "too weak-minded or crude-
minded" to contemplate the physical body. It was high time to overcome
this terror of the body, such as that which drove Jonathan Swift mad when
he thought about his mistress: "But—Celia, Celia, Celia s***s." In fact,
Swift did not go mad (he suffered from Ménière's syndrome), nor did he
intend to humiliate Celia (his satire is aimed at Celia's lover who is so
troubled by defecation). Nevertheless, Lawrence directs his outrage at what
he takes to be Celia's humiliation—"made to feel iniquitous about her
proper natural function, by her 'lover'" (84–86). Mann, Joyce, Huxley, and
Lawrence shared the view that no part of the body can be ignored, much
less feared, if lovers are to realize the pleasure and grasp the meaning of
embodied love.

The history of the body in literature changes from the facial peep-show of
the Victorians to the revelations of twentieth-century novelists who ventured to describe not only undressed bodies ready for pleasure but deficient,
detumescent, awkward, funny-looking, smelly, oily, and diseased bodies
that nevertheless held their erotic interest: Clarissa's "beaked" face, Ellen's
well-traveled eyes, Mellors's fourth kind of hair, Rhoda's "strong wrists,"
Connie's "alert legs," Rosemary's four-beat crawl, Molly's "large, soft
bubs," Leopold's "languid floating flower," and Clavdia's pathological tissue. Far from diminishing the possibilities of embodied love, these realities
expanded them in the direction of greater authenticity, as men and women
could include simply more of what they were and hence more awareness of
themselves as human beings in love.

5 Desire

IN ART AND letters after 1900 the beloved was seen in more bodily detail and deeper penetration beneath the visible surface of clothing and skin. The history of desire followed a similar course toward more explicit reference to anatomy and physical processes. In *Les Misérables* Victor Hugo celebrated Victorian reserve:

> In that first stage of their love, the stage when physical desire is wholly subdued beneath the omnipotence of spiritual ecstasy, Marius would have been more capable of going with a street-girl than of lifting the hem of Cosette's skirt, even above her ankle. When on one occasion she bent down to pick something up and her corsage gaped to disclose the top of her bosom, he turned his head away.
>
> What did take place, then, between those two? Nothing. They adored each other . . . There was a whole world, that of the flesh, from which their innocent love recoiled with a kind of religious awe. (846)

Sixty years later Joyce's hero stares *at* the world of the flesh with religious awe. Leopold is talking to a friend about the death of another friend Paddy Dignam when he notices across the street the white-stockinged legs of a woman getting into a coach. In the following passage, Leopold's distraction and desultory "Yes" contrast with his voyeuristic obsession.

> High brown boots with laces dangling. Well turned foot . . .
> —*Why?* I [Bloom's friend] said. *What's wrong with him?* I said.
> Proud: rich: silk stockings.
> —Yes, Mr Bloom said.
> He moved a little to the side of M'Coy's talking head. Getting up in a minute.

—What's wrong with him? he said. *He's dead,* he said . . . *Is it Paddy Dignam?* I said . . . *Yes,* he said. *He's gone. He died on Monday, poor fellow.*

Watch! Watch! Silk flash rich stockings white. Watch! (74)

Leopold's voyeurism peaks later that day as he watches Gerty on the rocks, and neither turns away. "His eyes burned into her as though they would search her through and through." She raises her skirt to show Bloom what she knows he needs to see, and she feels "the warm flush . . . surging and flaming into her cheeks." Voyeur and exhibitionist arouse each other. "It was he who mattered and there was joy on her face because she wanted him." His eyes "set her tingling in every nerve . . . He was eyeing her as a snake eyes its prey. Her woman's instinct told her that she had raised the devil in him and at the thought a burning scarlet swept from throat to brow till the lovely colour of her face became a glorious rose" (360). In sharp contrast to Hugo's reverence for Marius's prudish "religious awe," Joyce irreverently tears away the sublimating veil of religion and celebrates Leopold's masturbating to the cadence of Gerty's swinging foot, which she consciously synchronizes with the singing in a nearby church, while her face is "suffused with a divine . . . blush." Joyce underlines the irreligiosity of their desire by juxtaposing Canon O'Hanlon's eyeing the Blessed Sacrament in church with Leopold's eyeing Gerty's underclothes, "drinking in her every contour, literally worshipping at her shrine." After Leopold's climax, "their souls met in a last lingering glance and the eyes that reached her heart, full of a strange shining, hung enraptured on her sweet flowerlike face" (356–367).

This contrast between two responses to the body-as-seen takes its meaning from the underlying desire. Hugo's lovers turn away from it, while Joyce's lovers gaze unabashedly into its heart. This chapter will explore five questions concerning the history of desire: what is the function of desire in human existence generally, what is the bodily source of sexual desire, are there distinctive gender modes of desire, what is the value of desire, and what is the connection between desire and creativity?

I

After the mid-nineteenth century the role of desire in philosophies of human existence expanded and deepened. Until the late nineteenth century desire was a problem for ethics. For Hobbes ethics was a matter of reconciling or mediating between conflicting desires. Kant based his ethics on the activity of rational wills that renounce the hegemony of desire out of a sense of duty. Fourier grounded his utopian socialism on a philosophy that harmonized the conflicting "appetites" that had been so much trouble for the ethical philosophy of eighteenth-century associationists. Hegel expanded the function of desire by viewing it as crucial to the development of self-consciousness. Desire takes the subject beyond itself toward another self, negates the consciousness of that other self, and returns the self to itself dialectically at a higher level of self-awareness. For Mill the natural desire of the pleasure-seeking individual was the basis for ethics, which had as its goal the greatest happiness for the greatest number of people.

Phenomenology identified a number of basic tendencies akin to desire as the foundation of consciousness and hence of human existence. In 1874 Franz Brentano argued that the most distinctive feature of a mental phenomenon was its "intentionality," or a directedness toward something outside itself, which was nevertheless also part of itself.[1] For Husserl intentionality grounds what is most characteristic of human existence—acts of consciousness, which constitute every human experience ranging from simple perceptions to complex judgments. For Heidegger human existence is "ahead-of-itself-Being-already-in-the-world-as-Being-alongside-entities-encountered-within-the-world." He gives the name "care" to this unifying existential and unpacks it to disclose the primordial foundations of human existence. Human beings do not first exist and then learn to desire, rather they exist primordially in "care," which grounds all specific desires (237–241). Other notions of a basic human directedness include Scheler's "love," Freud's "libido," and Jaspers's "Existenz," all part of a broad cultural reorientation of thinking about human existence as intentional, as directed beyond the self in expressive and communicative movements that resemble the more sexual aspects of desire.

II

Victorian renderings of the anatomical sources of desire were vague. Elizabeth Barrett Browning's *Sonnets from the Portuguese* (1850), which inspired a generation of lovers, rendered the physical sources of desire with metaphors of euphemism and circumspection. She hears "footsteps of the soul" and waits with "trembling knees." The hand of love is "soft and warm" and brings "souls to touch." Her heart opens wide to "fold within the wet wings of thy dove." Passion is there, because her own pulse and her beloved's "beat double," and "no child's foot could run fast as this blood." There is an awkward first kiss that "sought the forehead, and half missed,/ Half falling on the hair." But most loving desire is deadly serious as in "Let Me Count the Ways." Her count includes loving "to the depth and breadth and height/ [her] soul can reach, when feeling out of sight/ For the ends of Being and ideal Grace." Her love is free and pure, with "passions put to use" in "old griefs" and with "childhood's faith." And "if God choose," she concludes, entombing sexual desire, "I shall but love thee better after death."

Victorian novelists routed sexual desire through such ethereal organs as the soul, spirit, or heart and sublimated it into "spiritual ecstasy," "religious awe," and "ideal grace." In *Ranthorpe*, when the hero's cheek gently brushes Isola's hair, her perfume "thrilled his soul with vague voluptuous ecstasy" (335). In *Far from the Madding Crowd*, Boldwood's "heart began to move within him" at the sight of Bathsheba (168). Hardy's transitional *Tess* points both ways. He describes Angel's sexual desire for Tess with conventional euphemism, as contemplation of her lips "sent an aura over his flesh, a breeze through his nerves"; but then Hardy adds, with unethereal humor, that it "actually produced, by some mysterious physiological process, a prosaic sneeze" (127).

Twentieth-century novelists and painters eagerly explored such sobering physical realities and returned the sources of desire from anatomical euphemisms and heavenly spheres to the loins, genitals, and bowels of sensate flesh. Two paintings contrast this basic shift.

Jean-Léon Gérôme produced some striking images of women undressing for men or being undressed by someone else.[2] His most spectacular disrobing was *Phryné before the Aeropagus* (Figure 10, 1861). Phryné was an exquisite Athenian courtesan and artist's model once caught bathing naked in the sea, which caused her to be tried for impiety. Gérôme depicts the moment when her lawyer whisks away her robe before a tribunal, the Aeropagus, to support his defense that no one so beautiful could possibly be guilty of impiety. Her twenty-eight judges are rendered like a composite physiognomical illustration, an A to Z of male desire. Interpreting the bottom row from the left we see paralysis, horror, perplexity, adoration, curiosity, shock, prayer, dumbfoundedness, disbelief, reflection, and exhaustion. In the second row four lechers lean forward to get a closer look, three raise their right hand in astonishment, one withdraws. In the top row three twist away but retain fixed stares, two sit calmly in judgment, and one stands and raises both hands as if the spectacle had lifted him out of his seat. Phryné's pose reveals frontal nudity only to viewers of the painting but gives her gallery of judges something more to look for, as several lean to their left to catch a better view. Her white body seems to absorb the light in the chamber and reflect it into our eyes. Gérôme intensifies the visual seat of desire by having her cover her own eyes.[3] The faces of the judges peer out of bright red robes which conceal any bodily evidence of deeper libidinal stirrings, but the color betrays the judges' lust.

In 1929 Salvador Dali and Luis Buñuel made a movie, *An Andalusian Dog*, which cut open the eye of Western art and with it a host of aesthetic and sexual conventions. The famous prologue scene in which a razor slices open a woman's eye and fluid gushes out has been interpreted as a metaphor for cinematic montage or the cutting of film and its vision of reality, a symbol of sexual penetration or castration, an assault on the viewer, or an emblem of surreality itself. It also suggests the transformations of sexual desire that structure the remainder of the film in which a man's passion for a woman bores a hole into the palm of his hand (out of which swarm devouring ants), switches the woman's breasts into buttocks, penetrates beneath the visible surface of her body, and cuts off the hair in her armpit and patches it on the man's own mouth in a final surrealistic transfiguration of the conventional sources of sexual desire.[4] The film contrasts with the Victorians' preoccupation with the surface of the body as seen and discloses subcutaneous and unusual sources of desire.

In 1929 Dali joined the Surrealist movement and assimilated its fascination with Freud's ideas about sexuality. The last issue of its journal *La Révolution Surréaliste* in December of that year reproduced Dali's *Accommodations of Desire* (1926) and *Illumined Pleasures* (1929)—both paintings of the secret depths and abnormal channels of desire. His *Dismal Sport* (1929) combines some disturbing childhood memories, Freudian symbols, and recent sexual problems with his new lover Gala to make a composite image of overwhelming sexual desire, phallic worship, coprophilia, masturbation guilt, and castration anxiety.[5] For the next several years his paintings reveal the intense, terrifying, and (so far as he could fathom them) unconscious origins of his own sexual desire.

The Specter of Sex-Appeal (Figure 11, 1932) transforms both the conventional object of desire and its normal sources. In place of the idealized beauties that inspired artists such as Gérôme and titillated his patrons and view-

10. Jean-Léon Gérôme, *Phryné before the Aeropagus*, 1861.

ers, Dali portrays a brutally amputated and decapitated, savagely
eviscerated creature propped up on crutches, with a dilapidated pillow over
her sex organs and two sacks of grain for breasts. She strikes the eye of
desire like the slashed eye in his and Buñuel's film, forcing viewers to exam-
ine precisely what arouses them. This is no *memento mori;* Dali wants to
show what living sex-appeal emphatically *is*. He indicates the deceptiveness
of desire as well as its monstrosity with the tiny boy in a sailor's outfit who
must somehow grow into the awesome destiny that awaits his advances. A
confirmed Freudian, Dali believed that the earliest stirrings of child sexuality are polymorphous perverse. He represents the bisexual nature of pregen-
ital sexuality by having the boy hold a feminine hoop and a phallic thigh
bone with bulging protuberances, manifesting in his short-panted way more
forthright sexuality than Gérôme's amphitheater of older men breathing
hard under their red robes.

Twentieth-century literature probes the sources of desire beyond vision
and deep in the lover's flesh. For Proust sexual desire is not stimulated by
vision alone, because "the senses follow one another in search of the various
charms, fragrant, tactile, savorous . . . and are able, thanks to . . . the genius
for synthesis in which desire excels, to reconstruct beneath the hue of cheeks

11. Salvador Dali, *The Specter of Sex-Appeal*, 1932.

or bosom the feel, the taste, the contact that is forbidden them" (I, 953). Mann equates the processes of life and desire that charge Hans's love for Clavdia. "It was a stolen and voluptuous impurity of sucking and secreting; an exhalation of carbonic acid gas and material impurities of mysterious origin and composition. It was an unfolding . . . of something brewed out of water, albumen, salts and fats, which was called flesh, and which became form, beauty, a lofty image, and yet all the time the essence of sensuality and desire" (276). Thus does the twentieth century count the ways. Hans romances Clavdia in similar terms with eroticized disquisitions on sexual physiology. He concludes one feverish outburst with a seriocomical string of fantasies: "Let me breathe in the odour of your knee-joint, beneath which the ingenious jointed capsule secretes its slippery oil! Let me devotedly touch with my mouth the femoral artery which pulses at the base of your thigh and which separates further down into the two arteries of the tibia! Let me smell the odor of your pores and feel your downy coat." To add a touch of intimacy Hans speaks in French, but Clavdia exits with the dubious compliment that he is *"un galant qui sait solliciter d'une manière profonde, à l'allemande"* (343).

The manner was not exclusively German: in England Lawrence also probed the inner recesses of desire and with even greater boldness. In *The Rainbow* the sight of Lydia grips Tom "in his bowels" (33). His adopted daughter Anna and her husband Will are as estranged as her parents, so sexual love becomes their sole and terrifying connection. Will taps into Anna's sensuousness to fill the void, systematically exploring "the many little rapturous places," each of which drives him mad with delight and stimulates his desire to know more. "He would say during the daytime: 'To-night I shall know the little hollow under her ankle, where the blue vein crosses.'" With that knowledge comes further anticipation of all "the undiscovered beauties and ecstatic places of delight in her body," even "the instep of her foot, and the place from which the toes radiated out, the little, miraculous white plain from which ran the little hillocks of the toes, and the folded, dimpling hollows between the toes." Their sensuality ranges from innocent toes as seen and touched to the "pure darkness" of "all the shameful things of the body" (233–235). The novel concludes a generation later with their daughter Ursula, who responds to Skrebensky's kiss from the depths of her body. It "flowed over the last fibre of her, so that they were one stream . . . and she clung at the core of him, with her lips holding open the very bottommost source of him" (447). Lawrence's final intercellular analysis of their bliss as the "nucleolating of the fecund darkness" borders on self-parody.

The "pent-up aching rivers" of desire, aptly described by Walt Whitman, were typically mid-nineteenth-century, when literary censorship maintained a sharp distinction between sexual desire (which might be described with suitable euphemism) and sexual activity (which could only be hinted at). Novelists concentrated on desire in lovers who must await sexual pleasure throughout a novel. By the twentieth century censorship was less restrictive and the distinction between desire and sexuality less sharp. The detail of Lawrence's descriptions of desire increased along with the increasing varieties of sexual experimentation, as in *Women in Love,* when Ursula puts her arms around Rupert's loins, her face against his thigh, and with her fingertips traces down his flanks, establishing "a rich new circuit . . . released from the darkest poles of the body . . . at the back and base of the loins." The stimulation of desire is also reciprocal: "a living fire ran through her, from him darkly . . . flooding down her spine and down her knees." Ursula traces desire to its genital-anal center with a frankness unthinkable for a Victorian heroine. "She had thought there was no source deeper than the phallic source. And now, behold, from the smitten rock of the man's body, from the strange marvellous flanks and thighs, deeper, further in mystery than the phallic source, came the floods of ineffable darkness and ineffable riches" (306). For a reader of the 1990s this prose may seem somewhat euphemistic, but in 1920 it was a daring revelation of the sources of sexual desire.

In *Ulysses* Leopold's response to pornography is polymorphous perverse. While standing in a bookstall picking something for Molly, he begins to read to himself. Joyce quotes what Leopold is reading in parenthesis. "Warmth showered gently over him, cowing his flesh. Flesh yielded amid rumpled clothes. Whites of eyes swooning up. His nostrils arched themselves for prey. Melting breast ointments *(for him! For Raoul!)* Armpits' oniony sweat. Fishgluey slime *(her heaving embonpoint!)* Feel! Press! Crushed! Sulphur dung of lions!" (236). Joyce recreates the physical processes of desire emerging with a rush, mixing sensations of heat, touch, sight, and smell with the written word and erotic fantasies—a decisive contrast to the reserve imposed by Victorian literary sensibilities and outright censorship.

III

The theme of gender modes of sexual desire takes me into a complex debate about nineteenth-century sensibilities that includes at least six questions: did men and women of that time actually experience sexual desire differently from the way it was experienced in later years? did women experience less desire? or was it triggered differently—by the sexual initiation of a man, by marriage, or by childbirth? did women experience the same kind and intensity of desire but hide it from their lovers? did women also hide it from themselves? did women experience the same kind of desire as men and express it freely to their lovers and to themselves, only to have novelists and artists interpret it as different if not deficient? Although my analysis will not answer these questions directly, it will treat how novelists interpreted desire and may in that way suggest some possible answers.

Victorian novelists were reluctant to envision female desire as active or initiatory. The accuracy of literary representations of heroines is sometimes supported with sex-negative assessments of female desire by Victorian physicians such as the notorious British gynecologist William Acton: "As a general rule, a modest woman seldom desires any sexual gratification for herself." Although Acton concedes that a woman may experience moderate arousal in response to the man's "positive and considerable excitement," her feelings do not arise from any inherent desire on her part. He concludes with the haunting image of female desire run amok—"nymphomania, a form of insanity which those accustomed to visit lunatic asylums must be fully conversant with." [6] The Victorian heroine, however passionate her feelings for a man, hid the anatomical sources and physical processes of desire from her man and herself and sublimated eros into spiritual devotion or what Martin Greene has aptly termed "a sorrowing ethical religiosity." [7]

In contrast to the pent-up aching rivers of Victorian desire, modern heroines broke loose with imagination and energy. While Jane Eyre, Catherine Earnshaw, Dorothea Brooke, and even Anna Karenina had to sublimate desire into morally respectable sensibilities, if not proper otherworldly ecstasy, and describe it with suitably discreet literary language, their modern counterparts could express themselves more directly. Hardy's transitional Sue Bridehead wants desperately to feel desire but is preoccupied, she tells Jude, with "that inborn craving which undermines some women's morals almost more than unbridled passion—the craving to attract and captivate" (280). Victorian heroines indulged in such captivation as a substitute for the sensuous fulfillment of their own desire, which was regulated by public codes. Many Victorian heroes and heroines viewed desire in moral/religious terms, tinged with a sexually paralyzing sense of sin, while the moderns strove to transcend that context altogether.

Mrs. Dalloway includes a daring description of Clarissa's autoerotic orgasm, stimulated by lesbian fantasies of an intimate conversation with a woman. "It was a sudden revelation, a tinge like a blush which one tried to check and then, as it spread, one yielded to its expansion, and rushed to the farthest verge and there quivered and felt the world come closer, swollen with some astonishing significance, some pressure of rapture, which split its thin skin and gushed and poured with an extraordinary alleviation over the cracks and sores! Then, for that moment, she had seen an illumination; a match burning in a crocus; an inner meaning almost expressed. But the close withdrew; the hard softened. It was over—the moment" (47). Strikingly modern are Woolf's metaphor for clitoral excitation (match burning in a crocus), her reference to the orgasm's "inner meaning," and its incompleteness ("almost expressed").

Lawrence reconstructs the history of desire from Victorian self-consciousness to modern self-awareness and more forthright expression.

The Rainbow traces its history across three generations of Brangwens (Tom and Lydia c.1865, Will and Anna c.1885, Ursula and Anton c.1905), alternating between male and female experiences in the same paragraph, sometimes even in the same sentence. A disappointing encounter with a prostitute, "so nothing, so dribbling, so functional," left the Victorian Tom with a distaste for the directly sexual. He was the more self-conscious and passive lover, more concerned than the woman with public expectations of courtship as opposed to exploring the private stirrings of desire. He insisted on an "honourable courtship" and on a "sanctioned, licensed marriage." Lydia took charge of sex. "So she came to him and unfastened the breast of his waistcoat and his shirt, and put her hand on him, needing to know him." Lawrence concludes bluntly—"he bungled in taking her" (51–52). But Lydia was no typical Victorian, since she was a Polish divorcée, several years older than Tom. Her daughter Anna grappled in the dark with her equally estranged husband Will. "It was a duel: no love, no words, no kisses even, only the maddening perception of beauty consummate, absolute through touch" (233). Anna and Will began to explore together the depths of shame that constricted and yet energized their eroticism. Their daughter Ursula took the redistribution of female activity in desire beyond the religious context and even beyond gender reciprocity. "She was weary of the Ursula Brangwen who felt troubled about God." She actively caressed Skrebensky and made love to him. When six years later they tried to rekindle their love, all other sources of communication had broken down and sexual desire remained the only open channel. Ursula engineered what is perhaps the first rape of a man in Western literature. She "seized hold of his arm, held him fast, as if captive . . . her mouth sought his in a hard, rending, ever-increasing kiss." Ursula "seemed to be pressing her beaked mouth till she had the heart of him . . . She held him pinned down at the chest, awful. The fight, the struggle for consummation was terrible. It lasted till it was agony to his soul, till he succumbed, till he gave way as if dead, lay with his face buried" (479).

Although many of Lawrence's Victorian women are more sexually self-aware than their men and more forthright about their desires, his literary history condemns all sexual oppression and tracks men and women struggling toward self-realization and the fuller intensities of reciprocal sexual exchange. In *Point Counter Point* Huxley modeled Mark and Mary Rampion after the Lawrences, retaining in Mary the assured pleasure in sexuality that D. H. found in his wife Frieda. At first Mark is shocked by Mary's matter-of-fact way of talking about sex and "her great and whole-heartedly expressed capacity for pleasure," which his mother had taught him was "horribly sinful." "Later, when they had been married several years and had achieved an intimacy impossible in those first months of novelties . . . he was able to talk to her about these matters" (116).

In *The Vagabond* Renée is at first offended by the unabashed desire of Max who, she realizes, "does not want my well-being, this man, he merely wants *me*" (22). The Victorian heroine would have transformed such bald desire into something loftier and more sublimated, but this quiet desiring man transforms *her* into something earthier and simpler, as she explains. "He forces me to remember, too often, the existence of desire . . . [and] that I am alone, healthy, still young" (62). In *The Last of Chéri* (set in 1919) Colette describes the post-war generation of men "free from the burden of themselves and being frightened—empty-minded, innocent; the women, given over to a pleasure far greater than any more definite sensual delight, to the company of men: that is to say, to physical contact with them, their smell, their tonic sweat, the certain proof of which tingled in every inch of their bodies" (45). The redistribution of active and passive roles between men and women in the stimulation of sexual desire during the war years is part of the general history of gender depolarization, which I will treat more fully in the chapter on gender.

Nineteenth-century seductresses used supernatural powers to stimulate desire in men and secretly entice them into ultimate ruin. Twentieth-century heroines are desirable and desiring in a more natural and less toxic way. Mary Rampion is "matter-of-fact" about sex; Renée rekindles her "healthy" desire. In *Ulysses* Leopold (Poldy) recalls the time his son was conceived, also the high point of his sex life, when Molly, turned on by the sight of two dogs coupling, said to him, "Give us a touch, Poldy. God, I'm dying for it" (89). In *The Thibaults* Rachel simply grabs Antoine, pulls him into her flat, slams the door, reaches up, and kisses him. The next morning, when Antoine suggests they leave her flat separately, she replies nonchalantly, "I'm quite free and make no secret of anything I do" (340). Her appeal is grounded in her firm stance and direct approach. Du Gard alludes to the historical significance of their encounter, for "hitherto it had been he who, as a man of science, by veiled allusions . . . set others in a quandary. Rachel had turned the tables on him; beside her Antoine felt atrociously small-boyish" (449).

For all the erotic daring of the Surrealist artists, they were reluctant to show an actual erection. In *The Specter of Sex-Appeal* male desire is represented only symbolically with the enlarged thigh bone held by the boy. One simple reason artists do not depict men with an erection is because they look funny; an aroused woman does not have such a comical and errant protuberance. Female desire is more aesthetically focused, because an aroused women does not appear to be as needy or as incomplete by herself as does a man with an erection. Whether or not she desires to have a penis or to be penetrated by one, her *appearance* is one of greater self-sufficiency. Although the depictions of female sexuality have been regulated by these universal features of sexual anatomy, artistic interpretations have also been influenced by sexual mores and artistic conventions which clearly reveal historical change.

Victorian artists allowed female desire to burn hottest when far away or long ago. Burne-Jones's painting *Laus Veneris* (1878) shows a sleepy, long-limbed Venus swooning in a medieval dreamland. In Böcklin's *Playing in the Waves* (1883) sea nymphs sport with aquatic centaurs in the spermatic foam of surging waves, displacing female desire to a marine never-never land.

How nudes touch themselves is one index of desire. Victorian nudes usually touch no part of their bodies. When they do it is primarily the hair, occasionally their face (or veils or vases located around the head), and some exceptional few touch below their waist. They never touch their own genitals. The reclining nude in Edouard Blanchard's *Le Buffon* (1878) grazes her hair with one hand and pets a sleek doberman with the other; Böcklin's Nereide in *Triton and Nereide* (1873) clutches her hair with one hand and fondles the neck of a monstrous phallic sea serpent in the other. One hand of Manet's *Olympia* (1863) rests on her thigh as frankly as her direct stare confronts the viewer. T. J. Clark sets up his estimate of the historical significance of this painting with a summary of the significance of the female nude at that time. "Her sex, one might say, is a matter of *male* desire: those various fauns, bulls, falling coins, enfolding clouds, tritons, goats, and *putti* which surround her. There they all are for the male viewer to read and accept as figures of his own feelings; and there *she* is, somehow set apart from her own sexuality, her nakedness not yet possessed by the creatures who whisper, stare, or hold up mirrors." *Olympia* marks a beginning of change by suggesting that sexuality is "nowhere but in the body" and that "desire itself" is the property of "the female subject herself." [8]

More typical of the mid-century is Courbet's *Nude with a Dog* (Figure 12, 1868). The woman's one hand rests calmly on her thigh while the other pets

12. Gustave Courbet, *Nude with a Dog,* 1868.

a fleecy white poodle that she is about to kiss. There is some sexual titillation in that the dog's paws rest on her right knee which is tilted to one side, but the painting exudes innocence. When contrasted with the partly clad woman in Schiele's *Kneeling Model with Deeply Bowed Head* (Figure 13, 1915), Courbet's nude appears to be a historically remote expression of female sexual desire. In the Schiele both of the woman's hands (one over the top and the other from underneath) are engaged in desperate self-gratification which involves the entire body, radiating through the hard-working muscular arms that lead to the center of passion. Fingers, labia, and folds of her underclothing intermingle to accent the confusion, anguish, and crisis of intense sexual desire. Courbet's nude is posed for comfort and leans forward effortlessly, while Schiele's is twisted forward and down into herself with a tension that offers no repose. The weight of her torso is supported like a wheelbarrow on the top of her head. Her hurriedly raised dress accentuates the urgency of the moment. Courbet hints at sexual excitement with his model's flexed right toe, while Schiele expresses it forthrightly with his model's booted feet rising off the ground as she approaches climax. Courbet poses the woman's sexuality out of view, while Schiele targets the source of desire and the woman's bringing about her own pleasure. The ar-

13. Egon Schiele, *Kneeling Model with Deeply Bowed Head*, 1915.

tificiality of Courbet's studio setting in a conventionalized landscape further subverts any suggestion of real desire, and just in case anything might heat up his subject cools her feet at the water's edge. In fact, backgrounds pale during peak excitement, and to avoid distraction Schiele leaves the background out, framing the woman's masturbation with her dark stockings and boots whose angular heels and high lacing accentuate the exposure of her sex organs as well as the emotional unlacing of autoerotism. Dark dogs may be phallic, but Courbet's white lamb-like poodle is a suitably discreet Victorian metaphor for animal desire, with just a hint of voyeurism in that the dog can see that most intimate part of the woman's body which is posed out of view. The desire of Schiele's woman is manifestly observable, fully centered in and for the woman herself, neither triggered by the presence of a man nor symbolized by an animal.

Schiele's watercolor was no isolated example. Klimt anticipated Schiele's daring treatment of female desire around the turn of the century in a series of paintings and drawings that show ever more explicit modes of sexual desire and fulfillment, most characteristically with women being swept along in a watery stream of ecstasy. German Expressionists celebrated male and female Eros from spacious woods to cramped Bohemian flats. Mueller, Pechstein, Heckel, and Kirchner met outside of Moritzburg in 1910 to paint eroticized couples in dazzlingly bright colors, expressive poses, and lush natural settings far from the constraints of civilization. They reworked classical and religious motifs to express the spirit of their erotic artistic movement. Kirchner's *Leda and the Swan* (1919) shows Leda reaching up eagerly to embrace the swan's flapping frenetic desire, and as he pecks one of her enormous nipples, she responds with a blissful toothy leer. In Corinth's version of 1902, Leda bends forward and rolls her eyes upwards in ecstasy as the swan mounts her from behind. Corinth painted Joseph and Potiphar's wife three times before painting Joseph out altogether. In this final version, *Potiphar's Wife* (1914), the would-be adulteress smiles eagerly into a blaze of light that floods across her animated body, as if Joseph's flight had released and illuminated her sexuality. Schiele's own work around this time abounds with images of sexual craving, masturbation, and heterosexual fulfillment rendered with a style that sought to disclose the subcutaneous processes of desire.

Less explicitly sexual but nonetheless venturesome in the celebration of male and female Eros are paintings by Suzanne Valadon that show herself and her lover as Adam and Eve. In an earlier version Adam is shown with explicit frontal nudity, although Valadon painted a fig-leaf on Adam for a public exhibition. This *Adam and Eve* (Figure 14, 1909) shows Adam in a supportive pose, sharing in the seizure of self-fulfillment by holding up Eve's wrist as she takes the (no longer) forbidden fruit. His gesture is somewhat ambiguous because it is at right angles to his visual focus, set apprehensively as if on the look-out, while Eve (a daring nude self-portrait) is calmly intent on plucking the ripest apple. Between the original and the final version Valadon painted an unusual *Adam and Eve* (1910): it shows the primal couple playing together with a fig-leaf (making sport of the symbol of sin) required for the public exhibition. By making light of the Christian view of sexual desire as sin that had to be cloaked in an absurd "garment," her frontal portrait of a sexualized Adam and Eve reaching out for pleasure, stepping forthrightly toward the viewer and the future, marks a transition to my next theme—the value of desire.

IV

The primordial urge that guides two squirrels in tandem through the branches in spring, like some miraculously choreographed *pas de deux*, is timeless. There is an analogous transhistorical raw desire in human beings,

14. Suzanne Valadon, *Adam and Eve*, 1909.

but one mediated by values that change in unmistakably historical ways. In this period those values shift away from the moral and religious toward the existential.

While the ancient Jews, Greeks, and Romans proscribed forms of sex to protect the family and the community, not until the Christian era did morality center on the regulation of desire, as sex life became an important basis for one's relation to God and one's fate in the hereafter. The unique new concept was "sin," which Paul linked with sex and made prominent in the moral foundation of Christendom. He put the matter succinctly: "It is good for a man not to touch a woman" (I Cor 7:1). Saint Augustine equated sex and sin, and his *Confessions* chronicled the way to God as a struggle to quash desire. His rhetoric has sounded throughout the ages. As a young man his "body's appetites plunged [him] in the whirlpool of sin." Without God he was "wallowing in filth and scratching the itching sore of lust." At Carthage he steamed in a "hissing cauldron of lust." His suffering was a punishment for "a host of grave offenses over and above the bond of original sin, by which we *all have died with Adam.*"[9] But a merciful God saved him by inflicting pain, mortifying his flesh, and thereby teaching the higher good of the spirit. After his conversion, he confessed, pleasures of the flesh continued to tempt. He had to maintain vigilance against enjoying the harmonies of Church music or the perfume of ceremonial incense which detracted from the absolute love of God through whom, he wrote, one may hear "sound that never dies away" and breathe "fragrance that is not borne away on the wind." By the fifth century, the Church Fathers institutionalized this ethic with the apotheosis of celibacy, further stigmatizing sex and all sensual pleasures.

The sex-negative ethic of Western Christendom showed remarkable staying power. Threats about damnation from unregulated desire abounded in Victorian sex manuals, perhaps most notoriously in *Satan in Society* (1870) by Nicholas Cooke (pseudonym "A Physician"), who wrote about masturbation, that most blatant form of self-indulgence, as if it were urged upon young men and women by a devil with a pointed tail. Cooke dramatized the importance of Christian salvation with the classic Christian threat—if you masturbate you will die and go to hell. It must be noted, however, that in a society which had no reliable way of diagnosing, let alone curing, syphilis (which has a latency period of anywhere from five to twenty years before the deadly tertiary symptoms may appear), even a reputable physician might have suspected as a possible cause of the horrors of tertiary syphilis any sexual activity not necessary for procreation.

Although novelists avoided such sex panic, they viewed desire in a Christian framework. In *Jane Eyre* Brontë assesses the moral worth of major characters in terms of their respective resolutions of the tension between sexual desire and Christian faith. On her deathbed, Helen Burns looks forward to a time for "putting off our corruptible bodies; when debasement and sin will fall from us with this cumbrous frame of flesh, and only the spark of the spirit will remain" (91). The head of Lowood School, Mr. Brocklehurst, explains his mission "to mortify in these girls the lusts of the flesh" (96). Sounding like a post-baptismal Augustine, St. John Rivers shares with Jane the thinking behind his repudiation of beautiful Rosamond's love: "Fancy me yielding and melting, as I am doing: human love rising like a freshly opened fountain in my mind and overflowing with sweet inundation all the field I have so carefully and with such labour prepared—so assiduously sown with the seeds of good intentions, of self-denying plans. And now it is deluged with a nectarous flood—the young germs swamped—delicious poison cankering them" (399). Jane and ultimately even Rochester turn to God to justify their final union. The moral foundation of Brontë's ideal hero in *Villette,* Paul Emanuel, is the regulation of desire, which he managed "like a knight of old, religious in his way, and of spotless fame." "He had vivid passions, keen feelings, but his pure honour and his artless piety were the strong charm that kept the lions couchant" (474).[10]

In 1850 Hawthorne created perhaps the most memorable literary image of sin, Hester Prynne's scarlet letter "A" for adultery, embroidered on the breast of her gown. The novel, set in seventeenth-century New England, dramatizes the plight of a woman condemned by the sexual morality of that time, although that historical displacement thinly disguises Hawthorne's call for an undoing of the abiding severity of the Puritan character in his own time. While mindful of the need for obedience to the laws of man and for recognition of "higher truth," Hawthorne celebrates "the sympathy of Nature" that surfaces when Hester throws away the scarlet letter and removes the cap that confined her hair. "Her sex, her youth, and the whole richness of her beauty" tumbled out of long confinement along with her rich dark hair (220).

Like Hawthorne, Eliot sides with natural desire against the demands of religious fanaticism or excessive moral restraint, although both recognize the need for self-control and some accommodation to the sensibilities of others. In *The Mill on the Floss* Maggie seeks peace from the conflicting demands of desire in the philosophy of the Christian ascetic Thomas à Kempis, which teaches her "that all the miseries of her young life had come from fixing her heart on her own pleasure" (384). In order to change she resolves upon a program of renunciation. She rejects an uplifting book from Philip because "it would make [her fall] in love with this world again" (402). But the tingle following her first meeting with Stephen reveals that "after years of contented renunciation, she had slipped back into desire and longing" (482). When Maggie and Stephen are literally swept away while boating, they are obliged to spend a glorious night under the stars. The next day Maggie turns her back on the "tremulous delights of his presence" that made life an "easy floating in a stream of joy instead of a quiet resolved endurance and effort" (607). She leaves Stephen and returns to society, but to no avail. The townsfolk do not believe her explanation for having spent the night with him and banish her from their community. Eliot sweeps Maggie to her death in a flood, which, like the current that carried her and Stephen to their night of bliss, represents the overwhelming force of desire as well as the overwhelming force of runaway public opinion.

The title of *Sentimental Education* is a euphemism for learning how to love. The internal conflict that tormented many Victorian characters Flaubert divides between his hero's contrasting desire for two women. Frédéric longs for Mme. Arnoux but is "restrained by a sort of religious awe." He cannot imagine her otherwise than clothed, he trembles at the slightest brush of her finger, and he never has sex with her. In contrast he does not love the courtesan Rosanette with whom he freely undresses and enjoys sex uncomplicated by guilt. He thinks of the saint while ravaging the courtesan and longs for the courtesan when Mme. Arnoux's saintly restraint becomes unbearable.

Jane, Hester, Maggie, and Frédéric confront the asceticism that pervaded the mid-century, but they do so in a Christian context which made sexual pleasure into a moral crisis. Nietzsche's announcement in 1882 that "God is dead!" signaled the undoing of that context. Although he substituted a "will to power" for the utilitarians' pleasure principle as the mainspring for human existence, he celebrated the creative function of *Lust,* which in German means both desire and pleasure.

In *The Sleepwalkers* (1931) Hermann Broch reconstructed Victorian sexuality against the background of Nietzsche's philosophy. In a wild seduction scene set in 1888, a reciprocal undressing, which begins with Ruzena ordering Joachim to undo the back of her dress, symbolizes release from the sexual-moral constraint of the time. "'Open that,' she whispered, tearing at the same time at his necktie and the buttons of his vest." She fell on her knees and, with her head pressed against the foot of the bed, unfastened his shoes. She then flung back the covers, but his starched collar still cut her chin. "Put that off," she commanded, and finally they felt release with "their delight rising out of their dread" (39). Unmarried lovers in an earlier age might have dreaded being discovered, but Joachim and Ruzena dread their own desire and pleasure itself. It is tempting to speculate that they may also have experienced some piquant intensities of delight unique to that hysterical time, but at a high cost which Freud subsequently interpreted as the "civilized" sexual morality that was responsible for a rise in the frequency and severity of nervous illness.

This shift in the evaluation of desire is not of course a disjunct. Victorians knew the joy of sex and recoiled from fanatical religious asceticism, and moderns did not throw off all moral restraint or completely bury the Christian god. But modernists were far more diligent in loosening the constricting values and dismantling the religious framework.

The nourishment that Gide calls for in *Les Nourritures terrestres* (1897) comes from desire and yields resurrection of the flesh. This preachy monologue addressed to an imaginary lover, Nathaniel, mixes a love of God with a celebration of the appetites, for "the most beautiful thing I have known on earth," he tells Nathaniel, "is my hunger" (32). Gide's private, and at that time still secret, struggle with homosexuality gave *Les Nourritures terrestres* its revolutionary fervor. In *The Thibaults* Du Gard underscored Gide's heavy moralizing through the character of Daniel, who was spiritually transformed while reading Gide's erotic call to arms. Gide no doubt captivated many a youth like Daniel, who was resurrected by Gide's urgent and urging rhetoric: "I have boldly laid my hands everywhere, and believed I had a right to every object of my desire." Du Gard explained that "in a flash the burden that [Daniel's] upbringing had laid on him—the obsession of moral standards—had been lifted; the word 'sin' had changed its meaning . . . In the brief period of a night the moral values which from his earliest days had seemed immutable went up in flames" (276).

As twentieth-century writers substituted aesthetic or existential interpretive language for religious and moral language, failures to check desire became rather failures of being, failures to realize possibilities of experience. And while earlier writers evaluated the failure to contain desire as a way to moral improvement if not back to God, modernists interpreted it as a stimulant to creative work and fuller love.

"Death in Venice" (1911) is the story of a famous German writer, Gustav von Aschenbach, who embodied the highest values of Western civilization. While vacationing in Venice, he was overwhelmed by a forbidden homoerotic love for a young boy. His love intensified, and was perhaps only possible, precisely because it was so immoral and heretical. He welcomed a cholera epidemic that provided a moral cover for his forbidden desire. "These things that were going on in the unclean alleys of Venice . . . gave Aschenbach a dark satisfaction [because] the city's evil secret mingled with the one in the depths of his heart" (53). Mann did not point out a moral or invent a way out for Aschenbach, who was eventually destroyed by his all-consuming passion. Before love killed him, Aschenbach repudiated Christianity in a dream of Dionysian frenzy, in which a voice heralded as "The strange god!" called to him, and wild women with their heads flung back uttered loud hoarse cries and danced, stumbling over hairy pelts that dangled from their girdles, shrieking and holding their breasts in both hands. Aschenbach was determined to "uphold his own god against this stranger who was the sworn enemy to dignity and self-control," but when the celebrants unveiled the "obscene symbol of the godhead . . . monstrous and wooden [a fascinus]," Aschenbach was suddenly "in them and of them, the stranger god was his own." "Yes, it was he who was flinging himself upon animals, who bit and tore and swallowed smoking gobbets of flesh" (67–68). However immoral, un-Christian, and dangerous the driving passion of this story, it ended not with a moral breakthrough or religious conversion but with Aschenbach, after seeing his beloved Tadzio abused by a bully, dying of a broken heart already weakened by cholera. The sympathetic ending reminds the reader of Aschenbach's abiding humanity despite his pathetic vanity, moral corruption, and social irresponsibility, all driven by a hopeless passion.

The difference between the first lovers of Frédéric in *Sentimental Education* and Paul in *Sons and Lovers* highlights the re-evaluation of desire over the years between these novels. Mme. Arnoux is a religious woman who resists Frédéric because of her marital status, only reluctantly agrees to a rendezvous, is "saved" by her son's illness which she takes as a judgment from heaven, and years later affirms that it had been good that they had never loved carnally. Flaubert presents her as one aspect of love that is split sharply between passion and reason, the world of the flesh and the world of God. Frédéric does not renounce his desire for her or question its value, he simply goes to a brothel. For Lawrence, however, the split is not so sharp. Paul learns to transcend the values of his first lover Miriam, one of Lawrence's several brooding asexual sex theoreticians who is torn between her passion for a man and her will to possess him. *Sentimental Education* ends with Frédéric's snicker about one good time in a brothel, while *Sons and Lovers* ends with Paul's lonely search for fulfilling sexual love.

The difference between the two women and the response of their respective lovers is partly due to a difference between the authors' temperaments, to be sure. Flaubert sought to achieve a dispassionate depiction of passion; he wanted to show that even adultery could become tiresome. In contrast Lawrence banged the drums of change and sought to replicate in his prose the passion his characters experienced. But the different values attached to desire within a fluid moral-religious context also offer evidence of historical change. If we cannot entirely separate out the personality of authors from their works to isolate their historically representative content, we can on occasion take authors at their word. Lawrence merits such interpretive indulgence because he consciously tried to recreate the history of love, and because the ideas and emotions of his characters became an important part of that history.

From across the Atlantic and the war years, Fitzgerald articulated similar ideas of a "new generation." In the end of *This Side of Paradise* his protagonist Amory looked back on four troubled romances which he saw as a collective effort to surmount the moral context of desire. "The problem of evil had solidified for Amory into the problem of sex," and the proper response, if not solution, to both would be their separation. During an overnight hike back to Princeton, he comes to terms with his own atheism, for "there was no God in his heart." Deprived of God and disillusioned in love, Amory, like Paul Morel, began to accept his responsibility in loving or believing, and he walked on thinking these final words: "'I know myself,' he cried, 'but that is all.'" Across these years the moral and religious context of desire gave way to the existential; instead of being a source of moral weakness or religious temptation, desire became a way to self-knowledge of what it means to be in love—to exist loving. In place of the moral disjunct of good/bad we find a cluster of existential gradations: rich/impoverished, protracted/brief, varied/repetitive, repressed/disclosed, routine/creative.[11]

In Western art the Crucifixion is the most powerful reminder of mankind's sinfulness. The injustice of an agonizing punishment for the quintessentially innocent son of God, which was necessary to save mankind from the eternal damnation it deserved, showed believers the extent of their depravity. Jesus' preaching from the cross to love one's enemies and forgive one's persecutors sharpened the moral disparity between divine kindness and human wickedness. Although Jesus was not so preoccupied with sexual sin as some of his disciples, he shifted the moral sanction from external shame to internal guilt: "If a man looks on a woman with a lustful eye, he has already committed adultery with her in his heart" (Matt. 5:28). From its inception there was no exit from Christian sexual guilt, graphically depicted in numerous Biblical themes. Around 1900 the inertial weight of almost two millennia of reverent guilt was lightened in a variety of ways as the theme of sin was secularized, eroticized, exaggerated, mocked, naturalized, and overturned.

In Corinth's *Adam and Eve* (1893) the couple both stroke Eve's luxurious hair as if it were strings of a harp. In Corinth's version of the temptation of St. Anthony (1897), the saint is too frightened to carry any moral weight, and his seducers are too sexy to be judged in a religious context. Viewers would be even more hard pressed to think Christian sexual morality when viewing his *Paradise* (1912), in which Eve pets a pair of lambs and Adam scans the horizon of adventure beyond the tree of knowledge that they have just passed. Coiled up in its branches the serpent stares wide-eyed at the backs of the primordial couple, like a dumbfounded apple salesman wondering why no one is buying.

Von Stuck reworked his painting of *Sin* in the course of these same years, with Eve and the serpent in ever cozier intimacy. A 1910 version shows Eve fully in control of the sexuality of Christendom, with a python of desire coiled around her shoulders, his head resting like a jeweled brooch above her right breast, and with her erect nipple silhouetted against background shadow. The python, notoriously dangerous for squeezing rather than biting, stares like a protective lover directly at the viewer, and the woman's alluring gaze suggests the caption, "He's with me." The implied message is more an invitation to sin than a moral injunction against it, although the image dramatizes perils as well as pleasures. Like much of Von Stuck's iconography of desire and conflict, *Sin* draws from Christian tradition for substance but interprets it with impious erotic vigor.

The turn-of-the-century secularization of desire was energized and complicated by a contemporaneous feminization of desire, which also looked to other mythologies for exciting but threatening lubricious subjects. Bram Dijkstra has documented how "literally hundreds of painted and sculpted versions of Lilith, Salammbô, Lamia, and assorted other snake charmers came to blend as generic depictions of Woman, the eternal Eve." [12] But if potent snake-kissing women brought new weaponry to the battle of the sexes, they were welcome in the battle men and women fought together against two millennia of sexual guilt.

The German Expressionists sought to return desire to nature. Mueller's half-clad gypsy hangs an angular arm around his dark lover who casually exposes her sagging breasts and stares languidly at the viewer. Kirchner's primitives gave form to the spirit of Ludwig Klages's "cosmogonic Eros," splashing and dancing around the earthly paradise of the Moritzberg lakes. German New Realists exposed the brutality and sometimes murderous violence of raw desire. Grosz chronicled the Weimar years in Germany as a sexual free-for-all, with raw desire seeming to dissolve the dresses on women, whose sexual parts are exposed as if they had sat in a puddle of acid. Dix and Grosz depicted brothel scenes, savage rapes, and sex murderers complete with severed limbs and blood-splattered walls. But far from calling for Christian clamps to control lust, they implied that excessive suppression and repression had caused it.

In Picabia's *Edtaonisl (ecclésiastique)* (1913) Cubist forms obscure the explicit moral comment on sexual desire. The meaning of the painting, like its title, is only apparent with commentary.[13] During a transatlantic voyage Picabia had noticed how the gyrations of the ship's star dancer had aroused a Dominican priest (the ecclesiastic referred to in the subtitle). Picabia rendered the priest's pounding heart with undulating, geometric shapes of blood and flesh tones contrasted with white Cubist pieces of the ecclesiastical collar. In Chagall's *Adam and Eve* (1912) temptation and sin are muted iconographical allusions in the delicately balanced, stained-glass Cubist forms. In *Promenade* (1913), *The Birthday* (1915), and *Over the Town* (1918), Chagall showed one or both lovers taking flight, all stunning inversions and repudiations of Christian imagery of the fall. These are among the happiest celebrations of love in modern art.

These diverse techniques for assessing the doctrine of original sin and loosening its grip on Western values shared the goal of restoring desire as a wholesome part of love. That important thematic message was accompanied by a more significant formal artistic development central to the emergence of modern art itself—the identification of desire as the energy for artistic creation. However innovative these depictions of love in art, the big news was the emergence of love as art.

V

No discussion of desire can avoid recent analyses by art historians of the convention that associated artistic creation with male desire and relegated to women the merely inspirational role of muse or model.[14] This traditional dichotomy was assailed, if not entirely rejected, in the early twentieth century as artists increasingly acknowledged the erotic sources of creative inspiration and focused ever more on the creative process itself. Artists also rejected the corollary notion that female nudes were an ideal model *of* love and instead began to view the reciprocal erotic exchange between artist and model as the more important subject of their paintings.

Conventional gender dichotomies structure William Frith's *The Sleeping*

15. William Frith, *The Sleeping Model*, 1853.

Model (Figure 15, 1853), which is clearly divided between artist and model, subject and object, activity and passivity, male and female. This self-portrait shows Frith standing securely positioned at his easel with brushes in hand. He is the complete artist depicted in the act of painting, fully absorbed in and defined by his activity. The woman has fallen asleep in the chair. She is a part-time model and an orange-seller but is neither successfully. She cannot stay awake or sell her two oranges, which she still holds absurdly in each hand. In contrast Frith's subjectivity is supremely free, unchallenged by her consciousness. He looks intently at her, while her gaze is lost in dreams. Her passivity is accented by the floppy lay figure behind her, which artists at that time used to form into any shape as a prop for showing the fall of drapery.[15] And behind that lay figure the suit of armor further symbolizes the artist's ability to make human forms take any shape desired. He is the confident subject, artist, and seer, poised in the act of fulfilling his creative urge; she is the vulnerable object and model, the one who is slumped helplessly and

16. Otto Dix, *Self-Portrait with Muse*, 1924.

whom he will resurrect like a god into the wide-awake smiling face that is already visible on his canvas.

Strikingly, disturbingly different is Otto Dix's *Self-Portrait with Muse* (Figure 16, 1924), which is ambiguously split between artist and model, subject and object, even conventional male and female traits. The artist is clearly Dix with paint brush in hand, but the model seems to be taking charge by raising her left hand as if signaling when to begin or stop and doing so with a Christ-like gesture. Her identity as a model is ambiguous, because it is not entirely clear whether he is painting a portrait of her on a canvas, or miraculously painting her into existence, or indeed whether she is somehow bringing him into existence. Is she a vision or a visionary? One of her pendulous breasts hangs over the diaphanous blue material around her midriff through which her dark pubis shows vividly, so there is no doubt about her sex, but there is some ambiguity about her "feminine" deference to "masculine" power. She has wild black hair, a trace of moustache, and a formidable face that seems to overpower the fair and diminutive artist, who is constrained by the tightness of his smock. Even her large breasts appear to be more instruments of power than of allure or nourishment. Unlike Frith's sleeping model, Dix's muse is wide awake, fully conscious, capable of godlike domination over the painter, who clutches his maulstick defensively. The dichotomies are not fixed. Although he has the brush and maintains a piercing gaze, it is not clear whose hand is in control or which of the two is the source of creative energy, and desire seems to flow equally between them. Dix shows not the painting of desire, but painting as desire.

Dix had company in the modern era. In the 1890s Munch emphasized the link between sexual desire and artistic inspiration, as I argued in Chapter 3. In the early twentieth century his work influenced the sensuous line of Art Nouveau, the explicit eroticism of German Expressionism, and the Surrealists, whose preoccupation with the themes of Pygmalion, Oedipus, and the myth of Androgyne supply abundant evidence for the modern connection between sexual desire and art. Picasso explored the connection throughout his life. For example, in an oil painting titled *The Sculptor* (1931; cover photo). Picasso depicted himself in profile, thoughtfully holding his chin with his hand, contemplating a sculpted bust of his beloved Marie-Thérèse Walter. Her face is an early version of the one in his *Head of a Woman* (Figures 29 and 30), here painted with an alert blue eye that looks back at the artist, suggesting a sharing of the visionary and creative function of the artist and model, one which Picasso appears to be intent on figuring out. His profile overlays a frontal mirror image of himself, also a work of art, which looks back on, if not also into, himself.[16] Its features are those of the artist but its coloring, that of his beloved, implying a reciprocity between the creative roles of artist and model, mutually energized by desire.

There was an analogous emphasis on the creative function of sexual desire in literature. In 1909 Ann Veronica's emergence as a New Woman included a "new-born appetite" for the sight and sound of beauty which, Wells explains, "interwove with her biological work" (187). Evolution, education, and emancipation fueled the cosmic creative urge that her lover-instructor Capes stimulated further with lectures on butterfly markings and the patterning of tigers. Mann's interpretation of Aschenbach's love for Tadzio moves in a circle linking desire and creativity. Beauty, Aschenbach reflects, is the artist's way to the spirit, but it is a way of "perilous sweetness, a way of transgression," a way inspired by physical desire, detoured by social conventions, and constricted further by the demanding conventions of art which, however, ultimately enable beauty to emerge as art and in its turn stimulate sensual desire.

While nineteenth-century artists and novelists were mindful of the way love inspired creative work, they did not paint or describe that inspiration as vividly or as frankly as did those in the twentieth century. Where the nineteenth century had teased and titillated, the twentieth century shocked with imagery that critics rejected as pornography. The new evaluation of desire sent a pair of messages. It was "elevated" as the mainspring of artistic inspiration, but "lowered" by the representation of its unmistakably sexual function. The irony of those messages became ever more apparent in the twentieth century, as the older moralistic terminology became increasingly unsuited to reveal the meaning of desire and was gradually displaced by the aesthetic and existential terminology of continental philosophy. Once again Nietzsche charted the shifting winds of change which were blowing beyond good and evil.

In the modern period philosophers, novelists, and artists explored more fully than had the Victorians the nature and extent of desire. They offered more detailed accounts of the anatomical sources of sexual desire, emanating not from the "heart" and "soul" but from the entire surface of the skin or even the instep of a foot as well as the nipples, loins, genitals, or anus. Moderns reversed the gender dichotomization of sexually passive females and active males, specifically focusing on women as more active in initiating sex or masturbating. They threw off the remnants of the Victorians' fear of desire itself as a mortal sin and celebrated the connection between loving desire and the creative process, ultimately replacing the traditional approach to love in art with an emphasis on love as art.

These changes made desire more authentic in that they enabled moderns to understand and experience the forward moving and visceral dynamic of love with fewer restrictions and inhibitions. But has all this clearer seeing and more direct understanding and more open discussion of desire undermined its mysterious joy? In the most explicit treatment of that subject—language—we find a similar historical movement in the direction of greater openness and frankness and, yes, understanding about what it means to be a human being in love.

6 Language

AT A CERTAIN moment all lovers must begin to speak, and they do so according to historical conventions. More than twentieth-century characters, those in the nineteenth-century novel observed distinctively male and female rhetorical formalities, delayed use of familiar pronouns until protocol allowed, followed the proper sequence for avowals with the man's coming first, relied on mediators and written communication (even for marriage proposals), veiled powerful feelings with euphemism and cliché, and avoided talking about sex.

Theoretical grounding for the analysis of the problem of language in the modern novel can be seen in developments in the philosophy of language. Philosophy was always fundamentally concerned with language. In the twentieth century Wittgenstein's bold stroke was to claim that many traditional philosophical problems arose from a misunderstanding of the logic of language. That is, traditional philosophical questions about the good, the true, and the beautiful were not so much about human experience as about the language used to pose them. Wittgenstein did not deny the importance of ethics, epistemology, and aesthetics, but viewed them as fundamentally about language. Allan Janik and Stephen Toulmin interpreted the analysis of language in Wittgenstein's *Tractatus Logico-Philosophicus* (1921) as a key to the superficiality of early twentieth-century Vienna: aristocratic formalism and ceremonial protocol, bourgeois social pretense and moral hypocrisy (especially about sex), aesthetic eclecticism and sentimentality with its "conventional and meaningless decoration," and a general preoccupation with verbal propriety and surface appearance, all topped with "waltzes and whipped cream." [1]

Among phenomenologists, Buber, Heidegger, and Jaspers explained ways in which the spoken word constituted the "I-Thou relation," "Being-with," or "Communication," which were central to human existence. Buber's analysis of the two ways man relates to the world begins with "the two basic words he can speak." There is a suspect nostalgia in Buber's speculative journey back to primary relatedness, especially evident when he praises the undifferentiated language of "primitive" peoples, which, he insists, preserves the wholeness of primary relatedness. "The Fuegian surpasses our analytical wisdom with a sentence-word of seven syllables that literally means: 'they look at each other, each waiting for the other to offer to do that which both desire but neither wishes to do.' In this wholeness persons are still embedded like reliefs without achieving the fully rounded independence of nouns or pronouns. What counts is not these products of analysis and reflection but the genuine original unity, the lived relationship." [2] Why a language unable to make analytical distinctions surpasses one that does, Buber does not explain. His position in history is transitional. His praise for communication with looks alone sanctions the kind of painful reticence that impoverished many a Victorian love, while his focus on the language of love points to the emphasis on the constitutive function of language in twentieth-century phenomenology.

In place of older philosophical interest in semantics and conceptual analysis, phenomenology was concerned with the way people actually speak to one another. Heidegger was particularly concerned with the sharing that is a co-understanding of existential possibilities. Authentic discourse *(Rede)* includes listening to or "being-open" to others in a caring exchange, or in an exchange in which one is "in thrall" to the other.[3] Love is possible because human beings can talk and listen enthralled. In contrast to authentic discourse is inauthentic "idle talk" *(Gerede),* which communicates everyday babble, half-consciously passing it along. Authentic discourse is possible only because we can choose (or not choose) to express our unique feelings with language that is our very own. Lovers' discourse is thus a continual choice between disclosure and closing off, between originality and cliché.

The difficulty of such choices intrigued Jaspers, who made communication the center of his philosophy of human existence *(Existenz)*. In *Philosophy* (1932) he argued that *Existenz* does not relate to others as an object of cognition; rather *Existenz* craves others, is deceived by others, is overjoyed by others, and so on. The "loving struggle" is a boundary situation which brings *Existenz* up against the critical realities of being. "The love in this communication is . . . the fighting, clear-sighted love of possible Existenz tackling another possible *Existenz,* questioning it, challenging it, making things hard for it." Chivalry will not do. Unlike the Darwinian struggle, the loving struggle is nonviolent. It involves utter candor and the elimination of all kinds of power and superiority. Both combatants "dare to show themselves without reserve and allow themselves to be thrown into question." There are no victors; both jointly win or lose. Love is an "evolving communicative struggle" in which two people fight to be with one another in spite of the unending conflicts (II, 59–61). Jaspers identifies the intensely combative though nonviolent nature of even the gentlest murmurings of love, which he puts at the center of his philosophy of existence—we communicate, therefore we exist.

I

In contrast to modern novelists who were increasingly troubled by the deficiency of language, some earlier novelists took a positive attitude toward it. Maeterlinck rhapsodized about the unique communication of lovers' silence. In *Crime and Punishment* (1866) Dostoevski made a special effort to keep Raskolnikov and Sonya from ever expressing their love.[4] In *Les Misérables* Hugo was suspicious of speaking about love and recommended other means of communication. Young Cosette had never heard the word love spoken in an earthly sense. In her convent "it was always replaced by some scarcely adequate synonym such as 'dove' or 'treasure trove.'" "She had, in short, no word to express what she was now feeling." Hugo then asks, "Is one the less ill for not knowing the name of the disease?" His answer dates the novel. "She loved more deeply because she did so in ignorance." But unlike a disease, love *is* mediated by consciousness, *is* structured by language, and *is* experienced in degree as more or less, and the metaphor itself smacks of the notion that love is like a disease that strikes out of the blue. Hugo then evaluates: "love had come to her in precisely the form that best suited her state of mind, in the form of worship at a distance, silent contemplation, the deification of an unknown" (774). But without talking. On page 809 she hears Marius's voice for the first time. After an hour's exchange, "everything had been said." "Everything" includes "breaths and nothing more . . . murmurs destined to be borne away like puffs of smoke." Hugo concludes: "Is that really all?—mere childishness, things said and said again, triteness, foolishness and reasonless laughter? Yes, that is all, but there is nothing on earth more exquisite or more profound" (845).

Hugo embeds this wordless exchange into a classic novel that provides a compelling portrait of an era. By the twentieth century the wordless exchange is parodied: in *Ulysses* Joyce winds up the silent communication between Gerty and Leopold across the sands of Sandymount Strand with Leopold masturbating while gazing up her dress. The exchange between them closes with the streaming of Leopold's consciousness that sweeps from the thought "Lord, I am wet" to his reflection that their unique discourse was "a kind of language between us" (372). That modest appraisal contrasts sharply with Hugo's exaggerated appraisal of a communication solely from an exchange of looks. One can almost hear the passage of sixty years of history in the resounding difference between these dramatizations of the silent communication of love.

While Hugo memorialized popular nineteenth-century views of language, Flaubert was the century's skeptic. He accentuates Emma Bovary's failures by contrasting them with her impossible hopes for happiness, expressed with clichés that progressively lose their punch. Even her callous lover Rodolphe tires. When Emma begs him to tell her that there are no other women, he suddenly sees "the eternal monotony of passion, which always assumes the same forms and always speaks the same language." Flaubert analyzes the language of love beyond Rodolphe's insight and concludes with the memorable simile: "human speech is like a cracked kettle on which we tap crude rhythms for bears to dance to, while we long to make music that will melt the stars" (216). That frustration is, of course, his own. He explores its nature in a novel celebrated for its melodious language, as if to underscore how difficult it is to say what one means. The similarity between Flaubert's insight and the linguistic skepticism of a number of modern novelists threatens the historicity of my subject. If lovers never quite understand what the other means and, like novelists, always fail to make music to melt the stars, then where's the history? It is a movement in the direction of greater sensitivity to the problem of communication and modest gains in overcoming it.

Some Victorian lovers who had trouble speaking used someone else to do it for them. A transitional moment separating them from the moderns is marked by a short story and a play from the 1890s: both tragedies that occur when a third person mediates. Hardy's "On the Western Circuit" (1891) turns on a misunderstanding that arises when the pretty but illiterate housemaid Anna receives a letter from a barrister, Charles, whom she met at a local fair, and asks her mistress, unhappily married Edith, to reply in her name. Although Hardy sympathetically crafts his account of the intensity of Anna's feelings, he does not idealize her inability to express those feelings. The epistolary romance that develops between Edith and the unwitting Charles valorizes the words lovers use. Anna's pretty smiles clash more and more with her verbal clumsiness, Edith eventually must disclose her deception, and the story ends in the honeymoon carriage after Anna asks her husband what he is doing: "Reading over all those sweet letters to me signed 'Anna,' he replied, with dreary resignation." This story is transitional because the epistolary romance, however much compromised by deception, is fulfilling, and because the capacity of the written word to communicate love does not come into question.

A similar philosophy informs Edmond Rostand's *Cyrano de Bergerac* (1898). Christian is beautiful but stupid and cannot speak what he thinks he feels. Cyrano is ugly, but oh, can he write and talk. They both love the beautiful Roxanne, but Cyrano, thinking he doesn't have a chance with his big nose, agrees to romance beautiful Roxanne for Christian with poetic love letters which Christian is incapable of writing. She falls in love with the fake composite of Christian's face and Cyrano's language and runs the showdown scene like a poetry contest. When Christian tries to speak for himself, Roxanne is quickly disenchanted and slams the door in his face. She reappears on her balcony and responds finally to a fresh metaphor from Cyrano, who is prompting Christian from the shadows. In frustration Cyrano, still in the shadows, begins to speak for himself, taking the opportunity to comment on the artificiality of love poetry. "Love hates that game of words!" he says. "There comes one moment . . . when Beauty stands/ Looking into the soul with grave, sweet eyes/ That sicken at pretty words!" (109). Rostand's didactic drama criticizes the stale conventions of courtly love, the artificiality of love poetry,[5] and the folly of getting someone else to write or speak for you. He also underscores the difficulty of communicating love, whatever the medium. Roxanne only discovers Cyrano's secret love years later as he lays dying, waving his sword but more effectively weaving his words while in delirious mortal combat against his ancient enemies—falsehood, prejudice, compromise, cowardice, and vanity.

The century turns with this rousing call to authenticity, this determination to write and speak the language of love for one's very own self, but it is mixed with dated chivalric imagery. With his last breath Cyrano boasts to Roxanne that he takes with him before God "One thing without stain,/ Unspotted from the world . . . My white plume." Twentieth-century lovers attempted to speak the language of love for themselves, and they did so even when they were as stained and spotted as was Leopold on the Strand.

In nineteenth-century literature there is a sharp difference between the awareness of the problem of language by novelists and by characters in their novels. Flaubert eloquently expressed his struggle to make music on the cracked kettle, while his characters rarely gave a thought to the crude instrument with which they beat out the rhythms of love. Few of his contemporary writers thematized the problem of expression as clearly. Most labored over their phrasings but considered language an adequate instrument and proceeded to write as omniscient narrators, fully in charge of their language and their stories. By the twentieth century such confidence in the adequacy of language erodes. Even the omniscient narrator gives way to the searching if not "unreliable narrator," and Gide, Ford, and Proust search along with their characters how to make sense out of love. The remainder of this chapter will trace modernists' increasing impatience with the deadening effect of cliché, the inability of lovers to express themselves, and finally the search for new ways to speak about love.

II

Art is the studious avoidance of cliché. For the man who immortalized the phrase "life imitates art," the way we speak about love *is* the way we live it. Wilde believed that most people love as they speak, in a cliché-ridden trance. He ridicules that way of loving in *The Importance of Being Earnest* (1895), when, after Algernon tells Cecily, "ever since I first looked upon your wonderful and incomparable beauty, I have dared to love you wildly, passionately, devotedly, hopelessly," she brings him down with the delightfully inappropriate semantical correction, "I don't think that you should tell me that you love me wildly, passionately, devotedly, hopelessly. Hopelessly doesn't seem to make much sense, does it?" (286). In Shaw's *Man and Superman* (1903) after Jack expounds on the measures he will take to see that his upcoming marriage will be free of clichés, he is interrupted by Violet and then urged on by his fiancée, "Never mind her, dear. Go on talking." Jack brings down the final curtain with his exclamation—"Talking!"

What Wilde and Shaw shot down with witty quips, others attacked with tragic self-disclosure, bitter irony, historical analysis, and heavy moralizing.

From the depths of degradation in the alleys of cholera-infected Venice, the aristocratic Aschenbach murmurs his tragic avowal far out of earshot: "quivering from head to foot [after Tadzio smiled at him] and quite un-manned he whispered the hackneyed phrase of love and longing—impos-sible in these circumstances, absurd, abject, ridiculous enough, yet sacred too, and not unworthy of honor even here: 'I love you!'" (52). The degra-dation of this master of language is underscored by the uncanny suitability of the hackneyed phrase he uses to express his passion.

Wharton's "age of innocence" refers to youth but, more importantly, to the 1890s, when she came of age in love. She accents the pastness of that time by setting the first part of her novel back in the 1870s. Her ingenue May Welland speaks for youth and the *fin de siècle*. When Archer suggests that they travel after marriage, May exclaims, "You're so original!" Archer despairs because he realizes "that she was making the answers that instinct and tradition taught her to make—even to the point of calling him original." "Original!" he responds, "We're all as like each other as those dolls cut out of the same folded paper" (83).

Two works by Musil revolve around the creation of value which depends on the avoidance of cliché: the marriage of a conventionally married woman needs perfecting, and the man without qualities needs to acquire some qual-ities of his own. Tradition, protocol, and habit have locked love for both protagonists into empty routines. In "The Perfecting of a Love" Claudine senses the promise of "a love in quest of its own perfection—a love for which there are still no words." To achieve it she will have to start from scratch with a stranger, perhaps even by actually scratching him. In *The Man Without Qualities* Ulrich is revolted by "the preformations passed down by generation after generation, the ready made language not only of the tongue but also of the sensations and feelings" (I, 149). When Ulrich takes his sister in his arms to reconstitute the qualities of love, he realizes that he cannot call her "angel" and that he must invent new words and phrases. Their incestuous love is anything but a cliché.

Over the years Lawrence's moralizing about the need for a revolution in the language of love seems itself to have become clichéd, but in its time it was original and bold. In *Women in Love* Rupert urges on Ursula the au-thor's own philosophy. "'The point about love,' he said . . . 'is that we hate the word because we have vulgarized it. It ought to be . . . tabooed from utterance, for many years, till we get a new, better idea'" (122). Their con-flict centers on words as much as feelings. Ursula begs him, "Say you love me, say 'my love' to me." Rupert fights the cliche. "I love you right enough

. . . but I want it to be something else . . . We can go one better." She insists
that there is nothing better and again pleads: "Say 'my love' to me, say it,
say it." He concedes grudgingly. "Yes—my love, yes,—my love. Let love be
enough then. I love you then—I love you. I'm bored by the rest" (145–146).
But Rupert holds out for something better, which in the end turns out to be
precisely his determination to hold out. For various reasons Cecily, Aschenbach, Archer, Claudine, Ulrich, and Rupert are loath to use commonplace
words for what seems unique.

III

Nineteenth-century lovers occasionally balked over clichés, but they had too
many objective problems to devote much time to the problem of language.
Before Rochester and Jane could begin to worry about inventing fresh metaphors, they had to overcome the palpable obstacles created by Rochester's
vast wealth, imposing mansion, social status, extensive travel, physical
strength, and greater age in addition to the attentions of beautiful Blanche
Ingram and the complications of his still binding marriage to Bertha. Their
love also had to be worked out within a complex institutional framework
that included polar gender roles, strict laws regulating marriage and divorce, a deeply entrenched hierarchical social system, and an exacting God.
Rochester's first proposal of marriage does include an implicit reference to
language, but it is not about the difficulty of communicating his feelings. He
urges Jane: "Say, Edward—give me my name—Edward—I will marry you"
(283). The history of the language of love is marked by the contrast between
his unquestioning confidence that Jane will be thrilled to be given a new
name packaged in this courtship cliché and all the uncertainty about the
possibility of communication itself in the novels of Colette, Wharton,
Woolf, and Forster.

In *The Vagabond* Renée reflects on the anguish of her new vulnerability
to a quasi-literate but sensuous man who has stirred her desire. But, she
thinks, "I shall not tell [him] that because, like those who have got to the
tenth lesson at the Berlitz School, we only know how to exchange elemen-
tary phrases where the words *bread, window, temperature, theatre*, and *family* play a great part." She is torn between her technically correct "*personal
language*" and her other "slovenly, lively idiom, coarse and picturesque,
which one learns in the music hall." The chapter concludes decisively: "Unable to decide, I choose silence" (82–83). In *Villette* Lucy also has two lan-

guages: "the dry, stinting check of Reason" and the "full, liberal impulse of Feeling." She explains what happened after she received a letter from the man she loved. "Feeling and I turned Reason out of doors, drew against her bar and bolt, then . . . poured out our sincere heart." But after giving expression to her feelings, "Reason would leap in, vigorous and revengeful, snatch the full sheets, read, sneer, erase, tear up, re-write, fold, seal, direct, and send a terse, curt missive of a page. She did right" (334–335). Lucy, in cahoots with Reason, kept one letter unmailed and judged her decision to be right, not because she despaired over the possibility of communicating it but because she feared that it would be understood all too well. While modern heroine-writers like Renée knew how to choose silence, Victorians knew rather how to keep quiet.

The problem was not just woman's. Wharton's age of innocence was also an age of reticence that crippled relationships, as men and woman lived "in a kind of hieroglyphic world, where the real thing was never said or done or even thought, but only represented by a set of arbitrary signs" (45). She indicts an entire historical age through Archer's son, who tells his father that his mother knew about his old love for Ellen but did not speak out. "You never did ask each other anything, did you? And you never told each other anything. You just sat and watched each other, and guessed at what was going on underneath. A deaf-and-dumb asylum, in fact" (356).

One recurring theme in Woolf's novels is the inability of her characters to understand one another, let alone express their love. Although she viewed that inability as part of the abiding human condition, there is a historical perspective on it in the relationship between Mr. and Mrs. Ramsay in *To the Lighthouse*, which was patterned after that of her parents. Her father was a distinguished Victorian scholar and family patriarch, Sir Leslie Stephen, who seems almost to have preferred writing biography to living, and who struggled, like Mr. Ramsay, against the terror of expressing love. The Ramsays avoided the clichés of love not because they wanted to be original but because they were afraid to say anything at all.

Woolf leads up to their ultimate non-exchange with trifling episodes about hiding thoughts and being found out, which show the extent of their fear. She further accents her characters' failure to disclose their inner thoughts by concealing them even from the reader. Mr. Ramsay wants to tell his wife something as he walks on the terrace but does not speak, and we never learn what it was he wanted to say. We even wonder whether *he* knew. Mrs. Ramsay is also uncommunicative. "She [Mrs. Ramsay] had been reading fairy tales to [her son] James, she said. No, they could not share that; they could not say that." *Did* she tell her husband that she had been reading fairy tales? If not, then why in the world could she not say *that*? And if she did say it, then what *was* it they could not say? Woolf digs further into their quiet suffering. "Had she known that he was looking at her, she thought, she would not have let herself sit there, thinking. She disliked anything that reminded her that she had been sitting thinking" (104). But there is no place to hide, because they are very much in love. Finally, as if their inability to speak has become too much to bear, Woolf works it into one of Western literature's most poignant failures to express love:

> So they sat silent. Then she became aware that she wanted him to say something.
>
> Anything, anything, she thought, going on with her knitting. Anything will do . . .
>
> "You won't finish that stocking tonight," he said . . . That was what she wanted—the asperity in his voice reproving her . . . And what then? . . . He wanted something—wanted the thing she always found it so difficult to give him; wanted her to tell him that she loved him. And that, no, she could not do. He found talking so much easier than she did . . . A heartless woman he called her; she never told him that she loved him. But it was not so—it was not so. It was only that she never could say what she felt. Was there no crumb on his coat? Nothing she could do for him? [She moves to the window] She knew that he was thinking, You are more beautiful than ever. And she felt herself very beautiful. Will you not tell me just for once that you love me? He was thinking that, for he was roused . . . but she could not do it; she could not say it. Then, knowing that he was watching her, instead of saying anything she turned, holding her stocking, and looked at him. And as she looked at him she began to smile, for though she had not said a word, he knew, of course he knew, that she loved him. He could not deny it. And smiling she looked out of the window and said (thinking to herself, Nothing on earth can equal this happiness)—
>
> "Yes, you were right. It's going to be wet tomorrow. You won't be able to go [to the lighthouse]." And she looked at him smiling. For she had triumphed again. She had not said it: yet he knew.

The possibility of a history of the language of love hangs on the significance of this exchange. If not speaking works as well as speaking, then it is impossible to distinguish loves by their differing articulations. And if one cannot distinguish loves by the way lovers speak, then how can one write a history of love with the evidence of dialogue as I have undertaken to do? Although Woolf is generous in evaluating the Ramsays' prison of silence, there is irony in her account. Mrs. Ramsay realizes her supreme happiness as she utters her last words in the novel, which give up the argument she had sustained with her husband from the opening pages. Woolf then explains that Mrs. Ramsay's happiness, which either allowed her to make this insincere capitulation or was made possible by it, was also her supreme triumph, which was a refusal to say she loved him. This double renunciation of the word (the argument she had been verbalizing as well as—and more important—what she did not say) is her triumph. Her one source of power is withholding speech to counter the overpowering Victorian patriarch, whose command of language is so maddeningly precise. Woolf's heroine, like her mother on whom the character was based, could only triumph by insincerity and passive-aggressive silence. To her conclusion that nothing *on earth* could equal Mrs. Ramsay's happiness, Woolf might have added, nothing *in her time*.

The novel articulates what Woolf's parents (and so many of their generation) did not say and is evidence for historical change. Her parents did not speak, so she spoke for them. And if her own lyric prose was inspired by their years of silence and guesswork loving, her moving reconstruction of it is testimony to the value of saying over not saying. Twentieth-century lovers understood a bit more than Victorians that hearing the words of love, even clichés, is more interesting, more distinctly human, than having crumbs brushed off your coat. Monkeys groom each other. Authentic love is only possible because of the language through which it can be expressed. Lovers can mask genuine feeling with empty chatter, but without speaking they cannot be open to the beloved, willing to risk being known and to discover what they mean together.

In *Orlando* (1928) Woolf theorizes about the history of communication in a sketch on the condition of England during the first day of the nineteenth century. "No open conversation was tolerated. Evasions and concealments were sedulously practiced." A few minutes after Orlando meets Shelmerdine they became engaged. "Though their acquaintance had been so short, they had guessed, as always happens between lovers, everything of any importance about each other in two seconds at the utmost." Of course they knew nothing about one another, and Woolf is bitterly sarcastic about the survival into her own age of this myth that lovers can know all without speaking. "Our modern spirit can almost dispense with language; the commonest expressions do, since no expressions do; hence the most ordinary conversation is often the most poetic, and the most poetic is precisely that which cannot be written down. For which reasons we leave a great blank here, which must be taken to indicate that the space is filled to repletion." Woolf leaves eight lines blank. She then "interrupts" her lovers' inexpressible nothings with a sample of what was actually being said. As Shelmerdine used precise technical language (map readings, compass bearings, rigging of the sails) to explain his passion for sailing, Orlando listened to every word, "interpreting them rightly, so as to see . . . the phosphorescence on the waves; the icicles clanking in the shrouds." This sort of mutual *mis*understanding continues as the lovers discuss many other things without understanding in the slightest what each other is saying, as Woolf narrates. "All this and a thousand other things she understood him to say, and so when she replied, Yes, negresses are seductive, aren't they? he having told her that the supply of biscuits now gave out, he was surprised and delighted to find how well she had taken his meaning" (143–161).

In *A Passage to India* Forster queries the expressive capacity of language itself: his characters cannot communicate their love because they cannot distinctly hear or understand anything clearly. Was Adela attacked by Aziz or was it a hallucination? The novel turns only superficially on that mystery but more importantly on the ultimate meaning of the mystery of life hidden in the Marabar Caves, which make of all sounds a single mesmerizing echo. "Hope, politeness, the blowing of a nose, the squeak of a boot, all produce 'boum,'—utterly dull" (147). Mrs. Moore thinks how she had come to India to witness Adela's marriage to her son but left in despair that love was possible, that anything would ever make sense to her again. "All this fuss over a frightened girl! Nothing had happened, 'and if it had,' she found herself thinking . . . 'there are worse evils than love.' The unspeakable attempt presented itself to her as love: in a cave, in a church—boum, it amounts to the same" (208). The resounding "boum" is a symbol of the incessant echoing that confuses human understanding. Forster's dramatization of the problem of communication belongs to an age that tried to decode the "hieroglyphic world" of its parents' generation, when couples "never did ask each other anything," and when frustrated wives achieved their triumphs with words of love unspoken.

This growing awareness of the difficulty that men and women had expressing their feelings included sensitivity to distinctive gender modes of language. One theme of Dorothy Richardson's *Pilgrimage* (1913–1931) was
the development of a distinctively female consciousness. Its heroine Miriam
concludes that "by every word they use men and women mean different
things." And not just different: "In speech with a man a woman is at a dis-
advantage—because they speak different languages. She may understand
his. Hers he will never speak nor understand."[6] While Richardson's comparison is ironic, viewing bilingual women at a *dis*advantage up against mono-
lingual men, Rilke in *The Notebooks of Malte Laurids Brigge* (1910) explicitly argued that women's superior command of the language of love
underscored men's deficiency. For centuries, he maintained, women have
"taken upon themselves the entire task of love; they have always played the
whole dialogue—both parts" (133). He calls upon modern men to speak
their love as he urges the modern poet to learn to see. The men who
struggled to love the women of Gilman's *Herland* also had to deal with
"Herlanguage." After repeated misunderstandings the men realized that the
problem was language itself. "It was not that [the women] did not love us;
they did, deeply and warmly. But what they meant by 'love' and what we
meant by 'love' were so different" (122).[7]

The difficulty men found in understanding women or expressing their love
to them was intensified by the war. In *A Room of One's Own* Woolf recalled
how the war "changed the value of words themselves" and the language of
love. It seemed ludicrous to her that a prewar lover might have hummed
Tennyson's line, "She is coming, my dove, my dear" (13, 16). The violence
of war blasted away the delicacy, the patience, and the platitudes of long
Victorian courtships. Prewar concern about the denial of sex changed into a
postwar obsession with sex. Hemingway's revolutionary simplification of
language came out of his combat experience, the effects of which he projected onto several love-starved veterans. The young ex-marine in "Soldier's
Home" returns to Kansas in 1919, unable to court the girls because they
were "too complicated," and, unlike the German and French girls he had
known, the hometown girls wanted to talk. "But it was not worth it . . .
he would not go through all the talking." In *The Sun Also Rises* Brett tells
Jake: "There isn't any use my telling you I love you." When he replies, "You
know I love you," she closes out the discussion: "Let's not talk. Talking's all
bilge" (55).

While writers examined the communication of love directly in dialogue, painters implied it with imagery. Victorians painted lovers in conversation (greeting, flirting, questioning, explaining, pleading, arguing, proposing, rejecting, even not speaking to one another) but did not make communication itself the theme.[8] It was not until more conceptual art came into vogue in the twentieth century that a painting about the difficulty of communicating itself was likely.

The title of William Windus's *Too Late* (Figure 17, 1858) suggests several reasons for this scene of love failed.[9] The man has returned too late to revive his own love and too late to save the life of his former beloved, who is dying of tuberculosis. Many Victorian paintings cry out for captions, sometimes given in titles, as in this one in which all four figures seem to have a lot to say and yet are unable to speak. The dying woman stands speechless in contemplation of the many things she said to herself instead of to the errant man over the years while he was gone, the child swallows some burning question that might clear up her own bewilderment, the woman's friend is an icon of consolation, and the man recoils in self-imposed muteness, desperately blocking his own sight and organ of speech. The exhibition catalogue of 1859 includes a quotation from Tennyson's poem, "Come Not, When I Am Dead," which contains the dying woman's response to her beloved's tardy return: "I am sick of time; / And I desire to rest." The melodrama turns on his timing: had he returned in time, he would have known what to say and language would have been adequate to resurrect love. But he was, alas, too late. All four figures are speechless, but the painting does not explicitly thematize or question the efficacy of language itself.

While this *love* is in ruins, it is the possibility of communication itself that seems to be breaking down in Giorgio de Chirico's *Conversation among the Ruins* (Figure 18, 1927). The artist was profoundly influenced by Nietzsche's philosophy, which had identified man's spiritual crisis consequent to the "death of God" as a terrifying confrontation with the void. De Chirico, the founder of "metaphysical painting," wrote: "Art was liberated by the modern philosophers and poets. Schopenhauer and Nietzsche were the first to teach us the profound meaning of the absurdity of life, and to show us how this absurdity can be transmuted into art."[10] The absurdity and the emptiness of life in a world without God are intensified in love. In *The Joys and Enigmas of a Strange Hour* (1913), two human figures stand facing each other at the far end of the deserted street, their long shadows lying parallel but clearly separate on the street, exaggerating their isolation from each other. The shadow figures, like a pair of black worms, appear in

17. William Windus, *Too Late*, 1858.

nine other paintings in the piazza series as a symbol of the isolation of persons from each other in the surrounding emptiness of modern life. In 1913 De Chirico began a series of paintings of dressmakers' mannequins in classical poses of love. In *The Duo* (1915) the male mannequin has a heart like a valentine painted on his chest, but both he and his beloved are without genitals, arms, or faces. He is an absurd modern lover stalwartly posed in loving intimacy but unable to desire, touch, or speak.

De Chirico commented on the difficulty of trying to communicate love in *Conversation among the Ruins*. The couple sits on the stage of life in their fragmentary home which is surrounded by a void of barren hills. Their differing period attires translate time into place and suggest that the lived distance between them is far greater than the measurable space that separates their bodies, for they are struggling to converse across the ages—classical

18. Giorgio de Chirico, *Conversation among the Ruins*, 1927.

woman must somehow speak to modern man. In contrast with Windus's *Too Late*, there is no melodrama, no fateful wrong turn or misunderstanding, because this couple has been staring at one another since antiquity, indicated by a portrait of the man who is De Chirico himself on an antique column and by the woman's Grecian dress, as if to say, "thus has it always been." Windus suggests that his lovers' tragedy might have been avoided if only the man had done the right thing in time, while De Chirico questions whether ordinary people, let alone lovers, are able to communicate their meaning at all. The breakdown of language is not caused by a word, a visit, or a response that was too late but is an abiding feature of the human condition. De Chirico's conversation among the ruins is about conversation in ruins.

Matisse's *Conversation* (Figure 19, 1908), a frank self-portrait with his

19. Henri Matisse, *Conversation*, 1908.

wife, probes the origins of communication between man and woman, starkly silhouetted against unshaded blue, posed in simple geometric forms, positioned in a basic hierarchy of standing and sitting, at the start of day, awakening to confront the primordial challenge of communication. Their argumentative positions are as rigid and inflexible as their postures, and their confrontation, whatever the specific issue, has been going on from the beginning of their relationship, from the beginning of time. They are separated by the window's iron grillework that bars escape and spells the word "NON" from him to her and from her to him, a word which visually precedes and therefore appears to preface every utterance in their conversation.[11]

The minimum of narrative detail that separates De Chirico and Matisse from Windus is apparent in the foliage. Windus offers a botanical museum of meaning: the overgrown ivy of faithfulness symbolizes the woman's abiding loyalty; the courting wall it now smothers betokens happier times past; the dead leaves at the woman's feet, the broken twig the young girl holds, the leafless pollard behind the man, and the broken tree struggling to send out new shoots collectively leave no doubt about the meaning of this tragic story. But precisely that narrative detail obscures the fundamental problem of language that is thematized by De Chirico and especially Matisse. De Chirico's defoliated background is a composition of forms that do not narrate. Matisse's garden is a framed painting, a work of art that separates the conversationalists but also draws them together in the painting. Matisse's trees are in absurdly full bloom, their sap flows freely like the artistic inspiration that enables them to be. Unlike Windus's flora they cannot die, because they do not live in a story or point a moral; they are not a stand-in for language but visual elements of the expressive process that is art. They are colored forms that communicate by uniting the fragmentary pieces of human existence into an aesthetic whole, however disunited the parts may seem to be "in reality." The powerful double irony of Matisse's painting is that it depicts a most unconversant couple under the ironic title *Conversation* and achieves with color and form a masterful communication between artist and viewer.

IV

Just as modern artists developed a new artistic language of love in the materials and the act of painting itself, modern writers developed new ways of writing about love.

A cardinal rule of psychoanalysis is that all experience, however painful, must be put into words. The first name for Freud's method was "the talking cure," and his earliest formulation emphasized the curative function of speaking. Each symptom disappeared when he "succeeded in bringing clearly to light the memory of the event by which it was provoked and in arousing its accompanying affect, and when the patient had described that event in the greatest possible detail and had put the affect into words." [12] The three major psychoanalytic techniques—dream interpretation, free association, and analysis of the transference—all involved a struggle to overcome resistance against putting experience into words. A major goal of psychoanalysis, the disclosure of unconscious mental processes, required that pregrammatical primary process thinking be put into some intelligible linguistic form to make it accessible to the conscious mind and hence to psychoanalytic therapy. Much of the resistance Freud encountered was from the "conspiracy of silence" that enshrouded talk about sex in the nineteenth century. Among his greatest contributions was the development of a language to interpret pathological resistance and repression. [13]

The goal of mental health called for the freer articulation of the language of *libido* (a Latinate euphemism for the sex drive), which screened the embarrassing language of love. For all his daring, the Viennese doctor had his own embarrassment and censored his own language. His first formulation of the phrase "anatomy is destiny" referred boldly to the anal-expulsive origin of the sadistic component of the sex drive, but he left the crucial body referents in Latin: "The excremental is all too intimately and inseparably bound up with the sexual; the position of the genitals—*inter urinas et faeces*—remains the decisive and unchanging factor." [14] No one at that time did more to enable neurotics to speak about their suffering than did Freud. Traumatic experience, whether in the genesis of a mental illness or in the loss of love, cuts an individual off from part of himself. Freud explained how necessary it is not just to recollect that experience but to describe it in the greatest possible detail and put the affect into words in order to restore that lost part of the self.

Modern novelists also appreciated the need for more precise words of love. The homosexual lovers in Forster's *Maurice* had to fashion "a new language" out of the "humblest scraps of speech" to express "a passion that few English minds have admitted" (83). *Remembrance of Things Past* is a search for lost love and the language to make it endure. Proust lost that love as a child the night he feared that his mother would not kiss him goodnight, though instead she delighted him by sleeping the entire night at his side. Her indulgence made him realize that his suffering was an inescapable part of life. His chronic failure to recapture such unqualified love fueled the search for a literary vocation (a language of love) which he realizes, seemingly along with his readers, only at the end of a million and a half words. Although his narrator never achieves a fulfilling love in the story, he comes to love the language of writing itself.

Lady Chatterley's Lover is about how the word became deed and *the* deed became word. For the young Connie "passionately talking" to men not only preceded but took precedence over the deed. After she marries, the word displaces the deed altogether. Lord Clifford Chatterley is an allegorical figure who stands for the idle chatter that prevailed in avant-garde aristocratic circles of his time. He transforms everything into words. "Violets were Juno's eyelids, and windflowers were unravished brides. How [Connie] hated words, always coming between her and life." Clifford's outlook is antisexual, and a stint in the trenches leaves him paralyzed and impotent. She must therefore find a potent man and learn to speak about love. Mellors guides her into sexual fulfillment and teaches her to speak about it with his earthy Midlands dialect.

While lounging in the woods in postcoital delight, Connie calls out to him, "Where are you? Speak to me! Say something to me!" Mellors responds in a dialect which Connie also attempts to use. He directs their talk to the physical goal of his desire, using language that until that time was viewed as obscene.

> "Th'art good cunt, though, aren't ter? Best bit o' cunt left on earth. When ter likes! When tha'rt willin'!"
> "What is cunt?" she said.
> "An' doesn't ter know? Cunt! It's thee down theer; an' what I get when I'm i'side thee, and what tha gets when I'm i'side thee; it's a' as it is, all on't."
> "All on't" she teased. "Cunt! It's like fuck then."
> "Nay nay! Fuck's only what you do. Animals fuck. But cunt's a lot more than that. It's thee, dost see: an' tha'rt a lot besides an animal, aren't ter?—even ter fuck! Cunt! Eh, that's the beauty o'thee, lass?"   (166)

Mellors also uses the playful personifications "John Thomas" and "Lady Jane" for penis and vagina, but he does not shrink from slang. He believes that it is necessary to use sex slang, because, although those words do not capture all the conflicting associations of sex, they express essential aspects that no other words convey. In the moment of passion men do not desire a vagina or "a round goblet that wanteth not liquor." Except for the most bizarre of perverts, sexual pleasure does not occur *inter urinas et faeces*, not even "between urine and feces." Sex slang is never entirely fitting, because it is at the edge of vulgarity, but it provides a hard-hitting alternative to the evasiveness of Latin, the antisepsis of medical terminology, or the ornamentation of metaphor. "If I use the taboo words," Lawrence wrote in "A Propos of *Lady Chatterley's Lover*," "there is a reason" (110). We must be able to use "the so-called obscene words, because these are a natural part of the mind's consciousness of the body." Lawrence ventured beyond the bounds of linguistic respectability to restore that part of sexual love which had been killed by the refinements of polite language. "Obscenity," he wrote, "only comes in when the mind despises and fears the body, and the body hates and resists the mind" (86). The melodious sexual dialogue between Connie and

Mellors contrasts with the clash with censors that Lawrence endured to write it, for his books were banned and burned as obscene, and the public outcry drove him into exile.

Joyce was also driven into exile from reaction to his even more ambitious effort to remake language. *Ulysses* revolutionized the modern novel with neologisms, spoonerisms, puns, anagrams, local wit, ventriloquy, stream of consciousness, parodying styles, linguistic indirection, and a dazzling display of metaphor. It was also, like the Homeric epic on which it is based, a love story in which all three major characters expressed different aspects of Joyce's search for a language of love.

Early on Molly asks Leopold the meaning of "metempsychosis." To his stuffy dictionary definition she responds with a command that Joyce will honor throughout the novel: "—O, rocks! . . . Tell us in plain words" (64). But Joyce also adds lots of not so plain words, journeying through lexical and semantic maneuvers that eclipse Odysseus's prototypical adventures and lead back to Molly's final unraveling of the fabric of language. Like Penelope, she also undoes her day's weaving, her tryst with Blazes, to entertain the possibility of reunion with Leopold, which she affirms with her own and the novel's final plain word—"Yes." *Ulysses* restores directness and potency to the language of love.

Stephen Dedalus's search for a literary vocation and a father is linked with his quest for absolution from his mother, whose funeral he refused to attend. His nagging guilt is intensified by her overbearing maternal love, which he realizes in an interior monologue that recalls a visit to her bedside. "She was crying in her wretched bed. For those words, Stephen: love's bitter mystery" (9). Toward the end of the novel he confronts her again: "Tell me the word, mother, if you know now. The word known to all men" (581). The word and the theme of the novel is "love." [15] While Mrs. Purefoy is in labor, Stephen comments on the connection between sexual desire, giving birth, the incarnation of God, and the vocation of the writer: "In woman's womb word is made flesh but in the spirit of the maker all flesh that passes becomes the word that shall not pass away" (391). Joyce rivals the maker by making the flesh word.

The chapter titled "Oxen of the Sun" uses the history of the English language as a metaphor for the growth of Mrs. Purefoy's fetus. To suggest verbal equivalents of the embryonic recapitulation of the species, Joyce recapitulates the history of English, imitating numerous styles from old Anglo-Saxon to modern slang. "Nausicaa" captures the inner workings of

Gerty's sentimental yearning for love with an inventive style that Joyce described as "namby-pamby jammy marmalady drawersy." [16] He salvages authentic expressiveness from the most worn-out romantic gush when he has Gerty respond to Leopold by showing him her innermost flesh, thus breaking out of her dream world of cliché.

In "Sirens" Joyce musicalizes language. He takes apart memories, fantasies, visual images, background noises, internal sensations, and pieces of barroom conversation and recombines them with lines from singing to achieve the verbal equivalent of melody and even, by simultaneously sounding different parts, harmony. The chapter is set in a bar where Leopold watches Blazes leave to meet with Molly. Leopold's interior monologue captures the moment when he realizes that Molly's affair is being consummated:

> Flood of warm jimjam lickitup secretness flowed to flow in music out, in desire, dark to lick flow, invading. Tipping her tepping her tapping her topping her. Tup. Pores to dilate dilating. Tup. The joy the feel the warm the. Tup. To pour o'er sluices pouring gushes. Flood, gush, flow, joygush, tupthrop. Now! Language of love.   (274)

This stream of consciousness does not describe or explain so much as offer up Leopold's consciousness in words, even parts of words and made-up words, before lexical meanings and syntactical rules have changed that raw experience into a rational, sequential thought process. Joyce's language here comes closer to capturing the lived actuality of love than did earlier renderings, a historical argument that can be best made by comparing this passage with Eliot's account in *Middlemarch* of "love-making" (which means courting) between Lydgate and Rosamond.

> Young love-making—that gossamer web! Even the points it clings to— the things whence its subtle interlacings are swung—are scarcely perceptible: momentary touches of finger-tips, meetings of rays from blue and dark orbs, unfinished phrases, lightest changes of cheek and lip, faintest tremors. The web itself is made of spontaneous beliefs and indefinable joys, yearnings of one life towards another, visions of completeness, indefinite trust.   (238)

Joyce and Eliot are both trying to express how people think about sexual desire and anticipate sexual excitation. Joyce is rendering Leopold's sexual fantasy laced with jealousy; Eliot is rendering how Lydgate and Rosamond experience immediate although frustrated sexual desire while anticipating something more sensuous. Joyce's direct interior monologue more accurately captures the prereflective, pregrammatical experience of sexual love, at least the way Leopold imagines it, than does Eliot's omniscient and polished authorial description. Eliot does not venture inside the mind of love as directly as Joyce and is therefore unable to describe the immediacy of sexual experience. Her well-crafted language distances readers from the earthiness and impulsiveness of sex. She identifies the hesitancy and miscommunication of "young love-making" by referring to them, while Joyce tries to build out of lexical rudiments the unconscious countercurrents, irrational ideation, disruptive memories, raunchy fantasies, and spatio-temporal craziness that shapes the ways of love. Eliot's ornamental metaphors clash with the stripped simplicity of sex, even its anticipation for her young lovers, while Joyce's linguistic coinages evoke sexual fantasies and sexual processes in action. If Joyce were to evoke the immediate sensation of "momentary touches," he would have tracked them back to their bodily roots or followed up their consequent tipping, tepping, tapping, and topping. Eliot refers to her lovers' "unfinished phrases" in skillfully finished sentences; Joyce believed that all the phrases of human existence were unfinished, as he showed with sentences, even words, that stop before they are finished.

The sex itself is different. Instead of Lydgate's and Rosamond's faint tremors Leopold sees lovers pouring "o'er sluices pouring gushes." Both authors refer to the ineffable—for Eliot it is the "scarcely perceptible," for Joyce, the "secretness." But their attempts to give it some expression are in sharp contrast: Eliot locates human contact with an unsuitable image of "points" to which a "gossamer web" clings, while Joyce fleshes out the stickiness of sexual connection with a rhythmic evocative image of the "warm jimjam lickitup secretness flowed to flow."

Eliot's observation about love's "indefinable joys" refers to her young lovers' inability to define what they feel but not to her own inability to define and describe. She would no doubt have conceded that the joy of love remains beyond the expressive capacity of even the most accomplished novelist, but her concession would be grudging. Joyce would not distance himself as much as did Eliot from her characters' inability to express their love. He would rather see such a struggle as more akin to his very own, at the heart of his literary vocation. Joyce's rendering of lovemaking comes closer to capturing the sensuous actuality of lovemaking than does Eliot's, a difference that reflects not only a change in style but also a change in the way lovers in these two periods were able to talk about their love.

I find the novels of Eliot more engaging than *Ulysses*, but my argument here is not about the accessibility of the novels nor about their dramatic force, but about the language of love in them. Eliot relied on language that exalts and embellishes the rhetorical conventions of the language of love in her time. She did it with great subtlety and insight, inspired by her own passionate commitment to the written word. Joyce fought his way through those conventions at considerable personal cost to create new and, I believe, more honest and accurate and hence more expressive words and phrases than those passed on to him. His struggle to find a new language of love is thus the more authentic, because it is a dangerous going-beyond that involves the more sustained and profound reflection on the creative possibilities of language, one that also parallels the dangerous crossing to another person that is the essence of love itself.

7 Disclosure

LOVERS HAVE an extraordinary opportunity to learn about being with another person. Their artful communications and coquettish posturings, their honest revelations and downright lies, their self-disclosures and self-deceptions create the pitch and roll of truth on love's high seas.

In contrast to the traditional notion that truth pertains to propositions that correspond to "the facts" or cohere within a system of knowledge, Heidegger argued that truth is a fundamental way of being—a "disclosure" or "uncovering"—terms which suggest how truth is an extraction from untruth (265). The lover first encounters the beloved (as well as his or her own self) all covered up. The dialogue of love is therefore not only an inquiry into secrets about the beloved, it is also a self-inquiry. There are four subelements: the lovers' sex pasts, their modes of disclosure, the value attached to disclosure, and self-disclosure.

I

As soon as a couple meet, they begin to investigate each other's sexual past, however diplomatically. Although many questions are investigated, the most tantalizing is "have you loved before?" It is the basis for all derivative inquiries about virginity and the other's sex past which indicate prospects for love to come.

Victorian men and women were reluctant to talk about something that seemed so confusing and dangerous. Hortatory and religious tracts warned men that masturbation, even nocturnal emissions or "pollutions," as they were called, might produce impotence. Men could also worry about the imaginary disease spermatorrhea (leaking of sperm), which was supposed to make them run out of sperm and become sterile. Neurologists believed that

female insanity was caused by a woman's sexuality, and some surgeons removed clitorises as a treatment for "nymphomania"—a medical diagnostic
category that did not survive into the modern period. "Experts" on birth
control counseled that women, like animals, were most fertile during menses, while others cautioned that having sex during menses might cause gonorrhea.

At mid-century the iron law of love for women was that prior to meeting
their man they ought to have had no past sexual experience, not even a Pla-
tonic attachment. Most women complied. At that time there were sound
medical reasons behind the frantic adherence to this law, which dictated
some of the excesses of Victorian prudery. No accurate test for syphilis existed until August von Wassermann developed one in 1906. No symptomatic treatment was available except the highly toxic iodides of potassium
and mercury until Paul Ehrlich discovered the less toxic salvarsan in 1909.
No complete and certain cure came about until penicillin (discovered in
1928) was first used to treat it in 1943. In 1859 Rudolph Virchow had hypothesized that syphilis was a systemic disease that could attack internal
organs, and by the 1870s medical researchers had strong evidence linking
the primary infection with the deadly tertiary infection sites of the heart,
spinal chord, and brain; but it was not until 1913, when Hideyo Noguchi
verified microscopically the presence of syphilis spirochetes in the brain of a
diseased victim, that clinical proof connected the relatively harmless primary symptoms to the fatal tertiary symptoms that sometimes did not appear for twenty years. That delay made it tempting to include masturbation
and "sexual excess" among the possible causes of syphilis, because no direct
connection could be made between sexual contact and the disease. Who
knew? Widespread ignorance about the disease on the one hand, and discoveries about its contagious nature and dangerous symptoms on the other,
drove the vulnerable population to greater mendacity. Among all the avant-
garde lovers in the novels I read up to 1934, none confessed to having ever
had a venereal infection before Frederic told Catherine in *A Farewell to
Arms* (1929).

Although syphilis could kill, gonorrhea was more prevalent and caused
arthritis, meningitis, peritonitis, and blindness. It was a special terror to
women, who were often asymptomatic but became sterile from infection
contracted from their husbands, who may have also been asymptomatic.
Under such circumstances prudent Victorians understandably tried to avoid
coitus with anyone whom they did not know to be a virgin.

Men were as vulnerable to venereal disease as women, but having sex was uniquely dangerous for women, since it also invited the life-imperiling risks of pregnancy and childbirth. Conforming to moral or religious proscriptions against sex was for most wives the only way to avoid such risks and free themselves to develop beyond the role of motherhood. Morally upright Victorian wives did not, however, consciously become pious to avoid becoming pregnant, for that would have violated the Victorian apotheosis of motherhood. Rather they adopted the regnant ideology as an unconscious screen for the life-preserving and liberating possibilities that came with living according to restrictive Christian sexual morality. They could not insist on separate bedrooms to be less sexy, but they could, to be more pious.

At the mid-century many obstetricians still examined pregnant women without looking directly at their vagina, but it was impossible to diagnose and treat properly without looking. Bloodletting was used to combat infection from puerperal fever, which physicians continued to spread on their dirty hands long after its contagious transmission was known. Shock, hemorrhage, and infection from high forceps or cesarean deliveries made giving birth a moment of supreme danger.

Whether the risk of venereal disease, pregnancy, or childbirth was the decisive factor it is impossible to know, but the literary record reveals that women, understandably, restrained themselves far more than men. Jane Eyre not only had had no prior sexual experience before meeting Rochester, she had scarcely seen more than a handful of men whom she could possibly love. Cathy was as pure as the wind-swept moors she roamed with Heathcliff. Even Hester Prynne was a virgin bride. Emma Bovary and Cosette were raised in convents. Isabel Archer, for all her American pluck, brought her husband a sexual blank page. Lucy Snowe, Clara Middleton, Dorothea Brooke, Anna Karenina, Bathsheba Everdene, and Effi Briest all remained virgins until marriage. Hester, Emma, Dorothea, Anna, Bathsheba, and Effi eventually had sex with either a lover or second husband, but they did not experiment sexually beforehand.

Men enjoyed a "double standard," to be sure, but it was more a loophole than a different set of values. Prospective husbands may have had past sexual experiences, but these were part of a shadowy background, less than a conscious choice, and their disclosures were accompanied by excuses. Rochester justifies his marriage to insane Bertha as a consequence of his father's plotting, pressure from other competitors, deception by Bertha's family, and his own youth. He tells Jane that while dutifully housing his insane wife, for ten years he sampled "English ladies, French countesses, Italian signoras, and German Gräfinnen." He then adds that he "tried dissipation—never debauchery," probably indicating that he never went to whores, which was a coded Victorian reassurance that he had not contracted a venereal disease. His explanations for these escapades ("I . . . was thrust on a wrong track" and "fate wronged me") evade responsibility.

Prospective Victorian husbands heralded the virtues of virginity. Casaubon's letter proposing to Dorothea underlines the prevailing anti-sex code for "proper" men and women. He pads his offering with a boast of triple negativity: "I can at least offer you an affection hitherto *unwasted,* and the faithful consecration of a life which, however *short* in the sequel, has *no backward pages* whereon, if you choose to turn them, you will find records such as might justly cause you either bitterness or shame" (28, italics added). These self-abnegating erotic credentials underscore the restrictiveness demanded of Victorian women: if *he* was that pure, then what must he have expected *her* to be? In this spirit, Meredith has *The Egoist*'s hero demand a bride who must come to him "out of cloistral purity" and present herself to him like "fresh gathered fruit in a basket." [1]

Although my literary evidence comes largely from fiction, now and then evidence from real life seems appropriate, as, for example, the marital debacle of John and Effie Ruskin. It was caused by lack of experience and frank communication and is especially relevant to the history of love in literature and art because Ruskin was a distinguished aesthetician, and taught Victorians how to write about and see beauty in art. In 1854, after six years of marriage, Effie wrote her parents, "I do not think I am John Ruskin's Wife at all." Prior to marriage she "had never been told the duties of married persons to each other and knew little or nothing about their relations in the closest union on earth." On their wedding night John talked about sex but didn't do it. "He alleged various reasons, hatred of children, religious motives, a desire to preserve my beauty, and finally this last year told me his true reason (and this to me is as villainous as all the rest), that he had imagined women were quite different from what he saw I was, and that the reason he did not make me his Wife was because he was disgusted with my person the first evening." [2]

Effie's letter reveals the horrors of marriage for sexually innocent young women, but it also mirrors male experience. What did disgust Ruskin that first night? Some scholars have speculated, following her clue, that he had imagined women the way he saw them in art and was disgusted when he first saw pubic hair on his bride. But even if the famous art critic never entered a studio with a live model, he must have seen sketches of nudes with pubic hair, however carefully Victorian artists and sculptors removed it from finished works. Yet even if he had seen pubic hair in art, the sight of hers may have nevertheless caused his disgust, because the pubic hair of a bride on her wedding night is experienced far differently from its presence on models or its representation on a canvas. Effie's pubic hair was a striking reminder that she was physically mature and undressed, ready for sex. Its visibility was also a preliminary uncovering of her mysterious inner depths, a symbol of the link of her fertility with the sexual prehistory of the species. We may conclude from its timing on the wedding night that Ruskin's disgust was triggered by a first viewing of his naked wife, who was innocent about the nature of sex and nervously awaited his sexual advances. These were supposed to begin according to a public timetable and readjust to a religious code that called for an instant reevaluation of sexual desire, turning it from a sin into a sacrament. His other professed reasons were covers for his reaction to the truth before his eyes: the quintessential aesthetician could not stand the sight of the living actuality of what for millennia had been synonymous with beauty in the Western world—a young woman's body—whatever the target of his gaze. Ruskin's sexual debacle was caused by precisely what Effie reported he said it was: "he had imagined women were quite different from what he saw I was." He was, Effie concluded, "disgusted with my person." His was a failure to understand and accept the reality of the other person in all her nakedness and sexual preparedness, if not sexual experience, and a failure to respond with his own naked desire. And for an intellectual like Ruskin such a combination must have been devastating.

By the 1890s the imperative for women not to have a sex past begins to break down. In 1895 Sue tells Jude forthrightly of "a friendly intimacy" she formed at the age of eighteen. That relation, never sexually consummated, was complicated by the young man's sexual overtures and her sexual aloofness, but Sue's openness about the attachment is historically significant. In the mid-1890s several plays centered on the woman with a past. In Arthur Pinero's *The Second Mrs. Tanqueray* (1893) and G. B. Shaw's *Mrs. Warren's Profession* (1893) neither past featured love, because both Mrs. had been prostitutes. Mrs. Tanqueray had tried to reform but committed suicide when it was revealed that her daughter's fiancé was one of her former lovers, while Mrs. Warren ran into conflict with her own daughter, who balked when she discovered the source of their wealth. The plays are transitional because although they treat the woman with a past, their sex was not a passion but a business, and neither woman was able to love again.[3]

By the war years men and women had greater opportunity to learn the facts of life. Fitzgerald's lovers in *This Side of Paradise* were like the author and his adventurous wife Zelda. "Isabelle and Amory were distinctly not innocent," and Isabelle warmed up for him sexually on dates with men she called "terrible speeds." Amory's next passion, Rosalind, lived for love. Her philosophy, Fitzgerald explained, was "*carpe diem* for herself and laissez-faire for others" (171).

In *The Age of Innocence* Wharton blasts the ideal of innocence. "What could [Archer and May] really know of each other," Wharton asks, "since it was his duty as a 'decent' fellow to conceal his past from her, and hers, as a marriageable girl, to have no past to conceal?"[4] "She was frank, poor darling, because she had nothing to conceal . . . and with no better preparation than this, she was to be plunged overnight into what people evasively called the 'facts of life'." Archer suffered too. "He felt himself oppressed by this creation of factitious purity, so cunningly manufactured by a conspiracy of mothers and aunts and grandmothers and long-dead ancestresses, because it was supposed to be what he wanted, what he had a right to, in order that he might exercise his lordly pleasure in smashing it like an image made of snow." Wharton suggests a piece of love's history in Archer's historical self-evaluation: "He could not deplore (as Thackeray's heroes so often exasperated him by doing), that he had not a blank page to offer his bride in exchange for the unblemished one she was to give him" (44–46). Archer's reluctance to deplore his sex past is also historical in the forward direction, because it is fueled by his growing fascination with the New Woman, Ellen, who, he is erroneously led to believe, had a sex past to rival his own. The secret love affair he had had with Mrs. Rushworth seemed paltry compared with Ellen's experience, which included her marriage to a rich Polish gentleman, her separation, her reputation of sexual adventures since then, and her "'drawing from the model,' a thing never dreamed of before" (60).

Joyce implies a historical meaning to *Ulysses* by reworking *The Odyssey*. Penelope's nocturnal unweaving had preserved her sexuality unsullied for Odysseus, who slew monsters to get home to her. Her epic achievement valorized fidelity, which she symbolized for over two millennia. Joyce questioned the value of such fidelity, if not Penelope's reputation, by replacing her spotless record with Molly's list of more than a score of pre-Leopold lovers including a professor, a farmer, an actor, a bootblack, an organ grinder, and the mayor of Dublin.

In a letter to his editor Edward Garnett on January 29, 1914, while working on a novel that would become both *The Rainbow* and *Women in Love,* Lawrence explained that to make the character of Ursula possible she must have had, prior to meeting Birkin, "some experience of love and of men." And so he resolves to give her "a love episode, a significant one." Ursula's affair with Skrebensky fills the last third of the first novel and prepares her for the mature love with Birkin in the second.

At age fifteen, before becoming Lady Chatterley, Connie lived in Dresden among the students, argued with men about philosophy, and hiked in forests. By eighteen she had a lover. Both were transformed: "the woman [became] more blooming, more subtly rounded, her young angularities softened, and her expression either anxious or triumphant: the man much quieter, more inward, the very shapes of his shoulders and his buttocks less assertive, more hesitant" (9). In "A Propos of *Lady Chatterley's Lover*" Lawrence substituted a more authentic, "accomplished chastity" for the devastating unpreparedness that was championed as virginity. "All this talk of young girls and virginity, like a blank white sheet on which nothing is written, is pure nonsense. A young girl and a young boy [are] a tormented tangle, a seething confusion of sexual feelings and sexual thoughts which only years will disentangle. Years of honest thoughts of sex, and years of struggling in action in sex will bring us at last where we want to get, to our real and accomplished chastity, our completeness, when our sexual act and our sexual thought are in harmony" (85). Lawrence echoes Heidegger in calling for an authentic constitution of chastity as a clearing, a self-reflective disentangling of the truth about one's sexuality from out of the "seething confusion" of youthful innocence. That disclosure also has a history.

II

The different values about male and female sex pasts increased the pressure on Victorian women to conceal. Disclosures at the mid-nineteenth century are often made by a third person, whereas later men and women make them more forthrightly on their own. That frankness lessens the agony of disclosures and makes possible a deepening of love rather than a histrionic termination of it. By the twentieth century disclosures also tend to increase rather than diminish the value of men and women as lovers. The history of these two subelements—the agency and value of disclosure—are so intertwined that they must be considered together.

A vivid starting point for their history is Augustus Egg's *Past and Present I* (Figure 20, 1858), the first of a set of three paintings. A marital infidelity comes to light when the husband intercepts a letter after returning from a journey unexpectedly early.[5] He squeezes part of (the truth of) the letter in his hand and crushes the remainder of it under his boot. This disaster is not caused by a woman's premarital sex past, for she is an adulteress, but it expresses, if melodramatically, mid-century values about any love past. We do not know who wrote the letter, but even if the wife wrote it, she did not intend it for her husband. The disclosure is thus not her own. Its impact is catastrophic, as Egg overdetermines with many hints. Their once happy home will collapse like the girls' house of cards, the father will be shipwrecked like the mastless boat tossed on seas in the painting that hangs over his portrait on the far wall, and the mother's sin will drive her to ruin as suggested by her serpent bracelet and the painting of the expulsion of Adam and Eve from the Garden of Eden that hangs over her portrait. For good measure a halved, wormy apple is pierced by a knife that points at the husband's heart. The anguished self-pitying husband bears no responsibility for anything that may have led to the adultery, and the wife, if she ever regains enough strength to stand up, has nowhere to go but out the open door that leads to perdition. An authentic self-disclosure and mutual self-revelation with a beloved scarcely applies to the message of this intercepted letter, and in the two other paintings in this triptych, Egg concludes his moral tale tragically. In *Past and Present II* (1858) the husband's portrait is in shadow, to show that he has died, and the older daughters comfort one another in despair; in *Past and Present III* (1858) the wife holds her dead bastard child, huddling under a bridge by the Thames into which she is no doubt destined to plunge. For Victorians, disclosure of any sexual love other than that which is reserved for the spouse exposes the guilty party and leads to ruin.

One vivid literary exposé is the scarlet "A" on the bodice of Hester Prynne's dress as a punishment for adultery in a novel that turns on the concealment and disclosure of sexual secrets. Hester keeps both her husband and her lover from knowing each other's identity, and she refuses to tell the townsfolk the identity of either. The final dramatic disclosure is made by Dimmesdale, who stands on the town scaffold to claim the paternity of Hester's child, tears away his ministerial garment to disclose his own

20. Augustus Egg, *Past and Present No. 1*, 1858.

mark of sin, and tells the crowd that Hester's letter is "but the shadow of what he bears on his own breast, and that even this, his own red stigma, is no more than the type of what has seared his inmost heart!" (268). Hawthorne surveys what people in the crowd thought they saw inscribed on Dimmesdale's chest but leaves the reader in doubt about what it was. The end transforms the secret of the scarlet letter into the mystery of Dimmesdale's "tatoo." His disclosure clears his conscience and the public record, but he and Hester are so overwhelmed by the condemnation of others that they are unable to learn any truth about their love apart from the fatal consequences of secrecy enforced by a conviction of sin.

The high drama of Victorian disclosures may be explained in part by the novel form, which sustained interest with tension created by deep dark secrets and fear of betrayal or by riveting mysteries and their solution; but the effectiveness of many climactic disclosures in novels came from the historically distinctive values that shaped their content—the uncompromising disapproval of premarital and extramarital loves. Readers of Dickens's *Bleak House* (1852) understood how urgent it was that Lady Dedlock hide from her husband that she had had a child out of wedlock. Her secret, hinted at by her name, is a dead bolt on the door of truth, and when the secret is leaked by a third party, there is no mutual illumination or deepening of love. Her husband has a fatal stroke, and she flees from the protection of the Victorian marriage to die in the open air, literally, as well as figuratively, of exposure.

In Ibsen's *The Wild Duck* (1884) Gina is unable to reveal to her proud husband Hjalmar that in years past she had had an affair with his benefactor, Haakon Werle, whose son Gregers finally discloses her past to Hjalmar in hopes of changing the foundation for his marriage from deception to truth. But Hjalmar is incapable of accepting what she has done and in a jealous rage wreaks havoc by turning against his wife and daughter, who accidentally kills herself while futilely trying to salvage her father's self-esteem and love for her.

Hardy was the master of disclosure. He captured the desperate compulsion of the investigator to know the truth and the desperate tenacity of the concealer to conceal it. *A Pair of Blue Eyes* centers on a woman's romantic misadventure, the disclosure of which becomes another man's obsession. Knight goes after Elfride's past like a dentist straining to extract a deeply rooted molar without anesthesia. It comes out in nine pieces.

The story begins years before she met Knight, when she ran away with

Stephen to marry, encountered some incidental difficulties, and the next day returned to London unmarried. During the early stages of Knight's courtship, before she had a chance to tell him about Stephen, Knight deadens whatever impulse Elfride might have had to confess by rhapsodizing about the supreme value of "a soul truthful as heaven's light," which to him is equated with a woman's "purity." Her presumed innocence is critically important because of his actual innocence, for he is twice sixteen and never been kissed. But his lack of experience is no matter, as he explains to Elfride, "because you know even less of love-making and matrimonial prearrangement than I, and so you can't draw invidious comparisons if I do my engaging improperly" (354). His erroneous presumption of her greater innocence will be his downfall. Their relationship is based on that misunderstanding, and its clarification will tear them apart.

The first disclosure comes after the courting pair meet Stephen by chance and Elfride realizes that she'd better tell Knight about her former relationship: "I want to tell you something . . . It is about something I once did, and don't think I ought to have done" (328). But she puts off telling and next day makes up a disclosure—that she had lied to him about her age. The second disclosure is inadvertent. Knight overhears her muttering in her sleep: "Don't tell him—he will not love me . . . We were going to be married—that was why I ran away . . . and he says he will not have a kissed woman . . . And if you tell him he will go away, and I shall die. I pray have mercy—O!" (356).

With the third disclosure the root starts to crack. Knight's suspicions compel him to ask if she ever had a lover, and she mutters several jerky responses: "Not, as it were, a lover; I mean, not worth mentioning . . . Well a sort of lover, I suppose . . . Yes; but only a mere person, and—. . . Yes, a lover certainly—he was that. Yes, he might have been called my lover . . . You don't mind, Harry, do you?" Knight replies feebly: "Of course, I don't seriously mind. In reason, a man cannot object to such a trifle. I only thought you hadn't—that was all" (362). Elfride concedes that she loved this other person (still unnamed) a bit but not as much as Knight, and she concludes with the wish that he were more experienced so that he would not be so demanding of her. Hardy skillfully shows how each disclosure, far from making truth known, demands greater concealment, because Knight and Elfride are both terrified of the truth. She is too ashamed to be forthright and so lets things out in dribs and drabs and only in response to his questions; he is humiliated at having to ask them and driven wild with jealousy over her answers, which uncover new areas of torment to probe and weaken his ability to compromise his rigid requirements.

The fourth disclosure is prepared by Knight's literary efforts, because he had published, of all things, a sermon which argued that any skill a woman may show in kissing proves that she has had prior experience. When Knight recalls that following his first kiss, Elfride had said, "We must be careful. I lost the other by doing this!" he realizes that his first kiss was not her first kiss and, further, that she must be laughing inwardly at his motto—"fresh lips or none for me" (368). These humiliating revelations trigger the fifth disclosure of the meaning of "the other" and what "doing this!" was all about.

Determined to find answers, Knight takes Elfride to a romantic spot where, as it happened, Stephen had first kissed her and she had lost her earring. Now Elfride sees the lost earring and attempts to reach for it unnoticed, but Knight observes her and realizes that it is what "the other" referred to. He then drags out of her that she was first kissed (the meaning of "doing this!") and became engaged at that very spot. Weary of the tortuous catechism into which they have become locked, Knight pleads, "You don't tell me anything but what I wring out of you," unaware that his exhortation to truth has been undermined by his hypocritical insistence on her innocence. This fifth disclosure concludes with a pointer to further morbid terrain. He asks where else the other man kissed her, and she replies, "Sitting on—a tomb in the—churchyard—and other places" (375).

On their way home as they walk by that very church, which is undergoing restoration, one of its towers collapses. That ruin is the site of Elfride's sixth disclosure, for he takes her back late that night and asks if one of the tombs was *the* tomb she sat on with her former lover. Elfride's "yes" sets Knight off on another lesson about how "everything ought to be cleared up between two persons before they become husband and wife." He adds perceptively, "a secret of no importance at all may be made the basis of some fatal misunderstanding only because it is discovered, and not confessed." To illustrate, he asks her to imagine how embittered he would become if her lover should suddenly turn up without her first having explained the relationship, and Elfride, trying to reply to his argument, blurts out "If he's dead, how can you meet him?" Increasingly anxious, Knight asks how could a dead man be her lover? Her answer—that she did not love or encourage him— touches another painful nerve when he recalls that she let the man kiss her. How could she do that without loving or encouraging him? Furthermore, he asks, "how, in the name of Heaven, can a man sit upon his own tomb?" Trapped, Elfride must explain: "That was another man. Forgive me, Harry, won't you?" His frantic reply is a moment of black humor: "What, a lover in the tomb and a lover on it?" When Elfride confirms that there were indeed two lovers, that she kissed the second man whom she did love while sitting on the tomb of an admirer whom she did not, Knight is pressed to the limit. When she indicates that there is still more, Knight warns that anything more "might make it impossible for me or any one else to love you and marry you." Elfride counters passionately that she never questioned his past and accepted him completely—"wherever you came from, whatever you had done, whoever you had loved"—and Knight retreats (381–383).

The seventh disclosure is a Hardyesque double disentombment. After sending Elfride home, Knight discovers widow Jethway's dead body under the tower's rubble and carries the corpse back to her cottage, where he finds several drafts of a letter the widow had been writing that promised to disclose some evil. The next day he receives the final draft, which is addressed to him and, by his way of thinking, comes from the other side of death. It reveals that the young man in the tomb was the widow's son and includes a list of Elfride's transgressions during her errant "elopement" and after. To her own letter the widow had attached a damning letter Elfride had written to her, begging her not to tell what she knew.

The next disclosure is the showdown. Without revealing his source of information Knight cross-examines Elfride about what he has already learned. By the time he reaches his final question, "Did you return home [with her first lover] the same day on which you left it?" Elfride is too exhausted by the long extraction to try and explain and replies simply "No" (400). Knight assumes that she had sex with the man and abruptly concludes the interrogation, seventy pages after he began, by withdrawing his proposal.

The ninth disclosure occurs fifteen months later, when Knight runs into his old friend Stephen and learns that he was the man to whom she had been engaged and that they had not had sex. Later that evening Knight agonizes over his mistake, as he wonders, with unintended irony, "Why did he not make his little docile girl tell more?" (429). In fact while straining to extract what turned out to be a tidbit of innocent gossip, he did everything he could to shut her up, simultaneously tormenting her with his own fantasies of female sexual innocence while firing accusations that deepened her sense of guilt.

This brutal interrogation is a compendium of the concealment and mendacity that were so magnified by the Victorian code of silence. The rules governing courtships were made to keep lovers from knowledge of past loves and, failing that, to keep anyone else from learning about them. Women were punished more than men for violations of the code, but both sexes made it work. The double standard that regulated the code was the pivot of *Tess of the d'Urbervilles,* on which turns the most famous disclosure of a woman's sex past in Victorian literature.

On their wedding night Tess and Angel exchange confessions. With characteristic male penitence over his premarital indiscretion, Angel confesses that he once "plunged into eight-and-forty hours' dissipation with a stranger." He never spoke to the woman again or repeated the "offence" with anyone else. Relieved that his disclosure might soften the impact of her own, Tess reveals that her "cousin" Alec raped her and made her pregnant and that then the baby died. In reacting, Angel summons up a century of masculine self-righteousness. He shrieks her name, she begs forgiveness, and he replies: "O Tess, forgiveness does not apply to the case! You were one person; now you are another. My God—how can forgiveness meet such a grotesque—prestigitation as that!" The remainder of this gruesome exchange centers on the connection between sex and selfhood. Tess pleads that she loves him, past and all, "because," she assures him, "you are yourself . . . Then how can you, O my own husband, stop loving me?" He replies, "I repeat, the woman I have been loving is not you." She asks, "But who?" and he says, "Another woman in your shape" (189–191). The poignancy of this scene comes from Angel's love of Tess. Hardy crafted their love as a romance that overcame several formidable obstacles only to come to this impassable barrier for reasons which, however crudely, Angel tries to explain as the transformation of her person as a consequence of her past sexual experience and pregnancy. Although Hardy does not reveal precisely what in her story most troubled Angel or what biological theories he may have known, some of the prevailing ideas about sexual physiology and hereditary transmission at that time help explain the theoretical climate for Angel's panicky exit from love.

In addition to ignorance about venereal disease, Victorians were also troubled by the theory that every sexual experience may leave its mark on a woman. In *Thérèse Raquin* (1867) Zola argued that men and women pollute each other's temperaments by kissing, breathing, and having sex: "These modifications, which have their origin in the flesh, are speedily communicated to the brain and affect the entire individual."[6] A likely source of popular thinking on the organic exchange between men and women in sex was the phrenology of O. S. Fowler, who explained how "all the secretions" of the body "partake" of the state of mind and body at any given time. August Weismann's refutation of the theory of the hereditary transmission of acquired characteristics only began to become known in the 1890s, and until then many scientists and moralists believed that any parental disease, vice, bad habit, or congenital defect could be transmitted to the offspring by the same confused hereditary process. Fowler emphasized the scope of hereditary transmission through the father's sperm: "*every element and function of both the mind and body* of parentage, and in *all their shades, and phases, and degrees of action and conditions,* are transferred to this secretion and through it transmitted to that physical and mental constitution of progeny derived therefrom!"[7] Others argued that "maternal impressions" such as a single shock during pregnancy could adversely affect a child, and moralists tended to believe that bad impressions were more likely to be transmitted than good ones. In 1857 the French physician B. A. Morel introduced his theory of degeneration—that the diseases and vices and "stigmata" of mankind were collecting and intensifying in a pool of corruption that undermined human goodness and threatened human survival. Degeneration theory attracted serious intellectual and artistic attention until the end of the century, as the German critic Max Nordau bemoaned in *Degeneration* (1893), a compendium of the evil consequences of hereditary degeneration in ethics, politics, and religion as well as sexuality, marriage, and parenthood.[8]

By including a pregnancy in Tess's past Hardy introduced a source of special anxiety, because the nature of the placental barrier was not well understood by scientists and was hopelessly confused by laymen. Some believed that a pregnant woman shares fetal blood and that consequently through this blood biological traces of the father continue to circulate in the mother's blood after she delivers, so that subsequent offspring sired by a second man might resemble the first father.[9] In 1886 a distinguished German philosopher theorized that during pregnancy the mother exchanges blood *(Blutaustausch)* with her fetus. Since half of the blood is determined by the father's hereditary makeup, postpartum traces of him remain "latent" in her blood. "The husband of a widow does not therefore find a blank page but one written on by his predecessor's organism, with whose hereditary tendencies his own must enter into conflict."[10]

Victorian men could thus be plagued by fear of "hereditary tendencies" as well as the venereal diseases of a woman's former lover. These ghosts of love past must be understood in the context of Victorian medical and biological knowledge. While novelists rarely elaborated this background, it shaped the individuals on whom these novels were based. Angel spoke for a generation of men for whom a woman's sexual disclosures, particularly when they included a pregnancy, spelled the end of love. Perhaps Angel did not consciously decide to stop loving because of a theory, but rather discovered with horror that he simply could no longer love Tess because her disclosure had transformed her very person—mind and body. In turn, her forgiveness of his sexual past might have been due to her ignorance of the disturbing theories to which the men in her life had greater access. The conspiracy of silence kept women from learning not only how to enjoy sex, but also how dangerous it could be. Men and women of the nineteenth century had only the vaguest ideas about what they were going to "catch" from sex, but men knew a little more, which translated into greater apprehension about a woman's sexual past. Arguments that premarital virginity or postmarital fidelity were demanded to insure the integrity of bourgeois status or the security of inheritance miss the crucial point in love relationships. And Angel did love Tess. He did not recoil from his beloved wife on his wedding night because of status or money. He was perplexed, terrified, disgusted. Without reducing the history of sexual disclosures to a mere consequence of advancing biological knowledge, I view that history as shaped in part by the discoveries of Weismann, Wassermann, Ehrlich, and Noguci as well the studies of the psychology of sex by Havelock Ellis and Freud, which helped sort out sexual fact from fiction and made possible the more forthright disclosures we find increasingly in modern novels.

One striking example of such disclosure is the series of revelations that Rachel makes to Antoine in *The Thibaults*. At first Antoine is charmed by her revelations that she had been a ballerina and a trick-rider, but soon he realizes that there are other troubling mysteries. Lying next to him in bed Rachel becomes irritated by his stare and shuts her eyes; he pries open her lids and provokes her remark about how eyes can give one away, as one of her past lovers, Hirsch, had done with a single look. She then tells of a horseback journey with Hirsch in Morocco for twenty-two days, during which time they were attacked and she received a bullet wound, hence the scar Antoine had seen on her waist. When Antoine quotes the description of a woman's breasts in the Song of Solomon, she performs: "Delicately she held them up, first one and then the other, with a tender little smile for each, as if they were two friendly little animals" (427). She then puts on a dressing gown, props a drawer full of old photos on her knees, and begins an illustrated monologue about her past. "Like to have a look at Hirsch? . . . he's fifty, there's lots of kick in the old dog yet . . . Loathsome creature! Look at that bull's neck of his wedged between his shoulders . . . his skull and that hook nose like a hawk's, the curve of his lips. Ugly, I grant you, but he's got *style*, all right . . . Hot-tempered and sensual as they're made. How that man loves life! . . . He's so ugly that he's a beauty! Don't you agree?" Another photo shows her with Hirsch on a shooting trip in the Carpathians. A picture of a baby makes her start. "No, leave that one alone! Drop it, there's a good man! I tell you, it's not a photo of me; it's . . . it's a little god-child, who died. Look at this one instead. It's . . . it was taken . . . just outside Tangiers. No, don't take any notice, Toine dear, it's over now; I've stopped crying; can't you see I've stopped?" When Antoine glimpses another photo of naked, tangled limbs, Rachel claps her hands over his eyes, sweeps away the photos, and locks them in the drawer, explaining that they belong to Hirsch (429–432).

The next disclosure takes place in a private box at a theater showing a movie about Africa. When the orchestra begins she mentions casually that the tenor Zucco was her first lover and explains how he dropped her when he learned that she was going to have a baby. Antoine is stunned and realizes that the child in the photograph that Rachel had snatched from him was her own. He unbuttons her blouse as he broods over his constantly slipping grasp on her life. When a female attendant opens the door to their box by mistake, and Antoine pushes Rachel away, he is then appalled by her outburst: "How silly you are! Perhaps she wanted to . . . Anyway she looks nice" (449). After the movie Rachel reflects wistfully over the freedom she felt in Africa—"No laws, nothing to tie you down! You needn't even bother what other people think of you." Her account of another escapade astonishes Antoine. She had pitched camp in the desert with Hirsch when a guide pointed out his two girls. Later that night the girls showed up in her tent ready to satisfy, as Rachel explains, "your least desire."

Another time she tells a scandalized Antoine that a black man crept in through the window of her hotel room at Lomé. "There he was! He slithered up the wall like a lizard. Without a word he let his one and only garment slide off his little body. I shall never forget it. His mouth was moist and cool . . . so cool!" Du Gard explores Antoine's unspoken thoughts about this disclosure: "Good God! A nigger—and not even vetted beforehand to make sure!" Oblivious of Antoine's fear that she may have contracted a venereal disease, Rachel continues, "They've such wonderful skins. Fine-grained like the rind of a fruit" (454). There are some final disclosures—that Rachel's ambition was to run a high-class brothel, that Hirsch had an incestuous relationship with his daughter, and that despite her repeated insistence that she hated Hirsch, he remained an obsession. These disclosures shock but do not alienate Antoine. They are not made freely, but when they do come out she rises in his estimation: "He clasped her in his arms; and then, from the depths of his unconscious life, a craving for adventure, like a new instinct, flared into sudden life. Ah, could he only swerve from the rut of a too orderly existence, make a new start, live dangerously and divert to free, spontaneous acts the energies which it had been his pride to lavish on laborious ends!" (483).

The difference between the disclosure of Rachel and that of Elfride marks a half century of change in the history of love. The sexual confusion and innocence of one contrasts with the erotic experimentation and pride of the other. Even the space of Elfride's pitiful failed elopement (Cornwall to London and back) is cramped, compared with the exotic settings of Rachel's global travels. Elfride remains ashamed and tells only when forced; Rachel is hesitant to tell because she does not want to lose her lover, but she ultimately tells and with some pride. Most significant is the response of each man. Knight is defeated and can only break off, while Antoine is inspired to live dangerously and undertake spontaneous acts. Rachel's past finally proves to be too much, but not for Antoine: their relationship ends only when she cannot resist her obsession and returns to Hirsch.

More evidence of forthright disclosure appears in the later period. In *The Age of Innocence* Ellen tells Archer "Ah, don't make love to me! Too many people have done that" (169). Although it is probable that she did not have any sexual involvements other than with her husband, her exotic reputation excites Archer, who is even more inflamed by her disclosure. In *Women in Love* Lawrence explains that Ursula "wanted to have no past." But hers is not a wish against experience; she wants to make experience her own. She wants to take charge of her life and commit it to love, and to do that she must expropriate her past as if she had "no father, no mother, no anterior connections" so that she might open to Rupert "in the heart of reality, where she had never existed before" (399). In response to Rupert's direct request, "Tell me about yourself and your people," Ursula tells him about her family "and about Skrebensky, her first love." Rupert listens respectfully and seems "to warm and comfort his soul at the beautiful light of her nature" (145).

If nothing else, Lucy Tantamount is frank. Her feisty counterpunch in

Point Counter Point is a sexual disclosure. She sends her jealous lover Walter a letter that discloses not her numerous past lovers, about whom he already knows all too well, but a recent fling. Walter had written her a letter that included the charge: "I suppose you've found some man you like more than me." Her reply, an epistolary smack in the face, is distinctly modern.

> Marvelous, my dear Holmes! And guess where I found him. In the street. . . . I liked his looks. Very black, with an olive skin, rather Roman. . . . I looked at him. After all, why not? Someone one has never seen before and knows nothing about—it's an exciting idea. Absolute strangers at one moment and as intimate at the next as two human beings can be. Besides, he was a beautiful creature . . . We hailed a taxi and drove to a little hotel near the Jardin des Plantes. Rooms by the hour . . . Sordid, but that was part of the fun . . . I hadn't let him touch me in the cab. He came at me as though he were going to kill me, with clenched teeth. I shut my eyes, like a Christian martyr in front of a lion. Martyrdom's exciting. Letting oneself be hurt, humiliated, used, like a doormat—queer. I like it. Besides, the doormat uses the user. It's complicated. He'd just come back from a seaside holiday by the Mediterranean and his body was all brown and polished by the sun. Beautifully savage he looked . . . The marks are still there where he bit me on the neck . . . I dug my nails into his arm so that the blood came . . . So now you know, Walter, why I've changed my mind about going to Madrid. Don't ever send me another letter like the last.   (361)

This disclosure does not move toward authenticity, because Lucy does not uncover so much as screen herself behind sexual boasting. The letter nevertheless reveals her pleasure in indulging and disclosing exotic sexual appetites in a way that was unthinkable for any Victorian heroine.

Men's history moves along the same track as women's in the direction of fuller disclosure and less critical moralizing about sex pasts. Levin lets Kitty read his diary to unburden himself of "the facts that were tormenting him," because, Tolstoy explains, he realized "what an abysm separated his tainted past from her dovelike purity." Her response closes off his past from any further discussion. "'Take, take those dreadful books back!' she cried, pushing away the note-books that lay on the table before her. 'Why did you give me them? . . . But no—it was best after all,' she added, pitying the despair on his face. 'But it is dreadful, dreadful!'" "She forgave him," Tolstoy concludes, "but after that he felt yet more unworthy of her" (372).

In *The Odd Women,* published twenty years later, Everard's disclosure to Rhoda marks some change. Troubled by gossip that he has had a lover, she asks him directly, "During the past month—the past three months—have you made profession of love—have you even pretended love—to any woman?" The reader already knows that Everard's much talked about escapade with a woman on a train occurred "some years ago," so his reply, "To no woman whatever" is in fact truthful. Rhoda closes the matter with her direct reply, "That satisfies me" (263). The historical significance of this exchange is not what he did as much as the framing of her question. In contrast to Kitty, she does not judge what he did before they met but is concerned exclusively about any attachments afterwards; and she has the presence of mind, half-way through her question, to correct the time frame from one month to three, the precise duration of their relationship. Her accommodating revision of the question points ahead to the diminishing insistence on virginity in modern novels.

A similar accommodation occurs in *Howards End,* following Margaret's discovery of Henry's affair that ended during his marriage to Mrs. Wilcox, long before Margaret met him. He does not tell her on his own, and when she finds out, he bows out with traditional decorum. "I am a man, and have lived a man's past. I have the honour to release you from your engagement." But Margaret is not traditional and will not let go.

> "So that woman has been your mistress?"
> "You put it with your usual delicacy," he replied.
> "When, please?"
> "Why?"
> "When, please?"
> "Ten years ago."
> She left him without a word. For it was not her tragedy: it was Mrs.
>   Wilcox's.   (233)

The chapter ends there, but not their relationship. Margaret has enough problems loving Henry as she finds him without troubling about what happened before they met.

The novels of Henry James unveil a world of secrets so convoluted that no character, not even the narrator, seems to understand them. *The Golden Bowl* turns on a secret romance between Amerigo and Charlotte which precedes his first meeting with his future wife Maggie but continues after their marriage. The "golden bowl" symbolizes deception and, in an everyday sense, the inauthentic, because it is not solid gold but gilded glass. Its crack symbolizes Amerigo's secret adulterous love which flaws his marriage to Maggie. Her discovery that the bowl is not genuine gold but gilded and cracked underneath unlocks this secret. When Amerigo sees Maggie standing over the pieces after her friend Fanny has smashed it on the floor, he realizes that Maggie knows. At that moment we read what seems to be Maggie's words spoken to Amerigo, "Yes, look, look," but James follows with an extraordinary narrative construction, "she seemed to see him hear her say even while her sounded words were other." Like so many Jamesian characters Maggie is locked in an inner world unto herself. Even when she makes so important a discovery she is unable to talk about it. Her *un*uttered words continue: "Look, look, both at the truth that still survives in that smashed evidence and at the even more remarkable appearance that I'm not such a fool as you supposed me." This outburst might have been Jane Eyre's unspoken thoughts after her discovery that Rochester had a wife, but Jane walked out and only returned after Rochester had been transformed in mind and body. Even though Maggie cannot confront Amerigo, she remains with him. Although her thoughts remain unexpressed, they are distinctively modern: "Look at the possibility that, since I *am* different, there may still be something in it for you—if you're capable of working with me to get that out" (427). The remainder of the novel is about how Maggie learns to act on her discovery. The novel's penetration of the labyrinth of concealment and the paths of disclosure is a landmark in literature about the way to truth in human relations.

James's characters are modern not because they have fewer secrets than the Victorians, for his are mired in secrecy, but because they are more resolved to accept painful disclosures. Whereas Kitty pushes Levin's diary away in disgust (and an important part of him with it), Maggie, who must deal not with an adolescent sexual spree such as Levin's but with her husband's adulterous romance still in progress, pulls together whatever bits of affection may survive her discovery. She does not break through to truth and happiness, and Amerigo does not slink into self-chastisement or public degradation. The two emerge as more authentic precisely because they come to understand the value of more forthright communication and because they ultimately resolve to live with a love that, like most, is not solid gold but gilded and cracked.

H. G. Wells did not ponder the labyrinth of concealment as thoroughly as James, and the heroine of his *Ann Veronica* glides to truth in love with suspect ease. The novel reads like a manifesto for sexual liberation, effectively dramatizing one disclosure and a modern response. Capes tells Ann straight out that he is married, to which she replies, "It doesn't matter." Unlike Rochester, he does not try to dismiss his own responsibility or early love. He explains that his wife was "one of the most beautiful persons in the world," she had a "proud and dignified temperament," and he "loved her and made love to her," although she did not respond with desire. In frustration he had an affair with another married woman whose husband found out and sued for divorce. At the trial a second co-respondent was produced. To this final humiliation, Ann says "Poor you!" Capes gestures toward withdrawal with conventional moralistic rhetoric, "I'm smirched . . . damaged goods," but Ann will not buy it. "I don't think it makes a rap of difference, except for one thing. I love you more" (317–320).

Hemingway crafts a classic World War I disclosure in *A Farewell to Arms*. Frederic's nurse Catherine is also his lover, and they have sex in his hospital bed. While prepping him for surgery, which requires that she catheterize and evacuate him, she is concerned that he will talk about their relationship while under ether and so asks him to think about something else, "even another girl." Their dialogue is brisk.

> "There, darling. Now you're all clean inside and out. Tell me. How many people have you ever loved?"
> "Nobody."
> "Not me even?"
> "Yes, you."
> "How many others really?"
> "None."
> "How many have you—how do you say it?—stayed with?"
> "None."
> "You're lying to me."
> "Yes."
> "It's all right. Keep right on lying to me. That's what I want you to do. Were they pretty? . . . I'm not afraid of them. But don't tell me about them. When a man stays with a girl when does she say how much it costs?"
> "I don't know."
> "Of course not. Does she say she loves him? Tell me that. I want to know that."

"Yes. If he wants her to."

"Does he say he loves her? Tell me please. It's important."

"He does if he wants to."

"But you never did? Really?"

"No."

"Not really. Tell me the truth."

"No," I lied.   (108–109)

With his impending surgery, with his catheter tube and enema bag lying nearby, and with Western civilization crashing down around them, what's a little white lie? In contrast to Victorian lovers who may have withheld the truth without actually lying, Frederic's lie has a ring of truthfulness, because he is a brutally honest narrator, and he already knows that she knows he's lying. Her easy-going questioning is part of a give-and-take that helps out a bit, even to the point of urging him to lie. This exchange also shows how much the value attached to sexual disclosure had changed from Levin's hang-dog reaction to being found out or Henry's obligatory withdrawal of his marriage proposal, because Frederic is not guilty and has no regrets. He knows that he loves Catherine intensely and that time is running out, so he lies to her with a wink.

For Lawrence there is no compromise with honesty; withholding the past is withholding love. His characters have to be able to speak freely about sex, so when Connie asks Mellors why he married, he begins a sexual life-history. At sixteen his first girl adored him but only let him have her reluctantly. The next one "loved everything about love, except the sex." Then came his wife Bertha Coutts, who loved sex. "That was what I wanted: a woman who *wanted* me to fuck her." (For Lawrence use of "so-called obscene words" is an essential part of full sexual disclosure.) But Bertha resented his pleasure. She put him off and then came on "all lovey-dovey." When he finished, he explains to Connie, "she'd start on her own account, and I had to stop inside her till she brought herself off, wriggling and shouting." As it got more difficult for Bertha to climax, she began to bear down on him "as if it were a beak tearing at me." "Self! Self! all self! tearing and shouting! . . . as if she had no sensation in her except in the top of her beak, the very outside top tip, that rubbed and tore." This is not mere self-pity. The truth about what he is involves disclosure of what he has been. He concludes with a list of female sexual attitudes—all deficient. Some women do not like sex, others pretend they do. A third type likes every kind of "cuddling and going off" except "the natural one," and they always make you "go off when you're *not* in the only place you should be." Then there is the "hard sort" like Bertha, and another type "that's just dead inside." A sixth type "puts you out before you really 'come,' and [they] go on writhing their loins till they bring themselves off against your thighs" (187–190).

Mellors's disclosure is unprecedented. No hero of non-pornographic literature prior to 1928 spoke so directly with his beloved about intercourse, and especially not about his own sexual humiliations and failures. But for all his daring openness, Mellors is closed to some of his share of responsibility. Commenting on the sexually unresponsive women, he says, "most men like it that way," although he quickly adds that *he* hates unresponsiveness, thereby dissociating himself from responsibility for his problems with women. Mellors does not believe, however, that authentic sexual loving is something you do *to* another person: it is an exchange, a way of "being-with." His partial self-reflection points to my final theme—self-disclosure.

III

Nineteenth-century lovers were reluctant to tell their beloved about a past love, because they feared that the beloved would be horrified and break off, as did Knight and Angel. But difficult as it is to be honest with one's beloved, it is even more difficult to admit to oneself that insurmountable obstacles to love come from within. Truth in love is a continual extraction of truth from untruth, not just about the beloved but also about one's own ability to love.

In the nineteenth-century novel, action turns on a lover's discovery about the beloved or how a lover learns to express a love which was felt all along. But such breakthroughs are largely about how to deal with the beloved or the world, and once the external impediments are removed, lovers may proceed toward fulfilling love. In modern novels the drama turns more on self-disclosures about how lovers can or, more often, cannot love.

The most famous epiphany in twentieth-century literature, Proust's moment of joy from tasting madeleines dipped in tea, initiates his search for a past which he began to lose as a child when he first felt his mother's love slipping away. The "exquisite pleasure" of the tea and madeleines, he reports, had "the effect which love has of filling me with a precious essence." That pleasure came from his momentary recapture of the past, which, like love, was fleeting and mixed with pain but also made him feel joyous and immortal. As the taste begins to fade, he thinks, "the truth I am seeking lies not in the cup but in myself" (49). That insight also applies to love.

Marcel's love for Albertine is fraught with external problems, specifically her lesbian lovers, whom she never discloses forthrightly; but his repeated discoveries of infidelities initiate a distinctively modern insight, because they reveal ever new regions of torture, which he comes to realize are located within himself. He compares these regions within to the two country paths he traveled to see his boyhood sweetheart Gilberte. "As, long ago, the Méséglise and Guermantes ways had laid the foundations for my taste for the countryside . . . so it was by linking them in my mind to a past full of charm that my love for Albertine made me seek out exclusively a certain type of woman" (III, 564). But always the wrong woman. His way of loving was forged in childhood by those two country paths as much as by his mother's love and his childhood sweetheart, and it reappears over the years projected onto successive women. All the discoveries he makes about other women are incidental to this self-disclosure about his inescapable penchant for disappointment in love.

Mrs. Dalloway is a protracted self-disclosure about love. The novel opens with Clarissa preparing for a party but thinking of a day thirty years earlier when she had been working in her garden and her beloved Peter had said something which she now cannot quite recall. "'Musing among the vegetables?'—was that it?—'I prefer men to cauliflowers'—was that it?" Woolf reveals Clarissa's uncertainty in the conclusion to this interior monologue. "He would be back from India one of these days, June or July, she forgot which, for his letters were awfully dull; it was his sayings one remembered; his eyes, his pocket-knife, his smile, his grumpiness and, when millions of things had utterly vanished—how strange it was!—a few sayings like this about cabbages" (4). In the Victorian novel pocket-knives are not as important as smiles and eyes, long-lost lovers never write dull letters, the month of their return is unmistakably marked, and love-starved women do not confuse cabbages and cauliflowers. That mistake, *in a single interior monologue,* underscores the confusion that obscures understanding of what love has been and still might be. In addition to her faulty memory, her openness to the possibilities of existence is further complicated by the logic of love, because, Woolf tells her reader, with a veritable motto of modernism, "She would not say of any one in the world now that they were this way or that." That motto also applies to love, because "she would not say of Peter, she would not say of herself, I am this, I am that" (11). For Clarissa no tag is adequate for her itinerant sensibilities. Each recollection of Peter alters another memory; each self-disclosure obscures another insight. No sooner does Clarissa think to herself, "If I had married him, this gaiety would have been mine all day!" than she thinks that it never could have been, because she became infuriated about the way he kept opening his knife.

Peter shows up later that morning, tells her that he is in love with Daisy back in India, and then breaks down crying. As he pulls himself together, Clarissa is overwhelmed by affection when she sees him revealing his feelings as no nineteenth-century hero would—by "blowing his nose violently." A momentary impulse that he take her away on a voyage is followed by the chilling realization that their love was over and, more important, that it had never been as deep as she had remembered it. Later in the day she imagines an exchange with Peter in response to his criticism of her parties. A self-disclosing interior monologue follows. "Who was Peter . . . always in love with the wrong woman? What's your love? she might say to him. And she knew his answer; how it is the most important thing in the world and no woman possibly understood it. Very well. But could any man understand what she meant either? About life? She could not imagine Peter or Richard taking the trouble to give a party for no reason whatever." Her parties were "an offering; to combine, to create; but to whom?" Every insight leads to another question, and this one she cannot fully answer. Her parties, she thinks, are "an offering for the sake of offering, perhaps" (184–185). Neither people nor parties nor lovers are entirely "this way or that." Clarissa is a Sisyphus of human relations who keeps giving parties. She is incapable of loving but does so incessantly. She gropes for understanding of her own way of loving, which is pulled together out of faulty memories, fluid personal identities, absurd incompatibilities, emotional instability, blinding self-pity, obedience to public decorum, and a profound feeling of isolation.

Peter's self-disclosures have their own blind spots. After leaving Clarissa's home that morning he begins to fantasize about an attractive woman whom he follows for a few blocks. When she suddenly disappears he realizes that his "fun" is over, "for it was half made up, as he knew very well; invented, this escapade with the girl; made up, as one makes up the better part of life, he thought—making oneself up; making her up; creating an exquisite amusement" (81). Between waking and sleeping on a park bench he recalls his break-up with Clarissa thirty years earlier and, as he proceeds toward his hotel, suddenly comprehends Clarissa's theory about "not knowing people; not being known" (231). Looking back on thirty years of "brief, broken" meetings, he realizes that she had influenced him more than anyone else. He regrets his failure with Clarissa, yet is relieved that their love did not work out. He gloats over Daisy's unqualified devotion but must admit that he chose her because she did not touch him the way Clarissa did.

Clarissa's party takes up the last fifty pages of the novel. Throughout it Peter communicates with Clarissa directly only when she says to him: "Come and talk to Aunt Helena about Burma" and then adds, "We will talk later" (272). They never do. He tries to speak with Sally Seton, but they connect only when talking about Clarissa and otherwise fail to listen to one another. Sally tells Peter that she has just read "a wonderful play about a man who scratched on the wall of his cell, and she had felt that [that] was true of life—one scratched on the wall. Despairing of human relationships (people were so difficult), she often went into her garden and got from her flowers a peace which men and women never gave her. But no; he did not like cabbages; he preferred human beings, Peter said" (293–294). Sally has no idea what Peter is talking about, we already know that Clarissa got the vegetable wrong, and now we must wonder whether he got it wrong and whether there might be something inherently unreliable about memories of love. Peter and Sally continue to talk past one another, exchanging precious confidences and everyday banalities. He works his way through the party, alternately uncovering and hiding his love. In the final moment of the novel he rises above the idle chatter of the party and sees a central "truth" about his love for Clarissa—that she is his "terror" and "ecstasy."

In comedy lovers surmount obstacles, in tragedy they fail. The novels of Proust and Woolf defy either classification. Their lovers have tragic flaws as well as irrepressible impulses to triumph over destiny. They give in to the inauthentic everyday mode of self-deception and boldly face up to their own responsibility for loving, however deficient they may find it. Like Marcel, they come to understand that the truth they seek lies not in the cup of tea but in themselves. Like Clarissa, they learn to give and enjoy parties as "an offering for the sake of an offering, perhaps." They learn that love thrives on the search for truth about oneself and about one's beloved, but that that truth is at the same time compromised by the evasions and self-denials that make love so devilishly sweet.

Proust and Woolf offer distinctively modern approaches to the disclosure of past loves and hence to the sort of truthful exchange that is the foundation of more authentic loving. Many Victorian novels turned on secrets about past lovers and moved to conclusion with contrived resolutions of the misunderstandings between lovers to which such secrets led. In the novels of Proust and Woolf sex pasts are largely incidental to the progress of love. Their novels turn on the way lovers work through self-deceptions and inner opacities that bar the way to understanding the meaning and possibilities of the characters' own ways of loving. Knight's worry that Elfride may have loved someone else before him seems shallow, self-deceptive, and downright trivial in comparison with Clarissa's doubt whether she could say of anyone in the world "that they were this way or that." The shift from a moral to an existential perspective is captured in these contrasting concerns about the possibilities and impossibilities of disclosure in love.

8 Kissing

IN ANY LOVE the first kiss is a pivotal moment when one dares to reach out toward greater intimacy, uncertain of the response. Although lovers throughout the ages have struggled with its terrors and thrills, it has a history. The brevity of a kiss and the many possible reactions to it make it particularly well suited to a comparative history. I found four subthemes—temporality, embodiment, morality, and gender.

I

There is a persistent myth that love comes naturally. The disastrous consequences of relying on such popular wisdom are particularly evident in kissing, which is not natural but a learned courting ritual fraught with perils. Even seasoned lovers find that a first kiss with someone new may transform them into timorous beginners.

On their first date, while walking down a New York street one evening, Alvy Singer (played by Woody Allen) suddenly turns and says to Annie Hall (played by Diane Keaton): "Listen, give me a kiss." To her bewildered "Really?" he answers, "Yea, why not, 'cause we're just gonna go home later, right? and there's gonna be all that tension, you know, 'cause we never kissed before, and I'll never know when to make the right move or anything. So, we'll kiss now and get it over with and then we'll go eat. Okay? . . . We'll digest our food better." They kiss and he concludes—"Okay, so now we can digest our food." *Cut to delicatessen scene.*

Allen's humor exploits the improbable mixture of lofty ideals and mundane reality, here applied to a bittersweet love. He has not abandoned belief in the miracle of love, but his star-crossed lovers meet on a tennis court. He does not want to wait months or weeks or even hours for that first kiss, because he is afraid, he knows that he is afraid, and he wants to stop being afraid right now, so he lets Annie know that he is afraid. His first kiss is unerotic but effective. He sacrifices sublime joy for a relaxing corned-beef sandwich. Digesting food is mundane, but it also symbolizes the daily life of love that Victorians postponed for so long. And sometimes those postponements actually interfered with their digestion—Heathcliff waited so long that Cathy starved herself and wasted away during her pregnancy, triggering a premature delivery which cost her her life.

Allen's scene, beyond the time span of my history, recalls a scene in *This Side of Paradise,* which is similar in spirit if not a direct influence. Amory is on a first date with Rosalind and tells her directly, "I'm afraid of you. I'm always afraid of a girl—until I've kissed her." Their exchange covers similar ground.

> He: Listen. This is a frightful thing to ask.
> She: *(Knowing what's coming)* After five minutes.
> He: But will you—kiss me? Or are you afraid?
> She: I'm never afraid—but your reasons are poor.
> He: Rosalind, I really *want* to kiss you.
> She: So do I.
>   *(They kiss—definitely and thoroughly).*   (175)

Whatever such first kisses lacked, they cut the tension that paralyzed Victorians. Amory kisses Rosalind *after* five minutes, whereas Heathcliff, after four years of waiting, breaks into Cathy's bedroom and kisses her *for* five minutes. They are observed by Cathy's maid Nelly, who relates: "He neither spoke, nor loosed his hold for some five minutes, during which period he bestowed more kisses than ever he gave in his life before" (194). While Brontë emphasizes the quantity of her lovers' kisses, Fitzgerald emphasizes the quality.

There is also a history of the duration of single kisses. Victorians "bestowed" them with dispatch as if pinning on a medal. Hugo is as tight-lipped in his account of the kiss that seals the love between Marius and Cosette as is that kiss itself. "How did it happen that their lips came together? . . . A kiss, and all was said" (810). By the 1890s there is evidence of change with Arabella's kissing Jude "close and long." By 1920, in *Women in Love,* Gudrun kisses Gerald with "a slow, luxurious kiss, lingering on the mouth" (168).

Forster dramatizes the meeting of two ages with the awkward meeting of a couple's lips. In *Howards End* Henry typifies Victorian reserve. One evening he summons up his courage, drops his cigar, and grabs Margaret in his arms. She is startled by the suddenness of these lips "pressed against her own," and after his swift exit, she is disappointed. "It was so isolated. Nothing in their previous conversation had heralded it, and, worse still, no tenderness had ensued" (184).

The Victorians waited long and then kissed quickly, making a fetish of the first kiss and complicating the course of love, as Hardy shows in *A Pair of Blue Eyes*. After Elfride refuses to let Stephen kiss her, he proposes marriage to get a kiss. "It was Elfride's first kiss. And so awkward and unused was she; full of striving—no relenting." She was unable to do it right, Hardy explains, because "a woman must have had many kisses before she kisses well." But women who kiss well were lost, as Elfride discovers with Knight, who is scandalized because she kisses more expertly than he. She was trapped, like so many Victorian women, because if she was a good kisser her love was suspect, and if she was a bad kisser her love was deficient. The happy scenario required that an experienced man teach her, but that scenario could not begin because there was no proper way for him to learn. Hugo's explanation of why Marius kissed Cosette is a series of sugar-coated questions—"How does it happen that birds sing, that snow melts, that the rose unfolds?" (810). To interpret the historical significance of such evasion we must consider another subtheme—embodiment.

II

Whether the Victorian kiss was a tender brush of the cheek or a peck on the lips or even an intense (and tense) "pressing" on the lips, it was invariably described in scant detail. After Rochester proposed to Jane, he followed up, she explains, by "pressing his lips to my lips." And that was that. Nelly emphasizes how many kisses Heathcliff gave Cathy, but for all their abundance and desperate intensity they are nondescript. After a breather, Heathcliff takes charge: "Kiss me again, and don't let me see your eyes!" (198). Although he has some special problem about her judgmental eyes, his command is distinctively Victorian. The governing sex etiquette, "look but do not touch," had its obverse among those Victorians who kissed with closed eyes.[1]

Speculation about the historical impact of the first motion pictures included the expectation that they would revolutionize kissing by enabling movie-goers to see how it is done, perhaps for the first time. As the article "Anatomy of a Kiss" from the *New York World* reported on April 26, 1899, "For the first time in the history of the world it is possible to see what a kiss looks like . . . [because] everything is shown in startling directness . . . The real kiss is a revelation." The impact of movies on kissing was sweeping enough by the late 1920s for writers to take note. In *Point Counter Point* Lucy spurns Walter's passionate kissing with the comment, "If you knew how like the movies you were! A great, huge, grinning close-up" (176).

The literary record, like the movie screen, reveals increasingly vivid detail of the fuller embodiment of kissing. The Victorian novel described the most passionate kisses without reference to noses, tongues, or teeth and with only the most reluctant acknowledgment that lips also play a role in eating.[2] A typical scenario begins with the man's first kiss on a woman's hand, sometimes preceded by a tantalizing removal of the glove, and then a respectful, if passionate, first kiss on the lips. In *On the Eve* Turgenev included such an archetypical scene with all the detail replaced by elision dots and a paragraph break.

> [Elena] trembled and tried to prevent him with the other hand: [Insarov] began to kiss the other hand. She pulled it away from him; he flung back his head, she looked into his face, and bent down . . . their lips met . . .
>
> A moment passed; she broke away, and stood up whispering "no, no"; then quickly went over to the writing-table.   (156)

In *Ranthorpe* Lewes offered standard melodramatic fare. "[Isola] rested [Ranthorpe's] aching head upon her bosom, and kissed his hot brow" (18). Hardy employs a similar use of metaphor in tracing the erotic surging throughout Bathsheba's body that followed Troy's first kiss. "That minute's interval had brought the blood beating into her face, set her stinging as if aflame to the very hollows of her feet, and enlarged emotion to a compass which quite swamped thought . . . The circumstance had been the gentle dip of Troy's mouth downwards upon her own. He had kissed her" (242). Hardy's intention is to contrast Troy's modest effort with Bathsheba's violent reaction, but the nature of the kiss itself remains a mystery. The symbolism of rational behavior overturned is obvious when Angel kicks over a milk pail in seizing his first kiss, and Tess responds with passionate intensity: "her lips parted, and she sank upon him in her momentary joy, with something very like an ecstatic cry" (127). The description of her parted lips violated the Victorian code of decency, and the reference to her "ecstatic cry" broke the code of silence that governed the typical Victorian kiss, but Hardy's role in the history of the kiss is transitional.[3] Among all of Tess's kisses the most freely given is described with worn-out metaphors. "She clasped his neck and for the first time [Angel] learnt what an impassioned woman's kisses were like upon the lips of one whom she loved with all heart and soul, as Tess loved him" (160). The reader never learns whatever Angel "learnt."

More than a hint of change is evident in Zola's *La Bête humaine* (1890), although Severine kisses under the atypical circumstances of urging Jacques to kill. "At once she glued her lips to his as though to seal this oath, and they had one of those deep kisses in which they mingled one with the other in the communion of their flesh" (276). Colette requires no murderous conspiracy in *The Vagabond* to elaborate the experimentation and irony missing from Victorian kisses. Max's moustache, Renée records, "brushes against my nostrils with a scent of vanilla and honeyed tobacco. Oh! . . . suddenly my mouth, in spite of itself, lets itself be opened, opens of itself as irresistibly as a ripe plum splits in the sun." Her metaphors do not hide, her elision dots do not censor. Her account of stimulation to the lower body caused by kissing conveys more than Hardy's worn-out metaphors. "And once again there is born that exacting pain that spreads from my lips, all down my flanks as far as my knees, that swelling as of a wound that wants to open once more and overflow—the voluptuous pleasure that I had forgotten." There are sounds too. "He understands and assents, with a happy little grunt." And tastes. "His mouth tastes mine now, and has the faint scent of my powder." His mouth also searches for a way to make their kissing artful. "Experienced as it is, I can feel that it is trying to invent something new, to vary the caress still further." Then she takes charge of the pacing. "But already I am bold enough to indicate my preference for a long, drowsy kiss that is almost motionless—the slow crushing, one against the other, of two flowers in which nothing vibrates but the palpitation of two coupled pistils." A final touch of verisimilitude: afterwards, in the mirror she sees that they both have the same "trembling, shiny, slightly swollen lips" (126–127).

By 1933 swollen lips were so routine that in *Tender is the Night* Nicole could complain that kissing led to nothing more. When she demands, "Kiss me on the lips Tommy," he complies, and then comments, "That's so American. When I was in America last there were girls who would tear you apart with their lips, tear themselves too, until their faces were scarlet with the blood around the lips all brought out in a patch—but nothing further" (295).

Proust compromises the sanctity of both motherhood and Christianity with his account of a kiss. "Albertine slipped her tongue into my mouth as if it were a gift of the Holy Ghost and conveyed to me a viaticum, left me with a provision of tranquility almost as precious as when my mother in the evening at Combray used to lay her lips upon my forehead" (III, 72, translation revised). In addition to turning two revered institutions upside down, Albertine's tongue could also turn bodies inside out. For she also ran her tongue over his neck and stomach in caresses which seemed to be "administered by the inside of her flesh, externalized like a piece of material reversed to show its lining, as it were the mysterious sweetness of a penetration" (III, 508).

In *Ulysses* Joyce follows one memorable kiss literally inside, down the alimentary canal. Surrounded by customers stuffing themselves at lunch, Leopold sees two flies stuck together buzzing on the window and recalls an afternoon on a hill when he and Molly kissed under the sun.

> Ravished over her I lay, full lips full open, kissed her mouth. Yum. Softly she gave me in my mouth the seedcake warm and chewed. Mawkish pulp her mouth had mumbled sweet and sour with spittle. Joy: I ate it: joy. Young life, her lips that gave me pouting. Soft, warm, sticky gumjelly lips . . . Wildly I lay on her, kissed her; eyes, her lips, her stretched neck, beating, woman's breasts in her blouse of nun's veiling, fat nipples upright. Hot I tongued her. She kissed me. I was kissed. All yielding she tossed my hair. Kissed, she kissed me.
>
> Me. And me now.
>
> Stuck, the flies buzzed stuck.   (176)

This is more than detail. Joyce uses words to convey direct experience—the stickiness of "gumjelly lips," the texture of half-chewed cake, the taste and sounds of her mouth "mumbled sweet and sour with spittle," and the "joy" of his swallow. The imagery of copulating flies, the other gluttonous luncheoners, and the glutinous contents of the kiss itself are emphatically unromantic. In contrast to Joyce's tracing of the tremors that Leopold's kiss sent throughout both their bodies, Hugo's account of Marius and Cosette's climactic kiss seems every bit sixty years old: "When two mouths, consecrated by love, draw close together in the act of creation it is impossible that this ineffable kiss does not cause a tremor among the stars" (1140).

Victorian kisses were indeed ineffable, if not also invisible. They were sudden, brief, and blind, intensely felt gestures, which novelists described with minimal detail. Heroes and heroines may have talked about the obligations that a kiss implied in the courtship scenario, but they never discussed the nature of the kiss itself. Victorian novelists seemed to share the deadly seriousness with which their characters approached a beloved's cheek or lips, and that reverence translated into the imagery of idolatry and perfection. Hugo's metaphor of starry perfection approaches caricature, even for the Victorians, but as a group they failed to acknowledge any imperfection or deficiency in the kiss itself.

A growing openness to that deficiency can be seen in art. The Pre-Raphaelites created a portrait gallery of women with full, shapely lips, as red as the deadly pomegranate held by Rossetti's *Prosperine* (1877) and idealized, if not fetishized, to perfection. The title of Rossetti's *Bocca Baciata (Lips That Have Been Kissed)* (1859) draws attention to the woman's perfect pucker that he drew with care and excludes the man whose presence would obscure a frontal view of her. She is one of many Pre-Raphaelite beauties awaiting lovers no doubt unworthy of kissing their exquisite lips.

When Victorian artists did depict kisses, they chose literary characters who exchanged them without any apparent signs of imperfection, or at least all the deficiency and danger that threatens to compromise them comes from without. Rossetti's *Paolo and Francesca* and Alfred Elmore's *Romeo and Juliet* depict lovers immersed in delicate kisses and gentle embraces that for the moment transcend earthly imperfection. All threat emanates from the outside: Francesca's jealous husband or the feuding Montagues and Capulets. In Francesco Hayez's *The Kiss* (Figure 21, 1857) the man's eyes are hidden by his hat, the woman's are closed. If there are any dangers, the lovers are blind to them. A strikingly different sense is conveyed by Picasso's *The Kiss* (Figure 22, 1925), where the lovers see all too clearly. Their eyes are wide open. The combination of facial and genital features suggests an inventive second kind of vision, for the man's kiss is delivered to the woman's vagina-shaped lips by a phallic-shaped nose, and his eye is positioned where his testicle should be, located visibly on the surface of his scrotum, which is itself in his head. He not only sees the object of his desire, his organ of sight is also his gland of desire.

Aside from the visible skin of hands and face, Hayez's lovers are covered

by a welter of clothing which narrows the focus on touching lips and obscures any distractions or complications from the rest of their bodies. Whatever the class differences implied by his rustic coat and her satiny dress,
whatever the difficulties indicated by the secretive and fleeting circumstances, their hands embrace and their lips touch in harmony. In contrast the
bodies of Picasso's lovers have been deformed, disjointed, and reassembled
in a way that does violence to traditional aesthetic norms. Clothing does not
hide the rest of their bodies, it frames their hybrid sex organs which are
endowed with the "higher" sensory powers normally located in the head—
smell, taste, and sight. Instead of the ethereal purity of Hayez's romantic
kiss, Picasso has suggested the earthy smells and tastes of a strikingly original "genital kiss" that simultaneously combines fellatio and cunnilingus.[4]
For Hayez the kiss itself is full of tenderness—all evil, all imperfection
comes from without, represented by the partial shadow figure framed by the
archway on the left. For Picasso the imperfection emanates from within. The
man's powerful left arm ends in a fist that crushes the woman's head toward
his own. Her right arm, which ends in tense fingers and sharp nails, lies
alongside the bristly hairs of his right arm. A second vaginal symbol, the
ultimate goal of the man's sexual desire, appears like a bright yellow egg just
below the woman's dress as if squeezed out from the crush of this suffocating
kiss.

Readers acquainted with Picasso's private life around 1925 may question
contrasting his painting with one by Hayez to document the history of kissing. Picasso's marriage had become a hell, something that can happen to
anyone at any time. But his response to that hell was distinctively modern.
Over the next few years he painted threatening women with tentacular
arms, pincer hands, spiked tongues, mandibular jaws, and toothed vaginas.
No Victorian painter, however tormented in love, could have expressed it
that way. And the changes that allowed Picasso's work to influence the art
world included historically distinctive attitudes about love and the meaning
of a kiss. His painting must also be viewed in the context of the Surrealist
movement, which showcased his work in 1925 and created a forum for its
exhibition, publication, and criticism. Picasso represented the search for
new possibilities of erotic experience among the Surrealists who believed
that the ironies of love secured its richness and that its deficiencies were
grounded in possibility and choice. Once Picasso's private love life revived
he again painted joyful lovers, their joy nuanced, though, by his passage
through a tempestuous marriage and by his understanding that the most

21. Francesco Hayez, *The Kiss*, 1857.

tormenting deficiencies do not climb stairs out of the shadows but are created by us out of our own way of loving.

Magritte's surreal *Lovers* (Figure 23, 1928) offers another riveting image of a deficient kiss. Although it has become an icon of alienated love in the modern world, it is in fact a provocative interrogation of the nature of love.

22. Pablo Picasso, *The Kiss*, 1925.

Is love blind or in hiding? Do lovers conceal themselves from themselves or from the beloved? Do the coverings merely suppress vision, or do they also occasion deeper reflection? These shrouds no doubt allude to Magritte's personal tragedy,[5] but they also symbolize the defenses that keep all lovers apart.

23. René Magritte, *The Lovers,* 1928.

By making sight impossible, Magritte underscores its vital function. The inability to see is accented by the lovers' uncanny exposure, for although they are in a room where they might expect privacy, one wall is missing, revealing a menacing, blue-black sky; so their kiss is open to the elements and to public view. The sense of surreality is further created by the relative position of the lovers, because they do not grope for one another as would a shrouded couple but come together serenely in an idealized pose. In showing lovers who cannot see but kiss as if they could, Magritte also suggests the opposite—that lovers who can see, may kiss as if they were blind.

Kissing can be authentic, like human existence itself, only if it can also fail to be authentic. And it falls into inauthenticity not when someone else interrupts but when the lovers fail to acknowledge that obstacles emanate from within themselves, not as shadowy figures coming out of the darkness, but as the lovers' own protective covers. This painting is not just of a failure, however, because although these moderns may lose the opportunity to project the responsibility for their failures in love onto someone else, they gain in the awareness that they are in control of their love. Their kiss may be deficient, but it's all theirs.

The modernist novel abounds in deficient kisses. In *A Room with a View*, the chapter that introduces Lucy's old-fashioned swain Cecil is titled "Medieval." With that period name Forster dates Cecil's clumsy first kiss. Fresh from the exhilaration of George's passionate kiss in Florence, Cecil's first effort seems to Lucy like an outdated relic. After a chatty, formal request for a kiss he proceeds. "At that supreme moment [Cecil] was conscious of nothing but absurdities . . . [She] gave such a business-like lift to her veil. As he approached her he found time to wish that he could recoil. As he touched her, his gold pince-nez became dislodged and was flattened between them" (124). Kafka accents the aberrant nature of a first kiss in *The Trial* (1925) by giving Joseph K's seducer a physical defect—webbing between her two middle fingers. In astonishment, K. tried to pull them apart and then kissed them. She became aroused. "She clasped his head to her, bent over him, and bit and kissed him on the neck, biting into the very hairs of his head." After they had sex, she gave him a final "aimless kiss" that landed on his shoulder (110–111). In *The Vagabond* Renée's persistent lover missed the target while hurrying a first kiss. He gave her "a badly planted, irascible kiss, a bungled kiss in short, which left [her] mouth punished and disappointed" (117). The next day Renée tells Max, "The fact that our mouths met yesterday, abortively, does not make me feel the least awkward at this moment. A bungled kiss is much less important than an understanding exchange of looks" (117). This postkiss evaluation documents a growing appreciation of the importance of talking about a formerly unspeakable topic. After Rupert's "soft, deep and delicate" lips kiss Ursula's "taut and quivering and strenuous" lips, he comments, "Your mouth is so hard . . . why do you always grip your lips?" And she replies, "Never mind . . . It is my way" (426). When in *A Farewell to Arms* Frederic makes his first move, Catherine pushes him away while protesting, "I just couldn't stand the nurse's-evening-off aspect of it." But he persists: "I kissed her hard and held her tight and tried to open her lips; they were closed tight." Eventually "her lips opened and her head went back against my hand and then she was crying on my shoulder" (26–27).

By discussing deficient kisses, moderns learned something about them. Victorians did not talk about them and idealized them, both at a high price. Their kisses were full of passion but lacking in artistry. They did not look while kissing, did not discuss kisses, avoided reference to the surrounding facial features or underlying physiological processes associated with the mouth and lips, and, I would speculate, consequently did not know much about kissing and hence did it badly. Conspicuously absent was any sense of irony, particularly evident in the displaced kiss.

The displaced kiss is literally in the wrong place. As such it is inherently ironic. When Victorians did kiss in the wrong place, it was because fear, guilt, or circumstance prevented kissing in the right place—on the cheek, forehead, or lips of the beloved. One of the most painfully delayed and tortuously displaced kisses in Victorian literature is in *The Scarlet Letter*. Hester's only power against the community that condemned her and especially against the husband she hates is the secret of Pearl's paternity. As the pillar of Christian virtue Dimmesdale cannot reveal his adulterous paternity even to his own child. He is divided from his beloved Hester by his guilt, by anticipation of the shame of disclosure before his parish, and by the eternally judgmental eyes of his God. To kiss Hester is impossible, so he kisses Pearl instead.

Mother, father, and child have escaped to the forest where Hester, excited by the "wild, heathen nature," tears off her scarlet letter and throws it away. But Pearl knows her mother only with the guilty embroidery and insists she put it back. After Pearl kisses the replaced scarlet letter, she asks Dimmesdale if he will walk back into town hand-in-hand with them. He refuses but promises to do so one day, and then kisses Pearl. Outraged at his cowardice, Pearl runs to the brook and washes her forehead "until the unwelcome kiss was quite washed off" (228). Dimmesdale kisses the child again only after he has disclosed his paternity to the townsfolk. Then Pearl lets his kiss remain. Dimmesdale finally earned the right to kiss his own estranged child's lips, which he once observed kissing the scarlet letter on his beloved's dress. That roundabout kiss costs him his life, and he must await the mercy of God to kiss Hester—maybe—in the hereafter.

Other Victorians put *ersatz* kisses in the strangest places. Stephen plants an impulsive first kiss on Maggie Tulliver's arm. In Howells's *A Modern Instance* Marcia kisses the door knob on which Bentley's hand had rested. By the twentieth century lovers kiss arms because they want to and not because it is the only part of the body they can get at or the first thing they happen to grab. And if a modern heroine were to kiss a door-knob, she might know what it meant. When in *Point Counter Point* Walter kisses Lucy's instep, she cools him off with the quip, "You're becoming quite oriental" (175).

III

Victorian idealization of first kisses not only caused them to be sudden, rushed, humorless, and disembodied, but so limited the conditions for their approval that many were the grounds for moral outrage. After Rochester first kissed Jane he said enigmatically, "It will atone." After Stephen first kissed Maggie she snatched her arm back and "glared at him like a wounded war-goddess, quivering with rage and humiliation. 'How dare you?'—she spoke in a deeply shaken, half-smothered voice. 'What right have I given you to insult me?'" (561). Afterwards Maggie expected that a "horrible punishment" would result from this single kiss that she described as a "sin" and "a blight—a leprosy" (562). These responses are, to be sure, complicated by Rochester's wife and Stephen's former attentions to Lucy, but the depths of guilt into which Rochester and Maggie are cast from kisses inspired by genuine love is historically marked.

In several modern novels a kiss generates similar moral anguish, but the authors present it as leftover from a bygone era. In *Strait Is the Gate* (1909) the fanatically religious Alissa's intense love for Jerome will not tolerate any imperfection, hence any physical or earthly expression. Her recoil after his first kiss becomes the focus of their tragic love which proceeds to exhaust the possibilities of self-denial. He attempts in vain to follow Christ's preaching that "strait is the gate, and narrow is the way, which leadeth unto life." But the straight and narrow, at least on earth, leads to Alissa's death. She tells Jerome that true communion and pure love are only possible in God, so she insists that they separate and correspond. At a later meeting he takes her hand but their hands unclasp and fall apart despairingly. To touch or even see him is too erotic. As she writes him, "I never before felt so clearly . . . by my embarrassment as soon as you came near me, how deeply I loved you; but hopelessly too, for . . . when you were away, I loved you more." To console him during his final banishment from her presence she writes, "To Him alone can we draw near with impunity" (82). After her death Jerome discovers a notebook in which she had recorded her anguish lest her own sensuousness corrupt his way to God.

Du Gard created a couple similarly divided by the woman's religious asceticism. Jenny loves Jacques but is sickened by sex. One evening Jacques is overcome with desire and positions himself to make the shadow of his lips kiss the shadow of Jenny's lips silhouetted against a moonlit wall. "Jenny stepped back hastily, as though to wrest her shadow from his lips, and vanished through the doorway." Her flight places her back in history as much as it displaces her from the kiss. "[She] ran and ran as though all the black and white phantoms haunting the eerie silence of the garden were at her heels." Back in her room she flung herself on the bed. "She was shivering in a cold sweat, there was a pain in her heart, and she pressed her trembling hands against her bosom, crushing her forehead against the pillow. Her whole will was bent on one aim only: to forget" (417). Such sexual guilt is possible in any period, but Du Gard implies a historical perspective in his story of the Thibault family by having Antoine inspired by the sexually adventurous Rachel while his brother Jacques is stymied by the sexually suppressed Jenny, who recoils in horror and is overcome with disgust over a shadow kiss.

In *Sons and Lovers* Paul is sacrificed to Miriam's purity, which, Lawrence explains, "felt more like nullity," and he must reassure her after they kiss. "Some sort of perversity in our souls," he says, "makes us not want, get away from the very thing we want." He must plow through centuries of guilt to convince her that they have done nothing wrong. "You don't think it ugly?" he asks. "No, not now. You have *taught* me it isn't," she answers. As they contemplate having sex, Miriam summons up her courage: "'You *shall* have me,' she said, through her shut teeth" (282–283). How very different the playful, acrobatic kiss (in *The Vagabond*), that Max gives Renée, which she describes as "his favorite game of lifting me up in his arms till I touch the ceiling, and then kissing my cheeks, chin, ears and mouth." Finally, "he tips me right over on his arm, head down and feet in the air until I cry 'Help'!" (138). That exuberant kiss is matched by Chagall's own in-flight kiss depicted in *The Birthday* (1915). He had rushed into his beloved Bella's room with a boquet and immediately gone to the canvas to paint their sense of elation. In the painting Bella is slightly elevated, and Chagall sweeps above her and twists his head down in anticipation of their jubilant kiss. The painting is one of the icons of love in modern art with Fauvist color, Cubist simplification of forms, Futurist motion, and even an anticipation of Surrealist invention.

IV

First kisses are always scary. In the Victorian period fear ran especially high, and to help men and women deal with it there was a rigid code, invariably adhered to, that men take the initiative. Men also assumed the commanding posture, as in Hayez's *The Kiss*, by holding the woman's face or head and by forcing the woman to cock her head to one side and arch her back, positions that underscored the man's superior muscular strength, larger stature, and active role.

As the fear of kissing lessened, the strict gender polarity of these conventions also began to erode. In *The Awakening* (1899) Edna leans over and gives Robert "a soft, cool, delicate kiss, whose voluptuous sting penetrated his whole being" (106). Ann Veronica tells Capes, "I want you to kiss me." In *The Age of Innocence* Ellen grabs Archer, flings her arms around him, and presses her lips to his. Léa tells the hero of *Chéri* (1920), "It's all too true that you've a pretty mouth, and, this time, I'm going to take my fill because I want to—and then I'll leave you." In *Point Counter Point* Mary grabs Mark's hand and lifts it to her lips for a first kiss. These counter-conventional gestures by women are symptomatic of the gender depolarization that also becomes increasingly visible in art.

Victorian artists sought balanced contrasts by opposing male and female characteristics that were visibly manifest in their respective heights, muscles, poses, faces, skin colorings, and clothing. Their renderings of the kiss drew on these conventional differences for meaning and aesthetic unity. Modern artists looked upon these conventions as a straightjacket and found new ways to unify their art. They came to believe that colors, textures, materials, and forms could kiss with as much artistic force as loving lips.

One of the sharpest contrasts of love in art is between two sculptures: Rodin's *The Kiss* (Figure 24, 1886) and Brancusi's *The Kiss* (Figure 25, 1912). Rodin's earliest version was intended for *The Gates of Hell,* a sculpted portal he began in 1880 and worked on until his death in 1917. It belongs in the transition period of my study, because it looks back to Victorian reliance on literary sources and moral-religious interpretation, but treats the themes of love and damnation in modern ways. In 1880 Rodin immersed himself in Dante's *The Divine Comedy* and sketched hundreds of episodes he intended to sculpt. Ultimately he obscured the literary and historical sources by rendering the figures in the nude, which many critics viewed as obscene. He replaced Dante's fervid religious motives with his own intense didacticism that showed numerous couples wriggling and writhing in hellish, though not specifically Dantesque, sexual indulgence.

Included in this masterpiece were Paolo and Francesca, the famous loving wrongdoers whom Dante banished to hell but whom Rodin rendered blissful and about to kiss. Sometime after 1889 Rodin took the sculpture of the

24. Auguste Rodin, *The Kiss*, 1886.

happy lovers out of the portal and replaced it with a suitably miserable pair.[6] The removed sculpture survived independently as *The Kiss*. In it the only reference to the original story is the book in Paolo's left hand, although there is a suggestion of the primordial sinners—a reluctant Adam and a seductive Eve. Her left foot rests on his left foot, and her right leg is slung over his left thigh. Her encircling arms aggressively pull him down in contrast to his right hand which only tentatively grazes her left hip. Her sexual initiative is not, however, an indication of modern equality, but a conventional symbol of female enticement. *The Kiss* is an erotically charged version of the romantic ideal, the culmination of a long artistic tradition.

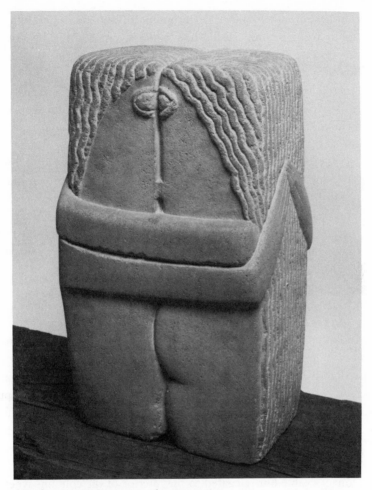

25. Constantin Brancusi, *The Kiss*, 1912.

Brancusi's sculpture reveals a number of revolutionary changes in modern art and contrasts with Rodin's in many ways. Rodin's kiss occurs at a precise moment in a love story; Brancusi's kiss is timeless. Rodin's kiss is climactic; Brancusi's is eternal. Rodin's is located in a realistic, if schematic, public space; Brancusi's is not located anywhere except in its own purely artistic space. Rodin's ethereal lovers are in glamorous white marble; Brancusi's earthbound lovers are in unglamorous stone. Rodin's assistants polished the marble to represent perfect skin; Brancusi's own direct carving left the surface rough. Rodin's lovers are young and beautiful; Brancusi's are ageless and beautiless. Rodin's innovative technique of allowing nude models to move about while posing created new expressive poses, but his couple is classically posed to accent the grace of a loving kiss; Brancusi's couple is not posed so much as arranged for strictly aesthetic purposes.[7]

The treatments of sex are strikingly different. Rodin's masterpiece is the apotheosis of love between a handsome man and a beautiful woman. Although she initiates, the man's superior strength, larger frame, sharply defined muscles, and more upright posture all emphasize sexual differences. Brancusi's lovers are almost androgynous. Aside from a hint of the woman's breast and longer, wavier hair, there is nothing to indicate sex. The man and woman are the same height and mass, their heads meet squarely on equal terms, and their hands and arms are the same size and hold one another with equal force. The parallel position of their arms and the single hyphen of stone that is the kiss both suggest equal signs. In place of the traditional union of two beautiful loving lips, Brancusi has created a more explicitly artistic, though no less loving, juxtaposition of material forms.

Even more important than the lips are the kissing, communicating eyes. While the eyes of Rodin's lovers are closed, those of Brancusi's are wide open, and in later versions of the kiss they become even more so. Brancusi's obsession with sculpting the kiss began around 1905.[8] In that version the eyes are slightly more differentiated than they are in 1912, but they do touch and begin to suggest a unified circular form. Over the years (in sculptures from 1908, 1909, 1912, 1919) he continued to simplify and unify the kiss until, in his most ambitious celebration of it—*The Gate of the Kiss* (Figure 26, 1938)—the eyes of the man and woman have become a single eye that is a geometric, purely formal harmony of two hemispheres in a circle. The lips are no longer visible but relegated to the interior of the columns where the lovers kiss in the mass of uncarved stone, but each of the eight visible eyes prominently displays the kissing and union of two lovers. These eyes also represent the sex act in purely geometric notation as a pair of hemispheres with a subdued phallic shape protruding from the stone in an unbroken female circle. And yet within that geometry of gender differentiation there is a perfectly androgynous symbolism, because each of the hemispheres represents, as Brancusi acknowledged, "the forms of two cells that meet and create life."[9] With a single sculptural form Brancusi has unified sperm and egg, penis and vagina, lips and eyes, eye and eye, man and woman, and perhaps even himself and the mystery woman who in years past may have refused his

26. Constantin Brancusi, *The Gate of the Kiss,* 1938.

kiss (see note 8). Brancusi's monumentally open-eyed celebration of the kiss is a long way from all the closed-eyed kissers in Victorian art and from Heathcliff's imperious command, "Kiss me again, and don't let me see your eyes."

Brancusi's forthright unification of kissing and seeing in a single geometric form embodies historically new modes of the four subthemes of kissing that I have traced in this chapter. The brief, stolen Victorian kiss is replaced by this composition of timeless geometric forms. In contrast to the Victorian blind kiss, the moderns opened their eyes ever wider and looked at themselves and at their lovers in order to see, understand, explore, and intensify new possibilities of love. The didacticism of Rodin's sculpture gives way in Brancusi to the dominion of aesthetic sensibilities of modern art. Moderns also sought to replace, or at least augment, the conventional objective of representing love in art with a newer conception of love as art—hence Brancusi's substitution of kissing materials and forms for actual lips. And finally the moderns sought new possibilities of aesthetic balance beyond contrasting gender roles. The cliche of a powerful man arching a woman's back, twisting her head, and pressing down on her lips in a clinch was replaced by an expandable set of androgynous kissing forms. Together these developments accorded artists an unprecedented sense of independence and responsibility for recreating this concise symbol of love.

9 Gender

SEXUAL difference is embedded in the pronomial system of all languages, woven into countless love stories, and ubiquitous in world art. In
the Orient it is the yin and yang that balances all forces in the universe. Men
and women dwell on the difference with rapt intensity in the pursuit of sexual pleasure, which is the driving force for the ultimate biological destiny of
human survival. Although gender grounds the institutions and values of all
societies, its modes vary and hence make a history of it possible.

Despite the Victorians' reserve about sex, they believed that the entire personality was structured by sharply dichotomous gender traits: men were
naturally polygamous, strong, rational, active, cool-headed, adventurous,
able to expend great quantities of energy in short bursts for vital activities,
while women were naturally monogamous, weak, intuitive, passive, impulsive, and flirtatious, less sharply defined than men in musculature and mental faculties, capable of long, sustained periods of low energy yield (a kind
of spiritual analogue to pregnancy), and destined to build nests and nurture
others. Such traits were rigidly fixed by an anatomical-psychological destiny
that only moral corruption or sexual perversion could alter. Nietzsche was
looking across this great divide when in 1883 he wondered, "Who can
wholly comprehend *how* strange man and woman are to each other?" [1]

A classic Victorian formulation is Ruskin's essay "Of Queens' Gardens,"
which insisted on the dichotomy of gender character. "Each has what the
other has not: each completes the other." The man's power is active, progressive, and adventurous; his intellect is speculative and inventive; his energy is for war and conquest. Woman's power is for rule but not for battle.
Her intellect is "for sweet ordering, arrangement and decision." Ruskin
omits woman's special energy but adds that her "great function is Praise."
His survey of polarities covers fifty pages. It often patronizes women but

occasionally waxes indignant over their subordination: "You bring up your girls as if they were meant for sideboard ornament and then complain of their frivolity. Give them the same advantages that you give their brothers— appeal to the same grand instinct of virtue in them; teach *them* also that courage and truth are the pillars of their being." But such affirmations of equality are compromised by his whimsical theorizing which affirms the supportive and subordinate role of women.

In *The Mill on the Floss* Eliot covers similar terrain but with barely disguised outrage. "While Maggie's life-struggles had lain almost entirely within her own soul, one shadowy army fighting another . . . Tom was engaged in a dustier, noisier warfare, grappling with more substantial obstacles, and gaining more definite conquests. So it has been since the days of Hecuba and of Hector, Tamer of horses: inside the gates, the women with streaming hair and uplifted hands offering prayers, watching the world's combat from afar, filling their long, empty days with memories and fears: outside, the men in fierce struggle with things divine and human, quenching memory in the stronger light of purpose, losing the sense of dread and even of wounds in the hurrying ardour of action" (405).

The conviction of gender dichotomy was pervasive. Most writers argued that each sex had special aptitudes and spheres of action, but the division was in fact a hierarchy based on female support of male privilege, as Eliot expressed it with bitter eloquence. Emma Bovary is doubly resentful of male privileges—because she does not have them and because her husband is unable to exercise them. She wonders: "Wasn't it a man's role, though, to know everything? Shouldn't he be expert at all kinds of things, able to initiate you into the intensities of passion, the refinements of life, all the mysteries? *This* man could teach you nothing; he knew nothing, he wished for nothing" (46). When Emma learns that her newborn is a girl she faints.

Victorians made a few qualified concessions to the superiority of women. They were believed to have a stronger moral fiber—affirmed ultimately, though, by the love of chivalrous men striving to serve them, as Eliot elaborates in *Middlemarch*. "The remote worship of a woman throned out of their reach plays a great part in men's lives, but in most cases the worshipper longs for some queenly recognition, some approving sign by which his soul's sovereign may cheer him without descending from her high place. That was precisely what Will wanted [from Dorothea]" (152). When a woman's high place was not a fabled tower, from which she could not escape, it was an equally mythic pedestal, from which she could not step down without falling.

Hawthorne makes an astute observation about the differing public and private tribunals for morality in women and men. Dimmesdale refers to Pearl as a "child of its father's guilt and its mother's shame" (137). Later in speaking to Hester he distinguishes the ways he and she, as man and woman, "wear" their misdeed. "Happy are you, Hester, that wear the scarlet letter openly upon your bosom! Mine burns in secret!" (209). Since women become pregnant and bear and nurse babies, evidence of their sexual experiences (adulterous or not) may become visible to others and hence experienced as public shame. Men's different role in reproduction enables them to hide their responsibility more than women, and Dimmesdale has noted this difference in identifying his burning regret as private guilt. Hester wears the mark of their sin openly on her clothing, while Dimmesdale's is inscribed on his chest in some mysterious fashion, concealed from others by his clothing. Although this difference has a universal foundation in reproductive biology, the intensities of shame and guilt vary historically and in the Victorian world were sharply divided between men and women.

Women of course were judged superior to men in child rearing and housekeeping, but in all worldly matters they were subordinate to men. Ruskin argued that "each has what the other has not," but men did not want what women had. The distribution of *desirable* gender privileges was especially uneven in education, as Eliot dramatized. Maggie thinks patchwork is silly and wants to study Latin and geometry like Tom. When she shows promise in her studies, Tom's teacher dismisses her along with all other women— "They've a great deal of superficial cleverness: but they couldn't go far into anything. They're quick and shallow" (220).

Victorian women were warned that too much learning would diminish their desirability, marriageability, fertility, or even milk supply. They might also become flat-chested, hipless, consumptive, degenerate, or "masculinized." In America, Edward Clarke's popular *Sex in Education; or, A Fair Chance for the Girls* (1873) cautioned that overworked female students were especially susceptible to "dysmenorrhea, chronic and acute ovaritis, prolapsus uteri, hysteria, neuralgia." [2]

Gender polarity can create powerful attractive forces that heighten the joy of union, or it can cause conflict so intense and gaps so wide that the poles are unable to reunite. Victorian lovers were sharply polarized by an uncompromising dichotomy that caused considerable conflict. This conclusion is based on the historical record of the late nineteenth and early twentieth centuries, which also reveals sweeping challenges to that dichotomy from genetics, endocrinology, embryology, gynecology, sexology, theology, evolutionary theory, feminist theory, psychoanalysis, sociology, and anthropology, as well as literature and art. The remainder of this chapter will sketch some of these challenges.

In the Victorian as in the modern period, assignments of sex were made on the basis of visual inspection of a newborn's external genitalia. The Victorians also believed, however, that an individual's gender identity (sense of belonging to one sex), gender role (behavior deemed suitable for that sex), and object choice (the sex to whom one is attracted) were determined completely, unambiguously, and permanently by the initial assignment of sex. Between the mid-nineteenth and early twentieth century these latter beliefs changed considerably.

Throughout the nineteenth century no one knew precisely how the introduction of a man's sperm into a woman's vagina determined the sex of offspring. Some theorized that the relative nutrition level of the parents determined sex, although there was disagreement whether the one with more or less nutrition prevailed. Others theorized that the age of the egg, or the sperm, or the parents' ages, or even the season of year at the time of fertilization were crucial. Still others focused on the fate of the fetus after fertilization. A correct understanding was possible only when the discovery of chromosomes in the 1870s (and specifically a sex chromosome in 1891) was coupled with Mendel's study of genetics, first published in 1866 but ignored until rediscovered in 1900. Then for the first time it could be established that sex was determined by one out of twenty-three minute pairs of chromosomes in the one sperm cell out of billions that fertilizes the egg.

This vast reduction in the scope of sexual determination further compromised the idea of an absolute sexual dichotomy, because other bodily cells, including the other chromosomes, are not sex-typed. Chromosomal theory also held that the sex of offspring had nothing to do with the apparent degree of manliness or femininity of either parent. The theory further dissolved an absolute sexual dichotomy, because it demonstrated that the sperm's sex chromosome could make mistakes in dividing or in recombining with the egg's sex chromosome and produce ambiguous sexual intermediate forms that did not have precisely either a normal female's XX or a normal male's XY chromosome. Finally, early genetics revealed that male and female sex chromosomes are fundamentally hermaphroditic and that sex determination is a process of developing one set of potentialities and suppressing the other.

Gender dichotomy was further assaulted by the discovery of "internal secretions" or hormones which proliferated the number of bodily sites, glandular processes, and biochemical substances that determined primary and secondary sex characteristics. Moreover, both sexes produce all three sex hormones—estrogen, androgen, and progesterone—although in different amounts and at different times. In 1921 Louis Berman, a biologist at Columbia University, summarized the historical impact of hormonal theory: "There is no absolute masculine or absolute feminine. The ideals of the Manly Man and the Womanly Woman were erected by the blind ignorance of the nineteenth-century illusionists." Rather, there is a gradation between the masculine and the feminine. Those in-between types, he concluded, are caused by "different admixtures of the internal secretions."[3] What Berman targeted as "blind ignorance" was state-of-the-art thinking about gender character throughout the nineteenth century.

Gynecologists gave increasing attention to hermaphrodites, who visibly and disturbingly contradicted an absolute gender dichotomy. The hermaphrodite Herculine Barbin kept a journal of her/his life which was published in 1874 (fourteen years after her/his suicide).[4] Her/his poignant recollections were repeatedly cited over the next twenty-five years and supplied material for several fictional works including Oscar Panizza's A Scandal at the Convent (1893). An article on another hermaphrodite, Josephine K., was illustrated by a striking frontal photograph that showed ample breasts looming from a woman's body that included a vagina through which she/he menstruated, a rudimentary penis through which she/he ejaculated, and a split scrotum with a testicle in each side, wedged between the labia majora and the thighs.[5]

Interest in hermaphroditism was intense at the Scientific-Humanitarian Committee founded in 1897 by Magnus Hirschfeld, the pioneer of German sexology. Its forum was a journal with the catchy title Yearbook for Sexual Intermediary Stages, which began to appear in 1899. The journal was intended to analyze homosexuality and defend it against moral condemnation and legal persecution, which were based on the presumption of a natural and absolute dichotomy of the sexes; so a number of articles documented a male-female continuum as illustrated by hermaphrodites and other intermediary types: "urnings," "inverts," "bisexuals," "androgynes," "intersexuals," "similisexuals," "transvestites," "transsexuals," and, Hirschfeld's own coinage, "the third sex."

A Dutch theologian surveyed androgynous images of God. Drawing from an impressive bibliography of 196 titles, he argued that "the deity embraces the active and passive, stimulative and sensitive, generative and vegetative, which also means by analogy manly as well as feminine powers."[6] Greeks, Armenians, Egyptians, Romans, and Indians had androgynous gods, and some Jewish and Christian mystics believed that Adam was a *Mannweib* and that Jehovah and Christ were androgynous. The universal imperative that god be a unity embracing disparate aspects of existence, he concluded, is what led religions to attribute both masculine and feminine qualities to their deities.

Bisexuality had been the subject of speculation for centuries, but in the 1870s it was supported by new findings in embryology and genetics and given notoriety by its inclusion in evolutionary theory. Darwin gave the theory special prominence in *The Descent of Man* (1871): "It has long been known that in the vertebrate kingdom one sex bears rudiments of various parts, appertaining to the reproductive system, which properly belong to the opposite sex; and it has now been ascertained that at a very early embryonic period both sexes possess true male and female glands. Hence some remote progenitor of the whole vertebrate kingdom appears to have been hermaphrodite or androgynous."[7] The theory was elaborated by August Weismann in 1892 and reiterated in the 1896 edition of Krafft-Ebing's *Psychopathia Sexualis*, which held that a latent bisexual disposition deriving from our animal predecessors is manifest in the human embryo, persists in the infant, and may reemerge in adult sexual pathology.

"Bisexuality" was part of a wildly speculative theory of human periodicity in the writings of an eccentric Berlin nose specialist, Wilhelm Fliess, who first suggested to Freud the psychological importance of bisexuality. In 1897 Fliess hypothesized that individuals were regulated by combinations of a 28-day female cycle and a 23-day male cycle, both of which function in both sexes but with one cycle dominant. Consequently men and women have a "double sexual disposition."[8] The theory was supported by the young Viennese physician Otto Weininger, who, in *Sex and Character* (1903), proposed a "law of sexual attraction" which dictates that healthy offspring are produced by the union of a "complete" male and female, although the completeness is always distributed between the sexes. Thus a woman with 1/4 male and 3/4 female characteristics will produce the healthiest child if she mates with a man who has 3/4 male and 1/4 female characteristics. Weininger's science was fanciful, but he added a scholarly veneer with current findings in genetics, embryology, and endocrinology. He popularized the ideas that "before five weeks the sex of a human embryo cannot be determined," that "sexual differentiation is never complete," and hence that "there is no blunt separation between males and females."[9]

In 1905 the German feminist theoretician Rosa Mayreder rejected the idea that every cell is sex-marked and dismissed derivations of female character from female sexual biology. "The task of sexual psychology will remain insoluble," she argued, "as long as one believes the sexes to be physically and mentally opposites."[10] The notion that men have to be "hard, uncouth, and lordly" is as destructive to male-female relations as the notion that women have to be "meek, passive, and coquettish." She concluded with an affirmation of the bisexual disposition of both sexes and a hope that new depolarized roles will bring about more humane and loving relationships.

The most significant psychiatric use of bisexuality was Freud's elaboration of it in 1905 at the heart of his developmental psychology, which was based on the presumption of a natural and innate bisexual disposition. Drawing from the articles on androgyny, bisexuality, and hermaphroditism in the *Yearbook for Sexual Intermediary Stages*, Freud observed that "a certain degree of anatomical hermaphroditism occurs normally" in male and female humans. Psychologically, all children are bisexual throughout the oral and anal stages or up to about the age of three. Since Freud believed that the basic personality was formed by the age of five (sometimes he put it at three), this bisexual disposition was fundamental to adult mental life—normal or abnormal. His controversial theory—that the childhood autoerotism of boys and girls during the phallic stage is "the same in both sexes"—extended bisexuality even later into childhood. He concluded that it would be impossible to understand the sex life of men and women without the notion of bisexuality.[11] Although Freud's quip "Anatomy is destiny" emphasized gender differences resulting from phallic excitation being centered in a penis or clitoris, he also emphasized similarities between the sexes by cutting loose a wide range of sensations and emotions from their conventional gender moorings.

Jung hypothesized that all ancestral experience of both sexes forms two collective images that are somehow transmitted to every man and woman at birth as archetypes or "subjective attitudes." He called the female archetype the "anima" and the male archetype the "animus." The subjective attitude of the anima, for example, is "an innate psychic structure" which makes it possible for a man to experience a woman. The man's anima is at first buried in the unconscious, from where it exerts its most powerful grip on his conscious and public *persona*. Unaware of his own repressed feminine side, a man will seek out his own anima projected onto a woman, "which is why a man, in his love-choice, is strongly tempted to win the woman who best corresponds to his own unconscious femininity—a woman, in short, who can unhesitatingly receive the projection of his soul. Although such a choice is often regarded and felt as altogether ideal, it may turn out that the man has manifestly married his own worst weakness." When a man falls in love quickly, he is able to do so only because he has known the woman (a projection of himself) all along. A more mature love is only possible following individuation—a life goal and also the goal of Jungian psychotherapy. It involves bringing to consciousness the unconscious archetypes of the anima and animus to achieve a union of opposites that leads to "the most legitimate fulfillment of the meaning of the individual's life."

While much of Jung's gender theorizing looks ahead historically, part of the content seems picked out of Ruskin's hat, especially when Jung interprets the fate of "masculine" qualities in a woman's mind: "The wide fields of commerce, politics, technology, and science, the whole realm of the applied masculine mind, she relegates to the penumbra of consciousness; while, on the other hand, she develops a minute consciousness of personal relationships, the infinite nuances of which usually escape the man entirely." Although these biases are distinctively Victorian, Jung dissolves the conventional gender roles with his theory about the "two crepuscular figures of the dark hinterland of the psyche"—the anima and animus.[12]

Anthropology revealed strikingly different cultures with institutions and values that challenged Western ethnocentrism, including its conviction of an absolute, permanent, and natural sexual dichotomy. Rosalind Rosenberg's apt title, *Beyond Separate Spheres,* graphically suggests what began to happen to the dichotomous world of men and women around the turn of the century, when venturesome feminist intellectuals crossed the barriers into graduate programs in anthropology (as well as sociology and psychology) at major universities and worked with men to refute theories formerly used to justify those barriers and maintain separate spheres. In 1931 Margaret Mead began research into the distinctive gender roles of three cultures of New Guinea, the very names of which suggested sexual exotica—Arapesh, Mundugumour, and Tchambuli. In *Sex and Temperament* (1935) she startled readers with her findings, which pointedly refuted the presumption of universal and Western-style dichotomies. She concluded that human nature was malleable and that "many, if not all of the personality traits which we have called masculine or feminine are as lightly linked to sex as are [the] clothing, the manners, and the form of head-dress that a society at a given period assigns to [each] sex." [13]

While Victorians suppressed sex, which they regarded as animalistic and unrefined, they exaggerated the extent, depth, and duration of gender difference. In the late nineteenth and early twentieth century the major genetic/historical approaches to human experience rested on some primordial unity of the sexes. In referring to these theories of the fundamental unity of the sexes as evidence of a growing emphasis on gender depolarization, I do not mean to suggest a complete breakdown of gender difference. Rather, a conception slowly emerged that took account of biological sexual differences and historical conventions of gender, both rooted in a human foundation that is shared by the sexes that makes the powerful attractive forces between them possible. I divide the history of this change into four subthemes: "masculinization" of women, "feminization" of men, acknowledgment of homosexuality, and fascination with the androgynous. "Masculinization" and "feminization" are in quotation marks to indicate the use of the nineteenth-century conceptions, which are of course historically variable. The use of these terms around the turn of the century to describe and sometimes decry changing gender roles only reaffirmed the older dichotomies.

I

Although Victorian heroines such as Maggie, Emma, and Hester envy the privileges of men, they remain irrevocably locked in conventional feminine roles. By around 1880 there are stirrings of change. In Ibsen's *A Doll's House* (1879) Nora slams the door on her condescending husband on the way out of her "doll's house," and two years later in *The Portrait of a Lady* Isabel travels to Europe (on her father's money) "with a fixed determination to regard the world as a place of brightness, of free expansion, of irresistible action" (51). In other words, Isabel aspired to live the way only a man of her age was entitled to live. By 1895 Sue Bridehead can make her way in a man's world without her father's money. She is university-educated, receives a "Queen's scholarship," and instructs Jude on the classical authors and architects he ought to know about. Neighbors tell Jude that Sue is "not exactly a tomboy" but can "do things that only boys do" (91). When she tells Jude that she is a "negation of civilization," he replies limply that the word "negation" is "profound talking." She tells him that she has "no fear of men, as such, nor of their books . . . I have mixed with them . . . almost as one of their own sex." But she seems distant with her "strange ways and curious unconsciousness of gender" (117–119). With this statement Hardy sides with the conventions of gender, because he does not see that a woman like Sue may have been intensely conscious of other ways of being a woman rather than altogether unconscious of gender.

In *A Room with a View* Forster captures a moment in the dissolution of gender polarities with his transitional pair—the tentative libertine Lucy and her incompetent chaperon Charlotte. Lucy wants to do "big things" and wonders why most of them are "unladylike." Charlotte explains. "It was not that ladies were inferior to men . . . they were different. Their mission was to inspire others to achievement rather than to achieve themselves." Although the dragons and knights have gone, Forster narrates, the "medieval lady" still "lingers in our midst . . . But alas! the creature grows degenerate. In her heart also there are springing up strange desires." The modern woman has noticed that the world is full of beauty and riches but that only men move freely over its surface. "Before the show breaks up she would like to drop the august title of the Eternal Woman, and go there as her transitory self." Lucy is no medieval lady, but she lacks a "system of revolt." When she travels to Florence she has a chaperon; she may transgress restrictions but "perhaps be sorry that she had done so" (46–47).

In *The Age of Innocence* Ellen travels on her own and feels less hesitant than Lucy about usurping conventional male privileges. In New York drawing rooms a lady was not permitted, Wharton explains, "to get up and walk away from one gentleman in order to seek the company of another. Etiquette required that she should wait, immovable as an idol, while the men who wished to converse with her succeeded each other at her side" (64). Ellen walks away from a duke to tell Archer how dull the duke was. She invites Archer to her apartment the next day and later flings her arms around him for a first kiss. When Archer hesitates to lay out his romantic plans, she guesses what's on his mind. "Is your idea, then, that I should live with you as your mistress—since I can't be your wife?" Archer is shocked. When Ellen finally resolves to have sex with him, she again takes the initiative. "Shall I—once come to you; and then go home?" (309). Her "unladylike" demeanor cannot undo the gender roles that hold her in her place. She crosses a room on her own to get away from a boring duke, but erroneous public opinion about her conduct ultimately drives her back across the Atlantic to Europe.

In *Howards End* Margaret forthrightly assumes "unladylike" roles.

When she proposes that she and Henry honeymoon at a currant farm near Calamata, he replies that it is "not the kind of place one could possibly go to with a lady." "Why?" she asks. "No hotels," he answers. When she tells him that she and her sister walked alone over the Apennines, he closes the discussion: "I wasn't aware, and, if I can manage it, you will never do such a thing again" (178–179). When consulting with Margaret about how to draw up his will, she naturally asks how much money he's got. "What?" he shrieks, astonished at her unladylike inquisitiveness. So she coolly clarifies. "How much have you a year? I've six hundred." And he replies finally, "My income?" aghast at her unladylike persistence. In *This Side of Paradise* Amory is stunned to learn that Rosalind is more at home than he in the world of high finance. She modestly explains that she does not own a corporation, "It's just 'Rosalind, Unlimited.' Fifty-one shares, name, good-will, and everything goes at $25,000 a year." And she apologizes for her own holdings when she explains further, "I'm not really feminine, you know—in my mind" (174). Women are not only up against men's ownership of material wealth but also against men's privileged entitlement to the attribute of monetary value itself.

Rosalind's explanation that she is "not really feminine" would not make sense to the women of Herland who own and run everything. Fifteen years before Mead found three cultures that undercut the primacy of European gender roles, Gilman imagined one. *Herland* clarified how the so-called "masculinization" of women was a homocentric misinterpretation of history, which held that women could realize their human potential only by becoming more like men. Gilman inverts the advantages and disadvantages of gender. The male visitors to Herland are miffed about being treated the way women are treated back home—as merely "the sex." One of the men realizes that "those 'feminine charms' we are so fond of are not feminine at all, but mere reflected masculinity—developed to please us because they had to please us, and in no way essential to the real fulfillment of their great process" (59). Gender traits are not divinely, inevitably, or ineluctably rooted in sexual difference but are cultural adaptations as malleable as human imagination.

II

There were analogous misinterpretations of the changing gender roles of men. Throughout the nineteenth century "feminization" of men meant weakness if not degeneration. One microscopic[14] example of change is in the description of how men cry. In the Victorian novel a man's tears are always copious (not weepy), and his sobbing is loud (not whimpery). In the novels that Emma Bovary read as a girl, men "wept copiously on every occasion" (41). Ranthorpe "sobs" convulsively. When Victorian heroes cry they do not get wet lashes, runny noses, or red eyes. Modern heroes show more delicacy, even frailty. In *The Vagabond* Max's "two lustrous tears" wet his eyelashes. When Renée tells him to be brave, he "blows his nose, rebelliously." Then he "dries his eyes, very slowly and carefully" (168–169). No doubt women writers were more attentive to the morphology of male tears. In *The Age of Innocence,* Archer stepped out of Ellen's carriage and ordered the driver on. "Suddenly he felt something stiff and cold on his lashes, and perceived that he had been crying, and that the wind had frozen his tears" (289). In *Mrs. Dalloway* Woolf explains how Peter "wept without the least shame, sitting on the sofa, with tears running down his cheeks" (69).

Joyce toyed with the conventions of sex and gender as irreverently as with those of religion and nationality. Leopold likes pornography, is aroused by Gerty's underclothing, and fantasizes about Molly's body. But on several occasions he also crosses the conventional gender line. He once took the role of a female impersonator in a high school play, *Vice Versa.* He has a "firm full masculine feminine passive active hand," and he fantasizes about being another man's wife. In the hallucinatory "Circe" episode Dr. Dixon pronounces Leopold to be an "example of the new womanly man" and "about to have a baby." Leopold responds to this news joyfully: "O, I so want to be a mother" (494). The whoremistress Bella Cohen (who herself turns into a man) transforms Leopold into a woman and threatens to subject him to humiliations commonly imposed on women—to be "wigged, singed, perfumesprayed, ricepowdered, with smoothshaven armpits . . . laced with cruel force into viselike corsets [and] restrained in nettight frocks" (535–536).[15]

In *The Man Without Qualities* Musil celebrates the feminization of man as well as the masculinization of woman. Among the qualities that Ulrich is without, conventional masculinity is conspicuous. His preparation for that "withoutness" began in childhood, when he longed to know what it was like "to be a girl himself" (III, 26). When Agatha moves into his apartment, first in a non-erotic sisterly role, her things become props for fantasizing about the gender reversal he longed for as a child. He observes the way gender differences are accentuated by her clothing, which he interprets as

"an ingenious contrivance of intermediate stations and fortifications surrounding expertly defended wonders and, for all their perverse artificiality,
a consummately curtained theatre of the erotic." With Agatha as a room-
mate he is able to "take pleasure in for once seeing the so-often desired from
the other side" (III, 331–332). He is not only without qualities, he is sick of
them, especially those dictated by conventional gender roles. When Agatha
wonders aloud whether "perhaps it's fun for you to play at brother and
sister, only because you're sick of playing at man and woman?" Ulrich
agrees and adds, "Love is basically a simple urge to get closer . . . It has been
split into two poles, male and female, with incredible tensions, frustrations,
paroxysms, and perversions arising between. Nowadays we've had enough
of that inflated ideology . . . I'm convinced that most people would be glad
if the connection between a local stimulus and the entire personality could
be cancelled out!" [16] Ulrich is sick of the idea that sexual differences permeate one's entire personality. He also wants to halt the lock-step derivation
of gender qualities from the unmistakably dichotomous "locus stimulus" of
penis or vagina. He looks forward to "an era of simple unassuming sexual
comradeship, when boy and girl will stand reconciled and uncomprehend-
ing, gazing at an ancient heap of broken clockwork springs that was once
what made Man and Woman tick" (III, 324).

The clockwork image conjures up the standardization and interchangea-
bility of parts imposed by conventional gender roles. The requirement that
a particular man and woman relate like all other couples is inauthentic.
When "man" and "woman" dutifully obey the same public and universal
codes for ways of being with one another, the thrilling uncertainty and creative possibilities of sexual attraction are lost. Ulrich and Agatha never entirely wipe out their conventional gender qualities, but their unique love enables them to fashion some new ones of their own.

III

The most threatening consequence of the "feminization" of men was "sexual inversion," although its notoriety around the turn of the century was not
a consequence of men trying to be like women. As Proust wrote, many homosexuals are denied love because "they are enamoured of precisely the
type of man who has nothing feminine about him, who is not an invert and
consequently cannot love them in return" (II, 638). Homosexuals are as attentive to gender as heterosexuals, perhaps more so, but they do not align with

the conventional gender dividers. There are masculine homosexuals who are attracted to masculine lovers, but some like feminine lovers. There are also effeminate homosexuals. Some like to wear women's clothing. There are various combinations of active/passive roles and a range of desires for oral, anal, or phallic sexuality. The unraveling of these varieties drew upon two new theoretical emphases around the turn of the century—the reduced scope of gender and the distinction between sexual aim and sexual object.

To the Victorians the initial assignment of sex at birth was believed to determine the entire personality, top to bottom, throughout life. Any subsequent hint of "inversion" implicated the whole person. In 1884 George M. Beard followed this theory to its logical conclusion: "perverted" men or women "hate the opposite sex and love their own; men become women and women men in their tastes, conduct, character, feelings, and behavior." [17] I have already surveyed some of the findings in the natural and social sciences that challenged the idea that gender governed the entire person. In a study of the impact of such research specifically on the study of homosexuality, George Chauncey, Jr. concluded that by the twentieth century gender came to be seen as more compartmentalized, and homosexuality therefore did not have to "invert" the entire personality. [18]

In 1905 Freud distinguished between the *sexual aim,* which refers to "the act towards which the instinct tends" (such as oral or anal, active or passive), and the *sexual object,* which refers to the sex of the person to whom one is attracted (male or female). [19] Nineteenth-century investigators had not made this distinction and had presumed that active sexuality was masculine and that passive sexuality was necessarily feminine. Thus if a man was sexually passive, regardless of the sex of his beloved, he was an invert. Freud's distinction clarified how many homosexuals need not act effeminate or desire effeminate lovers.

These two theories undermined the Victorian conviction that gender character permeated the entire existence of men and women and kept them poles apart. The increasing public debate about the morality of homosexuality created another set of challenges to confront a rigid gender dichotomy.

Around 1850 homosexuality was regarded as a sin and, almost everywhere, a crime. Its "medicalization" in the late nineteenth century eroded some of the religious, moral, and legal stigmas, and by the turn of the century sex reformers could take heart that it was being classified merely as a disease. Oscar Wilde's trial for homosexuality in 1895 and his subsequent two-year imprisonment intimidated its defenders, but they soon drew inspiration from his plight and began to argue that homosexual love was the highest form of love, because it had to be sustained against such fierce persecution and because it was not corrupted by the squabbling over dowry or inheritance that often compromised heterosexual love.[20] The continuing public alarm energized thinking about gender. Homosexuals discovered two powerful literary evocations of their difficulties in novels whose titles captured their sense of loss and loneliness.

In *A la recherche du temps perdu (Remembrance of Things Past)* Proust surveyed reasons why homosexuals seem to lose their own selves: they live "in falsehood and perjury" because their love is "punishable and shameful," they deny their God because before Christ they must "refute as a calumny what is their very life," and they are even rejected by fellow homosexuals "in whom they inspire only disgust at seeing themselves as they are." The *temps perdu* (time lost) that Proust sets out to recapture goes back to childhood, when his mother's love was unconditional and bountiful. The alienation of sons from that love was for Proust the bitterest loss of all. Homosexuals, he wrote, are "sons without a mother, to whom they are obliged to lie all her life" (II, 637–638).

In *The Well of Loneliness* (1928) Radclyffe Hall ventured to imagine what might happen when a mother found out that her daughter had lied. In a chilling confrontation the mother lets loose after discovering her daughter's damning letter. "All your life," she says to her daughter Stephen, "I've felt a kind of physical repulsion, a desire not to touch or to be touched by you [and] now I know that my instinct was right; it is you who are unnatural, not I . . . You are . . . a sin against creation . . . I shall never be able to look at you now without thinking of the deadly insult of your face and your body to the memory of the father who bred you." She thanks God that Stephen's father died before he was asked to "endure this great shame." "I would rather see you dead at my feet than standing before me with this thing upon you—this unspeakable outrage that you call love in that letter . . . [in which] you say things that may only be said between men and women, and coming from you they are vile and filthy words of corruption—against nature, against God who created nature. My gorge rises; you have made me feel physically sick." Outraged at this desecration of her love, Stephen pulls no punches in replying. "As my father loved you, I loved. As a man loves a woman, that was how I loved—protectively . . . I wanted to give all I had in me to give. It made me feel terribly strong . . . and gentle. It was good, good, *good*—I'd have laid down my life a thousand times over for Angela . . . If I loved her the way a man loves a woman, it's because I can't feel that I am a woman" (200–201).

Stephen challenges the conventional assumptions about gender that structured family and society. Although the assignment of her sex at birth correctly identified her genitals, it incorrectly indicated her subsequent gender identity, gender role, and object choice. Her thoughtful reply was more rational than her mother's rage, more humane than her mother's biting condemnation, more natural than her mother's stated preference for seeing her daughter dead at her feet rather than in a lesbian love. Stephen's *cri du coeur,* "I don't know what I am," centered the big existential question on gender and suggested that an uncompromising dichotomy might not properly classify anyone. Yet the power of the novel does not derive ultimately from such paroxysms of righteous indignation but from its sober realism, for in the end Stephen accepts that most people, and even some lesbians, must capitulate to the comforting "normality" of polarized gender roles. She realizes that her present beloved, Mary, has a great need to be "at peace with the world," to feel protected by its laws and codes, to marry and have children. So she lies and tells her that she had sex with another lesbian and thereby drives Mary into the arms of a waiting man. Stephen acknowledges an "inherent respect for the normal which nothing had ever been able to destroy" (430). In the battle for revision of rigid gender dichotomies, homosexuals and lesbians fought the hardest and lost the most. As Proust and Hall showed, they lost their gods, their homes, their mothers and fathers, often their lovers, and occasionally their minds. Although they had few contemporary defenders, their ordeals showed that the conventional gender dichotomies and the values attached to them were not universal.

IV

My final subtheme, fascination with the androgynous, emphasizes the adjectival form (as in "androgynous vision" or "androgynous ideal"), because no one was interested in actually becoming an androgyne.[21] But many artists and writers around the turn of the century drew inspiration from the concept to replace the divisiveness of polarized gender roles with an image of wholeness.

Androgyny means the union of male (andro) and female (gyne) in one being. It is an ancient concept in Western culture. In the *Symposium* Plato speculated that there were originally three sexes—men, women, and androgynes, who were a union of the two. When the gods cut them all in half, the halved androgynes became those men and women who sought the opposite sex to restore their wholeness. Plato supplied the classical links between androgyny, love, and wholeness: "Human nature was originally one and we were a whole, and the desire and pursuit of the whole is called love." The search for unity embracing disparate aspects of existence also led religious prophets and theologians to attribute androgynous qualities to their gods.[22] Throughout the nineteenth century mystic Christians associated with Gnosticism and Rosicrucianism believed in an androgynous Adam Kadmon, a primordial unitary being who was divided into two sexes after the Fall. For German Romantics and French utopian socialists the androgyne symbolized erotic liberation—one cure for the evils of industrialization, materialism, and patriarchy that plagued modern civilization. Novalis believed that primitive man before the Fall was androgynous and that the goal of life and art was a perfect, absolute, and eternal fusion of all antagonisms: body and soul, self and other, male and female. Around 1830 Saint-Simonians used the androgyne as a symbol for reunification in a society sundered by class conflict, industrialization, selfishness, and the oppression of women.

Although the concept of androgyny invoked erotic liberation in the early part of the nineteenth century, it was too disturbingly sexual to be a popular subject for art. A. J. L. Busst's extensive study offers no images of androgyny in nineteenth-century art prior to Paul Chenavard's *The Divine Tragedy* (Figure 27, 1869), which Busst described as "the finest pictorial expression of the optimistic image of the androgyne in nineteenth-century France." [23] And even though the androgyne is the key to Chenavard's painting, some contemporary viewers failed to interpret its significance. The official version of the *Salon of 1869* maintained that the painting represented the triumph of Christianity (represented by the Trinity) carried out by the Angel of Death (swooping down with a flaming sword) over pagan cults (represented by the crush of surrounding pagan gods and goddesses engaged in seduction, murder, and mayhem). That interpretation missed the significance of the androgyne, which represented the triumph of reason over the passion of all cults, including Christianity.[24] The androgyne wears a Phrygian cap (symbol of reason and liberty), is bright with a radiance behind its head (symbol of holiness), and plucks a celestial harp (symbol of harmony). It rides a mythological hippocamp (symbol of power and transmutation), and, most important, it has female breasts and a penis (symbol of the harmonious reunification of humankind). Its location in the uppermost part of the painting

27. Paul Chenavard, *The Divine Tragedy*, 1869.

indicates its superior position compared with that of all other cults, whose lower status implies earthiness, even though they seem to be on a cloud bank.

The image of androgyny remained ethereal and cerebral for the remainder of the century, even as its moral valence changed. After 1850, according to Busst, an optimistic image of the androgyne which symbolized human solidarity and trust in the future, in God, and in the fundamental goodness of man began to give way to a pessimistic androgyne which symbolized isolation, self-sufficiency, onanism, homosexuality, sadism, and masochism. But for all the sensuousness implied by these "vices," the *vice suprême* of the Symbolist androgyne was "cerebral lechery." [25] By the mid-1880s Victorian sexual reticence, Christian asceticism, and conventional gender polarities still governed the theory of the androgyne in the writing of Joséphin Péladan and its representation in the art of Fernand Khnopff.

Péladan's work embodied one goal of the order of the Rosicrucians: to substitute the purity of art for sexual love. In his novel *Le Vice suprême* (1884) one male character protests, "we seek the infinite [in woman] and she can only give a spasm." Péladan's lovers are disillusioned with the brevity and carnality of physical sex and seek eternal, absolute, asexual fulfillment in art, symbolized by the androgyne who combines both sexes and is hence self-creating and self-sufficient. His ideal lovers must be virile and virginal. They must maintain desire but also renounce it to achieve an "innocent voluptuousness" that can be fulfilled only in art. In the novel *L'Androgyne* (1891) Péladan creates an ideal love affair between a predominantly feminine gynander who exhibits herself in indecent postures before an open window and a predominantly male androgyne who watches her from across the street and "receives sexual initiation without contact." [26]

Péladan's link between art and asexual love, symbolized by the androgyne, inspired Khnopff's painting *Art or the Caresses* (Figure 28, 1896). The two figures represent characters from Péladan's play *Oedipus and the Sphinx* (1895), in which the Sphinx attempts to seduce Oedipus and urges him to draw close and kiss her "vermilion lips." [27] Khnopff does not invent new gender roles but recombines conventional ones. The Sphinx has some clear "feminine" qualities: a woman's face (that of Khnopff's sister Marguerite), vermilion lips, a demurely turned head, and an ethereal smile. There are also sexual ambiguities. Her powerful cheetah's body is furry and soft, it is balanced on its feet and not ready to pounce, and the phallic tail is up but waves harmlessly in the air. She also makes feminine gestures with a

28. Fernand Khnopff, *Art or the Caresses*, 1896.

powerful masculine body, does not actively touch his lips but poses passively cheek to cheek, and gently caresses with deadly claws dangerously near his genital area. Although Oedipus has the body of a man, it is a thin, hairless, effeminate, and off-balance body, with the surreal touch of flowers for nipples. He too has a feminine head (also resembling his sister's). In the play the Sphinx tells Oedipus that her caresses will make him feel godlike, but in the painting Oedipus's passive acceptance of the caress makes him more impotent than omnipotent.

This painting is transitional. It looks back to the nineteenth century in affirming dichotomous gender roles. Although Khnopff wreaks havoc with those roles by redistributing them between the sexes, he does not question the roles *per se*. By interpreting these new combinations as perverse, he has in effect sanctioned the very roles which these startling constructions were intended to interrogate, for perversion is only meaningful against a "natural" standard. While Khnopff looks ahead to the twentieth century with the incestuous brother-sister love which opens a way out of conventional gender roles, he cannot surmount the moral condemnation implied by that experimentation and therefore represents their love as asexual, because the caress itself, far from any voluptuous transgression of public morality, seems to be, as the cliché says, "about as exciting as kissing your sister." A second modernist feature in the Khnopff image is the equation of love and art, although even that is ambiguous because he retains Péladan's conception of art as a substitute for imperfect sex. That ambiguity is implied by the title of the painting, *Art or the Caresses,* which can be read historically backward or forward, depending whether it implies a choice between or an equation of painting and caressing.

In Péladan's *Le Vice suprême* the sculptor Antar is obsessed with the androgyne. Another character advises him to "make an angel, without sex, the synthesis of a young man and a young woman."[28] Antar portends Picasso's abiding fascination with the androgynous, although Picasso's imagery will be anything but angelic and will be emphatically sexed.

Already in Picasso's Blue Period of 1902–1903, poverty, hunger, alcohol, and aging erode many of his subjects' gender differences, which are further confused by the pervasive blue cast and low light. The subjects for his Rose Period of 1904–1905 are by profession of ambiguous gender roles—the actors cross sex lines, female acrobats vault over conventional roles, and female bareback riders trample those roles into the dust of center ring. His harlequins are sexually ambiguous men with frail bodies, delicate fingers, and beardless feminine faces, shown tending to children and hovering around more substantial women. The *Boy with a Pipe* has a garland of roses in his hair; the *Woman with a Fan* is shown in a determined, "masculine" profile. By his Cubist period gender becomes almost irrelevant. Aside from traces of long hair, geometrized breasts, and lack of male genitalia there is nothing to indicate the sex of his whores of Avignon. Picasso has repudiated with a vengeance the hyperfeminine odalisques in nineteenth-century art. His angular, muscular, savage whores shattered the conventional aesthetics of gender.

Among the many losses of World War I, the sexuality of men figured prominently. In literature Clifford Chatterley became a paraplegic and Jake Barnes got his penis shot off. Less spectacularly, many men lost the unquestioned presumption of their initiatory and more experienced part in sexual relations, while women, who took on active "masculine" jobs and social roles, applied their new skills in the bedroom when the men came home. How many soldiers wondered or dared to ask their women, "Where *did* you learn to do *that?*" The one art form to emerge specifically from the carnage—Dadaism—bellowed a resounding "no" to all prewar conventions, including gender. Surrealism transformed that nihilism into creativity with a movement, formally inaugurated by André Breton's Manifesto of 1924, which explained the Surrealists' goal to express "the real functioning of the mind." And the mind, they learned from Freud and confirmed by interpreting their own dreams, was brimming with libido, often not neatly divided between His and Hers. Picasso shared the Surrealist conviction that creative energy was stimulated (not drained, as the Victorians believed) by sexual activity, especially coitus. Since he had spent the prewar years as a Cubist cutting the human body apart and putting it back together, his own synthetic goal was a step ahead of the other Surrealists. He most fully realized that goal with an androgynous sculpture.

In 1931 Picasso sculpted a head inspired by his lover Marie-Thérèse Walter. He sculpted four more versions over the next year in ever more geometric and sexually androgynous forms. The largest version, *Head of a Woman* (Figure 29, 1932), achieved the unification of male and female sexuality he sought. The nose fused with the forehead has become a phallus; the soft open lips have become a vagina. The right cheek and the rounded form of the original model's bun of hair at the back form the two buttocks, which are penetrated by the shaft of the neck, making a powerful symbol of sexual intercourse. The prominence of the rounded buttocks suggest a man's ap-

29. Pablo Picasso, *Head of a Woman*, 1932.

proach to a woman from behind, which would avoid the distraction of eye contact between the man and the woman; but Picasso seeks to unify subject and object as well as male and female and so he includes a symbol of vision, the almond-shaped eye incised on the cheek/buttock. By situating this androgynous image of copulation in the head, Picasso has further accented the importance of knowing sex as well as seeing it. Eve disobeyed God by eating an apple from the tree of knowledge, and Christianity defined that disobedience as sexual transgression. Picasso's head looks back on that tradition with brazen contempt out of an eye located on the surface of a buttock that frames a sexual penetration.[29]

The similarity between Picasso's fascination with his androgynous sculpture and Brancusi's fascination with an androgynous kiss suggests that both may have reflected broad cultural concerns in addition to personal experience. In war and peace Picasso carted around casts or originals of his five sculptures of the androgynous heads, displayed them prominently in his homes, and reproduced versions of the "Great Head" in hundreds of oil paintings, drawings, etchings, and sculptures.[30] The different meanings of this head, which appears in twenty out of the forty-six etchings of *The Sculptor's Studio* (1933–1934), reveal how the unifying image of androgyny in Picasso's art linked the creative process, sexual union, and love. Three etchings show a young, a mature, and finally an old sculptor laboring intently upon the head, indicating that this image had been and might well continue to be a life-long preoccupation. In six other etchings the artist and model are naked, and both look with fascination upon the completed head displayed on a pedestal. In some of these they touch the head while examining it, as if preparing to make a collective judgment. In some the head gives off rays of illumination, signifying the magical and oracular power of art. Three other etchings are visions of fulfillment—the model lies in the artist's arms and they no longer look at the head. The creative process is completed, for a time. In one etching, *Sculptor and Model Viewing Sculptured Head* (Figure 30, 1933), the artist looks away as if his doubly creative acts have been discharged to satisfaction, though tinged with melancholy. The model stares forthrightly at the viewer and drapes a loving arm around the artist's neck. Both are rewarded for their labors with garlands in their hair. The androgynous head is rendered with a few simple lines. It anchors this image of fulfillment by unifying the most intriguing and tormenting dualisms that divide human experience—subject and object, mind and body, male and female, artist and model, sex and art. The opposition of the sexes is here momentarily quieted for the desirous man and woman, more abidingly resolved for them in their roles of artist and model, and permanently fused in the sculpture.

Androgyny pervades modern literature. Proust, Gide, Colette, Forster, Mann, Lawrence, Joyce, Hall, Musil, Rilke, and Hemingway reflect on the concept and create characters with depolarized gender roles. The key to *The Waste Land* is, ironically, the blind "spectator" Tiresias. He is also androgynous, because in him, as Eliot explains in notes to the poem, "the two sexes meet." Woolf repeatedly invokes the androgynous theme as a vision of unity in life and love. In *The Voyage Out* (1915) a woman describes her

30. Pablo Picasso, *Sculptor and Model Viewing Sculptured Head,* 1933.

husband as "man and woman as well"; in *Night and Day* (1919) Katherine and Cassandra "represented very well the manly and the womanly sides of the feminine nature"; in *To the Lighthouse* (1927) there is "manliness in [the Ramsay girls'] girlish hearts"; and in *Orlando* (1928) the hero becomes a woman but retains memories and sensibilities of her former sex. The most famous and most moving discussion is in *A Room of One's Own,* where Woolf ponders how the "androgynous mind" is necessary for the creation of an authentic literary style of one's own.

To appreciate the significance of that "androgynous vision" one must understand the extent to which Woolf's work is built around a critique of sexual dichotomies. She is incensed by the predominance of the masculinity that dominates her world and that she symbolizes variously by the Bank of England, the Indian Empire, Whitaker's Table of Precedency, and even the paltry meals typically served to women at British universities. She represents the conflict between the sexes with a number of masculine-feminine dichotomies: granite vs. rainbow; day vs. night; lighthouse vs. sea; surface vs. depth; fact vs. imagination; linear sentences vs. radial sentences; the House of Commons vs. the nursery; war vs. the feelings of women in a drawing room; Bennett, Galsworthy, and Kipling vs. Austen, the Brontës, and Proust.

A Room of One's Own addresses the question of why there have been no great women novelists. After surveying numerous reasons, Woolf moves toward her conclusion with a meditation on an imaginary novel by an imaginary female novelist, who engages Woolf's interest with an original crafting of a friendship between two women. Woolf imagines that her novelist was made possible by the progress women had made over the past fifty years: "Men were no longer to her 'the opposing faction'; she need not waste her time railing against them . . . Fear and hatred were almost gone." She wrote as a woman who had "forgotten that she [was] a woman, so that her pages were full of that curious sexual quality which comes only when sex is unconscious of itself." But she fell short of greatness. "Something tore, something scratched," Woolf writes. "First she broke the sentence, now she has broken the sequence." Just when the prose was about to probe the depths of a situation and allow Woolf to follow her into those depths, "the annoying creature twitched [her] away, as if the important point were just a little further on." But the novel never got to that point, and Woolf concludes her review with this modest hope—"give her a room of her own and five hundred a year, let her speak her mind and leave out half that she now puts in, and she will write a better book one of these days."

Woolf's final chapter is a moving evocation of the creative process, which centers on an interpretation of the androgynous mind. The problem with most novelists, male or female, is that they think too intently of their own sex and are therefore unable to do justice to the universal themes of great literature. "It is fatal to be a man or woman pure and simple; one must be woman-manly or man-womanly. It is fatal for a woman to lay the least stress on any grievance; to plead even with justice any cause; in any way to speak consciously as a woman." The most accomplished creative mind is not limited by the experience of one time, place, or sex—it is "resonant and porous . . . incandescent and undivided." It is open to experience but at peace with itself. It is a fusion of the passionate intensities of male and female sexuality, able to range freely across the sexual divide and return to "lie back and . . . celebrate its nuptials in darkness."

In documenting the many problems women writers face Woolf committed the very literary fatalities she was about to proscribe—stressing a grievance, pleading a just cause, speaking consciously as a woman. But she caught herself and opened up the essay with a commentary on what she saw when she stopped to look out the window—a man and woman came from opposite sides of the street, entered a taxi together, and drove off. A simple ordinary occurrence. Why did it give her such pleasure? She answers herself. "Perhaps to think, as I had been thinking these two days, of one sex as distinct from the other is an effort. It interferes with the unity of the mind. Now that effort had ceased and that unity had been restored by seeing two people come together and get into a taxicab." Amidst all the protesting about the history of patriarchal oppression, all the grievances and ambitious projects for reform, the artist searches for a simple, clear vision of the truth, as Picasso searched for a simple form to unify the abiding dichotomies of human existence with his androgynous sculpture. Woolf similarly shaped this simple narrative into a metaphor for the unity of the sexes. It gave her great pleasure not only because it relieved her of the tension she had sustained in keeping the sexes at odds, but because it was an image of joy itself. "One had a profound, if irrational, instinct in favour of the theory that the union of man and woman makes for the greatest satisfaction, the most complete happiness." This moment of simple happiness is the transition between Woolf's complex analysis of her imaginary novelist and her theorizing about the androgynous foundation of literature, because the vision of the couple suggests to Woolf that there may also be "two sexes in the mind corresponding to the two sexes in the body," which must be united to achieve happiness as well as great literature and art.

Picasso and Woolf searched for an image that would retain the magnificent differences between the sexes and still capture the naturalness and joy of their fusion. And it had to be simple. For both that image was inspired by the concept of androgyny, which they shared with many other writers and artists, as well as biological, medical, and social scientists who sought some way out of the rigidly codified gender dichotomy that constricted the relations between the sexes in earlier times. Woolf's title refers to the material necessities for great literature, but it also implies a spirit, equally necessary for the production of authentic love and art—that men and women learn to create gender roles of their very own.

10 Power

AUTHENTIC loving includes reflecting on the meaning of loving a unique other as free as possible from the unreflective routine of what the crowd of others do in love. To grasp the meaning of love requires an effort of will or creative power. The theoretical foundation for this element I have adapted from Nietzsche's philosophy of the will to power *(Wille zur Macht)*.

By 1870 several Western theorists speculated about the fundamental natural force that drove human activity. For Darwin it was a basic struggle to survive, for Marx it was biological need, and for Mill it was pursuit of pleasure. Nietzsche rejected these and instead suggested a will to power. How this concept functions in his philosophy is the subject of much scholarly debate. In places Nietzsche implies a cosmology with the will to power as the basic force of the universe. In other places he implies a psychology with the will to power as a motivating force in human activity.[1] And in still other places, central to his contribution to existentialism, he approaches the will to power phenomenologically and views it as a basic will to meaning.

The standard English translation of "power" misses the broader sense of the German *Macht*, which comes from *machen* and means "to make."[2] Before we can struggle to survive, satisfy biological need, or seek pleasure, we must be able to make something out of, or give form to, ourselves in the presence of what we encounter. That ability is the foundation for all derivative struggling, satisfying, and seeking. In *Thus Spoke Zarathustra* Nietzsche succinctly proclaimed the fundamentality of that creative will to meaning.

This profound philosophy of power grounds the derivative conception of power as a natural force that men wielded over women, often loosely referred to as "patriarchy."[3] Correctly understood, the will to power includes power over others, including physical power, but more importantly it involves power over one's self as one strives to reinterpret the world. It is thus power over one's own habits and meanings, over one's own past itself, which tend to become ingrained and hold back innovation. Such self-overcoming is most fully accomplished in one who is able to bear a great load, reconsider all hitherto ruling values, make new values, and affirm them with joy.

Deficiencies in the exercise of the will to power put one under the power of others. As Zarathustra proclaims: "Whatever lives, obeys," and "he who cannot obey himself is commanded" (114). Although all human beings have a will to power, individuals and cultures exercise it differently, and hence it has a history. Commanding others also has a history. As women increasingly realized their own will to power they diminished the ability of men to command them. Interpretation of the history of their struggle against "patriarchy" must be grounded in understanding of a more fundamental struggle that women *and* men fought to become victorious over themselves.

What does this have to do with the history of love? Nietzsche's exhortation to self-overcoming includes an exhortation to the highest love, which he believed was the foundation of virtue itself. He is unrelenting in criticizing the mindless, all-too-common marriage as a "wretched contentment in pair!" Love between men and women must be rather between two powerful, form-giving individuals—each "the self-conqueror." They must be commanders of their senses, legislators of their own meaning and virtue. As Zarathustra exhorts, "When you are above praise and blame, and your will wants to command all things, like a lover's will: there is the origin of your virtue" (76). Being "above praise and blame" does not mean being immoral. Nietzsche never exempts lovers from being good but rather identifies their "best love" as the source of their ability to understand what is good.

His conception of a "best love" is in accord with his larger philosophy of the way to the overman. Just as the individual can succeed or fail on that way, so lovers may also succeed or fail in love. Success in love involves awareness of the meaning of love, which is a function of the will to power.

Under historical circumstances in which public sanctions of power were unequally distributed between the sexes, women saw power as something to be wrested from men. Most men also did not distinguish between a creative will to power in the forming of the self in the presence of a beloved and a destructive will to power over a beloved that flourishes in the battle of the sexes. Whatever women got, these men reasoned, must be taken from men. In the heat of battle one does not think about the ultimate foundations or highest possibilities of human existence. The idea that women's increasing powers could facilitate a more meaningful loving for men emerged only slowly.

All men and women are born with the same fundamental will to power, the same potential ability to fathom the meaning of their existence. Access to power in the world, however, differs for men and women, and that difference changed historically as a result of developments in education, work, law, and politics. In the late nineteenth century the grudging admission of women to university education slowly opened up to them the power of knowledge and in consequence of that, the more respected professions. New laws also gave women control over their money, property, and bodies. In 1891, for example, English courts determined that "a husband had no right to carry off his wife by force or to imprison her until she submitted to his wishes." [4] In the twentieth century women's right to vote became a reality. These new sources of power changed the way women took command of themselves and loved men.

Throughout this period of dynamic feminist achievement, men's power over women diminished. This change is evident in three pairs of paintings. The first pair (showing a man with a female sphinx) and the second pair (showing a knight rescuing a woman) emphasize women acquiring a greater share of power in contrast to men. The third pair (showing a male watching a sleeping woman) indicates a growing realization of the creative will to power in loving.

I

Changing attitudes toward physical strength in women may be seen by comparing Gustave Moreau's *Oedipus and the Sphinx* (Figure 31, 1864) with Franz von Stuck's *Kiss of the Sphinx* (Figure 32, 1895). Although these paintings show different moments in the mythological confrontation, they both depict the power of the sphinx as a woman in relation to a man. They also share a fascination with woman's power, since in both paintings the sphinx is the more intriguing figure, magically compounded of distinctive parts of animals noted for special powers.

In Moreau's version every aspect of the sphinx's potential strength is compromised. She has a lion's body, but it is adorned by a seductive red waist chain. She has sprung onto Oedipus but cannot dig in her claws, because he is protected by his green chlamys. Her eagle's wings do not enable her to swoop down from great heights but merely maintain her balance. Her firm, conical breast seems more protecting than tempting, and Oedipus is shielded from contact with her breast by his chlamys. Her tiara beautifies more than it symbolizes power. Her face is not ferocious but placid, with eyes open wide in amazement at his clever answer to her riddle. Her lips are slightly parted in surprise, not pouted to deliver the fatal kiss. Her terrifying powers are implied by the rib cage of a former victim in the foreground cavern, but her appearance contradicts her reputation as a slayer of men. Her killer instinct is further impugned by the dark humor of the upward projecting foot and clutching dead hand of another recent victim.

Oedipus's head is positioned for a classical kiss, looking down at the sphinx's upturned face, but he is obviously not going to deliver it. He is securely balanced to turn away—strong, youthful, and armed. Despite her anatomical supplements from the king of the jungle and ruler of the skies, Oedipus is in command, for he has solved the riddle and, according to Theban myth, will destroy the sphinx.

In stark contrast Von Stuck depicts a variant of that myth in which the sphinx does not perish when Oedipus correctly solves the riddle but tries to seduce him with a kiss. Although she is wingless, her powerful shoulders and arms crush the man into abject submission, as indicated by his strained neck, arched back, flailing arm, and bent toes. Forced to kneel, his posture implies ecstatic adoration of the godlike sphinx on high. One of his hands rests on her powerful back while the other helplessly reaches into the air. Even his lips are forced open by her plunging kiss. She also has eight suffocating breasts, two of which bear down on the man's already overtaxed windpipe. With this image Von Stuck created an icon of the *femme fatale*, but her deadly force does not derive from conventional female seductiveness; the sexual content of this image is subordinated to physical strength.

In the thirty years separating these paintings, the feminist movements that sprang up in Europe and America made a visible impact. While the power of Moreau's sphinx is blunted, Von Stuck's moves in on her victim like a true queen of the jungle devouring its prey. The symbols and artistic quotations that adorn Moreau's crowded scene buffer the action from the actuality of a sexual fight between a man and a woman that is its central theme.[5] In contrast, Von Stuck has clarified the power struggle by simplifying the scene. His image is transitional. It shows no authentic will to power but simply a female sphinx overpowering a man. But that transition is part of a historical movement which saw women more willing to develop their physical strength, use it on men they loved, and reflect on its value.

In the mid-Victorian novel a heroine would rarely exert physical strength in the presence of a man she loved. Muscles were not ladylike. Jane Eyre lends a shoulder to support Rochester when he falls off his horse but there-

31. Gustave Moreau, *Oedipus and the Sphinx*, 1864.

after pursues him without a hint of physical strength. Rochester's wife Bertha shows demonic strength, but she is motivated by hatred, not love. The other female characters in the novel rely on conventional female sources of power—resignation (Helen Burns), self-control (Miss Temple), coquetry (Adele and Céline), high birth and beauty (Blanche Ingram).

In Gaskell's *North and South* Margaret admires men's "exultation in the

32. Franz von Stuck, *Kiss of the Sphinx*, 1895.

sense of power." Her one feat of physical strength occurs while she comes to
the rescue of her beloved Thornton. When he is besieged by angry workers,
she lifts the heavy iron bar of the door "with an imperious force" and faces
the workers. Then she throws her arms around Thornton and is struck in
the forehead by a rock. She faints, Thornton sweeps her into his arms, lays
her on a sofa, and declares, "Oh, my Margaret—my Margaret! . . . cold as
you lie there, you are the only woman I ever loved!" Their first touch from
her protective impulse is the turning point in their love, because Thornton
continues to fixate on her extraordinary daring, which he remembers as
a loving caress. "Everything seemed dim and vague beyond—behind—
besides the touch of her arms round his neck—the soft clinging which made
the dark color come and go in his cheek as he thought of it" (244). The

historical significance of her gesture is not its show of physical strength but Thornton's recollection of it as a caress.

Far different is Lena's show of strength in Conrad's *Victory* (1915). Ricardo, one of the three villains threatening Heyst, attacked Lena in her cabin. During the scuffle Ricardo's first words were, "You have fingers like steel. Jimminy! You have muscles like a giant!" She defended herself "by maintaining a desperate, murderous clutch on Ricardo's windpipe," and when he relaxed his hold, "with a supreme effort of her arms and of her suddenly raised knee, she sent him flying against the partition" (237). Unlike Margaret, whose saving gesture is witnessed by Thornton and immediately rewarded, Lena must hide her attack from Heyst and pretend complicity with the villains in order to help Heyst, even though she may have some doubts about his love. Since she and Heyst are without a weapon, Lena tantalizes Ricardo sexually in order to get his knife. In a final showdown another villain accidentally shoots Lena in the breast. Dying, she asks for the knife she had taken from Ricardo—a distinctively twentieth-century symbol of a woman's victory.

Lena uses the new women's powers for loving. She has fingers "like steel" and uses her strength, as Conrad explains, with "full, clear knowledge" of the danger as well as the meaning of her action. She uses her sexuality not to inspire a rescuing knight but to augment her limited physical strength in saving her man, and she is not morally devalued in the process. She is also able to express the meaning of her triumph in loving. "I've saved you!" she exclaims to Heyst, "Why don't you take me into your arms and carry me out of this lonely place?" (336). He makes a final loving gesture just before she dies, but to the end he is unable to express his love in words and seems far less able than she is to reflect on its meaning. Lena thus loves more authentically than Heyst, and her victory locates the frontal edge of this novel's place in history.

Her physical power is no isolated instance. In Gissing's *The Odd Women* Miss Barfoot delivers a feminist speech urging that women must "carry on an active warfare—must be invaders" (136). Ann Veronica is athletic and forthright in expressing the connection between her strength and her ability to love. One of the women of *Herland*, with some help from her friends, manages to overpower the most recalcitrant male chauvinist visitor who expected "to force her to love him as her master." He goes into a rage at having "the sturdy athletic furious woman rise up and master him" (142). The heroine of West's "Indissoluble Matrimony" has strong arms, and as her husband tries to drown her she resists "in turmoil, in movement, in action." When he returns home to discover that she had escaped and lies calmly asleep in their bed, he realizes that "bodies like his do not kill bodies like hers."

These women do not actually overpower men, but they do have muscles and flex them in struggles to protect love, to pursue love, or to free themselves from conventional ways of loving which devalued any expression of women's strength. There were other ways to experience the will to power in love and reflect on its significance, but to discover them men and women first had to kill the rescuing knight.

II

Changing values attached to knights rescuing women are illustrated by a second pair of paintings—Frank Dicksee's *Chivalry* (Figure 33, 1885) and Oskar Kokoschka's *Knight Errant* (Figure 34, 1915). The title of Dicksee's painting celebrates a code of conduct for medieval knights, who were supposed to fight for their lords, uphold the Church, protect the weak, and defend the honor of their ladies fair with courage, loyalty, and courtesy. Over the centuries the military value of the knight died out, but the code of behavior was still taken seriously and persisted in song, literature, and art. Throughout the nineteenth century the popular novels of Sir Walter Scott told of clanging armor and rattling drawbridge chains, of swooning maidens and knights with ladies' favors pinned to their helmet. Victorian art is full of sword-bearing, powerful men in suits of armor rescuing vulnerable women in various states of undress from ferocious monsters or evil knights—St. George and the Dragon, Perseus rescuing Andromeda (who is not only naked but chained to a rock), and a knight errant rescuing a maiden in distress (often shackled to a tree).

Rescue fantasies aim at power reversal. A man may fantasize about rescuing a woman with whom he feels powerless in order to put her in his debt and gain power for himself. But even actual rescues fail because, for a man's power to become genuine, he must develop it out of his own self and not "win" it in a contest with a rival by rescuing his beloved. Moreover, powerful women who make men feel powerless do not need rescuing. The prevalence of such fantasies in Victorian art and literature indicates not how powerful men were but how imperiled their powers were beginning to seem.

Since this art was produced by men, we must assume that it was intended

33. Frank Dicksee, *Chivalry*, 1885.

34. Oskar Kokoschka, *Knight Errant*, 1915.

to assuage their fears about that loss. Women may have shared in these fantasies for a time, but as they acceded to new sources of power, the maiden's fantasy of being saved by a knight lost its appeal. Monsters and evil knights symbolize forces beyond our control, hence the terror of their evil. As women became more powerful and more aware of their power, they did not accept the image of all worldly power embodied in rescuing knights. By the early twentieth century, love based on the chivalric code was becoming, like the armor that protected the rescuing knight, a museum artifact.

The undermining of that code is apparent in the differences between these two paintings. Dicksee's knight errant has all physical power—the evil knight has been vanquished and lies on the ground underfoot; the woman is tied to a tree. He has "won" the love of the damsel in distress by rescuing her from rape. In contrast, Kokoschka's knight cannot rescue anyone, for he has lost his power and is where no knight ought to be—on the ground, lying on his back. He has also lost his love. In fact, he has lost his self. The German title, *Der irrende Ritter,* captures the pervasive sense of loss the English translation does not convey. *Irren* means to be mistaken, lost, deceived, confused, delirious, even insane and not merely wandering or possibly misguided as the English "errant" implies. Kokoschka comments on the meaning of power in relation to love with this image of spectral disorientation and knightly failure. He shows that superior masculine physical strength is useless in love, that armor will not protect but weighs one down, that the chivalric code is obsolete, and that love cannot be "won" by rescuing a powerless woman. His painting interrogates the meaning of power itself.

The painting also refers to personal experiences concerning the two other figures—the small sphinx with Alma Mahler's face at the right and the flying creature with the artist's own face in the distant sky. As he worked on this painting in 1915, Kokoschka's three-year affair with Alma was about to end. Her refusal to marry him and especially her decision to abort his child against his wish precipitated the final rupture. The figure in the sky may symbolize the departed spirit of the aborted fetus.[6] These personal determinants do not diminish the broader historical significance of this painting, evident from its ironic title and from the humiliating position of the knight in dated historic dress.

The sole power of Dicksee's tethered maiden is her passive sexual allurement, tantalizingly revealed by her exquisite profile and bare shoulder. Alma has different resources. After her conquest she is resting and reflective with head in hand, strangely like Rodin's thinker. And although her way of getting ahead in the world was dependent on her husbands (Gustav Mahler, Walter Gropius, and later Franz Werfel) and liaisons such as this with Kokoschka, the power of these men did not come from conventional sources of patriarchal domination. Moreover, Alma was noted for her own intelligence and strength of personality as well as seductive beauty.

Kokoschka's *irrend* knight also has a lot to think about. Deprived of his "erroneous" knightly powers, he must contemplate the meaning of a love for a woman who tumbled him from the saddle and then aborted his child without his consent. She exercised power over her own body in a way that would have been highly unusual, if not unthinkable, for her Victorian predecessors. Although Kokoschka makes no explicit iconographical reference to women exercising such power, Alma's decision to exercise control over her reproductive power contributed to the downfall of Kokoschka's effort at courtly love, which is unmistakably evident.

In painting, eyes are the clearest index to consciousness. Dicksee focuses on an external object and symbol of combat—the mighty sword. The rescued woman looks toward it gratefully, the conquering knight proudly eyes its tip going into the scabbard, and the defeated knight (if he is still alive) stares at it in mortal terror. But in Kokoschka, there is no central focus or even external seeing, for all three figures focus within. The woman is absorbed in contemplation. The bird-child turns to look down upon himself as the toppled knight, whose crossed eyes seem also to turn inward, as if searching for a way to resuscitate new powers within. In authentic loving, consciousness is mightier than the sword.

Kokoschka's unhorsed knight is a reference to that last hurrah of chivalry—World War I. The first British cavalry charge was on August 24, 1914. There were no more.[7] After that the cavalry was used largely to deliver messages, and even that function was increasingly taken over by the telephone and wireless. Although the horsed rider quickly ceased to be a viable fighting force, the imagery of chivalry was ubiquitous, and throughout the war remained a potent, though mythic, resource of power. When the soldiers came home, the myth slammed into reality.

The mythology of the war was that powerful and courageous men were marching, shouting, and killing to protect weak women. But the reality of the war was otherwise. The men were in fact terrified by their powerlessness under machine-gun fire and artillery bombardments. They were exposed to filth, disease, pain, killing, and being killed, all of which obliterated their feelings and their identity. What remained of their sexual desire was channeled into masturbation, prostitution, and even some instances of sodomy (bestiality) in the cavalry. The war dirtied the soldiers' sexy uniforms, anesthetized their senses, mutilated their bodies, and provided various incomplete, unsatisfying, and dangerous sexual outlets that destroyed their ability to live up to or even identify with prewar masculine roles, let alone the mythology of the rescuing knight.

In the myth men were active and productive while women were passive and helpless, but in reality the men were doing nothing productive (killing was emotionally and morally destructive), while the women were actively seeking out the few eligible men at home, running households, educating children, and learning new "masculine" skills which required muscular strength—shoveling coal, shoeing horses, fighting fires, chopping down trees, making shells, digging graves.[8] The horizon of men was narrow, often not more than a few hundred yards of no-man's-land where they lived from moment to moment, while women were running ambulances at the front and driving buses back home, where they could also read about the war and conceive of it in a broader geographical and historical perspective. For the nurses, even watching and attending the wounded assumed a more active and productive form than in past wars. Alonzo Foringer's Red Cross Relief poster, *The Greatest Mother in the World* (Figure 35, 1918), captures the war's triple overpowering of man as casualty, child, and sacrifice. In this visual echo of a *pietà*, a truly pitiful soldier, miniaturized and infantilized, with bandaged hands and eyes, is cradled in the powerful arms of *the* greatest mother in the world—a formidable composite image of nurse, mother, and Madonna.

These contrasting wartime experiences shaped the profound revision in power relations that emerged afterwards as women, so long separated and protected from their own men, emerged with stronger characters and more aggressive functions in areas that had formerly been exclusive male preserves. In addition many men, crippled from the shelling and from the overwhelming powerlessness of trench warfare, needed women as they had never needed them before, especially to resume normal sexual functions and restore or create meaningful loves. The reality of war redistributed to women public outlets for the expression of their will to power, and in the immediate postwar years gender roles and love relations were a composite of both the reality and the mythology and moved contrapuntally across the landscape of the war and its aftermath, intensifying the discourses of power and gender that had arisen in the prewar period and creating the distinctively new love relations that persisted into the next decade.

Red Cross
Christmas
Roll Call
Dec. 16-23ᵈ

The
GREATEST MOTHER
in the WORLD

35. Alonzo Earl Foringer, *The Greatest Mother in the World*, 1918.

The erosion of the chivalric code in literature can be traced in three novels. In *Ranthorpe* it is still in place. Percy and Harry do not fight physically
over Isola, but they negotiate her fate chivalrously. Harry says to Percy:
"Tell me that she rejected you, because her word was pledged to me—and
she is yours!" Momentarily bewildered, Percy then realizes what to do and
"recovering himself he walked up to him, holding out his hand in silence. In
silence it was taken, and one long significant pressure was all these two
bruised hearts could find to express their emotion" (311). Fifty-two years
later, in *The Awakening*, Edna will not allow men to dispose of her love with
a gentlemanly handshake. She chastises her lover for requiring that her husband set her free. "You have been a very, very foolish boy, wasting your time
dreaming of impossible things when you speak of Mr. Pontellier setting me

free! I am no longer one of Mr. Pontellier's possessions to dispose of or not. I give myself where I choose. If he were to say, 'Here Robert, take her and be happy; she is yours,' I should laugh at you both" (106). In *A Room with a View* both the author and his hero George agree about the obsolescence of the chivalric code. Forster comments: "The only relationship which Cecil conceived was feudal: that of protector and protected. He had no glimpse of the comradeship after which the girl's soul yearned" (179). Then George adds a moral twist when he tells Lucy: "He [Cecil] daren't let a woman decide. He's the type who's kept Europe back for a thousand years. Every moment of his life he's forming you, telling you what's charming or amusing or ladylike, telling you what a man thinks womanly." When Lucy charges George with also wanting to control her, he concedes: "Yes . . . I'm the same kind of brute at bottom. This desire to govern a woman—it lies very deep, and men and women must fight it together before they shall enter the garden" (194–195). George echoes Nietzsche's insight that in the "best love" the impulse to command one another must be fought by men and women in order for them to become victorious over themselves.

III

In the art of antiquity and revived in the Renaissance, one popular theme was a sleeping female observed by a desirous male, frequently a nymph observed by a lewd satyr. Leo Steinberg has documented the history of this theme and interpreted its power relations: "Inevitably in these situations a helpless sleeper is exposed to the relative omnipotence of an intruder; and the imbalance of power provides the whole plot." [9] In William Etty's *Sleeping Nymph and Satyrs* (Figure 36, 1828) one satyr's sexual desire is but momentarily restrained by a companion, who also no doubt has plans of his own. Etty distributes the power of desire unequally between the sexes, not only by depriving the female of consciousness but also by veiling her genitals and by figuratively veiling her eroticism with his title, because the sleeping "nymph" (supposedly a guardian of chastity) is actually a maenad—a devotee of Dionysian orgies, indicated by her ankle bracelet and tambourine. Her languorous body is twisted improbably in sleep to enable the viewer of the painting to observe both satyrs indulging their erotic fantasies uncomplicated by even the slight interference of a returned gaze. Etty contrasts the dark, hairy, horned, hoofed, and muscular forces of masculine sexual desire with this luminous, large-breasted woman rendered unconscious and vulnerable, if not entirely powerless, in sleep.

Etty's painting is early for my periodization, but it captures mid-Victorian sensibilities, exaggerated by the mythological actors.[10] Picasso was fascinated with sleepwatchers and painted them throughout his career. His *Sleeping Nude* (Figure 37, 1904) contrasts sharply with these earlier sleepwatchers and provides a distinctly modern image of a redistribution of power between the sexes.

The power of Etty's "nymph" is her ability to evoke desire in her observers, even though her pubis, the seat of her own desire and focus of theirs, is covered. The pubis of Picasso's nude is not covered, but her powers do not seem to originate there so much as in her mind. In contrast to the satyr's muscular animalistic body, Picasso's sleepwatcher is thin and weak. His hands are crammed uselessly in his pockets. His height does not suggest towering masculine strength but great distance from a seemingly untouchable naked woman. The angular thrust of his head is like that of a broken twig. But he has another source of power—reflection. While the satyr's eyes bulge toward the nymph, the eyes of Picasso's sleepwatcher, dark and deepset, seem to look within, as if searching for a way to deal with the overwhelming presence of a beloved who lies naked and yet unattainable in sleep. Ironically, his "advantage" is useless—he must wake her up or wait. But if he renounces the bogus advantage of wakefulness, which might give him momentary physical power over the sleeping nude, there is another more abiding power of creation, one which Picasso portrays in a companion watercolor (also from 1904)—*Woman Sleeping (Meditation)*—which shows the sleepwatcher seated at a desk with head in hand, thinking but looking away from the same peacefully sleeping woman, now clad in a nightgown. By giving this sleepwatcher his own face, Picasso has transformed the will to power in love as a subject of painting into the will to create itself. The sleepwatcher-artist is shown summoning his own creative energies, and the sleeping female is no longer an opportunity for sexual indulgence but one for reflection on the possibility of art as well as love.

Literature covers the same ground. Hardy crafts a classic Victorian seduction in *Tess of the d'Urbervilles* by having his heroine taken by Alec while she is asleep. Hardy tells his reader, with typical Victorian euphemism, that "upon this beautiful feminine tissue, sensitive as gossamer, and practically blank as snow [was] traced such a coarse pattern" (62–63). But Tess does not realize that she has had sex until some time later, when she discovers that she is pregnant. When Victorian women slept under the gaze of desirous males they were powerless.

Already in the 1890s, according to Nina Auerbach, the powerless "Angel

36. William Etty, *Sleeping Nymph and Satyrs*, 1828.

in the House" began to recapture the demonic powers that had been wrested
from the imposing, and originally male, angels of early Christendom. Auerbach argues that the supposedly mesmerized, mastered, hypnotized women
in George Du Maurier's *Trilby* (1894), Bram Stoker's *Dracula* (1897), and
Freud's *Studies on Hysteria* (1895) actually controlled their magus/masters,
whose very fascination with their "helpless" and quasi-sleeping female subjects was a token of the masters' own subjugation. Beneath the manifest
powers that male characters had over females in these works, women were
granted considerable latent powers: "the victim of paralysis possesses seemingly infinite capacities of regenerative being that turn on her triumphant
mesmerizer and paralyze him in turn."[11]

     Three twentieth-century literary works question the power available to a
man observing a woman asleep. In the volume titled "The Captive" from
Proust's *Remembrance of Things Past* Marcel takes Albertine into his apartment and attempts to regulate her movements in order to minimize the jealousy that her lesbian affairs cause him. He partially succeeds in controlling
her activities but is unable to regulate her errant consciousness, which seems

37. Pablo Picasso, *Sleeping Nude,* 1904.

to be "captive" only when he observes her asleep. "[Then] her personality was not constantly escaping, as when we talked, by the outlets of her unacknowledged thoughts and of her eyes. She had called back into herself everything of her that lay outside, had withdrawn, enclosed, reabsorbed herself into her body. In keeping it in front of my eyes, in my hands, I had an impression of possessing her entirely which I never had when she was awake" (III, 64). Marcel's rumination is distinctively twentieth-century, because it interrogates those bombastic nineteenth-century phantasies of the power of the sleepwatcher and because his claim to possess "entirely" the sleeping

Albertine is patently erroneous. The novel emphasizes how elusive or over-whelming Albertine could be in sleep or even after her death. In this passage Proust becomes momentarily an incompetent narrator, proclaiming his pos-session of a consciousness that could not be possessed and that even in sleep rather made *him* the captive.

Marcel's more active involvement with Albertine's sleeping mocks the tra-ditional fantasy of the sleepwatching male in some mythic land, preparing for his triumphant sexual indulgence. Marcel acts out the fantasy in his stuffy Paris apartment and reports the pathetic details; for in addition to sleepwatching, Marcel would cozy up to Albertine, clasp her waist in one arm, kiss her cheek, and, he confesses, place his "free hand on her heart and then on every part of her body in turn." Sometimes his "embarkation" on her tide of sleep afforded him another pleasure that was "less pure." This possession was not just of her tamed unconsciousness: "The sound of her breathing, which had grown louder, might have given the illusion of the panting of sexual pleasure, and when mine was at its climax, I could kiss her." At such times he claims to have "possessed her more completely, like an unconscious and unresisting object of dumb nature" (III, 67). But that last description applies rather to the jealous quasi-necrophilic himself.

Marcel's "possession" of Albertine's sleeping mind and body both fail. He is as captivated by her asleep as he is by her awake. His sexual potency, so devastated by her affairs, is further degraded by his nocturnal naughtiness with her sleeping body. Proust's account of the illusory power of the sleep-watching male reflects, as it reinterprets, a historical redistribution of power between the sexes.

In "Indissoluble Matrimony" the physical strength that Evadne used to escape her murderous husband continued to overpower him even after he returned from the lake and found her asleep. Her jaws and throat appeared powerful and threatening; her breasts and hips seemed mountainous. He stood before this "great lusty creature" and "sneezed exhaustingly." Lusty satyrs and Victorian lovers did not sneeze. West's final description of Evadne's husband contrasts sharply with the image of powerful satyrs: "Now his soul was naked and lonely as though the walls of his body had fallen in at death, and the grossness of Evadne's sleep made him suffer . . . He had thought he had had what every man most desires: one night of power over a woman for the business of murder or love. But it had been a lie." West and Proust dramatize the realignment of power between the sexes in emphasizing how even the sleeping woman is not vulnerable but potent and self-sufficient: she presents to the sleepwatching male not an opportunity for sexual indulgence but an occasion for reflection on the impossibility of possessing anyone.

Colette's Renée allows herself to fall asleep in the presence of three male visitors to her study. She grows sleepy, changes into a kimono, and dozes off. When she awakens only her zealous suitor Max is present. Her description of him is remarkably like one of Picasso's sleepwatchers—"Standing beside me, the Big-Noodle [as she calls him] looms as high as the room . . . His face is so far above me in the shadow that I can't make it out." As he begins to move back she is relieved: "I had had enough of seeing him towering so close to me!" He is astonished that she had the temerity to fall asleep with three men present. He charges, "It's crazy to fall asleep like that! Before Hammond, and even before me! It's obvious that you've no idea how you look when you're asleep." He is unnerved by the "joy" on her sleeping face. "You haven't the face of a woman asleep," he says, "you . . . well, damn it, you know very well what I'm trying to say! It's revolting. When I think that you must have slept in that way before a heap of people, I don't know what I couldn't do to you!" His double negative is revealing, for he is paralyzed by her self-possession and thoroughly unable to do anything about it.

Renée gives her own reaction to waking up under his looming face. "I am not afraid; on the contrary it is a relief to me to find him sincere." Their brief post-nap confrontation breaks into a shared reflection on the deficiencies and glories of their respective ways of loving, and she begins to respond warmly. "Once again," she explains, "there reappears before me, with his childish rage, his bestial persistence, his calculated sincerity, my enemy and my tormentor: love." This thoughtful personification of love distinguishes her waking moment from the way we might expect Etty's nymph to awaken, at the mercy of satyrs venting primordial sexual rage. Colette's last reference to Renée's waking underscores her heroine's independence. As Renée takes the mirror to powder her nose Max asks: "Whoever d'you want to put powder on for, at this hour?" And she replies, "For myself, in the first place. And then for you" (105–107). Mythic nymphs, nineteenth-century women, and other powerless women powdered only for others.

In the course of a historical period in which women fought for and won concrete new powers from men in education, work, law, and politics, the battle of the sexes to triumph *over* each other overshadowed the ultimately more rewarding triumph of gaining more power for each when together *with* one another. Winning the vote shaped the ways of love, to be sure, but it also tended to distract men and women from the equally difficult non-combative exchanges of tenderness, vulnerability, and downright silliness that are only possible between those who are secure in themselves, willing to reflect on the meaning and limits of their respective powers, and able to share those reflections with a beloved. The men and women depicted in my first two pairs of paintings were too busy with the battle to see the possibility, let alone the desirability, of a shared conquest of themselves together in love.

The final pair of images and the literary accounts of sleepwatchers illustrate movement toward a distinctively modern mode of the will to power in love, which centered in reflection rather than in muscles or sex organs. The woman watched sleeping, traditionally an icon of powerlessness, emerges in the twentieth century with as much power of reflection as her male observer if not more. And with that change this disturbing imagery of the opportunity for love, which was for so long actually a rape contemplated, begins to appear passé. It is replaced by an image of a woman on her own, a seasoned entertainer, awakening calmly and securely in the presence of her vulnerable beloved, sharing with him her anxiety not about being manhandled but about her own vulnerability in loving. Colette ingeniously symbolizes the will to power not with a lion's claws or a mighty sword but with a powder puff. She gives a final touch of verisimilitude to this pivotal exchange by having her vagabond casually powder her nose first for herself, then for her beloved, and then—maybe—for everyone else.

11 Others

SO FAR I HAVE considered love between two people, with others making occasional appearances from a shadowy background. In this chapter that background becomes foreground.

Love between even the most hermetic couple is shaped by others. One agency for that shaping is public opinion; and observers after the mid-nineteenth century believed its influence was intensifying. When Mill published *On Liberty* in 1859 democracy was by no means triumphant, but he nevertheless pitched his defense of individual liberty against a growing "tyranny of the majority." For centuries, he argued, individual liberty had to be protected against the tyranny of political rulers, but with the rise of democracy, as those rulers came to represent the people, the threat to liberty came increasingly from society as a whole, peering into private life with the "eye of a hostile and dreaded censorship." Improvements in communication and transportation wiped out individuality formerly preserved by remoteness, and society formed "a mass of influences hostile to Individuality" (69). Mill's solutions were legal protection of a private realm for society as a whole and "nonconformity" for the individual.

Nietzsche's *Thus Spoke Zarathustra* added an elitist spin to this growing concern about the coercive force of the masses, those "flies of the market-place" that poison whoever aspires to greatness. He preached self-overcoming and, when the crush of others became too great, getting away to solitude where the air is raw and strong.

Heidegger approached the matter differently—instead of asking what caused the growing influence of others or how to minimize or overcome it, he asked how such influence was possible. He began with the simple claim that one is always aware of others as different. Caring about such differences makes one subject to others. He interpreted that subjugation without dramatic examples such as Mill's political tyrants or Nietzsche's poisonous flies. He rather identified a universal, subtle, and yet profound subjugation of an individual not by an invading army but by the mere presence of others. And these others are not definite others. *Who* are they? No one in particular. "The 'who' is the neuter, *the 'they'*" (164).

"The 'they'" is an awkward, but by now standard translation of *das Man*, which is one of the existentials of Dasein. "The 'they'" is not exactly the opinion of others, because it is what I am, what I think myself, but in a way that is not entirely my own. Heidegger elaborates. "We take pleasure and enjoy ourselves as *they* take pleasure; we read, see, and judge about literature and art as *they* see and judge . . . we find 'shocking' what *they* find shocking." "The 'they'" makes everything public, "insensitive to every difference of level and genuineness"; it averages sensibilities and accommodates to everyone and therefore to no one (164–165).

Heidegger invites misreading by using political language with historical and moral implications ("subjugation," "domination") in order to elucidate this existential, which, like all existentials, is universal and essential and calls for no concrete morality. In one such memorable usage he describes how the impersonality of others establishes "the real dictatorship of the 'they'." This political metaphor is misleading because the "dictatorship" is not distinctive to the twentieth century; it is not even imposed from without by a political ruler but arises from within by my acceptance of what "they" do. In fact it is effective only when "they" have no precise identity. Heidegger uses the metaphor to emphasize the enormous power of others when their influence is hidden, when the "dictatorship" is enforced by myself, and when I am unaware of where it gets its power. And when the individual is unaware of himself, he is inauthentic.

Heidegger offers another memorable definition of inauthentic Being-with-others: when "everyone is the other, and no one is himself" (165). This condition is what he calls the *inauthentic they-self*, which takes as its own the everyday world that lies most conveniently close at hand and obscures what one is. The other mode of Being-with-others is that of the *authentic self*, which reflects on the way one is (or loves a beloved) in a world with others. Heidegger insists that this is not an ethical distinction and that he is not intending to point out a way to authentic selfhood. These are simply two modes of being in the world with others. One is not better than the other, and human existence is not possible without both. The individual encounters the inauthentic (impersonal) mode of "the 'they'" first. Only after re-

flecting on the meaning of human existence does he begin to realize the authentic self. The inauthentic they-self grounds the authentic self, which is a
specific (and never fully realized) instance of the they-self, because one is
always in the world of others and always partially distracted from absolutely personal self-reflection.

I have been unable to assess the history of love from a position of ethical
neutrality because many aspects of Victorian love, as opposed to modern
love, merit moral disapproval. I nevertheless believe that Heidegger succeeded in identifying fundamental aspects of being human, however much
their modes may vary historically and elicit ethical evaluation. The remainder of this chapter surveys some of those changing modes—specifically how
lovers became aware of the dominion of "the 'they'" by coming to understand that the ways of love are shaped by their own acceptance of what
"they" do. The chapter will proceed from impersonal society to more identifiable others: parents and God.

I

The novels reveal society in five structuring roles: keeping lovers apart,
bringing them together, condemning existing loves, preventing separation
(or divorce), and authentic bonding.

In *North and South* the public witnessing of Margaret's rescue of Thornton (discussed in Chapter Ten) becomes the major barrier to her love, which
the remainder of the story will work to remove. Reflecting on the publicness
of her act, Margaret agonizes that others might realize she loves Thornton:
"Oh how low I am fallen that they should say that of me!" Her love is
choked off by everyone else suspecting. When the next day Thornton declares his love, Margaret is offended by his presumption of her love and
says: "You seem to fancy that my conduct of yesterday was a personal act
between you and me; instead of perceiving, as a gentleman would—yes! a
gentleman, that any woman, worthy of the name of woman, would come
forward to shield, with her reverenced helplessness, a man in danger from
the violence of numbers" (253). It takes almost three hundred pages for
Margaret to overcome the shame caused by what "they" will think. Finally
she and Thornton declare their love hurriedly, almost inadvertently, during
a business transaction which concludes with their gleefully anticipating
what others will say. "'How shall I ever tell aunt Shaw?' she whispered . . .
'Let me speak to her.' 'Oh, no! I owe to her,—but what will she say?' 'I can

guess. Her first exclamation will be, "That man!"' 'Hush!' said Margaret, 'or I shall try and show you your mother's indignant tones as she says, "That woman!"' The novel ends with this exchange between the lovers, who remain unaware of how such preoccupation with what others will say about their love diminishes their own responsibility for it.

In *Middlemarch* Eliot explains that Dorothea is hemmed in by "the intolerable narrowness and purblind conscience of the society around her" (23). After Casaubon's death her love for Will Ladislaw is blocked by Casaubon's meanspirited will, which contains a codicil that she must forfeit all inherited property if she marries Will but not if she marries anyone else. The codicil implies that Casaubon had reasons for suspicion and therefore makes it difficult for the lovers to act on their feelings, because it creates the threat of a malicious public opinion if they marry. The most historically revealing aspect of this episode is how the codicil frustrates the lovers, so terrified by public opinion, from acknowledging their love even to themselves, at least for several years. In the end they cannot be kept apart. Dorothea marries Will, gives up her inheritance, and lets the tongues of Middlemarch wag. Eliot concludes with a defense of the lovers' prolonged deference to the threat of gossip—"there is no creature whose inward being is so strong that it is not greatly determined by what lies outside it" (577). True, but in the twentieth century the inner resources of lovers were stronger and public opinion about them was less judgmental; hence they were less intimidated by appearances.

Ann Veronica walks out on public opinion almost too effortlessly. When her lover reminds her that to live unmarried with him is "wrong in the eyes of most people," she replies, "Who cares for most people," and adds, "To have you is all important . . . Morals only begin when that is settled. I sha'n't care a rap if we can never marry. I'm not a bit afraid of anything—scandal, difficulty, struggle . . . I rather want them" (327). Connie Chatterley takes the same defiant stance in opposition to the initial caution of her lover Mellors, who reminds her about the danger of "folks" finding out about their affair—"Think about it! Think how lowered you'll feel, one of your husband's servants . . . It's not as if I was a gentleman." To Connie's blithe dismissal of the threat of scandal, he replies: "I'm afraid. I'm afraid o' things." "What things?" she asks. And he answers, "Things! Everybody! The lot of 'em." But then he talks himself out of all the bother as Margaret and Thornton or Dorothea and Will had been unable to do. "Nay, I don't care . . . Let's have it, an' damn the rest" (116).

In the nineteenth century public formulas also work more effectively to bring lovers together. Meredith's *Egoist* is, paradoxically, lacking in ego: "he is dependent for his self-assurance on the good opinion of others, and to gain and keep that he must always make the appearance of being successful in terms of the prevailing fashion" (12). Even in love. He is drawn first to Clara's public aspect, which he learns about from rumor. "Hints were dropping about the neighbourhood; the hedgeways twittered, the tree-tops cawed" (65). He is a caricature of the inauthentic they-self: "the world's view of him, was partly his vital breath, his view of himself" (449). When his romance with Clara sours, his primary concern is appearances. Hardy's Jude is corralled into becoming involved with Arabella because on their first date he was seen with her on three occasions—when he picked her up and someone within her cottage saw him; when they were out walking and two strangers noticed them; and when they returned that night to be greeted by her parents and several neighbors, who "all spoke in a congratulatory manner and took him seriously as Arabella's intended partner" (41). Their expectations, combined with her subsequent feigned pregnancy, ultimately force him to propose.

This transitional novel of 1895 also shows some effort to resist the influence of others. Later in the story, when Sue leaves her husband in order to live with Jude, she justifies her act by citing Mill's *On Liberty*: "He, or she, 'who lets the world, or his own portion of it, choose his plan of life for him, has no need of any other faculty than the ape-like one of imitation.' J. S. Mill's words, those are. I have been reading it up. Why can't you act upon them? I wish to, always" (178). But Sue cannot act on them for long. She is driven back to her husband after public pressure on her adulterous liaison leads to one of the most grisly tragedies in all of Victorian literature—her own children's suicide by hanging.

Victorian society also condemned consummated loves. *The Scarlet Letter*, a classic novel about malevolent public opinion, opens with Hester standing in front of the town pillory, suffering "under the heavy weight of a thousand unrelenting eyes, all fastened upon her, and . . . on her bosom. It was almost intolerable to be borne" (84). One guardian of public morality wanted Hester's "A" to be branded not on her dress but on her forehead, so that she could not cover it with outer clothing. But Hester wears it uncovered on her bodice, thus internalizing the town's condemnation of her love. In the end the letter becomes, ironically, a "mystic symbol" of integrity which Hester cultivated out of the humus of the towns' decomposed moral condemnation of her.

In *The Mill on the Floss* (1860) Maggie energetically justifies the public condemnation of any love that undermines public mores. She explains to her beloved Stephen that his courting of Lucy and her promise to love no one but Philip make their own love wrong: "the real tie lies in the feelings and expectations we have raised in other minds" (570). If there is conflict between duty and love, the latter must be sacrificed. Maggie makes the "right" choice for duty to others and decides not to remain on the boat with Stephen, but the river sweeps them away and she is unable to return home until the next day. Stephen warns her that she cannot return unmarried, that no one will believe her story, and he is right. Her brother banishes her from his home, and the people of St. Ogg, who make allowances for Stephen's indiscretion, bring down the full force of their outrage on her. She rejects Dr. Kenn's advice to leave town and, like Hester, decides to stay. "I will not go away because people say false things of me. They shall learn to retract them" (626). She resolves to correct the town's misinformation about her but defends the moral ground for its condemnation.

Thirty-five years later another heroine attempted to reject that public morality but was destroyed. In Allen's *The Woman Who Did* Herminia offers Alan her love but refuses to marry and justifies her decision with a litany of feminist arguments. She continues her defiance by giving birth and raising their child out of wedlock. After Alan dies Herminia loses her job, friends, family, and reputation; she then learns that the illegitimate daughter she raised to do battle for her cause in the next generation has instead fallen in love with a rich aristocrat and wishes her mother out of the way so that she can become his wife. When Herminia realizes how ruthless society can be, she commits suicide to make it possible for her daughter to marry.

Both Maggie and Herminia are destroyed, but with one difference which implies a changing dominion of "the 'they'." Maggie lives more in the mode of the inauthentic they-self, because she accepts as her own moral code the logical foundation for what "they" think. Herminia is also destroyed by what "they" think and to some extent accepts their decision by killing herself, but only because she grows weary of the lonely fight and is undone when she realizes that her own daughter is against her. But she never accepts her daughter's way of thinking as her own and hence remains more in the mode of the authentic self, albeit defeated by others.

In the world described by Musil the dominion of "the 'they'" is ubiquitous. People cannot remember "how they managed to arrive at themselves, their amusements, their point of view, their wife." They adopt public standards for dress and facial expressions, even for emotions. Ulrich questions "the goals, the voices, the reality, the seductions" of life; he turns icy before the "pre-formations passed down by generation after generation, the ready-made language not only of the tongue but also of the sensations and feelings" (I, 150). He is not just unwilling to accept public morality as his own—he is unable to. He is the man without *(their)* qualities. He at first criticizes what is generally approved, the lacquered finish to everything, but eventually determines "to create obligations of his own." That creation gets under way at first tentatively but then with greater determination in a scandalous love with his sister (I, 173).

Loveless marriages dramatize the fourth function of society—preventing separation. After Anna Karenina publicly displays her love for Vronsky, her husband announces the new rules: "'I demand that the external conditions of propriety shall be observed till'—his voice trembled—'till I take measures to safeguard my honour and inform you of them'" (194). Since Russian law required ocular evidence of adultery, Karenin knew he would be unable to obtain it, and even if he could, his own "refinement" would not allow him to bring such evidence into court. To preserve appearances he demands that Anna remain with him, threatening that if she leaves she will never again see her son. Karenin's main emotion, he confesses, is not regret for the loss of Anna but "feeling ashamed before others" (463). In *The Portrait of a Lady* free-spirited Isabel capitulates to similar public pressures after she realizes that her husband does not even like her and that she is wretched. But, she acknowledges, "I can't publish my mistake. I don't think that's decent. I'd much rather die" (488).

In *The Age of Innocence* Ellen has left her philandering husband in Europe and returned to America, intending to get a divorce, but discovers that New York Society functions like "a powerful machine" to keep even bad marriages together. She falls in love with Archer, who resolves to back out of his impending marriage to May and be free to love her, but he is immediately foiled by a telegram from May that reads: "Parents consent wedding Tuesday after Easter at twelve Grace Church eight bridesmaids please see Rector so happy love May" (175). This clicky language conveys essentials largely about others; its style accents the speed and efficiency of the machinery of society which effectively blocks Ellen's divorce. At her farewell dinner, on the eve of her return to Europe, New York Society revved up the machine again, as Wharton explains: "The silent organization which held [Archer's] little world together was determined to put itself on record as never for a moment having questioned the propriety of Madame [Ellen] Olenska's conduct, or the completeness of Archer's domestic felicity. All these amiable and inexorable persons were resolutely engaged in pretending to each other that they had never heard of, suspected, or even conceived possible, the least hint to the contrary" (338). Ellen's threatened disruption of that silent organization passed into oblivion like the wake of her ship in the North Atlantic.

In Fontane's *Effi Briest* the absurdity of slavish devotion to public opinion is evident behind Innstetten's explanation to a friend of why he must duel with a man who, he has just discovered, cuckolded him six years earlier. The rhetoric, sentiment, morality, and duel itself are distinctively nineteenth-century. "We're not isolated persons, we belong to a whole society and . . . we're completely dependent on it. If it were possible to live in isolation, then I could let it pass . . . But with people living all together, something has evolved now that exists and we've become accustomed to judge everything, ourselves and others, according to its rules . . . I don't want to have blood on my hands merely for the sake of the happiness I've been deprived of, but that *something* which forms society—call it a tyrant if you like—is not concerned with charm or love, or even with how long ago a thing took place. I've no choice, I must do it." His friend argues that a six-year-old injury is no grounds for a duel, and Innstetten agrees but adds that since he has now told his friend, "the game passed out of my hands. From that moment onwards, there was someone else who knew something of my misfortune." Therefore he must fight the duel. His friend concedes—"It's terrifying to think that you're right, but you *are* right" (216). Innstetten's commitment to the "cult of honor" shows how insidious "they" can be. Even though only one other person knows about the stain on his honor, he must have "satisfaction." He kills his opponent and then divorces Effi, who is banished from her parents' home and dies. His happiness conflicts with society not just incidentally; in the larger picture individual personal interest is necessarily in conflict with the impersonal duty which society imposes at whatever cost.

The dominion of society remains powerful into the twentieth century, but some lovers become less inclined to accept its dictates. In *The Awakening* Edna is torn between "that outward existence which conforms" and "the inward life which questions." This duality will kill her, but unlike Effi, who wastes away, Edna fights. Her husband capitulates to public expectation. He is troubled when his wife is not "at home for callers" and scandalized when she resumes her sketching. "He could not see that she was becoming herself and daily casting aside that fictitious self which we assume like a garment with which to appear before the world" (57).

Twenty years later Lawrence had created enough freedom from the dominion of others to envision an authentic love *with* others, which he called
a "further fellowship." In the foreword to *Women in Love* he criticized
Western sexual morality, which had bowed for so long to what "they" do
that it no longer knew why it was being done. "A fate dictated from the
outside," he wrote, "is a false fate." In the story Rupert prepares Ursula for
a unique love for which there is "no obligation, because there is no standard
for action." They must never be "dominated from the outside." As they
agree to marry, Ursula plans to get away from everyone, but Rupert sees
their friends as necessary to their own love. Their dialogue is a reflective
exploration of a way to love among others.

> "I know," he said. "But we want other people with us, don't we?"
> "Why should we?" she asked.
> "I don't know," he said uneasily. "One has a hankering after a sort of
> further fellowship."
> "But why?" she insisted. "Why should you hanker after other people?
> Why should you need them?"
> This hit him right on the quick. His brows knitted.
> "Does it end with just our two selves?" he asked, tense.
> "Yes—what more do you want? If anybody likes to come along, let
> them. But why must you run after them?"
> His face was tense and unsatisfied.
> "You see," he said, "I always imagined our being really happy with
> some few other people—a little freedom with people."   (355)

Ursula concurs tentatively but urges him not to run after others. The novel
ends in a reprise of this exchange. Ursula asks, "Aren't I enough for you?"
and he replies that "to make it complete, really happy, I wanted eternal
union with a man too: another kind of love." Their final words leave the
issue open.

> "You can't have two kinds of love. Why should you!"
> "It seems as if I can't," he said. "Yet I wanted it."
> "You can't have it, because it's false, impossible," she said.
> "I don't believe that," he answered.

Although there is evidence that Lawrence coveted a homoerotic bond in additional to a heterosexual one, the emphasis here is on "another kind" of love—something other than the grasping exclusivity of the heterosexual pair. The idea of "two kinds of love" further distanced Lawrence from the "one and only" love insisted on by the Victorians—private, conventional, exclusive, and immutable. This other kind would not be defined by an impersonal society but would be nevertheless open to the unpredictable and creative presence of specific others. While struggling to disencumber himself from the dominion of others, Lawrence also accepted the way love is inescapably shaped and enriched by others—only he wanted some say in the shaping.

II

The history of parents as others is complex. Victorian medical, psychiatric, and hortatory literature emphasized strong parental influence, ranging from hereditary transmission to moral modeling and external coercion over children's conscious choice of lovers. Victorian novels emphasized external parental influence, which made better material for literary treatment of love relationships than did the workings of invisible hereditary processes. Into the twentieth century novels reveal less of external and more of internal parental influence on the way children actually love.

Victorians were unable to distinguish clearly between the processes of hereditary, infectious, and cultural transmission from parent to child and hence confused the ways children got hereditary syphilis, tuberculosis, or sexual perversion from a parent. Moralists warned that the entire sexual prehistory of parents could shape the sexual constitution of children. A French educator observed: "There has been some time—a day, an hour—in which the fate of an entire family has been cast, so that mutual moral responsibility binds parents to children." An American essayist warned that the moment of conception was particularly important: "Never run the risk of conception when you are sick or over-tired or unhappy." The "vigor and magnetic qualities" of the child "are much affected by conditions ruling this great moment." A German physiologist took such biological reductionism to absurd lengths in claiming to have located parental love in a brain lobe, an *Organ der Kinderliebe* which he believed was larger in women.[1] These processes of transmission were understood to work within the body. By emphasizing such bodily influences, Victorian researchers avoided reflecting on the unconscious or even conscious psychological pathways of parental influence.

Misinterpretation of Darwin's metaphor for the "descent" of man and lack of a clear understanding of heredity engendered much alarmist speculation that "degenerate" forms were passing through the blood and rising in concentration from one generation to the next. Gerhart Hauptmann's play *Before Sunrise* (1889) turned on the nefarious biological and psychological influences of a father's indulgence in alcohol, tobacco, and incest. His daughter commits suicide after being abandoned by her lover when he discovers that she may "inherit" her father's alcoholism. Although Hauptmann identifies both physical and mental parental influences, they are external to the daughter's actual way of loving. She does not smoke, drink, or desire her father, and her swain abandons her not because of her behavior but because of his erroneous ideas about hereditary transmission. One of Freud's most important contributions to understanding of the parent-child relationship was to counter the vogue of speculative theories about hereditary degeneration and focus rather on how psychic remnants of parenting work away at the unconscious level to shape adult ways of loving.

At the mid-nineteenth century parental influence was potent. Victorian lovers were cramped in places where parental pressure was strong, as compared to twentieth-century lovers who could court over an area expanded by new transportation and communication technologies and new work and recreational opportunities. And young Victorian women especially remained at home where men came courting under parents' watchful eyes. In these circumstances children had little chance to see ways of loving other than the way their parents loved.

By the time of *Anna Karenina*, there were signs that change was under way. When Kitty's mother had married thirty years earlier, the match had been arranged by an aunt, but lately, her mother frets, "social customs had changed." Girls Kitty's age "went to courses of lectures, made friends freely with men, and drove alone through the streets; many no longer curtsied, and above all every one of them was firmly convinced that the choice of a husband was her own and not her parents' business" (40). Her mother was looking, however, at external influence. Although recent matches were not formally arranged, young lovers generally remained within the family fold and chose spouses in accord with the dominant erotic sensibilities that they had been exposed to—those of their parents.

As a secret homosexual Forster was particularly sensitive to the way parents sabotage "the love that dare not speak its name" by innuendo, sarcasm, and willful misunderstanding. In *Maurice* every member of the hero's family actually mispronounces his homosexual lover's name. As Forster observes, "home emasculated everything" (44). And even when parents are supportive, their influence may undermine children's responsibility for choosing and hence for more authentic loving. In *A Room with a View* George's father urges Lucy not to be like most young lovers who "march to their destiny by catch-words" but rather to marry his son whom she loves, even though, he concedes, "your mother and all your friends will despise you" (204, 240). The story ends, like *North and South,* with the happy young couple discussing what others might be saying about their love.

Later twentieth-century novels move parental influence to a farther horizon. In *The Counterfeiters* Edouard proclaims flatly: "It is to bastards that the future belongs" (114). In *A Farewell to Arms* Catherine and Frederic check into a cheap hotel in order to make love. Afterwards, with only his tunic covering her naked shoulders, she inadvertently mentions her father and provokes his question:

> "Have you a father?"
> "Yes," said Catherine. "He has gout. You won't ever have to meet him. Haven't you a father?"
> "No," I said. "A step-father."
> "Will I like him?"
> "You won't have to meet him."   (161)

There is no further reference to parents. In *The Man Without Qualities* Ulrich tells Agatha, "Family life is not a full life. Young people feel themselves deprived, diminished in stature, not in full possession of themselves, so long as they're in the family circle" (III, 58). Agatha rejects conventional parental advice in the extreme by becoming her brother's lover, following their reunion at her father's funeral. She also blatantly repudiates her father even in death by disobeying his wish to be buried with his medals. She substitutes fake medals. That gesture is of historical significance insofar as it highlights the contrast with the way Victorian children religiously obeyed the wishes of a dying parent.

There was thus an unmistakable historical shift with regard to external parental influence between the Victorian and the modern novel. But bastardy, avoidance, and even disrespect respond to the imperious otherness of parents only deficiently. Moreover these actions protest a bit too much. One of the most important revelations of psychoanalysis was that no matter how fervently children try and get away, parents remain in the unconscious.

At the heart of psychoanalysis is Freud's theory of the Oedipus complex, first mentioned in a private letter of 1896 and later elaborated systematically in a publication of 1905. Freud believed that boys and girls develop a powerful sexual love for the parent of the opposite sex that becomes the nucleus of all subsequent libidinous attachments, which may take the form of chronic inability to love anyone but that parent, repeated attachments to lovers who are like that parent, chronic rebellion against that type, or healthy resolution in mature love. Earlier psychologists had emphasized how parents provide conscious models—not unconscious memories and wishes—which shape the ways their children love. Freud explained further that the boy's sexual desire for his mother (and the girl's, until her love for her father intercedes) is subject to repression when it comes into conflict with a public morality that ruthlessly condemns such desire; when "the child's mother becomes his love-object the psychical work of repression has already begun in him, which is withdrawing from his knowledge awareness of a part of his sexual aims." [2] Psychoanalytic therapy, like hermeneutic phenomenology, is a process of restoring awareness of one's self, with the difference that Freud's method aims to uncover sources for a chronological priority while Heidegger's method seeks to elucidate an ontological priority in fundamental ways of being human. Although Freud's clinical obligations focused on the pathological consequences of unresolved Oedipus complexes, his discovery was equally about how childhood lays the foundation in the unconscious for fulfilling adult love.

Two contrasting paintings illustrate the historical change in awareness of such unconscious (or at least internalized) parental influence. In James Hayllar's *The Only Daughter* (Figure 38, 1875) that influence is largely conscious and external. There is a hint that the father has taught the daughter how to express love physically, for she holds his hand in the same reserved way as that of her fiancé. The daughter also momentarily expresses greater physical intimacy with her father than with her fiancé, but it is conscious, sexually tame, and dictated by the formal requirement of asking permission to marry. Moreover, the father, trying to hide his sense of loss, looks away, holds onto his newspaper, and absent-mindedly squeezes his daughter's fingers by reaching back over his shoulder without even turning around. Hayllar carefully records the external manifestations of this father's provisions for his daughter's marriage with all the props of a successful Victorian household—devoted wife, faithful dog, caged bird, potted fern, sewing machine, comfortable chairs, and ancestral portraits. But Hayllar gives no indication of repressed sexual tensions, unconscious Oedipal ambivalences, or serious emotional deficiencies. There is a whisper of remorse over this only daughter leaving home, but the father will soon return to his paper as will the mother to her needlework. The parents have taught their daughter how to love by explicit models, and she is showing the proper devotion demanded by her familial station and its duties.

The similarity of attire of the parents and the couple depicted in the portraits on the wall emphasizes the unchanging nature of their loving. Hanging from the daughter's waist (over her reproductive organs) is an anchor charm (of hope) from which hangs a watch (time)—together symbolizing hope for the continuing reproduction of this family's way of loving. Parental influence on the daughter's way of loving comes from the outside—it passes to her through the machinery of tradition according to the rules of proper decorum represented by furnishings and family portraits that frame this pivotal moment in the generational transmission of love.

Far different are the workings of maternal influence suggested in Francis Picabia's *Quadrilogy of Love* (Figure 39, 1932), which offers a striking image of lovemaking in the presence of others who are ambiguously either introjections into, projections from, or doubles of the lovers themselves. In 1928 Picabia developed a transparency style which enabled him to represent how echoes of the past—mythic, artistic, and personal—penetrate the present.[3] By 1932 he had used it in hundreds of paintings, some of which depicted several layers of experience showing through one another in a single image of lived time. *Quadrilogy of Love* suggests a *pietà* with the Virgin closing the eyes of Christ, a man and a woman embracing, a mother and child, or a young man with a whopping Oedipus complex. The mother figure continues to be loving and vigilant while the man sleeps, a time when unconscious childhood memories of the desire for maternal affection may surface to consciousness. Picabia offers unintentionally a glimpse of Freud's conception of how a parent may remain present at the unconscious level during adult loving, because this man's "others" are himself and a composite of his beloved in a mothering role.[4] Unlike Hayllar's father, whose handholding visibly demonstrates his past way of teaching by external influence, this mother's influence is not now visible and never was. The son has internalized her loving. Picabia reveals how a parent may remain in a sense visible through the transparency of consciousness and present during a grown-up child's lovemaking.

In the Victorian novel, when parents are overly in favor of a match or overly opposed, the story revolves around a resolution of the conflict between parent and child, but the parental intrusion remains external to the child's way of loving. In *The Egoist* Clara's father pushes her toward a man she does not love, but he does not modify how she loves. In *Les Misérables* Valjean first opposes the love between Cosette and Marius and then risks his life to make it possible, but his efforts do not alter Cosette's ability to love. In *The Mill on the Floss* Maggie remains more externally constrained than internally transformed by her father's opposition to Philip. How Heathcliff and Cathy love each other does not derive from any intense erotic attachment to either parent.

But in the twentieth century novelists explore how such attachments may shape children's loving at the unconscious level. The classic of such shaping is a novel whose title might have appeared under Picabia's painting: *Sons and Lovers*. Paul is drawn to Miriam, who embodies his mother's alert mind, deep religiosity, and sexual disgust. Miriam's offering of brooding sexuality is always a sacrifice. "She was slightly afraid—deeply moved and religious. That was her best state. He was impotent against it." She asks what's the matter, but as Lawrence explains, "he did not know himself what was the matter." As his mother's rivalry with Miriam intensifies, Paul is paralyzed by Oedipal guilt, as revealed in an exchange his mother initiates.

> "And I've never—you know, Paul—I've never had a husband—not really—"
> He stroked his mother's hair, and his mouth was on her throat.
> "And she [Miriam] exults so in taking you from me—she's not like ordinary girls."
> "Well, I don't love her, mother," he murmured, bowing his head and hiding his eyes on her shoulder in misery. His mother kissed him a long, fervent kiss.
> "My boy!" she said, in a voice trembling with passionate love.
> Without knowing, he gently stroked her face.   (213)

Paul is unable to love Miriam because of conscious guilt about his mother's opposition, because his mother's smothering has atrophied his desire, and

38. James Hayllar, *The Only Daughter*, 1875.

39. Francis Picabia, *Quadrilogy of Love*, 1932.

because he has unconsciously selected a woman like his mother whose sexual sacrifice conjures up his own forbidden incestuous love. Paul's criticism of Miriam's tormented offering of herself seems to be directed against his mother—even the way Miriam picks flowers. "Can you never like things without clutching them as if you wanted to pull the heart out of them? . . . You absorb, absorb, as if you must fill yourself up with love, because you've got a shortage somewhere" (218). Paul eventually returns to his mother. "There was one place in the world that stood solid and did not melt into unreality: the place where his mother was . . . It was as if the pivot and pole of his life, from which he could not escape, was his mother" (222). Just when his mother looms up as a love-devouring monster, Lawrence balances the account with a sympathetic sketch of the mother's genuine devotion to her son's happiness. For all her needfulness she accepted Paul's need for a young woman, and she wished "that Miriam had been a woman who could take this new life of his and leave her the roots" (223). But Paul fails to love Miriam because his own roots are smothered by his mother's stronger roots.

Even though Paul has a more sexually fulfilling affair with Clara, his successes are compromised by an unconscious maternal drain on his libido: "his love turned back into [his mother], so that he could not be free to go forward with his own life, really love another woman" (345). In the end, after his mother has died of cancer, Clara leaves him. He then fails with Miriam one more time and walks off, whispering the last spoken words of the novel—"Mother!—Mother!"

Nineteenth-century novelists accepted that a son may be strongly attached to his mother out of filial respect but not out of unresolved sexual desire, and none grasped how profound an effect that desire could have on the son's way of loving. With the mother-son relationship in *The Judge* (1922) Rebecca West provides another piece of evidence that internal parental influences are more fully appreciated by twentieth-century novelists. While still pregnant, Richard's mother Marion was abandoned by his father. Irate townsfolk tried to make her miscarry by throwing dung and stones at her, even poking her with a stick. Richard's guilt over this and subsequent suffering she underwent on his behalf make it impossible for him to love anyone else. She confides to Richard's beloved Ellen that he "frets about these troubles far too much," and adds, "I can see that you, my dear, are going to break the spell that, very much against my will, I've thrown over my son" (215). Richard's mother is more insightful and more willing to share her love than was Paul Morel's mother, but that generosity makes her sacrificial love all the more potent. Besides, there are critical moments when she clutches him tight, followed by paroxysms of remorse mixed with pride: "Of course! Of course!" she realizes, "He cannot love Ellen because he loves me too much! He has nothing left to love her with!" (346). Richard observes his mother looking at him "like a judge," and she concurs, with an explanation of the novel's title, "Every mother is a judge who sentences the children for the sins of the father" (346). But that partial disclosure screens the deeper unconscious cause of his inability to love Ellen—his guilty love for his mother, whom he had all to himself after his real father departed and his stepfather died. His mother's desperate remedy—suicide—only tightens her hold. Richard's step-brother Roger accuses Richard and Ellen of having caused his mother's suicide after she discovered the two "fornicating"— "you've killed my mummie with your wickedness!" (424). There is partial truth in that false condemnation because Richard believes that his love is wicked and leads to death, and Ellen realizes that "her love had not been able to reach Richard across the dark waters of his mother's love" (429).

III

In identifying how remnants of the parent-child relationship become unconscious sources of adult ways of loving, Freud focused his criticism on another powerful traditional mediator—God. He argued that three of religion's main tasks—exorcising the terrors of nature (protecting), making amends for suffering imposed by civilization (comforting), and reconciling one to the cruelty of fate or death (justifying existence)—replicate basic parental roles. He tagged religion as an "illusion" which grew out of the adult's wish to retain the circumstances of childhood, when love *was* generously supplied by a devoted mother, when protection *was* provided by a supremely wise and powerful father, and when the parents together *did* provide the meaning of existence. For the individual, excessive prolongation of such infantile wishes into adulthood creates neurosis; for society, prolongation of premodern and unscientific understanding of man and the world creates religion, which he interpreted as a "universal obsessional neurosis" with God substituted for the father. Published in 1927, the same year as Heidegger's *Being and Time,* Freud's *The Future of an Illusion* argued that religious faith is destabilizing because the individual believer is not allowed to verify the truth of its doctrines for himself and is hence unable to understand his own faith. Religion also undermines authentic morality. It would be preferable to leave God out of political and legal matters and "honestly admit the purely human origin of all the regulations and precepts of civilization." Freud also believed that it would be best to leave God out of love.[5]

For over a millennium of early Christendom God was believed to be immediately and directly present to nature, society, and the individual. In the Middle Ages believers held to an unswerving faith in God's love. God was the ultimate "other" in regulating the ways of temporal love, especially its legitimization, and the words of Jesus remained the essence of the Church's blessing—"What therefore God hath joined together, let not man put asunder" (Matt. 19:6). In addition to forbidding divorce, this injunction also sanctified the joining. Although many Victorians found it increasingly difficult to believe in a providential God who could make miracles happen, they believed that God was spiritually present in the miracle of love.

Jane Eyre explores several pitfalls of Christian faith—the resignation of moribund Helen Burns, the mean-spirited asceticism imposed on young girls by sadistic Mr. Brocklehurst, the arrogance and sexless love of St. John Rivers. But the ultimate love between Jane and Rochester is embedded in profound faith. Their budding love is first shielded from moral corruption, then mediated in the nick of time, and finally given its concluding form through faith in God. Reflecting on her rejection of Rochester's offer to live in France as his mistress, Jane reasons, "God directed me to a correct choice: I thank His Providence for the guidance!" (386).[6] When St. John presses Jane to respond to his marriage proposal, she entreats God: "Show me, show me the path!" Suddenly she hears a far-off cry—"Jane! Jane! Jane!"—which seems like the voice of God but sounds like the voice of Rochester, at the time two hundred miles away (444). Before rushing to his rescue Jane falls on her knees and prays. She returns to find Rochester repentant and devout. He reveals that in praying to God he called out her name three times and then heard what seemed like a reply, "I am coming; wait for me." She does not tell him that those were her exact words. Her faith is fortified by this sign of divine intervention and by Rochester's new reverence for his Redeemer, and throughout the story God protects, shapes, and sanctions love.

God could also be wrathful for all who forget the moral pivot of Christendom—the sin that is primordially equated with sex. *The Scarlet Letter* explored this dark side of divine presence in love. The dying Reverend Dimmesdale explains to Hester after she asks if they will ever meet again: "When we violated our reverence each for the other's soul,—it was thenceforth vain to hope that we could meet hereafter, in an everlasting and pure reunion." But there is hope because God is merciful. God has shown his mercy, Dimmesdale explains, "by giving me this burning torture to bear upon my breast! By sending yonder dark and terrible old man [Chillingworth] to keep the torture always at red-heat! By bringing me hither, to die this death of triumphant ignominy before the people!" (269). Dimmesdale's agonizing is extreme, but it expresses the conviction of many devout Victorians that sex between lovers who are not married corrupts their souls, and that God's mercy can be measured by the pain he inflicts on them for their sins. The form of Dimmesdale's reflection is authentic in that it ponders the meaning of love, but the content is inauthentic, because his thinking is regulated by a dogmatic religion and encompassed by values which are external to his love for Hester and which he is unwilling to question.[7]

Later in the century there is increasing evidence that many were not only willing to question such values but unable to sustain belief in them. That is the meaning behind Nietzsche's announcement in 1882 of the "death" of God. In *The Brothers Karamazov* (1880) Dostoevski insisted that in a world without God "everything is permitted"—everything except belief in a hereafter and the heavenly reward. Without the hope of God's eternal love, Dostoevski predicted, people will increase their expectations for earthly love: "Love will satisfy only a moment of life, but the very consciousness of its momentary nature will intensify its fire to the same extent as it is now dissipated in the hopes of eternal life beyond the grave" (764).

By the 1890s the divine presence was further dimming. In *The Awakening* Edna tells a friend: "I was running away from prayers, from the Presbyterian service, read in a spirit of gloom by my father that chills me yet to think of." During one service she is overcome with the "stifling atmosphere of the church" and leaves with Robert, who will eventually become her lover. In *Jude the Obscure* Jude and Sue struggle away from the spirit and even the architecture of religion. He suggests they go into a cathedral, and she replies, "Cathedral? Yes. Though I think I'd rather sit in the railway station . . . That's the center of the town life now. The Cathedral has had its day!" (108). Jude's reply, "How modern you are!" is premature. In the end her religiosity returns with a vengeance. He appeals to her, "But surely we are man and wife, if ever two people were in this world? Nature's own marriage it is, unquestionably!" "But," she says, "not Heaven's. Another was made for me there, and ratified eternally in the church" (278).

By the twentieth century the mediation of God in love diminishes as the religious framework for literature becomes further attenuated. Those lovers who still believe intensely are unable to love another mortal. Du Gard's Jenny, Gide's Alissa, and Lawrence's Miriam are throwbacks to nineteenth-century, if not medieval, piety. Religion has made them disgusted by any expression of physical love (Jenny is sickened when Jacques kisses her shadow; Alissa believes that just looking at Jerome is a profanation; and Miriam makes love, Paul charges, like a nun). For most modern lovers, however, what remained of their faith did not fundamentally structure the way they loved. In *Howards End* Margaret "was not a Christian in the accepted sense," and she believed that it is "private life that holds out the mirror to infinity; personal intercourse, and that alone" (81). In *The Well of Loneliness*, Hall explains, "God had grown so unreal, so hard to believe in since [Stephen] had studied Comparative Religion" (74). Musil's brother-sister lovers are atheists. "He and Agatha found themselves on a path that had a great deal in common with the ways taken by those who are possessed by God; they went along it without a faith, without believing in God or the soul, indeed without even believing in a beyond or another life" (III, 111).

Lawrence, Joyce, and Woolf express different aspects of this sweeping secularization of love. In *The Rainbow* Lawrence traces the history of the decline of religion's power to shape love. First-generation Tom Brangwen is deeply religious. While the second generation of Brangwens lament that even on Christmas "the passion was not there," third-generation Ursula bitterly resents the teachings of her parents' evangelical Christianity—the image of "Jesus with holes in his hands and feet" and the triumph of "Sorrow and Death and the Grave" over the "pale fact of Resurrection!" To free love from the deadly "mechanical action" of the contemporary church, Lawrence crafted a brief sexual exorcism of it in church. Ursula and Skrebensky stop to rest in a church and he tells her about a friend who liked to make love in a cathedral. He interprets Ursula's response, "How nice!" as a deliberate profanation, but she replies, "I don't think it a profanity—I think it's right, to make love in a cathedral" (295–296).

Joyce took this blasphemy a step further in *Ulysses* by celebrating a Black Mass in a brothel on a woman's naked body. His stage directions include bondage and scatology. *"(On the altarstone Mrs Mina Purefoy, goddess of unreason, lies naked, fettered, a chalice resting on her swollen belly.)"* During the ceremony the Reverend Mr Haines Love *"(Raises high behind the celebrant's petticoats, revealing his grey bare hairy buttocks between which a carrot is stuck)"* and says "My body" (599). Of course a Black Mass works only for believers. This one is the climax of a series of blasphemies Joyce included in the novel to exorcise the crippling effect he believed Catholicism had had on sexual love. Joyce also treated religion as the afterthought in love that it had become for so many.

Love loves to love love. Nurse loves the new chemist. Constable 14A loves Mary Kelly. Gerty MacDowell loves the boy that has the bicycle. M. B. [Molly Bloom] loves a fair genteman. Li Chi Han lovey up kissy Cha Pu Chow. Jumbo, the elephant, loves Alice, the elephant. Old Mr

Verschoyle with the ear trumpet loves old Mrs Verschoyle with the turnedin eye . . . You love a certain person. And this person loves that other person because everybody loves somebody but God loves everybody. (333)

The ordering of this list is significant: God's universal love comes last—not as final comforting embrace but after everyone else, even after Jumbo the elephant. Joyce makes a suspect defense of God with the raving of a slobbering drunk and the sound of his climactic flatulence:

"The Deity ain't no nickel dime bumshow. I put it to you that he's on the square and a corking fine business proposition. He's the grandest thing yet and don't you forget it. Shout salvation in king Jesus. You'll need to rise precious early, you sinner there, if you want to diddle the Almighty God. Pflaaaap!" (428)

In historical contrast to these attitudes stands that icon of Victorian faith— Holman Hunt's painting *The Light of the World* (1853). Hunt reported that he was inspired to paint the picture by a "divine command" which came while he was reading in the Bible, "Behold, I stand at the door and knock; if any man hear my voice, and open the door, I will come into him, and will sup with him, and he with me" (Rev. 3:20). The painting shows Christ standing outside a door which symbolizes one emphatically closed human soul; it is barred with rusty hinges and overgrown with ivy and brambles. Christ's offering of faith is symbolized by light that emanates from three sources: his lantern, which radiates the light of conscience on the closed door and illuminates some fallen apples of sin, the nimbus that silhouettes Christ's crown of thorns and is the light of hope, and Christ himself, who is the source of the "light of life." [8] Hunt doubles the emphasis on sexual sin by presenting this painting as a pendant to *The Awakening Conscience* (1854), in which an adulteress rises from her seducer's lap, having taken to heart the refrain of a song shown resting on the piano stand, "Sad memory brings the light/ Of other days around me." [9] The collective message of the two paintings is that the light of the world, in fact God's *heavenly* light, is for all who open the door of their souls to repent and be saved. Victorian love was a difficult and uniquely personal struggle, especially against the temptations of sin, but ultimately it was defined by public commandments inspired and secured by faith in God.

While Lawrence and Joyce had derided the crippling effect that an overly spiritual Christianity had had on sexual love, Woolf explored how belief was becoming a dispirited cliché. In *To the Lighthouse* Mrs. Ramsay's uplifting illumination emanates as much from within as from without, and the external source is very earthly. She sees it after putting her children to bed. "Turning, she looked across the bay, and there . . . was the light of the Lighthouse. It had been lit." Alone in the darkness and interrupted only by the intermittent sweep of light, Mrs. Ramsay was ready for adventure, the sort inspired by mundane activities and simple things. She stared "until she became the thing she looked at—that light, for example." In this pensive mood Mrs. Ramsay suddenly chastises herself for saying without thinking, "We are all in the hands of the Lord." As Woolf explains, "instantly she was annoyed with herself for saying that. Who had said it? Not she: she had been trapped into saying something she did not mean." Mrs. Ramsay looked into the third stroke of the lighthouse light "and it seemed to her like her own eyes meeting her own eyes, searching as she alone could search into her mind and her heart, purifying out of existence that lie." Holman Hunt's inspiration has become Mrs. Ramsay's lie. And unlike Hunt's adulteress in *The Awakening Conscience,* whose eyes are radiant with a vision of God that takes her out of herself and away from her sordid surroundings, the modern heroine sees herself in the real light of the everyday world. "[Mrs. Ramsay] praised herself in praising the light, without vanity, for she was stern, she was searching, she was beautiful like the light." Caressed by the lighthouse light, pondering the meaning of her life, Mrs. Ramsay found a love radiating from within, for "there curled up off the floor of the mind, rose from the lake of one's being, a mist, a bride to meet her lover." Reflecting once again on her earlier thought—"We are in the hands of the Lord"—she was troubled, Woolf explains, at "the insincerity slipping in among the truths." Mrs. Ramsay reasons that there could be no God because there was too much injustice and suffering in the world, and because no happiness lasted.

While Mrs. Ramsay meditates on the godlessness of the world, her husband walks by, feeling especially distant. But the lighthouse light will make love possible, at least Mrs. Ramsay will make it make love possible. She looks once again at the light and lets it in until "the ecstasy burst in her eyes and waves of pure delight raced over the floor of her mind and she felt, It is enough! It is enough!" Beatific visions are too much. The real lighthouse light, mediated by the miraculous incendiary powers of the poetic mind, is just enough to generate the ecstasy of love. Her meditative outburst is followed by a simple narrative of the love between Mr. and Mrs. Ramsay, stimulated by the generative power of ordinary things—"And again he would have passed her without a word had she not, at that very moment, given him of her own free will what she knew he would never ask, and called to him and taken the green shawl off the picture frame, and gone to him. For he wished, she knew, to protect her . . . She folded the green shawl about her shoulder. She took his arm" (94–100). Mr. and Mrs. Ramsay stroll out into the evening air, illuminated at intervals by the sweeping, saving arc of the lighthouse beam, their very own light of the world.

One distinctive feature of love in the twentieth century is how lovers became more aware of the ways society, parents, and God mediated love. The most explicit recognition of that growing awareness was about parental influence, as it was dramatized by several novelists and codified by Freud. The psychoanalyzed lover is no less attached to his parents than the unpsychoanalyzed lover, but in being more conscious of the attachment is less prone to neurotic repetition of infantile patterns of loving into adulthood. Modern lovers became increasingly troubled by the intrusion of society, parents, or God and increasingly determined to take more responsibility for building their love on their own. They joined with Lawrence's Rupert in trying to break both the intrusive presence of others and the exclusivity of the isolated pair in order to situate their love as "a little freedom with people." They joined with Woolf in trying to find the light of the world in the ecstasy of love, bursting from the eyes and racing across the floor of the mind.

12 Jealousy

NO MATTER how overbearing the influence of society, parents, or God, the loving pair remain bonded, often driven closer together in reaction against external meddling. The intrusion of another lover, however, erodes love from within and threatens the dual commitment altogether. This chapter on jealousy is located between chapters on *others* and *selfhood*, because its history involves a growing realization of the function of jealousy in maintaining selfhood while loving amidst others. It is one of three chapters that treat elements of love that are experienced in the positive mode as a deficiency, a way of being *without* a beloved: in *waiting,* love will be, but is not yet; in *ending,* love has been, but is no longer; in *jealousy,* love is now, but with someone who loves another.[1]

Among phenomenologists there is surprisingly little on jealousy. Heidegger does not consider it, although his interpretation of the existentials *anxiety, guilt,* and *being-towards-death* suggest how the more discomforting aspects of human existence come closest to revealing its meaning. Sartre gives no systematic analysis, but his philosophy of love suggests why jealousy is so painful. In love, Sartre argues, the lover desires that his beloved somehow return to him the subjectivity that was drained out of him by the objectifying gaze of others and thereby reunite him with his alienated self. He wants the idolatry of his beloved to canonize all the accidents of his existence, as if by God, as that-which-was-meant-to-be. He wants to fascinate his beloved and retrieve from her a free and absolute acknowledgment of his being. These grandiose desires, however, will not be satisfied. Love is undertaken in good faith (that is, without intending to flee the anguishing freedom of consciousness) but is doomed to failure, because it aspires to possess another's freedom, which is impossible: if he succeeds in possessing it, it is no longer free; and if it remains free, he cannot possess it.

Even though his beloved cannot entirely redeem his lost subjectivity, she is endowed with enormous power, and so any redirection of her love to someone else is devastating. Recognition that she loves someone else creates a hole in his existence through which his life-blood pours out. The despair of jealousy is about the loss of love, but that loss is itself grounded on the deeper and more devastating loss of one's self. The challenge of jealousy is to understand it as part of love's inevitable deficiencies. The history of jealousy turns on the changing modes of that understanding.

Victorians viewed jealousy as a disease to be avoided, a corruption of love, or a "contagion of evil." [2] In response they typically chose denial, flight, self-pity, or, in extreme instances, the retribution of murder or the "satisfaction" of dueling.[3] These responses had one thing in common—they projected the source of the grievance onto either the "unfaithful" beloved or the "third party" and therefore avoided reflecting on any sources of the grievance within one's own self. By the twentieth century artists and intellectuals began to think that the loss of oneself in jealousy was not so much an affliction or an evil as an unavoidable and important challenge, essential to retrieving oneself as a self and to tempering love as non-possessive and free.

This difference is evident in two paintings. Philip Calderon's *Broken Vows* (Figure 40, 1856) shows a jealous woman stricken with self-pity. She clutches her heart to locate the pain, and her eyes are closed in despair, with a tear on one cheek. The depth of her torment is suggested by symbols of a past love that is now lost: the initials "MH" carved on the gate frame, the charm bracelet with a sailor's anchor that lies on the ground, and the drooping flowers. In contrast Munch underscores the protean nature of jealousy by giving his painting three different titles—*Melancholy, Evening,* and *Jealousy* (Figure 41, 1893). The foreground figure is not so much self-pitying as contemplative, like Rodin's *The Thinker,* and holds not his heart but his head. Though his eyes are open, his vision is clearly inward. Whereas the jealousy of Calderon's woman is caused by the actions of a clearly identifiable man in a specific past, the jealousy of Munch's thinker has no clearly identifiable culprit or precise time: it comes from past memories as well as the evening air, even the seashore itself, which symbolizes ebb and flow, the endless concealing and disclosing that is the artist's life and work.[4]

Calderon overloads his painting with conventional symbols that locate moral responsibility as external to the wronged woman.[5] The cause of her suffering is out there in the world—the perfidious man offering a pink rosebud to a blond woman whose full red lips are framed in the hole in the gate,

40. Philip Calderon, *Broken Vows*, 1859.

41. Edvard Munch, *Melancholy*. 1891.

and who eagerly reaches for the flower. In contrast Munch locates the cause of jealousy more in the jealous man himself; the responsibility for it lies as much with this thinker's melancholia or even the ambient seashore as with any other person.[6] The two figures on the pier did have precise biographical referents,[7] but they are small and far away, as if irrelevant.

The world around Calderon's figures is intact. His realistic drawing, accurate proportions, correct color, single light source, and careful application of paint lead viewers to think that they are looking through a window of real space and seeing what has struck pain in the woman's heart. One need only be in the right position and open one's eyes to see and comprehend all, as has the woman herself, who has just spun away from a glimpse of the scene visible through the hole in the gate. For Munch the surrounding world is unstable and incomplete, lacking precise definition or uniform space. Our vision of that world is fundamentally different from that of the persons depicted in his pictorial space and includes an awareness of the artistic process.

What we see is ambiguous. The truth cannot be fully known by looking in the right place at the right time; it can only be approached by persistent reflection.

Calderon's title underscores the legitimacy of vows, and his messages are clear: the man broke his vows and is therefore wicked; the woman is a good woman who picked the wrong man. Munch, in giving his painting three different titles, de-centers the theme of jealousy and questions the moral evaluation of vows, jealousy, and love altogether. In his world human relations are unstable and compromised; public rituals such as vows are ineffective for holding people together; and jealousy is an inescapable component of all love relations, caused as much by self-betrayal as by the betrayal of others. Rather than trying to find someone who will keep his or her vows no matter what, one must experience jealousy head-on and overcome it in a trial-and-error groping similar to the artistic process.[8]

In many Victorian novels the *cause* of jealousy is a misunderstanding, the *responsibility* for it is projected onto someone else, its *value* is largely negative, and the *emotional response* to it is self-pity. *Resolution* comes from a clarification of the original misunderstanding about what the other person said or did, not from self-discovery. The remainder of this chapter will treat these five aspects of jealousy together and trace their changing modes into the twentieth century.

I

Wuthering Heights is typically Victorian. Cathy tells Nelly, "It would degrade me to marry Heathcliff, now; so he shall never know how I love him." Heathcliff leaves after hearing the word "now." He does not understand what she really means because he did no stay around long enough to hear the end of the sentence and darts off with the mistaken belief that Cathy views marrying him as merely a degradation. Cathy explains further to Nelly that she could not marry Heathcliff because they would both be beggars, and therefore she will marry Edgar Linton to "aid Heathcliff to rise, and place him out of [her] brother's power" (121–122). Heathcliff remains away for three years, wallowing in jealousy and self-pity, convinced that his misery was caused by Cathy's betrayal. He returns a rich man and uses his money and power to wreak vengeance on the entire Linton family, including marrying Edgar's sister Isabella out of spite, even hanging her pet dog. He gets only minimal clarification of the deeper reasons for his unhappiness when he breaks into Cathy's home, finds her on her deathbed, and embraces her for one last time, exchanging passionate kisses punctuated by accusations, apologies, and regrets. He discovers how intensely Cathy loved him but not why, nor does he discover his own responsibility for a burning jealousy that remains until his own death and is projected against everyone who, he continues to believe, did him wrong—even their children.

Jane Eyre's jealousy is also based on a misunderstanding which Rochester intentionally cultivates by feigning an affection for Blanche. Jane learns little about herself from jealousy and denies the intensity of her feelings, claiming that Blanche was "beneath jealousy." That denial involves a measure of self-deception, as do all denials, but especially because a high point of the novel and of her own happiness comes when Rochester dramatically discloses his ruse by way of proposing marriage.

In Gaskell's *North and South* misunderstanding also plunges Thornton into jealousy. From afar he sees Margaret speaking intently to another man—her brother, whom he takes to be her lover. Seventy pages later Margaret learns about Thornton's misinterpretation from his mother, but because the lovers are too proud to speak frankly, the misunderstanding and Thornton's jealousy persist for another three years and are resolved only when the couple is obliged to converse for financial reasons. During this climactic exchange Thornton discovers none of his personal deficiencies but only how wrong his judgment of Margaret had been. A similar jealousy based on misunderstanding occurs in *Middlemarch*. Dorothea sees Will with Rosamond and mistakenly assumes a romantic attachment. Her jealousy is explained away not by direct communication with Will but by a letter of clarification from Rosamond.

Charles Bovary misunderstands in his own way. His grief over Emma's death is so numbing that he is unable to feel jealous even when he discovers an incriminating love letter to her from Rodolphe. "'Perhaps they loved each other Platonically,' he told himself. In any case Charles wasn't one to go to the root of things: he closed his eyes to the evidence, and his hesitant jealousy was drowned in the immensity of his grief" (388). Charles, like many a Victorian lover, was especially disinclined to find the roots of jealousy in himself.

In *Les Misérables* Marius's misunderstanding is amplified by paranoia. Hugo trivializes the cause and significance of Marius's jealousy in a chapter with the suitably trivial title—"A Puff of Wind." While Marius watched Cosette and her father walking in the park, a gust swept up her skirt, revealing her leg, and Marius became "dismayed and furious." Hugo reconstructs the genesis of jealousy in Marius's feverish brain: "No one else was there to see her, but supposing there had been someone! A dreadful thought, and her conduct was disgraceful! The poor child was, of course, in no way to blame; the wind was the only offender; but Marius was determined to disapprove and ready to be jealous of his own shadow. Thus it is that without justice or reason the extraordinary and bitter flame of jealousy of the flesh flares up in the heart of man" (615). If a twentieth-century lover were to become incensed at the possibility of another man catching a glimpse of his beloved's accidental exposure, his love would be doomed and not fulfilled in the end as it is in this novel. But even more characteristic of the nineteenth century is Hugo's description of the emotion as "without justice or reason." Some of the more profound explorations of love in the modern period will reject the moral implications of evaluating jealousy as with or without justice, explore rather the reasons for its burning actuality, and identify the jealous person's own responsibility for it instead of projecting its cause onto a puff of wind.

Hugo's definition could apply to Anna Karenina's "fits of jealousy" over Vronsky's increasing detachment from her. She also misinterprets the situation: although her possessiveness did make him colder, there was no other woman. Both Vronsky and Anna believe that this powerful "demon" (their term for jealousy) destroyed their love as a visitation from without. Zola's jealous characters are destroyed by the same demon and likewise have no sense of their responsibility for it, hence little understanding of its workings. In *Nana* (1880) Muffat prowls the streets for an entire night like a madman outside a room where he believes his wife is being unfaithful. *La Bête humaine* (1890) opens with Roubaud's maniacal jealousy upon learning that his wife had been coerced into having sex with her godfather when she was sixteen, long before they were married. "He seized her head and banged it against a leg of the table. She fought, and he dragged her across the floor by the hair . . . gasping through clenched teeth, in savage, mindless fury." When he finished "there was blood and hair sticking on one corner of the sideboard" (36). Almost every other main character is done in by jealousy. Roubaud kills Severine's godfather, and the prosecutor assigns jealousy as the motive when he erroneously convicts Cabouche of the crime. Jealous Flore attempts to kill Jacques and his beloved Severine by making their train derail. They survive the crash, but later Jacques kills Severine in jealous rage, which Zola interprets as a "malady . . . passed down from male to male since the first betrayal in the depths of some cave" (179). Jealousy also inspires Pecqueux's attack on Jacques, resulting in both of them falling to their deaths from a moving train. *La Bête humaine* is a compendium of late Victorian thinking about the nature of this "malady" for which, at least in Zola's view, there seems to be no cure, only the consequences of madness, destruction, and murder.

Typical of his age, the hero of *The Egoist* becomes jealous over a mistake, is obsessed with his rival, views his woman as a lost possession, and takes no personal responsibility for his suffering. His mistake is over a misinterpretation of one meeting between his betrothed, Clara, and his intended best man, Colonel De Craye. His obsession is being "haunted in the heaven of two by a Third; preceded or succeeded, therefore surrounded, embraced, hugged by this infernal Third." He views Clara as "his possession escaping," and he projects the source of his misfortune onto others as a humiliating visitation of a "foreign devil" (282–283).

The treatment of jealousy in Gissing's *The Odd Women* marks a change. Rhoda becomes jealous over a mistake. She receives a letter informing her that another woman was seen knocking at Everard's door. Later she learns that he was innocent. While Rhoda's jealousy, the misunderstanding that triggered it, and its ultimate clarification structure the action of the novel, what is more important is how this incident of jealousy becomes the foundation for deeper exploration of other aspects of their relationship—the possibility of trust and the importance of their power struggle. When she confronts Everard with the incriminating evidence, he realizes that Rhoda has been misinformed, but he refuses to do anything to clear himself beyond denying the accusation. Why, he asks, won't she take his word? Why, she counters, won't he make a greater effort to find out why he was wrongly incriminated and give her an adequate explanation? They remain deadlocked. When Rhoda finally learns the reason for her mistake, she and Everard do not proceed to find happiness as did lovers in many Victorian novels, because the deeper issues remain unresolved. Her jealousy teaches them both how they love or, rather, how they do not love, and they realize that they cannot go on together.

II

Twentieth-century novelists are more resolute in viewing jealousy as a cause for personal introspection rather than interpersonal accusation, and they treat the resolution of love stories as the disclosure of self-deceptions rather than as dramatic corrections of mistakes about what a beloved actually said or did.

In *The Golden Bowl* Maggie's jealousy is not based on a mistake or revealed in a sudden dramatic disclosure; rather it emerges slowly and most subtly as she begins to suspect that her husband Amerigo is involved with Charlotte. The consequent action brings out her anger toward Amerigo and Charlotte but, more important, the discovery of truths about herself. Maggie's friend Fanny explains to her husband Bob that for the first time in her life Maggie is beginning to doubt her "wonderful little world." For Maggie the first step on the way to getting her husband back is "waking up to the truth that, all the while, she really *hasn't* had him." Before this incipient jealousy Maggie had been closed to the truth. Now she is coming to know "Evil—with a very big E . . . the daily chilling breath of it." Fanny predicts that jealousy will force Maggie to "understand one or two things in the world." When Bob suggests that they will be disagreeable, Fanny replies: "Oh, 'disagreeable'—? They'll have *had* to be disagreeable—to show her a little where she is . . . to make her sit up . . . to make her decide to live." Later Maggie confesses to Fanny, "I live in the midst of miracles of arrangement, half of which, I admit, are my own" (283–287, 375). Maggie assumes responsibility for her marriage and her jealousy as part of being responsible for herself. She comes to understand that jealousy is a deficient but real aspect of love, a painful rite of passage to the difficult reconstitution of herself in loving which occupies the last half of the novel.

In *Howards End* Margaret exhibits a modern understanding of jealousy, although her husband's Victorian attitudes, minutely shaded by more modern values, try her patience. Ten years earlier, when Henry had been married to Mrs. Wilcox, he had had an affair with another woman. Margaret's response to this infidelity has a modern directness. She writes to Henry:

"My dearest boy," she began, "this is not to part us. It is everything or nothing, and I mean it to be nothing. It happened long before we ever met, and even if it had happened since, I should be writing the same, I hope. I do understand."

But she crossed out "I do understand"; it struck a false note. Henry could not bear to be understood. She also crossed out "It is everything or nothing." Henry would resent so strong a grasp of the situation. She must not comment; comment is unfeminine. (240)

The new thinking about jealousy among moderns is captured by Forster's account of Margaret's excisions—what she thought and felt but was not quite ready to express publicly. She might also have cut out "It is everything or nothing" because of its dated melodramatic ring and because she and Henry eventually resolved the problem without black-and-white formulas— she did not send the letter but communicated some of its content verbally, she was troubled by Henry but her main feeling for him was pity, she believed that Mrs. Wilcox's wrong was her own but did not actually feel wronged, and she commented daringly but judged comment as unfeminine. When Henry formally released Margaret from their engagement she replied: "Leave it where you will, boy. It's not going to trouble us." Henry was annoyed at such reasonableness and, Forster explains, would have preferred her to be prostrated or enraged. He was troubled that "her eyes gazed too straight; they had read books that are suitable for men only" (244). But her straight gaze helped them both to put his transgression into perspective, and the modern books she read were the source of the modern thinking that made such resolution possible.

Jealous Victorians got some relief. If tragic, they died like Heathcliff, Anna Karenina, or Count Muffat. If comic, they discovered that there was no good reason to be jealous and loved again. Three modern classics show how jealousy can reveal positive truths about friendship, love, or art.

In *The Magic Mountain* Mann explores a relationship between a jealous lover and his rival. Hans is devastated when after Clavdia's long absence she returns to the sanatorium with her dying lover Peppercorn, but jealousy enriches the friendship between Hans and Peppercorn, who struggle to understand the mixture of rivalry, jealousy, and respect that stimulates their relationship. Too sick to get out of bed, Peppercorn asks why no one accompanied Clavdia to the village. Hans, reluctant to admit his love, avoids a direct answer and talks about how up there on the mountain where disease is rampant, suffering is privileged and chivalry is superfluous. Unconsoled by Hans's evasion, Peppercorn grabs his wrist, looks him in the eye, and demands the truth. Hans admits his love for Clavdia and adds, "I have long wished and hoped that there might be understanding between myself and the man for whom I entertained feelings of the most extraordinary respect" (607). When Hans begins to describe his feelings for Clavdia, Peppercorn interrupts. "Stop! . . . Is it not rather—common—of us to talk about her?" Hans counters, "I don't think so . . . These are human topics we are treating; human in the sense that they have to do with freedom and the spiritual" (609). When Peppercorn expresses concern about causing him to suffer, Hans explains that he has come to understand "the enormous privilege of knowing you," even though it is "indissolubly bound up with suffering" (609).

As the dialogue becomes more intimate Hans reveals how his love for Clavdia has "bewitched" and "enchanted" him beyond reason. "For love of her, in defiance of [the rationalist] Herr Settembrini, I declared myself for the principle of unreason, the spiritual principle of disease . . . and I remained up here, I no longer know precisely how long. I have broken with everything, my relatives, my calling, all my ideas of life" (610). Peppercorn is moved. Were it not for his infirmity, he would give Hans "satisfaction, man to man, weapon to weapon," but instead he proposes friendship, offers Hans "the brotherly thou," and adds: "the satisfaction which age and incapacity prevent me from giving you, I offer in another form, in the form of a brotherly alliance . . . let us swear it to each other in the name of our feeling for somebody [Clavdia]" (611). In this historically distinctive gesture the jealous man and his rival celebrate their love for the same woman and offer each other the authentic satisfaction (what they actually want) of a handshake and "the brotherly thou" instead of the inauthentic satisfaction (what they are supposed to demand) of a duel.

One of the most eloquent—and certainly the most long-winded—of jealous lovers was Proust. In *Remembrance of Things Past* Swann's love for Odette is so interwoven with jealousy, Proust explains, "that it would have been impossible to eradicate it without almost entirely destroying him; as surgeons say, his love was no longer operable" (I, 336). Jealousy brushes Marcel's love for Gilberte but takes over his obsession with Albertine, which Proust recreates in exacting detail—days spent traipsing all over Paris to track down her lesbian haunts and refute her repeated lies, the fascination with names and details about all his male and female rivals, hours spent in pathetic interrogations which reveal the imagery and dialogue that cause him only greater anxiety, the unpredictable associations that inexorably lead back to her betrayal, and the bitterest revelations of greater deceit that come to light after she leaves him and that continue to torment him even more after her death. But unlike Victorian jealousy, Marcel's does not prove to be either based on a mistake that can be corrected or lived as a reality that must kill love or lead to death. In the end Marcel cashes in on his jealousy, which proves to be, like all his suffering and disappointments, the stuff of art. And for a man seeking his vocation as an artist, the truth that reveals the way to art leads to the self.

The final two hundred pages of the novel focus on the sources and processes of creativity, which turn on the stimulating possibilities of jealousy. "In love, our fortunate rival," he writes, "is our benefactor," because the suffering of jealousy reveals the meaning of love. Around the time when Heidegger interpreted truth as an extraction from untruth, Proust explained how truth and art were extracted from the unhappiness of jealousy through which "we are brought back time after time to a perception of the truth and forced to take things seriously, tearing up each new crop of the weeds of habit and skepticism and levity and indifference." "Women who make us unhappy," Proust declares, "are the cause of our writing books." Moments of grief force us into new situations and therefore oblige us "to enter more profoundly into contact with ourself, these painful dilemmas which love is constantly putting in our way teach us and reveal to us, layer after layer, the material of which we are made." And he concludes flatly: "The happy years are the lost, the wasted years, one must wait for suffering before one can work" (III, 943–947).

In the concluding dramatic action Marcel has five involuntary memories in rapid succession that enable him to discover the meaning of the joy that comes from recapturing *le temps perdu* and finding a way of making that joy endure by putting the story of its recapture into a novel. These involuntary memories, he realizes, go back to suffering in love, in his case back to the first stirring of jealousy in childhood on that night when he was afraid that his mother would not give him her customary goodnight kiss. *Le temps perdu*, like love, is experienced most intensely when it has been retrieved, and both can be retrieved only after they have been lost. The most intensely felt loss of love is jealousy, which, Proust believed, spurred his creativity.

In a famous short story, a bold play, and an epic novel Joyce explored some distinctly modern jealousies. "The Dead" (1914) leads up to Gretta's revelation that throughout her marriage to Gabriel she has been secretly, and far more passionately, in love with a young man who died long ago. Gabriel is awed by this disclosure as much as jealous, and he sensitively interrogates his wife for the details about her former love. After she falls asleep he stretches out next to her in bed and recaptures his love in a more understanding way than ever before. "Generous tears filled Gabriel's eyes. He had never felt like that himself towards any woman but he knew that such a feeling must be love."

Gabriel deals with jealousy reactively. In *Exiles* (1918) Richard intentionally seeks out jealousy so as to understand love better by experiencing its
most painfully deficient mode, and to liberate his marital love from conventional bonds. His wife Bertha is pursued by Richard's best friend Robert.
Richard wants to know all, so he interrogates Bertha about Robert's advances and learns how and where he kissed her, that she kissed him in return, that he did not have nice lips, and that she was excited. Richard wants
to use his jealousy to understand and transform his own love for her. He
explains to Robert that no one can take Bertha from him because she is not
a possession. Love does not mean, as Robert suggests, to possess a woman
in the flesh but rather "to wish her well." If Robert's love for Bertha, Richard
tells him, were based on "the luminous certitude that yours is the brain in
contact with which she must think and understand and that yours is the
body in contact with which her body must feel" (63), then he would go
away and leave them for each other, convinced that Robert was her deserv-
ing lover. Later Richard gives a deeper motive for pushing them together: "I
longed to be betrayed by you and by her—in the dark, in the night—secretly, meanly, craftily. By you, my best friend, and by her" (70). With this
exchange Joyce dramatizes Richard's search for the foundation of love out
of the ruins of a self-induced shame.

That search probes deeper with the concluding dialogue between Richard
and Bertha.

> BERTHA: Do you not wish to know—about what happened last
>   night?
> RICHARD: That I will never know.
> BERTHA: I will tell you if you ask me.
> RICHARD: You will tell me. But I will never know. Never in this
>   world.
> BERTHA,   *moving towards him:* I will tell you the truth, Dick, as I
>   always told you. I never lied to you.
> RICHARD,   *clenching his hands in the air, passionately:* Yes, yes.
>   The truth! But I will never know, I tell you.   (102)

Richard and Bertha reconstitute their love out of this doubt, which jealousy
made into a living reality. He confesses that his experiment did not entirely
work, that he still has a deep wound of doubt which can never be healed.
And he has an unfulfilled desire, he tells her—"To hold you by no bonds,

even of love, to be united with you in body and soul in utter nakedness—for this I longed." Not only can he never know for certain whether she was unfaithful or untruthful but, more importantly, he realizes that he can never know for certain anything about another person. As he stretches out to rest, Bertha takes his hand, asks forgiveness, and delivers the curtain line—"O, my strange wild lover, come back to me again!" (112). For Richard and Bertha love must be a coming-back, a recapture of something that, as with Proust, must be lost in order to be experienced with greater intensity.

Richard crudely pushed his wife into the arms of another man and she returned, but in the end he doubts the sincerity of his rejection, the truthfulness of the reasons he gave for it, the fidelity and honesty of his wife, the genuineness of her feelings, even the genuineness of his own jealousy. And yet, Joyce implies, their love seems stronger precisely because they lived through and became more aware of those deficiencies.[9]

On June 16, 1904, the day when *Ulysses* takes place, Leopold ogles the swinging hips of the girl next door and a strange woman's white stockings as she steps into a coach, masturbates in his pants while peeping at another woman, buys some pornography, revels over a letter to him from an admirer, bemoans the fact that he and his wife have not had sex in ten years, becomes aware that his wife that very afternoon is having sex with another man, laments further that she has had a string of other lovers, goes to a brothel, returns home late that night to crawl into the same bed where his cuckoldry took place, and goes to sleep after barely speaking to his wife. And yet *Ulysses* is a love story—one of the most profound and moving love stories of the twentieth century.

The love of Leopold and Molly is deficient in many ways. At its center is Leopold's jealousy, which Joyce recreates with a distinctly modern interpretation. Leopold feels most jealous when he sits in a bar listening to Simon Daedalus sing a love song. He watches his rival Blazes leave the bar and imagines him traveling arrogantly to have sex with Molly: "By Bachelor's walk jogjaunty jingled Blazes Boylan, bachelor, in sun, in heat, mare's glossy rump atrot, with flick of whip, on bounding tyres: sprawled, warmseated, Boylan impatience, ardentbold" (269–270). Moments later, upon hearing Simon sing the line "All is lost now," Leopold returns to his increasingly fragmented and painful thoughts: "Yes, I remember. Lovely air. In sleep she went to him. Innocence in the moon. Still hold her back. Brave, don't know their danger. Call name. Touch water. Jingle jaunty. Too late. She longed to go. That's why. Woman. As easy stop the sea. Yes: all is lost" (273). During the song's concluding line, "Come!—to me!", Leopold also hears the crowd's applause and imagines the sexual climax of Molly and Blazes:

>—*Come!*
>
> It soared, a bird, it held its flight, a swift pure cry, soar silver orb it leaped serene, speeding, sustained, to come, don't spin it out too long long breath he breath long life, soaring high, high resplendent, aflame, crowned, high in the effulgence symbolistic, high, of the ethereal bosom, high, of the high vast irradiation everywhere all soaring all around about the all, the endlessnessnessness . . .
>
> —*To me!*
> Siopold! [Simon plus Leopold]
> Consumed.
> Come. Well sung. All clapped. She ought to. Come. To me, to him, to her, you too, me, us. (275–276)

Jealous Victorians suffered alone. Leopold does not share his jealousy with anyone, and his isolation is intensified by the conviviality of a barroom crowd unaware of his suffering. At this moment the burning actuality of jealousy is too intense for Leopold to do anything but feel it. Only later will he be able to think about it as a universal problem and incorporate it into his love for Molly. But Joyce is not jealous. He crafts a direct interior monologue that universalizes jealousy by associating it with the singer, the crowd, the unhappy lover in the song, Leopold's distress, the pleasure of Molly and Blazes, and the idea that Molly ought to "come" to (and with) everyone. Joyce also raises his evaluation of jealousy above its traditionally low, pathetic status by merging it with the beauty of the singing and the joy of sex as an occasion for the crowd's unified applause—"Bravo! Clapclap. Goodman, Simon. Clappyclapclap. Encore!" (276).

Later that night Leopold reflects on the "eternal question of the life connubial" which involves jealousy: "Can real love, supposing there happens to be another chap in the case, exist between married folk?" (651). The remainder of the novel shows that although there is always another chap around, the answer is "yes." As Leopold settles next to Molly in their bed which still smells of Blazes, he reflects on the folly of the male fantasy that he always be "first, last, only and alone." He realizes that he, like every man, is "neither first nor last nor only nor alone in a series originating in and repeated to infinity" (731). That cosmic rationalization is followed by an earthy listing of the twenty-five names of Molly's lovers. But before falling asleep, Leopold puts to rest, if he does not fully resolve, the question of jealousy. He excuses Blazes for a number of reasons, but especially because, like himself, he is but one of the eternal series that must naturally pursue the Great Mother and Eternal Woman that Molly represents. He considers the four sentiments that make up his reaction: envy, jealousy, abnegation, and equanimity. He envies Blazes's sexual prowess; he *is* jealous because Molly made love to Blazes; he excuses them both for extenuating circumstances including Blazes's young age; and he feels equanimity, because what happened was natural, far less calamitous than many other crimes, and simply irreparable. Leopold rejects drastic reactions such as dueling and lists numerous reasons for trying to accept Molly's affair: the "frangibility of the hymen," variations in the ethical code, the endless production of semen, the futility of protest or vindication, and "the inanity of extolled virtue" (734).

What does he do? In the end he literally kisses Molly's ass. But this gesture, described with playful Joycean language, signifies not his ultimate degradation but the resiliency of his love: "He kissed the plump mellow yellow smellow melons of her rump, on each plump melonous hemisphere, in their mellow yellow furrow, with obscure prolonged provocative melonsmellonous osculation" (734–735). Thus does Leopold offer a benediction to the two hemispheres (and opposing principles) of the world of earthly delights, "redolent of milk and honey and of excretory sanguine and seminal warmth." By describing far more than his reticent literary predecessors, Joyce left even more to the imagination.

The history of jealousy can be summarized by contrasting its five subelements—its cause, responsibility, value, response, and resolution. Victorian jealousies were caused by contrived misunderstandings: Heathcliff misinterpreted what he heard, and Dorothea and Thornton misinterpreted what they saw. By contrast modern jealousies (such as those of Hans, Marcel, and Leopold) were caused by correctly interpreting what was seen and heard. Victorians projected the responsibility onto others (Willoughby blames Colonel De Craye, Marius imagines voyeuristic rivals, Calderon's wronged woman blames the man who broke his vows), while the moderns came to understand that jealousy was more their own responsibility. Victorians evaluated jealousy as an unqualified corruption of love or "contagion of evil," while moderns found it a stimulus for self-knowledge, art, friendship, and even love. The emotional response also changed. Although Victorian women might have panicked more than modern women, because they had fewer options and because their lives were more intensely focused on finding a man who would honor his vows, the initial hurt for men and women remained similar, since in all periods, I assume, jealousy causes a terrifying sense of annihilation. But the meaning, perhaps even the lived reality, of that experience changed. Victorians, finding no value in jealousy, indulged in self-pity as if they had contracted a disease, while the moderns used the suffering as a stimulus for self-examination and the reconstruction of love. The Victorian resolution was primarily negative, the modern one, more positive: the only resolution for Victorians was a comic clarification (hence removal) of the misunderstanding that caused the jealousy, or a tragic end of love itself by separation or death. On the other hand, the moderns resolved jealousy by keeping it alive, transmuted for their various purposes: jealousy gave Maggie the knowledge to take power in a compromised marriage, enabled Margaret to put Henry straight, forged a friendship for Hans, became the inspiration for Marcel's novel, and rebuilt Richard's marriage. It forced Leopold to think about the deficiencies of loving which are the foundation of its possibilities—from the weakness of the hymen and the endless production of semen to the insatiability of desire and the infinite range of human consciousness.

Jealousy also became more authentic. Victorians, by trivializing or projecting their responsibility for it, denigrating their experience of it, and failing to resolve it inwardly, turned jealousy into an experience that was alike for everyone, a "foreign visitation" that remained distant from their understanding of themselves even though it might be eating them up with anxiety and self-pity. The moderns, by accepting responsibility for jealousy, evaluating it as constructive (if nevertheless agonizing), and resolving it more self-consciously, experienced jealousy as a meaningful revelation of the deficiencies and possibilities of their unique ways of loving.

13 Selfhood

THE FOCUS OF the history of selfhood in loving is on awareness of oneself *as a self*, which varies between the extremes of fusion and autonomy. Fusion with a beloved tends toward the inauthentic, because it seeks loss of self-awareness. Autonomy tends toward the authentic, because it involves reflecting on what it means to be a separate self while still remaining drawn to the beloved. Although no lover can be entirely fused or autonomous, every love falls somewhere along this gradation. This chapter will show how the history of selfhood reveals an increasingly favorable estimation of struggling to resist the lure of fusion and remain autonomous.

I

The archetypal Romantic lover, yearning to lose himself in love, is Goethe's hero in *The Sorrows of Young Werther* (1774). After one meeting with Charlotte, he finds the entire universe blotted out—except for her. After hearing her play the harpsichord, he is exalted: "I feel like blowing out my brains" (47). "My imagination," he continues, "calls up no other image than her, and I see everything in the world only in relation to her" (69). By the mid-nineteenth century the Romantic ideal of a love that unified everything—mind and body, man and woman, rich and poor, sexual desire and love of God—could make lovers hyperventilate. In *Wuthering Heights* Cathy exclaims, "I *am* Heathcliff—he's always, always in my mind—not as a pleasure, any more than I am always a pleasure to myself—but as my own being" (122). After her death Heathcliff's own existence, so fused with hers, loses all purpose. He explains how, without her, "I have to remind myself to breathe—almost to remind my heart to beat!" (354).

In *Jane Eyre* the fusion of Jane's and Rochester's souls in love is symbolized by the chestnut tree, which is split by lightning moments after Rochester first proposes marriage and appeals for divine sanction even though, unknown to Jane, he is already married. Brontë would have us believe that God split only the trunk, for later Jane interprets the tree as a symbol of their underlying union. Although the tree was split and the branches would soon die, "the cloven halves were not broken from each other, for the firm base and strong roots kept them unsundered below . . . [and] they might be said to form one tree—a ruin, but an entire ruin" (304). That invisible root is a symbol of the Victorian ideal of fusion in love. Although the surface structure (and reality) appears sundered, the lovers are organically unified. In fact she and Rochester had very different roots, and love only became possible in the end after those deeply rooted differences were removed *unor*-ganically by her inheritance and by his financial ruin and physical injuries. In the end the lovers do fuse, or so Jane tells her reader in Biblical language: "I am my husband's life as fully as he is mine. No woman was ever nearer to her mate than I am: ever more absolutely bone of his bone, flesh of his flesh." [1] This fusion raises questions about the authenticity of their freedom, solitude, and communication. "To be together," she proudly proclaims, "is for us to be at once as free as in solitude." Their talking is not a struggle between independent selves to communicate but more like a single "audible thinking" (476).

The cultural high point of Romantic fusion is the love duet from Wagner's *Tristan and Isolde* (1859).[2] Tristan and Isolde are divided by their different nationalities and, most important, by their different loyalties to King Mark: she is supposed to marry him, while Tristan has sworn to serve him. The real world, symbolized by the light of day, thus forbids their love, which can only come forth in darkness and secrecy, as the couple sings together: "O sink down upon us, night of love / make me forget I live: / take me into your bosom, / free me from the world!" Their wish for annihilation builds as they yearn to flee the real world and forget their past. They hope to become "one breath" and to "die, undivided . . . ever at one in unbounded space." At the climax they long to fuse, not even separated by names *(ohne Nahmen)*, and become "infinitely, eternally, one consciousness" (Act II, Scene II).

Their words alone do not convey the power of Wagner's music, which evokes a sense of harmonious unity with the magnificently contrasting male and female voices that together span the emotions of lovers attempting to transcend the differences and imperfections of their worldly existence by aspiring to become one if only in death. But their hope to die together, however exquisitely scored, is inauthentic because it seeks to avoid responsibility for their own necessarily separate deaths and spare them from facing up to the everyday problems of living that in fact make fusion impossible. I am not arguing that the opera is inauthentic, only the love it celebrates. Victorian artists, writers, and composers produced numerous masterpieces about inauthentic modes of loving, I would speculate, precisely because the reality of love from which they drew was so constricted by conventions that they were driven to envision the most heroic efforts and sacrifices in order to achieve love. Like Tristan and Isolde, Victorian lovers were forced to flee from seeing one another clearly in the light of day, and in seeking to fuse in secret places of darkness, sometimes even in death, they were seeking ways to escape from themselves as selves.[3]

Victorian novels are full of lovers aspiring or expiring to fuse. Writing to Cosette, Marius praises a love that has "melted and merged two persons in a sublime and sacred unity" (805). Hugo adds approvingly, "love is the melting-pot in which man and woman are fused together" (1139). Flaubert is more cynical about the genuineness of such yearning but includes it in *Sentimental Education*, as Frédéric exclaims to Mme. Arnoux, "I can no more live without you than without the air of heaven. Can't you feel my soul yearning for yours? Don't you feel that they are destined to mingle?" (269). His rhetoric is as excessive as his love is impatient, but both lovers take the rhetoric seriously.

Sometimes the desire for fusion was one-sided. Already by 1873 Tolstoy presented such desperate longing as one cause of the tragedy of Anna Karenina, who herself comes to realize as much: "If I could be anything but [Vronsky's] mistress, passionately loving nothing but his caresses—but I cannot and do not want to be anything else" (690). Anna identifies one reason for the longing for fusion that was a particular problem especially for middle-class women in her time—the lack of other life choices. In *A Pair of Blue Eyes* Elfride faces the same dilemma, as Hardy explains: "Clinging to [Knight] so dependently, she taught him in time to presume upon that devotion . . . A slight rebelliousness occasionally would have done him no harm, and would have been a world of advantage to her. But she idolized him, and was proud to be his bond-servant" (369). Hardy's recommendation—that she play hard to get—underestimates the enormity of Elfride's dilemma.

Around the mid-century Heathcliff and Cathy, Jane and Rochester, Tristan and Isolde, Marius and Cosette unabashedly yearn for fusion. Around 1870 the deficiencies of fusion begin to surface with Flaubert's irony and with the lonely, tragic deaths of Anna and Elfride. Meredith ridicules it in *The Egoist* with Willoughby's demand that Clara swear to "be true" to him "dead as well as living!" (86). Willoughby's elaboration caricatures the ideal of fusion. "Women think the husband's grave breaks the bond, cuts the tie, sets them loose. They wed the flesh—pah! What I call on you for is nobility; the transcendent nobility of faithfulness beyond death" (86). Willoughby's love for Clara is, as we have seen, overwhelmingly mediated by prescribed emotional posturing, and his appeal for everlasting fusion is similarly shaped by conventional *patterns*.[4] By making such an impossible demand for love beyond death the pivot of a struggle that occupies a great portion of the novel, Meredith underscores the persistent vitality of the ideal of fusion in his time.

In Allen's *The Woman Who Did* (1895) Herminia repudiates the ideal of fusion in searching for a love that is free from external constraint. She loves Alan but rejects marriage because it is an institution that asserts a man's supremacy and ignores a woman's individuality. As she explains to him, "If I love a man at all, I must love him on terms of perfect freedom. I can't bind myself down to live with him to my shame one day longer than I love him" (41). If he were to leave, she continues, "I shall go away, and grieve for you, of course, and feel bereaved for months, *as if* I could never possibly again love any man. *At present* it *seems* to me I could never love him. *But* though my heart tells me that, my *reason tells me* I should some day find some other soul I might perhaps fall back upon" (59). Herminia believes that Alan is the love of her life, "the man who I know by immediate instinct, which is the voice of nature and of God within us, was intended from all time for me." That conviction makes her rejection of the hope for fusion so anti-Victorian, because her qualifying words (which I have put in italics) contradict the unqualified rhapsodic expressions that poured out of mid-century lovers who anticipated eternal bereavement at the loss of a beloved. Victorians did not grieve "as if" they would never love again. After Alan dies, Herminia continues to search in vain for an ideal man who does not aspire to fusion, a man who can say to her: "Be mine as much as you will, as long as you will, to such extent as you will; but before all things *be your own*" (183, italics mine).

Four years later in Chopin's *The Awakening* Edna's own awakening includes rejecting the unreflective fusion of her friends the Ratignolles, who appear to understand each other perfectly. "If ever the fusion of two human beings into one has been accomplished," Edna explains, "it was surely in their union." The Ratignolles depress Edna, for she sees their union as "but an appalling and hopeless ennui" (56).

In *The Odd Women* Everard and Rhoda reject the suffocating love that will not permit any withholding of emotion or even withholding of attention between lovers. Gissing contrasts their craving for independence with Monica's idolatrous love for Bevis. Monica believes that she could "make his will her absolute law, could live on his smiles, could devote herself to his interests" (222). In contrast Everard wants rather a "free union" that presupposes "equality of position." He wants a woman who would be capable of "resuming her separate life" if necessary (145). Rhoda wants a man who will respect her individuality. But their wants are ahead of their time, because her passion for autonomy and his inability to accept it keep them apart. They are both oddballs who do not fit in with their age or with each other's demands in love.

In the twentieth century novelists begin to create lovers who not only survive a failure to fuse but could thrive on it. For James fusion is an impossibility, and the desire for it, "a lost art." His "golden bowl" is the first of a number of strikingly modern images of autonomy. Like Brontë's tree, the bowl is cracked. But whereas the tree is whole under the ground and only split above it, the bowl appears whole but is cracked beneath its gilded surface. The love story turns on the disclosure of the truth about the marriage between Maggie and Amerigo, symbolized by the bowl that looks elegant but is basically unsound. Their marriage can only begin to be repaired as the truth about the crack underlying their love becomes known, and that knowing must remain incomplete.

James underscores the historical significance of his symbol with an exchange at the antiques shop where Charlotte finds the golden bowl and comments that the technique of gilding is "a lost art," and the antique dealer (most likely James himself)[5] adds that it is also from "a lost time." He does not mean that people have lost the art of gilding but that buyers (that is, lovers) have a better eye for artifice and are better able to perceive underlying flaws. Even Amerigo, whose infidelity is the crack in his impending marriage to Maggie, is wary of the gilded bowl. Charlotte offers to give it to him as a wedding present, but he does not want to risk the truth being known and declines. One implication of this story is that all loves are cracked somewhere, like the golden bowl.

Ann Veronica (1909) abounds with the current feminist rhetoric of autonomy. In rejecting Manning's proposal of marriage the heroine writes: "I want to be a person by myself, and to pull my own strings. I had rather have trouble and hardship like that than be taken care of by others. I want to be myself" (112). By the end of the novel she does find a better suitor, but she also falls blissfully into the stew of fusion—married, pregnant, well-dressed, and without a care in the world, waited on by her parlormaid and taken care of by a loving husband.[6]

In Rilke's *The Notebooks of Malte Laurids Brigge* (1910) the hero does not just talk about being autonomous; he is sickened by fusion and reconstitutes all relationships to avoid being loved too much. In the opening pages he wonders whether the entire history of the world may have been misunderstood "because we have always spoken about its masses . . . instead of talking about the one person" (23). Malte elaborates his call for recognizing the singularity of existence with his interpretation of the story of the Prodigal Son as "the legend of a man who didn't want to be loved" (251). When the Prodigal Son was a child, everyone loved him, but in so doing they smothered him by fashioning his life according to their own desires. Their love was "careless and trivial." His greatest terror was "the thick sorrow of those embraces in which everything was lost." He resented how love made him feel "drained of all meaning, without the right to even the slightest danger," and he went away to escape a suffocating, generalized love that denied his singularity. He was able to return because in staying away he came to understand how much he had been misunderstood and how consequently the love that others wanted to shower on him had nothing to do with him. "How could they know who he was?" Upon returning, with an "incredible gesture which had never been seen before," he threw himself at the feet of those from whom he had fled "imploring them not to love." To his relief no one could understand. He consoled himself that some kind of love may be possible, but only from one who understood who he was. But such love was not likely even from God. "He was now terribly difficult to love, and he felt that only One would be capable of it. But He was not yet willing" (254–261). Whether that "One" was a God, his own deified self, or a perceptive beloved is unclear, but his insistence on the singularity of love is unmistakable. Maintaining distance and danger in love, imploring people not to love too much, and finding comfort in being difficult if not impossible to love were aspects of greater value attached to autonomy of the self.

Musil begins his story "The Perfecting of a Love" (1911) with a claustrophobic love at the point where Brontë leaves Jane and Rochester. Claudine and her husband have clung to each other "uniting like two wonderfully well-fitting halves in the act of fusion." Every room in their home was like a crystal, with the couple in the center "blissfully communing." But whereas Brontë saw happiness in her couple's "perfect concord," Musil sees a couple "exhausted by the weight of their happiness." The *im*perfection of their love becomes apparent when Claudine tells her husband how she became desperate one night when he held her in his arms and she realized that there could be something other than him. They gaze at one another, "both of them swaying as with the tension there is in the bodies of two tightrope acrobats close together on the rope"—another inventive modern image of love as an autonomous, if perilous, connectedness (127–128).

Claudine's affair with the stranger she meets met on a train reveals the deficiency of fusion and allows her to reflect on the possibilities of being her own self. "The wonderful, dangerous intensification of feeling that came with lying and cheating in love" liberated her from the routine and safe bond of marriage. "For the first time she had felt her being, down to its very foundations, as something indeterminate, had apprehended this ultimate faceless experience of herself in love as something that destroyed the very root, the absoluteness, of existence." For Musil, a single root cannot even unite the individual, let alone a pair of lovers. Stripped of her home, husband, morality, past, and reputation, she is free to explore the "possibilities of real love" instead of the illusory love of her marriage, which involves "existing solely by virtue of another human being." Such an illusory fused love is actually as empty as "a gliding between two mirrors behind which nothingness lay" (168–169).

Musil's image of fusion as the nullity created by two gliding mirrors shatters, almost literally, one meaning of the mirror as an instrument for reflection. In traditional art a woman contemplating herself in a mirror usually symbolized vanity. That convention, represented in numerous paintings of "Woman at Her Toilette," did not of course indicate genuine self-contemplation, because the woman always saw herself *for someone else,* as an object and not as a subject.[7]

Colette challenged that conventional meaning by invoking the mirror to suggest not vanity but authentic self-reflection. *The Vagabond* opens with Renée contemplating herself in a mirror. As a mime and dancer she must make herself up to perform for an audience, but she also uses her time at the dressing-room mirror, her "dangerous, lucid hour," to study herself. She does not worry about what others will see but ponders whether there "really is me behind that mask of purplish rouge" (7). She sees evidence of the passage of time but consoles herself that her face "depends on the expression which animates it" (12). She does not await redemption in a man but accepts the inevitability of being alone, as the mirror shows her. Redemption must come out of isolation after a loss of love. "What numbers of women have experienced that retreat into themselves," she wonders, "that patient withdrawal which follows their rebellious tears!" (31). With her first lover she had tried to efface herself, but she resists her new lover. "His belief in me," she explains, "enlightened me about myself that evening just as an unexpected mirror, at a street corner or on a staircase, suddenly reveals blemishes and saggings in one's face and figure" (76). The mirrors that turn her toward herself as a self are everywhere.

In moments of strength she can put herself first, but the joy of loving threatens to weaken such resolve. Colette keeps her heroine always at the edge of that temptation. There is a hesitation before every plunge, a qualifier in every delirious exclamation, a disappointment behind every thrill. After resisting Max's persistent courting she finally lets him stay for a while, but eventually goes off on tour. He begs her to return, but she resists, recalling the self-effacement of her first love. "The momentary grace which touched me now withdraws itself from me, since I refused to lose myself in it. Instead of saying to it: 'Take me!' I ask it: 'What are you giving me? Another myself? There is no other myself. You're giving me a friend who is young, ardent, jealous, and sincerely in love? I know: that is what is called a master, and I no longer want one.'" Her soliloquy concludes with another question and answer: "A look of his can arouse me and I cease to belong to myself if he puts his mouth on mine? In that case he is my enemy, he is the thief who steals me from myself" (214–215).

Renée's love is distinctly un-Victorian. She is not an exquisite courtesan, a demonic seductress, a husband hunter, a diligent governess, a courageous heiress, a devoted sister, a fresh ingénue, a convent flower, or an angel in the house. She is an entertainer and a vagabond. She is divorced from a man who fooled and seduced her and, instead of finding goodness, truth, or God, continues to fool and seduce other women. Her new lover has no profession, and her work takes her away from him. He is still under the sway of parental influence; she is not. She is salaried and does not need to inherit a fortune to become eligible for fulfillment in love. She is thirty-four years old, her lover is thirty-three, and she does not value his ardent loving, because it is a manifestation of his annoying naivete. She can lose herself in delirious sexual pleasure but is able to tear herself away. Her reflections on the importance of a strong sense of self are convincing, although the next moment she can yearn for fusion. Her reflections in a mirror show her to herself ever more revealingly.

II

Victorian novelists did not all fail to question the value of fusion, but they did so rarely and were aware of going against the governing sensibilities of their age. In the modern period the desire to fuse with a beloved did not disappear, but it was increasingly interpreted as an illusion, a failure, or a projection of oneself.

Fitzgerald and Hemingway explore the illusory nature of fusion. In *This Side of Paradise* Rosalind wallows in the rhetoric of fusion: she tells Amory that she wants to love him eternally with all her heart, have his babies, become one with him. "We're *you*—not me," she cries incoherently. "Oh, you're so much a part, so much all of me." But even at that high point of elation Amory is skeptical: "Wouldn't it be awful if this was—was the high point?" (186, 188). He questions the possibility of fusion and its illusory joy, as does Frederic in *A Farewell to Arms*. When Catherine cries out for oneness, "Oh, darling, I want you so much I want to be you too," Frederic replies unconvincingly, "You are. We're the same one." She proposes finally that they "go to sleep at the same moment," and he agrees. "But," he explains flatly, "we did not. I was awake for quite a long time" (310–311). Hemingway concludes the chapter with the ruminations of this sleepless lover—a mundane reminder of the impossibility of fusion.

Ford and Musil dramatize the failure of fusion. In *The Good Soldier* Ford theorizes that "the real heat of passion long continued and withering up the soul of a man is the craving for identity with the woman that he loves. He desires [not so much sexual union but] to see with the same eyes, to touch with the same sense of touch, to hear with the same ears, to lose his identity, to be enveloped, to be supported." In anticipation of Sartre's theory that the lover in aspiring to fuse seeks in vain to have his beloved restore his lost self to himself, Ford writes, "We are all so afraid, we are all so alone, we all need from the outside the assurance of our own worthiness to exist." The need is so desperate that the illusion works for a time, though eventually it fails. That is why, he explains, "this is the saddest story." But the failure to fuse is only a prelude to the even sadder and more destructive consequence of the desire to fuse, because after repeated failures one day some woman will "set her seal upon his imagination . . . for good." Then he will stop seeking new horizons in love, not because he has found someone with whom he can fuse but because as a human being "he will have gone out of business" (114–115).

While Ford's hero fails to fuse tragically, Musil's brother and sister lovers fail comically. First Ulrich surveys some ancient myths of love as a search for wholeness after primordial separation. He comforts his sister with the thought that as brother and sister they are partly reunited. She responds that twins would go one better, and Ulrich voices their defiant affirmation: "We declare ourselves twins!" He explains further that their happy theorizing comes from the universal desire to move "in the imaginary direction towards a love unadulterated with estrangement and not-love" (III, 280–285). While they're at it, Agatha adds, they might as well go all the way and declare themselves Siamese twins. Ulrich becomes troubled by this fantasizing and frets over such practical physiological difficulties as how he would live with a shared blood-stream or nervous system. He plunges back into reality brooding about how disquieting it would be if another man kissed his Siamese-twin sister. Their playful dialogue on fusion is its *reductio ad absurdum*.

Proust and Gide emphasize the projective nature of fusion. Proust, ever the pessimist about love, states categorically that we are always detached from others. "When we are in love with a woman we simply project onto her a state of our own soul." Marcel explains that "Albertine was scarcely more than a silhouette; all that had been superimposed upon her was of my own invention" (I, 891, 917). The joy of love is the delusionary pleasure we get from believing that we are united, not detached, but since we are irremediably detached and merely project our own scarcely understood soul onto another human form, that joy cannot last long.

In *The Counterfeiters* (1925) Gide labels his characters, their emotions, even his own novel as counterfeit and so, in good Cartesian style, wipes clean the slate of conventional truths. This updated universal doubt about what is genuine enables Gide to disclose a deeper understanding of the possibilities of truth, even if he does not hold up some entity, character, morality, or emotion as the ultimate truth. When he turns his withering skepticism to love, the projective nature of the lover's passion for imposture becomes apparent. Edouard's journal speaks for Gide in explaining how Edouard and Laura "abandon all sincerity" in loving each other. "So long as he loves and desires to be loved, the lover cannot show himself as he really is, and moreover he does not see the beloved—but instead, an idol whom he decks out, a divinity whom he creates" (72). But the projecting cannot be sustained. "A day comes when the true self, which time has slowly stripped of all its borrowed raiment, reappears, and then, if it was of these ornaments that the other was enamoured, he finds that he is pressing to his heart nothing but an empty dress." Truth in loving is, ironically, realization of its tendency toward the counterfeit, as Edouard announces: "Ah! with what virtues, with what perfections I had adorned her!" (70).

Gide formalizes his theory of the "decrystallization" of love and clarifies its historical significance by contrasting it with the famous theory of "crystallization" that Stendhal had presented a century earlier in *On Love* (1822). Stendhal compared love to a bough left for several months in the saline pools of the Salzburg salt mines, where it becomes "spangled with a vast number of shimmering, glittering diamonds." He defined psychic "crystallization" as "that process of the mind which discovers fresh perfections in its beloved at every turn of events" and concluded that "it is sufficient to think of a perfection in order to see it in the person you love" (6). In contrast to Stendhal who was fascinated by such projection as a creative source of joy in love, Gide is interested in "decrystallization"—the process by which the wear of daily life removes the shimmering crystals and exposes once again the unadorned original bough (the real nature of the beloved). "What an admirable subject for a novel—the progressive and reciprocal decrystallization of a husband and a wife after fifteen or twenty years of married life" (72).

Although Gide's primary commitment is to aesthetics, he does moralize about fusion and autonomy. He shared a measure of Stendhal's admiration for the way love unleashes one's imagination and then makes one captive of those projected imaginings, but Gide's admiration had limits. He argued that one must learn "to love a little less" in order "to detach some of the crystals from one's love" (72). The temptation to crystallize must be countered by an effort to decrystallize, which gives the lover some room to breathe and provides the artist with the distance to craft his passion into a work of art.

Gide's theory of decrystallization identifies the projective nature of fusion and underlines the importance of maintaining some measure of autonomy. Other modern novelists were more emphatic about the necessity of autonomy, although they were wary of the tendency of the newly autonomous to indulge in overblown moralizing. In *The Thibaults* Rachel caricatures the

New Woman's conception of the will to power as the ability to withhold love from a beloved, as she tells Antoine: "'I haven't always had my independence; two years ago I hadn't it. But now I've got it—and I mean to keep it.' (She believed she spoke sincerely.) 'I set so much store by my freedom that for nothing in the world would I abandon it. Do you follow me?'" (348). Du Gard might have added the same parenthetical clarification after Antoine's feeble reply—"Yes"—because both lovers protest too much that they sincerely want to be free and avoid all misunderstanding, as if polemics could protect them from the dependencies of love.

Woolf and Lawrence create numerous pairs of lovers who invent ways to remain autonomous. Already in Woolf's first novel, *The Voyage Out* (1915), lovers strain to retain personal space. When Terry proposes to Rachel he vows: "Oh, you're free! . . . and I'd keep you free. We'd be free together" (244). That outburst is the theoretical basis of the plot for *Night and Day* (1919), in which Ralph weans Katharine away from a loveless engagement to another man by offering an unbinding friendship which would allow her time, friends, work, and a room of her own. He secures her agreement and eventual love by his strong commitment to freedom.[8] In the end they discover an enchanted region of autonomous loving. "Together they groped in this difficult region, where the unfinished, the unfulfilled, the unwritten, and the unreturned, came together in their ghostly way and wore the semblance of the complete and the satisfactory" (506).

In *To the Lighthouse* Lily admires the love of Mr. Banks for Mrs. Ramsay—"a love that never attempted to clutch its object" (73). In *Mrs. Dalloway* such non-possessive loving is the source of Clarissa's resiliency. The novel is full of people who clutch and destroy others—the doctor (Sir William *Brad*shaw), the evangelical (Miss *Kil*man), and the philanthropist (Lady *Brut*on), who, as their names imply, nail, kill, and brutalize in the name of high ideals. There is also Peter, who in years past clutched at Clarissa's soul. "With Peter," she reflects, "everything had to be shared; everything gone into." Thirty years earlier she had rejected Peter because of his insistent demand for fusion and chose instead to marry Richard, who offered her a greater measure of autonomy, although dependencies eroded it over the years.

Her party, which concludes the novel, is like a dramatization of Heidegger's remark about how in the inauthentic everyday self "everyone is the other, and no one is himself" (165). But in the final scene Clarissa emerges magisterially on her staircase in a striking pose of autonomy amidst others, the object of Peter's admiration. From that commanding position she presides over the live-and-let-live spirit that made her parties and her marriage work.

Among the many issues that preoccupied Lawrence, resolving the tension between fusion and autonomy was paramount. Ursula wrestles with it throughout *The Rainbow* until she finally rejects a cozy capitulation to Skrebensky, who offers the wifely happiness that "had been enough for her mother." She insists rather on "creating life to fit herself" (484). In *Women in Love* Ursula takes that determination and the historical change that it implies into her relationship with Rupert, although he takes the lead in working out an autonomous love.[9]

When Rupert tells Gerald early on that he aspires to a "perfect union with a woman" (51), he seems to be repeating the longing for fusion that had resounded over the centuries. But in conversation with Ursula he explains that the perfection of love is not fusion, that love is only part of any relationship. To Ursula's anti-historical claim that love "always means the same thing," Rupert counters that its meaning has changed, and he urges that they "let the old meanings go." She asks what he means by it, and he replies tentatively, "I don't know—freedom together" (124).

Three days later in his room they have another chat. Once again he seems to invoke the language of fusion. "If we are going to know each other, we must pledge ourselves for ever." It must be "final and irrevocable." But then he adds, "I can't say it is love I have to offer—and it isn't love I want. It is something much more impersonal and harder—and rarer." After a tense discussion about the meaning of love, he insists that the root of his love is "a naked kind of isolation, an isolated me, that does *not* meet and mingle, and never can." These sobering remarks infuriate her. "If there is no love," she asks, "what is there?" Rupert has worked so hard to get her to ask that question that he is not quite prepared to answer. He begins with what love is not. It is not based on any obligation or standards for action. It is something between "two utterly strange creatures," whose love is impersonal and beyond speech. He then seems to affirm the ideal of fusion but with a crucial reservation—love is a willingness to lose oneself in order to regain a deeper sense of oneself as autonomous. "There needs be the pledge between us, that we will both cast off everything, cast off ourselves even, and cease to be, so that that which is perfectly ourselves can take place in us" (136–138). His perfection is not fusion but an exquisite tension created by a full commitment of the autonomous self. In other words, a crucial aspect of autonomy can only be realized, paradoxically, when one is willing to throw oneself into love without holding back.

Frustrated and apologetic by the abstraction of his language Rupert offers a vivid image of the love he wants. It must be not a mingling "but an equilibrium, a pure balance of two single beings—as the stars balance each other." In explaining he uses the word "orbit," but Ursula, altering the word to "satellite," charges: "You want a satellite, Mars and his satellite!" He protests that he did not say or imply a satellite. "I meant two single equal stars balanced in conjunction." Rupert explains its larger significance. "One must commit oneself to a conjunction with the other—for ever. But it is not selfless—it is a maintaining of the self in mystic balance and integrity—like a star balanced with another star" (139–144). With this image Lawrence deftly takes a cliché among clichés, the star that symbolized the bonding force governing the fate of the original star-crossed lovers, and transforms it into an image of attraction, equality, balance, and autonomy.

As his love for Ursula heats up, Rupert pulls away. "Fusion, fusion, this horrible fusion of two beings," he thinks, "was it not nauseous and horrible anyhow, whether it was a fusion of the spirit or of the emotional body?" He recoils from Ursula's suffocating "bath of birth, to which all men must come!" "Why could they not remain individuals, limited by their own limits?" (301). In the end he marries Ursula and both begin to give without reserve in sexual loving, each compromising their uncompromisable demands. As Lawrence explains, "they were never *quite* together, at the same moment, one was always a little left out" (427). She never got all of him, and he never got enough of the freedom component of his ideal "freedom together."

Lawrence's image of love as a pair of orbiting stars belongs with a group of unfused, if not entirely autonomous, twentieth-century love images: James's golden bowl, Rilke's Prodigal Son, Musil's tightrope acrobats and Siamese twins, Colette's mirrors, Hemingway's war-weary insomniac, Proust's silhouette lover, and Gide's decrystallization. The diversity of these images is itself evidence of the singularity of the respective conceptions of love that they were designed to express. And when loves are unique, they cannot be fused, because fusion obliterates uniqueness.

Jane Eyre, Heathcliff, and Marius were each likewise one of a kind, and their struggle to find love was genuine. But they did not emphasize individuality as did so many twentieth-century lovers who lined up to insist upon autonomy—not because the moderns were overly cautious, but because they believed that autonomy must be maintained to allow each lover to re-main open to the fuller intensities of passionate love.

Throughout history many powerful systems of thought emphasized the necessity of privation or deficiency as a necessary foundation for transcend-ence. For the Stoics self-denial was the way to truth and goodness; for Chris-tianity subduing the flesh was necessary to liberating the spirit; for Kierke-gaard despair preceded faith; for Nietzsche nihilism and the death of God preceded the way to the overman; for Freud neurotic misery preceded psy-choanalytic insight; and for Heidegger anxiety preceded the disclosure of the self as a self. Absorbed in the world of others, I can flee from myself as a self, but anxiety forces me back to myself. In anxiety I am aware of peril but forced to accept its cause—my own existence and nothing else. Anxiety brings me close not to some threatening beast out there in the world but to my own self as a continual temptation to lose myself in what "they" do. Similarly, in love, the presence of the beloved offers me a chance to flee from myself by fusion with the beloved, but the authentic lover resists that temp-tation. As I have shown, many twentieth-century writers called for such re-sistance.

14 Proposal

FUNDAMENTAL elements of love are essential, which, strictly defined, means necessary to all possible loves. I have relaxed that definition in order to include the proposal—along with kissing, wedding, sex, and marriage—for three compelling reasons. First, they are important experiences of many lovers and reveal the meaning of love precisely because one can choose them or not. Secondly, since they take place in a relatively discrete moment (aside from marriage) and are easy to isolate from the sprawling time span of the love story, their modes can be brought into sharp contrast with modes from other periods. Finally, the proposal, wedding, and marriage involve other people who also structure love in historically distinctive ways.

On the modern side of this history much of the evidence is missing. Whereas images of proposals abound in Victorian painting, they all but disappear in the modern period along with the decline in narrative painting generally. Although modern novels continue to narrate love stories, proposal scenes in them become increasingly ironic, if they are not omitted altogether. The examples I did find are deficient in revealing ways: Lawrence creates a mock proposal, Colette elaborates a rejected proposal, and Joyce's heroine rethinks a proposal she had accepted sixteen years earlier. These deficiencies are themselves of historical significance in that they reflect an increasing devaluation of public ritual. They also explain why I introduce my interpretation of some of the subelements with only the Victorian mode and leave the historical contrast to Molly's concluding interior monologue, which bears on them all. The history of the proposal may be divided into eight subelements: motivation, others for permission, others for mediation, others for sanction, gender polarity, intimacy, climacticality, and choice.

I

The motives for proposing and accepting a proposal shift from concern about money, class, status, and security to a greater emphasis on self-realization. In Hardy's *Far from the Madding Crowd* Gabriel promises Bathsheba "a piano in a year of two" and offers as collateral his "nice snug little farm" (77–79). Angel proposes to Tess with the savoir faire of a personnel manager: "I shall soon want to marry, and, being a farmer, you see I shall require for my wife a woman who knows all about . . . farms. Will you be that woman, Tessy?" (144). In *Daniel Deronda* Grandcourt's motive in proposing to Gwendolen is "to have the right always to take care of you" (168). Wells caricatures such chivalry in *Ann Veronica* with Manning's proposal "to take you up, to make you mine, to carry you off and set you apart from all the strain and turmoil of life." She can hardly keep a straight face as he elaborates his intentions "to shield, to protect, to lead and toil . . . to be your knight, your protector" (56). Manning exemplifies Heidegger's definition of inauthentic solicitude—a leaping in for the other in such a way as to take away the other's "care" and leave the other "dominated and dependent."

In 1895 Oscar Wilde mocked one hallmark of the Victorian proposal—earnestness. *The Importance of Being Earnest* involves a subterfuge: Jack, who lives in town, has invented an imaginary younger brother Ernest who lives in the country. Jack uses Ernest, who is always getting into scrapes, as an excuse to get away from town. In the country Jack goes by the name of Ernest. He runs into unexpected difficulty while trying to propose to Gwendolen, who lives in the country, when he discovers that she has a fetish about the name Ernest, which she thinks is his name. He is shocked to learn that ever since their friend Algernon told her that he had a friend named Ernest, she felt destined to love this man. Flabbergasted, Jack asks, "But you don't really mean to say that you couldn't love me if my name wasn't Ernest?" She replies that that's not a problem, since his name *is* Ernest. For a number of delightfully frivolous reasons Gwendolen is determined to marry a man whose name is Ernest. She is not concerned that he *be* earnest, only that he be *named* Ernest. Gwendolen mocks three hundred years of sympathy with Juliet's woeful question, "What's in a name?" She further inverts conventional gender roles first by reminding him to put the question and then by accepting before he has a chance to do so. When he finally does propose she gives him another spin by ridiculing the conventional reverence for love's one-and-only climactic moment, as she says derisively, "I am afraid you have had very little experience in how to propose" (Act I).

Wilde marks a transition in the history of the proposal by mocking the way the entire courtship ritual had been observed throughout the Victorian era. Henry James dramatizes that transition with a character who has modern goals but Victorian means. In *The Golden Bowl* Charlotte explains her motives for accepting Adam's proposal: "I should like to be a little less adrift. I should like to have a home. I should like to have an existence. I should like to have a motive for one thing more than another—a motive outside myself. In fact . . . you know, I want to *be* married. It's—well, it's the condition" (175). As a consequence of advances in education, employment, and law, women were becoming increasingly able to consider marrying for personal affection, sexual pleasure, common interest, and mutual respect rather than for protection and security. But Charlotte is caught in the middle. Her education, temperament, and expectations are feminist and modern, but she has no profession or money and thus marries for money and status in the hope of achieving "the condition," which she thinks of as wanting any one thing more than another.

Her motives are inauthentic and self-contradictory: one cannot realize oneself as a self by giving oneself over to a motive outside oneself. Such external pressures shape all proposals by providing permission, mediation, or sanction, although the intensity of those pressures changed over the years I am covering.

II

In the Victorian era requests for permission generally went as follows. The suitor met privately with the father, respectfully presented his qualifications, demonstrated his ability to care for the daughter, affirmed his undying love for her, and then, if permission was granted, met with her and proposed. Every element of this scenario is satirized by Lawrence in *Women in Love*.

Rupert has come to propose to Ursula and meets with her father, but only because she is not at home. In the Victorian novel the daughter is always at home. The father, instead of an imposing authority, appears to Rupert as "a roomful of old echoes." Rupert tells her father casually, "As a matter of fact . . . I wanted to ask her to marry me." Rupert is not dutifully asking permission to propose, rather he is trying it out on the old man, who, already scandalized, asks, "Was she expecting you then?" Rupert's negative reply further miffs the father, who realizes that his daughter's privileges as well as his own paternal rights are being slighted. Since Ursula was not expecting him, her father cautions, perhaps this is rather sudden: "I shouldn't want her to be in too big a hurry either. It's no good looking around afterwards, when it's too late." Rupert outrages her father by replying: "it need never be too late . . . If one repents being married, the marriage is at an end." So much for the once-in-a-lifetime momentousness of the proposal and the commitment to undying love. Lawrence's evaluation of seeking permission from others before proposing is evident in this clash between Rupert's temporal flexibility and the rigid scheduling of Ursula's father, in particular his notion of what might be "too late."

Rupert subverts the final steps of the conventional scenario after Ursula returns. Her father, instead of granting permission, finds himself mediating by aping Rupert's own inadvertence in explaining that he had come to propose. Rupert attempts to reassure Ursula that "there's no need to answer at once," to which she replies indignantly, "Why should I say anything? . . . You do this off your own bat, and it has nothing to do with me. Why do you both want to bully me?" (248–253). Lawrence thus ridicules asking someone else for permission by constructing one of the most powerful love stories of twentieth-century literature around this botched request for permission.

III

The second function of others is their mediation in the actual proposal. Five such mediations in nineteenth-century novels testify to the vast lived distance between prospective couples, their lack of communication, and the resulting doomed unions that required such assistance. In response to Charles Bovary's hint that he wants to marry Emma, her father suggests that *he* ask Emma and then inform Charles by slamming shutters against the outside wall of their home if she agrees. Waiting outside at a safe distance down the road Charles observes the shutters slam and returns to the Rouault farm the next morning when, we are told, "Old Rouault [not Emma] embraced his future son-in-law." In *Middlemarch* Mr. Brooke proposes to his daughter Dorothea on behalf of Casaubon, and she accepts by letter. In *The Portrait of a Lady* Isabel is at first scandalized over Mrs. Touchette's theory that Madame Merle had arranged her marriage to Gilbert, but as the marriage disintegrates, she realizes that Mrs. Touchette was right. "Madame Merle had married her" (517). These three mediated proposals portended ruinous marriages, but none was more destructive than that of the heroine of *Effi Briest*, whose mother dropped the news on her seventeen-year-old daughter when she had just come inside after playing with friends. "Baron Innstetten has just asked to marry you . . . You saw him the day before yesterday and I think you liked him, too . . . He's a man of character [and] has a good situation, and if you don't say no, which I can hardly imagine my clever Effi doing, then by the age of twenty you'll have gone as far as others have at forty" (24). Effi was engaged by sundown. When in *The Well-Beloved* Pierston asks Avice's mother to propose to her for him, he goes one better than Innstetten, since Pierston had not only proposed to Avice's mother but to her grandmother as well. This mediated proposal concludes with the dying mother melodramatically placing her daughter's hand over Pierston's. Hardy uses the passive voice to emphasize the force of public pressure behind such mediated proposals: "No more was said in argument, and the thing was regarded as determined" (165).

I found no mediated proposals in the modern novels.

IV

The third function of others is to provide public sanction for the proposal, that is, how proposals were influenced by others. In *Daniel Deronda* Gwendolen discovers that in spite of her attempt to retain a choice in the face of Grandcourt's courting, social forces are overwhelming. "But as to her accepting him, she had done it already in accepting his marked attentions [for a couple of weeks]" (169). Anna Karenina's husband was similarly corralled when Anna's aunt introduced him to her and "contrived to put him in such a position that he was obliged either to propose or leave town." When Karenin hesitated, her aunt explained "that he had already compromised the girl, and that he was in honor bound to propose" (461). In Meredith's *The Egoist* Willoughby, for all his self-involvement, is slavishly beholden to public opinion and finds himself engaged to Clara, to whom he proposed as if in a trance created by public opinion simply because she "was held to be" the most desirable woman around when he was of a mind to marry. Once again the passive voice expresses the inauthenticity of internalized public opinion pressuring someone to propose. In *The Odd Women* when Widdowson proposes to Monica he also asks if he can speak to her friends to try and win them over. But she replies that no one must know of the proposal because that alone would compromise her since they were not properly introduced.

"In this position," she explains, "I must either not speak to you at all, or make it known that I am engaged to you" (74).

The Age of Innocence begins in the midst of New York Society at the opera, the evening of the day when May had first let Archer know that she "cared," which was, Wharton explains, "New York's consecrated phrase of maiden avowal." The proposal is never actually articulated. "As [Archer] entered the box his eyes met [May's], and he saw that she had instantly understood his motive, though the family dignity which both considered so high a virtue would not permit her to tell him so. The persons of their world lived in an atmosphere of faint implications and pale delicacies, and the fact that he and she understood each other without a word seemed to the young man to bring them nearer than any explanation would have done" (17). At a ball after the opera May announces her engagement, and the next day the couple begins the "usual betrothal visits" to secure the venerable ancestral blessings they will require, because "the New York ritual was precise and inflexible in such matters" (27). With a chat between May's mother and grandmother Wharton hints at some prior historical change about the importance of intimacy: "'We must give them time to get to know each other a little better, mamma,' Mrs. Welland interposed, with the proper affectation of reluctance; to which the ancestress rejoined: 'Know each other? Fiddlesticks! Everybody in New York has always known everybody'" (30). Written in 1920, Wharton's scathing exposé of the New York Society of the 1870s, when public sanction overshadowed lovers' private attraction and obviated their personal communication, points up the historical distance between the two periods.

V

The decades before the 1920s saw a movement away from an extreme gender dichotomy between active and passive roles. In comparison, Rochester's first proposal to Jane is a caricature of the active male commanding an affirmative response: "Jane," he says, "I summon you as my wife . . . Jane, accept me quickly. Say, Edward—give me my name—Edward—I will marry you" (282–283). Her acceptance is marked by her first tentative utterance of his name, as per instructions. Even the quintessentially considerate Daniel Deronda exhibits a desperate, domineering activity in proposing to Mirah. After eight hundred pages of patience he insists: "Say you will not reject me—say you will take me to share all things with you. Say you will promise to be my wife—say it now . . . Say that now and always I may prove to you that I love you with complete love" (863).

The proposal, even when phrased as a polite question, is a vigorous intrusion that must bridge a vast distance between two people, and the Victorian proposer came on strong to help himself across. By the twentieth century the distance was no shorter or less frightening, but men could count on women crossing a bit more of it from their side. That shift also required that men recognize the power and the rights of women in the exchange. The author of *Dracula* (1897) envisioned such new powers even as his heroine Mina derided them in her journal: "Some of the 'New Women' writers will some day start an idea that men and women should be allowed to see each other asleep before proposing or accepting. But I suppose the New Woman won't condescend in future to accept; she will do the proposing herself" (99). In Eliot's "The Love Song of J. Alfred Prufrock," before Prufrock can ask the "overwhelming question," he is paralyzed with doubt. He wonders how he should presume, how he should begin, will he have the strength to face his crisis, one which Eliot elevates to cosmic proportions as Prufrock asks himself whether he should dare to "disturb the universe." There is still time to descend the stairs and go back down the street, but he pushes on tentatively, questioning not only whether to propose but also whether love (his visit) is at all possible.

Depolarization of the conventional gender roles is also evident in art, particularly in proposal scenes, so popular among Victorian artists.[1] William Frith's *The Lovers' Seat (The Proposal)* (Figure 42, 1877) is typical.[2] By the early twentieth century proposal scenes all but vanish from modern art. Marc Chagall's *Dedicated to My Fiancée* (Figure 43, 1911) is as close as I could come to finding a proposal scene in twentieth-century art.[3] Placed side by side the two paintings reveal how artists in different periods treated the distribution of power and eroticism between the sexes during the proposal or, in the instance of the Chagall, around the time when proposals are made.

Although the Victorian proposal inaugurated what was generally a brief interval (from ten minutes[4] to a few weeks) when the woman had the power to decide, the initiation of the proposal and its terms came from the man. Frith and Chagall show the distribution of power between men and women in strikingly different ways. In Frith, the man's posture is active and imploring, while the woman's is passive and tentatively receptive. His right hand hugs her shoulder, while hers lies in her lap as if anesthetized. Their left hands are a contrast between his grip on things and her compliance with his grip. Even their gloves, a symbol of hands and hence of effective work, imply different power roles. His have fallen with his hat onto the ground in the rush of his focused activity, while hers have been placed neatly on the stone bench, indicating a focus equal to his but also looking as if she had been waiting all her life to receive his advances. In sharp contrast, Chagall shows a seated man in a red dress-like garment holding in his hand his horned head (like that of an ox, goat, or bull) that symbolizes an ambiguous mixture of patience, sacrifice, mockery, cuckoldry, fertility, and animal desire. While Frith's woman is seated demurely, and her dress, cuffs, collar, and bonnet cover up as much of her body as possible, Chagall's woman has mounted the man and slung over his shoulders her naked and muscular legs, one of which he hugs absentmindedly with his right wrist. Although she has not entirely overpowered him, she is literally on top of him, and her elongated left arm arcs around his shoulders and extends down to his left elbow. Frith's woman has calmly put down her book, implying quiet spirituality prior to this moment, while Chagall's woman has kicked aside the man's palette and broken his paraffin lamp.[5] The eyes of Frith's woman are turned away from the man's inquiring gaze, while Chagall's woman not only looks directly at her man but spits into his face. The erotic overtones of this gesture are unmistakable; its specific source might have been a rural custom of Brittany.[6] Chagall celebrates the joy of a new betrothal with a free assemblage of Cubist forms, a riot of color, even a blast from the woman's horn. In his painting the conventions of gender polarity that governed the nineteenth-century proposal have been treated much the way Cubists treated the conventions that governed shape, color, and volume in nineteenth-century art—they have been simplified, streamlined, and rearranged at the artist's will. Once again, the primacy of love in art has been replaced by a more important emphasis on love as art.

VI

This redistribution of active and passive roles between the sexes is linked to the subelement of intimacy. One might expect that in a century famous for long courtships, proposals would be well anticipated and that when they occurred couples would be intimate with one another, but in novels that is not the case. In *Anna Karenina* Levin's first proposal to Kitty is so abrupt that he chokes on his own words (the ellipsis dots are Tolstoy's): "I want to say . . . I want to say . . . I came on purpose . . . that . . . to be my wife!" (44). By the time Levin gets around to proposing again years later he is still terrified and does it in code. They are at a table, and he takes a piece of chalk

42. William Frith, *The Lovers' Seat (The Proposal)*, 1877.

and writes a series of letters which are the first letters of each word of his question: "W, y, a: i, c, n, b; d, y, m, t, o, n?" Kitty decodes the meaning which is, "When you answered: *it can not be*; [referring to her first refusal] *did you mean then or never?*" The rest of his proposal and her reply are transacted with their chalk-scribbled code, and Tolstoy concludes that "everything" had been said in their "conversation." In fact, very little was said, just as a generation earlier, Kitty learns, when her father proposed to her mother, all was decided "by the eyes, by smiles" (504).

In *A Pair of Blue Eyes* Knight is so shocked at having kissed Elfride for the first time that "without having quite intended an early marriage, he put the question: 'Elfride, when shall we be married?'" (338). Such suddenness

43. Marc Chagall, *Dedicated to My Fiancée*, 1911.

came from a lack of intimacy. Hardy captures that deficiency with the most impulsive and impersonal proposal in all of Western literature—Bathsheba's proposal to Boldwood in *Far from the Madding Crowd*. She has purchased a valentine and tosses a hymn book to decide to whom to send it. If it falls open she'll send it to Teddy Coggan, if closed, to Boldwood. It comes down closed. She then picks up a letter-seal which she cannot read and *after* stamping the hot wax discovers that the seal reads "MARRY ME." She mails it nevertheless. Bathsheba does not love Boldwood, and he has scarcely noticed her, but the capricious proposal works like acid on his steely solemnity, transforming his indifference into obsessive love. When Boldwood finally descends on her to propose, he does so with the desperate assertiveness and brutal concision of so many Victorian suitors: "I feel— almost too much—to think . . . I have come to speak to you without preface. My life is not my own since I have beheld you clearly, Miss Everdene—I came to make you an offer of marriage" (177). Flaubert's "A Simple Heart" (1877) is a classic about the almost wordless love of Félicité, as, near the beginning of the story, she says to a man who has come to her with amorous intentions nothing more than "Ah!" The "resistance" of her taciturn manner "inflamed Théodore's passion to such an extent that in order to satisfy it (or perhaps out of sheer naivete) he proposed to her" (20).

In *The Rainbow* Lawrence looked back on the tragic deficiencies of impulsive Victorian proposals, such as that of Tom to Lydia, set around 1870. As she opened her kitchen door one night he stepped in gripping a bouquet of flowers. Lawrence's narration alternates between the terrified couple. "She stood away, at his mercy, snatched out of herself. She did not know him, only she knew he was a man come for her . . . He was watching her, without knowing her . . . She had flinched from his advance. She had no will, no being." To break the tension Tom blurts out, "I came up . . . to ask if you'd marry me" (39). He had appeared suddenly out of the dark armed with flowers, and he had rehearsed how to put the question, because "he knew, if he asked her, she must acquiesce," which after a momentary hesitation she did. Their ensuing conversation is punctuated by frightening silences and intense blind kisses. "They were such strangers," Lawrence explains, "that his passion was a clanging torment to him. Such intimacy of embrace, and such utter foreignness of contact!" (44).

In *Howards End* Henry's aversion to intimacy clearly points back to nineteenth-century formality. His proposal reveals his own reticence and Margaret's understanding of her lover's vast emotional needs and limited expressive capabilities. Henry stumbles into the crucial dialogue:

"Could you be induced to share my—is it probable—"
"Oh, Mr. Wilcox!" she interrupted, holding the piano and averting her
  eyes. "I see, I see. I will write to you afterwards if I may."

He began to stammer. "Miss Schlegel—Margaret—you don't understand."

"Oh yes! Indeed, yes!" said Margaret.

"I am asking you to be my wife." . . .

"You aren't offended, Miss Schlegel?"   (165)

Forster resumes narrating: "There was a moment's pause. He was anxious to get rid of her, and she knew it . . . He desired comradeship and affection, but he feared them, and she, who had taught herself only to desire . . . held back . . . 'Good-bye,' she continued. 'You will have a letter from me.'" And Forster concludes: "It had been a strange love-scene—the central radiance unacknowledged from first to last. She in his place would have said *'Ich liebe dich'* . . . He might have done it if she had pressed him—as a matter of duty, perhaps; England expects every man to open his heart once; but the effort would have jarred him, and never, if she could avoid it, should he lose those defenses that he had chosen to raise against the world" (166). Had Woolf recorded Mr. Ramsay's proposal in *To the Lighthouse*, it would no doubt have been similar to this exchange, with a sympathetic and intelligent woman protecting her lover's fear of intimacy even as she hungers to satisfy her own need for it.[7]

VII

The moderns reduced the climacticality of the Victorian proposal and instead allowed all sorts of lesser questions to be considered in a give-and-take that might lead gradually to deeper understanding, instead of compressing them all into a sudden, terrifying question and its seemingly irreversible answer. But in the nineteenth century, without the communication opportunities made possible in the later period by easier access to one another and by fewer social restraints, the proposal was highly climactic in two respects— it was a supreme moment of emotional intensity, either ecstasy or despair, and, especially for the woman, it was a never-to-be-repeated opportunity, the climax of a lifetime of waiting.[8]

Tolstoy captures the breathtaking climacticality of a nineteenth-century proposal scene between two minor characters in *Anna Karenina*. Koznyshev is haunted by a promise to a dead lover to remain true to her memory, but in Varenka has found someone who has all the qualities he would desire in a wife. Separated from her by a few paces during a walk, he finally decides.

He throws away his cigar and strides toward her "with resolute steps." The next chapter begins with what the reader supposes to be his words: "Mlle Varenka! When very young I formed my ideal of the woman I should love and whom I should be happy to call my wife . . . and now in you for the first time I have met what I was in search of. I love you, and offer you my hand." But this, Tolstoy informs us, was what Koznyshev said only to himself as he approached her. After he drew near, they walked a few paces together in silence before he began to speak aloud. Varenka realized that "now in a moment it must be decided . . . He must make his declaration now or never." The exchange that follows is unsurpassed in poignancy.

> Everything—Varenka's look, her blush, her downcast eyes—betrayed painful expectation. He saw it and was sorry for her. He repeated to himself the words with which he had intended to propose; but instead of those words some unexpected thought caused him to say: "What difference is there between the white boleti and the birch-tree variety?"
>
> Varenka's lips trembled with emotion when she replied: "There is hardly any difference in the tops, but only in the stems."
>
> And as soon as those words were spoken, both he and she understood that all was over, and that what ought to have been said would not be said, and their excitement, having reached its climax, began to subside.   (511–512)

Against the background of such scenes the historical significance of Rupert's remark to Ursula's father that "it need never be too late" is clear. Lawrence fashioned the most important proposal scene in all of his novels to diminish the desperate climacticality of such scenes in decades past.

VIII

For the final aspect of the proposal all eyes are on the woman. However overbearing the social forces that govern her options, however abject her passivity and powerlessness vis-à-vis the man, and however distant their relationship prior to this terrifying climax, the man holds his breath and must await a reply as the woman has, for one brief moment, an unprecedented measure of freedom to say "yes" or "no" if not to make a more authentic choice.[9]

Back in the nineteenth century the difference between mere consenting and more authentic choosing was already a cause for indignation. In 1855 Gaskell challenged the narrow limits of woman's freedom with a comment in *North and South* about her heroine's wide mouth—it was "no rosebud that could only open just enough to let out a 'yes' and 'no'" (48). In *Daniel Deronda*, somewhat less critically, Eliot observes the world historical role of women in the American Civil War: "They are the Yea or Nay of that good for which men are enduring and fighting" (160). But between Grandcourt's bulldog tenacity and her own family's pressure, Gwendolen is cornered. Grandcourt requests permission to call on her and she has fifteen minutes to reply to his servant. Her acceptance triggers an exchange that proceeds inexorably. The final "yes," Eliot explains, "came as gravely from Gwendolen's lips as if she had been answering . . . in a court of justice" (348). In *Anna Karenina* Dolly protests to Levin: "you men, having views on a girl, come to the house . . . observe her and bide your time, and when you are quite certain that you love her, you propose . . . But a girl is expected to choose for herself, yet she has no choice; she can only say 'Yes' or 'No'" (246). That distinction is conceptualized explicitly in *The Egoist*. In response to Vernon, who has just said to Clara, "you are in a position of your own choosing," she counters that he has "wrongly used the word . . . to call consenting the same in fact as choosing [is] willfully unjust" (197).[10]

If Victorian novelists were aware of the deficiencies of mere consent, their characters were not in a position to do much about it. By the twentieth century female characters show more effective indignation about those deficiencies and muster greater resources to expand their freedom to choose. Although twentieth-century men still do the proposing and demand ultimately a single answer, women show greater awareness of many of the considerations and alternative options that can go into agreeing to marry or not. In *The Vagabond* Renée takes the final thirty pages to arrive at her decision to say "no," and in *Ulysses* Molly's interior monologue ranges over a myriad of reflections before coming to her final "yes."

While Renée is on tour Max proposes in a letter which threatens her freely chosen vagabondage. If she marries him, he promises, "the whole world shall be yours, until you come to love nothing but a little corner of our own where you will no longer be Renée Néré but My Lady Wife." She resents these arrangements without her consultation and wonders, "What do I become in all that?" (191). But her irritation gives way to deeper reservations. She realizes that they are strangers to one another and that everywhere there are unknown dangers. At thirty-four, one year older than he is, she worries about aging. She resents Max's uncomplicated view of a love which she finds ambiguous and tormenting. She is afraid of betrayal. The prospect of going on tour to South America provides a convenient way out, back into her own self-chosen vagabondage rather than into Max's marital bondage. She imagines his further urging and her own response: "Come back to me, beseeches my love, leave your job and the shabby sadness of the surroundings where you live, come back among your equals. I have no equals, I have only my fellow wayfarers" (215). Finally she decides and writes to explain why she is going away. "In a few years' time the best of myself would be that frustrated maternity that a childless woman transfers to her husband." And there is another reason. "You will understand that I must not belong to anyone, and that in spite of a first marriage and a second love, I have remained a kind of old maid, like some among them who are so in love with Love that no love appears to them beautiful enough, and so they refuse themselves without condescending to explain." Moreover, she confesses, "I no longer dare, my darling, that is the whole trouble" (220).

Her letter is a mixture of honesty and feigned self-abnegation to soften the blow of her refusal. In a concluding soliloquy directed to Max she expresses the fiery intensity of her love and the relief of her escape from it. "I reject you and I choose . . . all that is not you. I have met you before, and I recognize you. Are you not he who, thinking he is giving, takes for himself? You came to share my life. To share, yes: *to take your share!* To be a partner in everything I do, to insinuate yourself at every moment in the secret temple of my thoughts, isn't that it?" One final argument brings her reflective "no" full circle, back to Max's original proposal of a marriage that would some day make her tire of travel. "I refuse to see the most beautiful countries of the world microscopically reflected in the amorous mirror of your eyes" (222). Her refusal is more of a choice than the typical Victorian's refusal, because hers is not a retreat from love and certainly not a retreat from life, which for the vagabond is symbolized by travel. Unlike her Victorian predecessors, she has somewhere else to go.

No one has treated the exquisite disequilibrium created by a proposal more exhaustively than the writer who first exploited this motif in the eighteenth century, the father of the English novel, Samuel Richardson. In a million words or so, his *Clarissa* conjures up a seemingly endless variety of ever more complex and conditional ways of saying "no." A hundred and seventy-five years later, the writer who almost brought the English novel to an end,

James Joyce, probed the extraordinary narrative and existential possibilities of saying "yes."

It is hard to imagine a more unconventional and unromantic setting for a woman to think about a proposal than he contrived for Molly. She lies in bed with her husband's corn-swollen toes a few inches from her ear, the couple being deployed head to foot—their customary sleeping position. To appreciate the significance of Molly's reply, we must interpret the first sound she makes in the novel, which is her response to Leopold's question whether she wants anything for breakfast. The "Mn" she utters, which he interprets as "No," is a comment on their entire relationship. At the end of her long interior monologue which is the end of the novel, Molly reconsiders her initial response to Leopold's proposal sixteen years before along with his question that morning.

> . . . the sun shines for you he said the day we were lying among the rhododendrons on Howth head . . . the day I got him to propose to me . . . 16 years ago my God after that long kiss I near lost my breath yes he said I was a flower of the mountain yes so we are flowers all a womans body yes that was one true thing he said in his life and the sun shines for you today yes that was why I liked him because I saw he understood or felt what a woman is and I knew I could always get round him and I gave him all the pleasure I could leading him on till he asked me to say yes and I wouldnt answer first only look out over the sea and sky I was thinking of so many things he didnt know of Mulvey and Mr Stanhope and Hester . . . and the Arabs and the devil knows who else from all the ends of Europe . . . and Gibraltar as a girl where I was a Flower of the mountain yes when I put the rose in my hair like the Andalusian girls used or shall I wear a red yes and how he kissed me under the Moorish wall and I thought well as well him as another and then I asked him with my eyes to ask again yes and then he asked me would I yes to say yes my mountain flower and first I put my arms around him yes and drew him down to me so he could feel my breasts all perfume yes and his heart was going like mad and yes I said yes I will Yes.

In this final passage each of the subelements of the proposal that I have contrasted across this period is given a distinctly historical sense as Molly searches for a way to say "yes" to her husband who is sleeping by her side.

Her *motive* for accepting is emphatically passionate. Leopold's proposal is not of the wordy, disembodied nineteenth-century variety, nor is her reply motivated by conventional considerations of money, security, or status. She replies with a kiss that seems to come directly from her body that squirmed under his first desperate kisses and that has remained active with many other men over the years. *Others* function not as obstreperous fathers, meddlesome matchmakers, or oppressive society, but as actors in a panorama of erotic adventures stretching back to her girlhood and across Europe and now streaming across her consciousness. The exclusive right of initiation by the man is tempered now, as she "got him to propose." *Gender polarity* is reduced, because one of Leopold's virtues is that he "felt what a woman is." Their *intimacy* has been forged by years of shared experience and by long stretches of alienation. The *climactic* now-or-never aspect of older proposals has been diminished, since she makes the final affirmation only after everything has been said again and again. Far beyond the narrow straits that had channeled so many of her predecessors to consent, Molly ranges over vast stretches of time and space and experience to make her final *choice*. As reckoned by public time it took less than a day for Molly's "Mn" to become a triumphant "Yes," but her interior monologue shows that experientially it took sixteen years for her earlier hurried and unreflective consent to mature and become a more authentic choice.

The experience of choice is at the heart of existential philosophy. The issue has a long history in Western thought in which freedom often meant the free will to do good or to believe in God. Existentialist philosophers argued that authentic choices were so free that one could not limit them to any specific moral or religious context. Even the Christian existentialist Kierkegaard insisted that authentic choices are terrifying because they must be made with a "teleological suspension of the ethical," that is, without reference to any specific ethical system and therefore on one's own. Such choices are not immoral, in fact they always involve some sense of good and bad, but they cannot be derived from ethical precepts or publicly formulated codes.

Human existence is a fundamental and perpetual choosing. In every choice we experience guilt, which is an awareness of responsibility for our own existence; we experience loneliness, which is a consciousness of the difficulty of human relations; and we experience time, specifically the future, which brings us face-to-face with the finitude of existence. Although choice is fundamental and universal, it can be evaluated in different ways and hence has a history. Indeed, choice is that aspect of existence which makes meaningful history possible. And so the contrasting ways Clara and Renée say "no" or the ways Jane and Molly say "yes" evince dramatic historical change.

Between the mid-nineteenth and early twentieth century the number of options open to women changed considerably. Although one might argue that the Victorian world offered an equal number of options, one would be hard pressed to explain away the many restrictions put upon women that I have surveyed throughout this study, especially the limited work and travel opportunities and the many social, religious, family, and moral restrictions that dictated how women should think, feel, and behave. But in arguing that the relaxation of these constricting rules opened up greater opportunities for women, as I have done, another, more challenging question arises about the increasing authenticity of choices made in this world of greater opportunity. If authenticity is a way of being that involves understanding one's own self as a self, then how can authenticity be increased by a changing external world for which one is hardly responsible and over which one has little control? One might argue, for example, that the freedom-conscious celebrants of F. Scott Fitzgerald's world of riotous parties and sexual liberation were inauthentic, because their new opportunities did not lead to reflection on the meaning of existence but rather to escape from such reflection. In contrast, Jane Eyre could be said to be more authentic in choosing, because her prison-like existence forced her, as all prisoners are forced, to think about the crushing pressures of the world and the meaning of freedom.

These arguments, however, are not borne out in the novels, because, as I have argued with respect to a number of the elements of love, the constrictions of the Victorian world limited not only the external options open to lovers but, more fundamentally, their ability to reflect on the meaning of being in love in that world. Jane may indeed have thought about freedom more than Molly did, as for example when she looked out of the third-story window of Rochester's mansion towards the horizon and "longed for a power of vision which might overpass that limit: which might reach the busy world, towns, regions full of life [she] had heard of but never seen." But Jane's longings come out of deficiency, so much so that she apologizes for it—"Anybody may blame me who likes," she writes. (Eighty years later Woolf was outraged at Jane's need to apologize.) And longing for some unknown possibility is not the reality of confronting choices for oneself *in the world itself.* The prisoner may dwell on freedom but does so as an obsession, endlessly repeated in the same context, stripped of the detail of living actuality. The prisoner's obsession with freedom becomes, paradoxically, a routine of the mind, and choices of action become empty dreams.

When Clara finally rejects Willoughby she does not choose freedom, for Vernon is waiting in the wings to sweep her off to marriage and a honeymoon in the Alps. In contrast, when Renée rejects Max she is not only terrified at the prospect of having to fend for herself but even more terrified that she will miss Max, as she already does, and possibly never love again. When Jane accepts Rochester's second proposal she does so effortlessly, and every shred of discord quickly disappears in the prospect of marital bliss. In contrast, when Molly reiterates her acceptance of Leopold, he is asleep and most likely will never be told, and she concludes her rumination, exhausted after years of serious deliberation, with a final choice that is as tentative as it is triumphant.

In the twentieth century, responding to a man's proposal of marriage became more authentic because changing circumstances made it possible for a woman to choose among more options rather than merely consent, and thus become better able to understand her response as her own.

15 Wedding

IN 1927, THE year in which Heidegger published *Being and Time*, Emily Post published *Etiquette*. One interpreted human existence poised between authenticity and inauthenticity, scrupulously avoiding any concrete morality; the other, a handbook of inauthenticity, codified and emphatically recommended rules for doing what "they" do. Post provides guidelines for the wedding list, invitations, flowers, music, cake, bridal gown, and groom's pants. There are directives about who opens doors, who passes out boutonnieres, and who looks for the ring if it falls during the ceremony. There are rules for displaying presents, seating guests, leaving the bride's home, timing the processional, returning to the wedding feast, and positioning family members on the receiving line—even sample comments to say while passing along it. This book is strangely moving, because it brings to mind the commendable, though unavailing, and often counterproductive, efforts of family and community to help their young with the perils of love, and because it reminds one of how desperately lovers try to sustain their private feelings in the midst of all the public fuss.

I

We all cry a little bit at weddings. They compress lifetimes of hope and regret, they mark one of the most comforting and yet frightening moments in family life, and they are important ceremonies unique to everyone concerned even though homogenized by decorum. A wedding is also the most public moment of love, which allows family and friends to witness an exchange of vows sanctioned by religious or civil authorities. During the ceremony the hands that often caressed one another freely in private are publicly held and brought together by others. That public aspect inclines weddings toward the inauthentic, because the vows are not authored by the bride and groom but are recited to them to be repeated phrase by phrase as if they were children just learning to speak. The authority of ritual discourages reflection on the meaning of those vows or the meaning of the love they consecrate. The groom chooses a ring, and the bride chooses her gown, but these choices are superficial and narrowly circumscribed by convention.

After 1847 weddings proceed unchanged with bewildered brides and nervous grooms, but into the twentieth century interpretations of them move in the direction of greater authenticity as brides and grooms think more critically about their weddings and show greater irritation with their sometimes humiliating public aspects. At the same time authors assume greater ironic distance from the fear and helplessness of the characters they put through these ceremonial travails.

The mid-nineteenth century marked a high point in the regulation of weddings by other people and external formalities. In Wagner's *Lohengrin* (1850) the wedding scene takes over an hour of the opera's running time. During that hour the love of Lohengrin and Elsa is celebrated in song not by the bride and groom but by the wedding party which leads the couple to the altar. The opening line of the famous bridal song is "Treulich geführt, ziehet dahin" (Faithfully led, proceed thither). Lohengrin and Else are alone together for the first time only after the wedding is over. In *Madame Bovary* Charles and Emma spend sixteen hours at the wedding table. Flaubert mocks their celebratory excess with brutal realism—for instance, in the description of the preposterously ornate wedding cake.[1]

The Victorian bride experienced the ceremony as if in a trance. The heroine of Tolstoy's "Family Happiness" recalled that the words given to her to repeat during her wedding "found no echo" in her heart. She looked "listlessly" at all the religious icons but did not respond. During the ceremony, as she recalled, "I only felt that something was being done to me" (41). In *Les Misérables* Cosette remained passive throughout the ceremony and emerged from the church with a look of "doubtful amazement." While riding back to the wedding feast in the carriage, she joyfully renounced her selfhood in whispering to Marius: "It's true. My name is now the same as yours. I'm Madame You" (1135).

During her wedding in *Anna Karenina* Kitty "understood hardly anything of the service and was not even listening to the words of the ceremony" (411). She was filled with thoughts about Levin. "The whole of her life, all her desires and hopes were concentrated on this man, still incomprehensible to her" (411). Kitty and Levin blundered through the ceremony with the priest prompting them in whispers. Tolstoy accents the passivity and uncertainty of the bride and groom by contrasting their confusion and tentativeness with the uncompromising certainty of the vows and the indissoluble union they are supposed to consecrate, collectively enforced by everyone whom the priest invokes as witness—God, ancestors, community, friends, and family.

Most Victorian painters depicted the bride's happy preparations or post-wedding celebrations surrounded by other people. Some rendered a bride's darker moments, although these were embedded in a narrative and triggered by a particular situation rather than by the act of wedding itself. Edmund Blair-Leighton's *Until Death Do Us Part* (Figure 44, 1878) shows a dejected bride who has just made the wrong choice by marrying the prosperous but aloof older groom at her side instead of her true love, who is staring intently at her from the left aisle. Fifty years of history separate this painting from one by the German artist Hannah Höch—*The Bride (Pandora)* (Figure 45, 1927). It shows a baby-faced yet contemplative bride surrounded not by other people but by images of her own thoughts, which are sustained in flight by various bird and insect wings, implying that they make up her streaming consciousness and take flight in different ways toward different ends. Höch's bride does not seem to be thinking about the rightness of her love choice but about the contrasting consequences of her choosing. Höch was critical of modern technology, and in many photomontages she associated technology with domineering men, but the image of an automobile tire in this painting is open to a positive as well as a negative interpretation: it may suggest the adventure and the uncertainty of the honeymoon or the more abiding mobility gained or lost in married life. The bright blue eye sheds a tear, but like the eyes of the bride herself, it is wide open. This bride may be in for some tragic disappointments, but she approaches her wedding with awareness. The nursing baby and the apple of sin complete with a hissing snake's forked tongue suggest further conflict about motherhood and sex. In the lower right corner a bright red blossom (the bride's sex, fruit, or love) is set in a prickly-leaved stem (the ambient danger and pain). The heart with exposed auricles and pulmonary artery is chained and weighed down, indicating the bride is no longer free to love anyone else, but other ambiguities suggest emotional contrasts—it is either being cut open or in the process of repair, it is either exposed and vulnerable or open to analysis and understanding. And over everything is a symbolic reference to the overarching act

44. Edmund Blair-Leighton, *Until Death Us Do Part*, 1878.

45. Hannah Höch, *The Bride (Pandora)*, 1927.

of judging—a weight from a scale sustained by a pair of outspread condor wings.

The painting's subtitle indicates further ambiguities associated with the Pandora myth. In different versions of the myth, Pandora, meaning "the all-giver," brings mankind either goods or evils. In all versions these gifts are in a large basket or urn; in no classical source are they in a box. In different versions either she brings the container down to earth with her, someone else brings it for her, or it is already on earth when she arrives. In some versions her husband opens the container that lets loose evils on mankind, while in others she lets them out. No classical source has her opening any container in defiance of the gods' warning not to. In all versions only hope remains after all the gifts or evils have been let loose.[2]

Höch represents many of these versions as multivalent images set loose not in the world but in the bride's own mind. True to the classical text, there is no box. The bride has succumbed to curiosity about marriage, and already the goods and evils of marriage are apparent, but she is a modern bride and a modern all-giver. She is thinking not so much about the wedding gifts she will get as about the gifts she will give. Whatever goods and evils she lets loose are within herself as contrasting possibilities. And unlike her mythic predecessor, she appears to have more resources left than just hope. She towers over the cipher of a groom, who stands as stiff as a wedding-cake figurine. She looks back in time and ahead, weighing the value of her own wedding amid these myriad possibilities, seeming to take charge in striking contrast to Blair-Leighton's bride, who appears as helpless as a sacrificial lamb.

Victorian men also went to the altar passive and bewildered, as the literary record shows. During one ceremony in *Anna Karenina* Levin realized that a wedding "was something he had never understood" (412). For David Copperfield, wedding Dora was like an "incoherent dream" (697).

The pressures on the typical middle-class Victorian groom contemplating his wedding-night responsibilities can be briefly summarized. Since adolescence he has been warned about the morally debilitating consequences of masturbation and the physically debilitating consequences of any sexual discharge. If he has had pre-marital sex it has most likely been with a "loose" woman or a prostitute, and if he has contracted a venereal disease he is worried that it might infect his bride and future offspring. If he has had no experience he is worried about his ineptitude. Either way he is unprepared to deal with a middle-class virginal bride. He has not been able to discuss sex with her, and their physical contact has been limited to an occasional embrace during a dance, formal kisses on the hand, and perhaps a kiss on the lips to seal the betrothal. If he has read a marriage manual it may have advised that his wife will not have powerful sexual desires and will await his advances passively, although he may also fear an explosion of passion which can erupt, some guardians of morality warned, when female eroticism is legitimized by marriage. Some manuals instructed husbands and wives not to undress in front of one another in order not to overstimulate desire and destroy the marriage on the wedding night by a rape. What *must* the Victorian groom have been thinking during the ceremony? Both the groom's lack of experience and the bride's innocence combined to make the Victorian wedding the prelude to a climax of sexual confusion, anxiety, and disappointment which they nevertheless seemed to anticipate from early childhood as the supreme consummation of love.

Three weddings from the mid 1890s evince increasing ironic distance by novelists, even though the actual ceremonies are outwardly the same as those a half century earlier. Tess is "whirled onward" to her wedding by the force of custom. On the way to the church she "did not see anything" aside from Angel, and she experienced the ceremony in a "luminous mist" (178). In Gissing's *The Odd Women* Monica's wedding is brought about entirely by "social and personal embarrassments" (121). In *The Woman Who Did* Allen charges that weddings of his time were barbaric practices in which the "most sacred and private event in a young girl's life" became "an opportunity for display of the coarsest and crudest character." Allen adds that only the "blinding effect of custom could ever have shut good women's eyes to the shameful indecorousness of wedding ceremonial" (70).

Into the modern period, criticism of the conventional wedding continues to mount. Wharton crafts a withering exposé of an 1870s New York wedding. "All the old ladies in both families had got out their faded sables and yellowing ermines, and the smell of camphor from the front pews almost smothered the faint spring scent of the lilies banking the altar." That image suggests how tradition and public opinion smothered the freshness and vitality of love. At a signal from the sexton, indicating that the bride's brougham was in sight, the groom stepped up to the chancel. During the wait for her appearance, Wharton explains, "the bridegroom, in proof of his eagerness, was expected to expose himself alone to the gaze of the assembled company; and Archer had gone through this formality as resignedly as through all the others which made of a nineteenth-century New

York wedding a rite that seemed to belong to the dawn of history." Such weddings generalized the emotions of the bride and groom by making them conform to ancient custom and putting them on public display. "Everything was equally easy—or equally painful, as one chose to put it—in the path [Archer] was committed to tread" (179).

In the opening scene from *Women in Love* Lawrence creates a sense of historical perspective on the wedding ceremony with a withering critique of a conventional wedding. As the bride and groom emerge from the church, the Brangwen sisters focus on the groom, who "looked rather comical, blinking and trying to be in the scene, when emotionally he was violated by his exposure to a crowd" (16). His exposure dramatizes the fate of all conventional wedding couples whose sense of privacy and personal identity is violated by the gaze of others.[3]

If that wedding looked back in time, the extraordinary "wedding" of Connie Chatterley and Mellors looked ahead. After making love in the forest Mellors piles flowers on Connie's breasts, places a pink campion in her navel, and weaves forget-me-nots into her pubic hair. Using the euphemisms "John Thomas" and "Lady Jane" for penis and vagina and with his lilting Midlands dialect Mellors begins the wedding benediction.

> "That's you in all your glory!" he said. "Lady Jane, at her wedding with John Thomas."
>
> And he stuck flowers in the hair of his own body, and wound a bit of creeping-jenny round his penis, and stuck a single bell of a hyacinth in his navel. She watched him with amusement, his odd intentness. And she pushed a campion flower in his moustache, where it stuck, dangling under his nose.
>
> "This is John Thomas marryin' Lady Jane," he said . . .
>
> He spread out his hand with a gesture, and then he sneezed, sneezing away the flowers from his nose and his navel.   (213)

This "wedding" is distinctively modern. It is not a serious public spectacle but a private celebration with mocking overtones, it is not a repetitive custom but an original creation, it is less artificial than natural, and it does not treat sexuality with conventional symbols but with direct reference, slightly decentered by playful euphemism. The flowers are not from a florist but from the forest floor, the bride and groom are not side by side but face each other directly, the bride's face is not hidden by a veil but is, like her entire body, naked and open, and in place of the high-minded seriousness of the conventional wedding Lawrence ends with an earthy sneeze. It was not, of course, an actual wedding, and it was in no way typical of 1928, but it does represent the values of a novelist who, deeply concerned about the celebration of love in his time, conjured up this "marryin'" as a challenge to current conventions. In that sense it represents the cutting edge of contemporary ideas about how to consecrate love in life and art.

In painting there was a formal shift of emphasis from painting love to loving paint, from trying to depict love in art to trying to make the creative process the subject of painting. This shift is evident in depictions of the wedding, which into the twentieth century become more a wedding of colors and forms than of brides and grooms. Van Gogh, who passionately loved thick oils, anticipated this change in a letter of 1888 to his brother, Theo, in which he explained his desire "to express the love of two lovers by a wedding of two complementary colors, their mingling and their opposition, the mysterious vibrations of kindred tones." [4] This shift can be seen in the contrast between Blair-Leighton's *Until Death Do Us Part* (Figure 44) and Fernand Léger's *The Wedding* (Figure 46, 1911). The former shows a wedding of two identifiable persons; Léger shows a wedding of colored forms. It is barely possible to discern the bride and groom from out of the riot of Cubist forms, but Léger sought to achieve a harmonious composition rather than a specific wedded couple.

The ethical content of these paintings is significantly different. Blair-Leighton's heavy moralizing over this "wrong" wedding is based on a reading of individual personalities, in particular the bride who is marrying for money or status instead of love, while Léger's main concern is formal and aesthetic and only incidentally targets the ritualized, public aspect of weddings.

The meaning of public witness also changes. Blair-Leighton shows a couple surrounded by identifiable judges. On the left there is an old woman, head in hand, depressed about what she is seeing. Behind her two elderly men gossip in critical poses. The spurned young man stands in disbelief. Next to him a mother holds her daughter tight as if to keep her from following the same wrong path as the bride. Even the best man, visible in the recessional just behind the groom, seemingly looks away in disapproval. The four faces at the right are somber. All witnesses, who would be expected to authenticate a good wedding, condemn this one as a bad match. In contrast Léger critiques the publicness of weddings *per se*, for his bride and groom

46. Fernand Léger, *The Wedding*, 1911.

have no identifiable age, status, or personality. His bride is not a symbol of
virginity in a halo of reverence but a sex-goddess on display. She stands not
"in the sight of God, and in the face of this company" but under the menacing gaze of at least nine angular faces peering out from the crowd pressed
around her naked breasts and buttocks. She is literally up for grabs. She
towers over everyone, and numerous hands, as if from drowning men,

clutch at her exposed body. The robotic forms at the right stand as mechanical witnesses to this mechanical ceremony, and their arrangement in a receding line is a mocking Cubist recessional. Léger's groom in the upper right corner is barely distinguishable from the throng of voyeurs who symbolize the remorseless public gaze of public weddings. The transparency of Cubist forms is one technique ideally suited to render the insatiable curiosity of wedding guests, whose probing vision has here stripped the bride of her wedding dress. The groom is wedged between her balloon breast and his own body and holds on for dear life as if he were also about to drown in the sea of impersonal, geometrical faces that make up the church aisle. In place of Blair-Leighton's realistically drawn Gothic church, Léger has created a church of Cubist forms, substituting the religion of art for religious architecture.

Using these two paintings to document a change in the experience of weddings is a bit forced, because the purpose of painting itself changed so markedly in the years separating them. Blair-Leighton's could well have illustrated a melodramatic Victorian novel, while Léger's is unthinkable as an illustration for any story. But that shift in the function of art also bears on its content.[5] In the course of these years greater value was attached to reflecting on the meaning of creating and existing as well as loving. To such reflecting Heidegger gave the tag of authenticity. Blair-Leighton rendered artistically the same conventions that Emily Post codified as proper behavior fifty years later. Our understanding of the historical significance of those generalized public codes can be clarified by contrasting them with the artistic self-awareness of Léger and the existential self-awareness of Heidegger.

II

The extreme publicness of the wedding is followed by the extreme privacy of the honeymoon, although that contrast itself has a history. In America, around 1850, the usual wedding trip was a visit to relatives in the company of friends or relatives. But around 1870, as Ellen Rothman has demonstrated, newlyweds began to travel alone to secret destinations. "The bridal journey was no longer a ritual designed to integrate a new pair into the community, but, instead, it self-consciously isolated the couple." After 1890 the honeymoon became less frightening for the bride because of the growing use of contraception and because the prospect of more work, education, and entertainment opportunities placed wives in the community and reduced their isolation in the home.[6] The increasing economy, safety, and comfort of railroad and ocean travel also popularized more distant and independent honeymoon tours.

Although during honeymoons the bride and groom are isolated from the public arena, public pressures may continue to dictate the most unreflective behavior and inauthentic escapism. The clichés are familiar—dashing off to Niagara Falls, carrying the bride across the threshold. Newlyweds adhere to these conventions to minimize the frightening choices that must be made in the transition from the publicness of the wedding to the privacy of the honeymoon, when they must begin to style their love in a uniquely personal way and reflect on its meaning. The history of that reflection is documented in literature.

In the Victorian novel there was little about honeymoons and nothing about their sexual purpose. Public morality and literary sensibilities allowed only vague reference to the newlyweds' sexual autodidactism. Descriptions of "happy" honeymoons were as discreet as the Victorian chapter's end following a kiss. The fights and resolutions of unhappy honeymoons provided richer literary possibilities and, since they were often chaste, could be explored without offending censors or public morality. Tolstoy offers no explicit details about sex in the one good marriage in *Anna Karenina* between Levin and Kitty, which gets off to a disastrous start. "The honeymoon . . . was not delightful, but remained in both their recollections as the most oppressive and humiliating time of their lives." In later years they tried "to efface from their memories all the ugly shameful circumstances of this unhealthy time, during which they were rarely in a normal state and rarely themselves" (439). The confusion of the typical Victorian honeymoon made it difficult for the bride and groom to be themselves. Eliot detailed two nightmarish honeymoons: Gwendolen's emotional enslavement to Grandcourt and Dorothea's sexless estrangement from Casaubon, for six weeks her escort around the ruins of Rome. Casaubon's lifeless commentary on Samothracian fertility gods was, like his own research, "lost among small closets and winding stairs." His way of explaining the glories of ancient Rome struck Dorothea "with a sort of mental shiver" (136–137). Toward the end of the century, Innstetten, with guidebook in hand, took his much younger bride Effi on a honeymoon to the museums and churches of Germany and Rome, overwhelming her with his knowledge. The most noteworthy sensual experience Effi reported was tired feet.

"The first real honeymoon in English fiction" [7]—that of Will and Anna in *The Rainbow*—is a classic about the emotional highs and lows of apprentice love, but it is also a historically specific portrayal of lovers dealing with the sensibilities, obligations, and possibilities of the 1890s. Lawrence's vivid description of this honeymoon was distinctively and, for many readers of 1915, disturbingly modern.

It began at the dawn of erotic consciousness with Will's impressions of his first blissful night in protective darkness, his shame in the morning when he realized that he was in bed while others were up and about, and his return to Anna's embrace. His vague notion of a woman's body, formerly all "skirts and petticoats," was shockingly clarified by Anna's carefree nakedness. He was stunned when one afternoon she stripped him naked in the daylight, undaunted by his ineptitude.

Anna struggled less than Will with the intimacy of sex and was sooner ready to return to the world. Their first fight was set off by her preparations for a tea party, which plunged Will into panic. He grew dark and hopeless, "his wrists quivered murderously." He felt burdensome and evil. Despite their deep longing for one another, a chasm opened between them, and, consumed by anger, he made her pay. She fled to her parents, but upon her return she and Will were still unable to break the painful silence. Lack of experience in talking hardened their pride and stubbornness. She softened slightly but Will took the opening to "lacerate" and "desecrate" her. The impasse continued. He felt compassion for her suffering and reached out, but his touch seemed to burn. Finally her convulsive sobs broke the tension. She responded tentatively to his touch, his blood started pounding, she clung to him, and he held her tight. As they kissed Will "felt his veins would burst with anguish of thankfulness, his heart was mad with gratefulness, he could pour himself out upon her for ever" (153). Their explosive fighting followed by mute sexual reconciliation did not solve problems for long, but for three days they were "immune in a perfect love."

Going to church triggered the next fight. Before they met, Anna had drifted away from the church because of its impersonality and "ready-made" faith. Sitting next to Will in church she became incensed by his longing for the gloom and mystery of faith, which also shaped his erotic passion. She wanted thought and lucidity, while he craved mystery and opacity. "The thought of her soul was intimately mixed up with the thought of her own self . . . Whereas he seemed simply to ignore the fact of his own self, almost to refute it." That smoldering conflict flashed to argument about the meaning of the *pietà*. She interpreted it literally: she was disgusted by "bodies with slits in them, posing to be worshipped." She did not want to see Will's chest cut open or to eat his dead body. Such literalness infuriated Will, who explained that the body of Christ is sacrificed and eaten as a symbol of the sacraments. But she would not accept even symbols of mutilation, and she recoiled at worshipping a sacrifice. Without speaking they headed out of Church in different directions. Later they reconciled by making love, although their deep differences remained unresolved, and in sex they were like clashing birds of prey. She "roused him like a hawk," and he came at her "like a hawk striking and taking her." No sooner was she carried off in pleasure than she began to retaliate. She too was a hawk and dashed at him savagely until he raged again.

Another fight started when Will discovered that his tools had rusted because Anna had put them away carelessly. She piqued his anger further by getting out her own tool—a sewing machine. He fumed at the clicking sound of the stabbing needle which she ran in defiance of his insistence that she stop. She continued to pump the pedal furiously as if stitching across his soul. They raged deep into estrangement over simple domestic activities. Will stormed out and his absence conjured up new fears for Anna. "She knew she was immutable, unchangeable, she was not afraid for her own being. She was only afraid of all that was not herself. It pressed round her, it came to her and took part in her, in the form of her man, this vast, resounding, alien world which was not herself. And he had so many weapons, he might strike from so many sides" (162). He returned and ventured a delicate touch; she resisted momentarily, clinging to herself, fearing his vast otherness, and the rising flood of desire carried her away. "So it went continually, the recurrence of love and conflict" (164). One day he was a god and life was glorious, and suddenly she was disgusted by the gulping sound he made when drinking. Next day he was the sun, moon, and stars.

They quarreled again, over religion, over sex. She began to feel that he wanted some "dark, unnatural" sex (possibly a reference to anal sex) and so struck back until he bled. It got downright cruel. "She wanted to desert him, to leave him a prey to the open, with the unclean dogs of the darkness setting on to devour him" (166). Such darkness was dispersed by sunbeams followed again by misery. Will tried asserting the old position of master of the house, which Lawrence dates historically as already passé by setting it against Anna's nascent feminism: "He asserted his position as the captain of the ship. And captain and ship bored her" (170).

This extended honeymoon is presented in a chapter titled "Anna Victrix," which refers to the minor victories Anna achieved in these daily skirmishes as well as her ultimate victory—pregnancy and the birth of Ursula, who would carry on her historical destiny. Anna's pregnancy caused another fight when she refused to have sex, and Will persisted in demanding it. "She did not want his bitter-corrosive love, she did not want it poured into her, to burn her" (178). Feeling vulnerable, invaded, and corrupted, Anna retaliated not only by turning away from Will but (and this must have scandalized the authorities who banned the novel) by turning on to God.

Anna's ultimate victory came when Will discovered her in front of a fire, naked and fully pregnant, "dancing his non-existence, dancing herself to the Lord, to exultation." Lawrence's explicit narration of this assault on traditional piety and patriarchy was the main reason for the ban. "Her fine limbs lifted and lifted, her hair was sticking out all fierce, and her belly, big, strange, terrifying, uplifted to the Lord. Her face was rapt and beautiful, she danced exulting before her Lord, and knew no man." Will watched transfixed, hurting as if he were burning alive at the stake. "After this day, the door seemed to shut on his mind" (181).

The tension built until she finally drove him out of her bedroom. "I sleep so well when I'm alone," she implored, "and I can't sleep when you're there" (186). Anna did need sleep, but her request was also a cover for refusing sex. Her action was different from that of Emma Bovary or Anna Karenina, who rejected their husbands to have lovers, and different from Gwendolen or Dorothea, who rejected their husbands because they could not stand them. Anna still desired Will, but not in late pregnancy. To dramatize her conflict Lawrence refers to a subject that was emphatically off limits to Victorian novelists—a woman's sexual desire during pregnancy. The Victorian conspiracy of silence made it especially difficult for Victorian wives to ask for sex forthrightly when they were aroused or to refuse it forthrightly when they needed rest.

Anna's rejection pointed toward the twentieth century not only because it accompanied desire and was in the service of love, but because it eventually led to a reconstruction of a more authentic, if less torrid, relationship. Will finally let go and accepted her need for privacy and his own loneliness. And once he let up on his insistent desire, she could let down her insistent denial. "They slept together once more, very quietly, and distinct, not one together as before." Her rejection became the basis for a new, deeper freedom. "Now at last he had a separate identity, he existed alone, even if he were not quite alone. Before he had only existed in so far as he had relations with another being. Now he had an absolute self—as well as a relative self" (187). Anna's role in this change is located ambiguously between what Heidegger would define as inauthentic and authentic caring. At times she seemed to leap in for

Will inauthentically to take away his "care" and in so doing made him "dominated and dependent." But she also seemed to "leap ahead" of Will "not in order to take away his 'care' but rather to give it back to him authentically as such for the first time" (*Being and Time*, 159). Anna was poised between these modes as she was between Victorian and modern loving. She also needed Will, especially as her delivery drew near.

When Emma Bovary learned that her baby was a girl she fainted. Thereafter she remained distant from little Berthe, who, she was convinced, was destined to repeat her own subordination in a man's world. Anna was also disappointed when she learned that she had had a girl, but only momentarily. Lawrence evokes Anna's bonding with a distinctively modern maternal exclamation: "'It sucks me, it sucks me, it likes me—oh, it loves it!' she cried, holding the child to her breast with her two hands covering it, passionately." No doubt Victorian mothers felt the deep visceral thrill of the first suck in just that way, but there is no evidence that they voiced its sexual overtones so candidly with their husbands present or that novelists recorded their outbursts.[8] After a few moments Anna looked blissfully into the eyes of her baby and said "Anna Victrix." Will did not fill with pride but "went away, trembling, and slept" (189).

Lawrence relentlessly counters conventional treatments of the wedding, honeymoon, pregnancy, and parenting. Connie and Mellors "wed" each other unofficially by weaving flowers in one another's pubic hair. The honeymoon of Will and Anna alternates between cruel fighting and blind sex. Anna's pregnancy culminates in a blasphemous erotic dance, her nursing begins with what Victorians would have regarded as vulgar sensuality, and Will's fathering begins with an unpatriarchal retreat. Lawrence concludes Anna's victory with an image of deficiency if not defeat. "She was a door and a threshold, she herself. Through her another soul was coming, to stand upon her as upon the threshold, looking out, shading its eyes for the direction to take" (193). Far off toward the horizon Anna saw a sign of fulfillment, a rather clichéd image of a rainbow, which Lawrence used for his title. That distant horizon, like the one that Jane Eyre longed to approach from the attic window of Rochester's mansion, still loomed for Anna. It was somewhat closer, but Anna was still a mere threshold across which another generation must pass. With that anticipated passage from one generation to the next Lawrence provides one of the most moving and compelling sources for the history of love.

16 Sex

"I want men and women to be able to think
sex, fully, completely, honestly, cleanly."
—D. H. Lawrence, "A Propos of *Lady
Chatterley's Lover*"

THE HISTORY of embodiment, desire, language, kissing, gender, and power shows how men and women saw and revealed more of their bodies, acknowledged deeper anatomical sources and more varied objects of desire, developed new ways to talk about sex, accepted the humor and deficiencies of kissing, and revised traditional gender roles of eroticism and power. The history of sex reveals a similar pattern of growing thoughtfulness, openness, and originality. At the mid-nineteenth century intercourse was a climactic moment that was charged with excitement, but compared with the early twentieth century it was also anatomically constricted, spatially confined, morally suspect, less satisfying, deadly serious, more dangerous, abruptly over, and less authentic. This is an extravagant set of claims about an age that rhapsodized over the glories of love, but it is justified by the way sex was portrayed in Victorian literature.

My ordering of elements is itself based on values that changed over time. By putting sex after the wedding I deferred to Victorian ethics. Among all the novels I read for this study, in none published before 1895 did lovers have sex and subsequently marry. That year in *Jude the Obscure* Arabella and Jude had sex before marrying, and in *The Woman Who Did* Herminia challenged the reigning ethic by having sexual relations without ever intending to marry. The relaxation of that ethic is revealed by the frequency with which early twentieth-century novels included lovers who have sex before marrying, if indeed they marry at all—Ann Veronica and Capes, Swann and Odette, Chéri and Edmée, Molly and Leopold, Frederic and Catherine, Ursula and Rupert, Connie and Mellors, Ulrich and Agatha.

I

Censorship reveals the bodily details of sex that public morality permits. An increase in that allowance is illustrated by a comparison of what the authorities attempted to censor from *Madame Bovary* in 1857 and from *Ulysses* in 1933. A comparison of descriptions of sex in those novels suggests that across this period the guardians of public morality were gradually permitting the curtain of censorship to rise. One of the scenes the French public prosecutor cited in charging *Madame Bovary* with "offenses against morality and religion" was Rodolphe's seduction of Emma at the start of their adulterous affair, a scene from which Flaubert had omitted any explicit reference to the sex act. Flaubert's first reference to physical contact between Emma and Rodolphe was literally cloaked in metaphor.

> The broad cloth of her habit clung to the velvet of his coat. She leaned back her head, her white throat swelled in a sigh, and, her resistance gone, weeping, hiding her face, with a long shudder she gave herself to him.
>
> Evening shadows were falling, and the level rays of the sun streamed through the branches and dazzled her eyes . . . All was silent; soft sweetness seemed to be seeping from the trees; she felt her heart beating again, and her blood flowing in her flesh like a river of milk.   (181)

Flaubert's upward displacement of sexual swelling from Emma's genitals to her throat, his use of metaphor for her capitulation, his eliding paragraph break for the sex act, and his further displacement of her sexual release and post-coital calm from her body to the surrounding forest are typical of Victorian treatments of sex. Far different was Joyce's description of Molly's thinking about adulterous sex with Boylan and its aftermath:

> . . . I wished he was here or somebody to let myself go with and come again like that I feel all fire inside me or if I could dream it when he made me spend the 2nd time tickling me behind with his finger I was coming for about 5 minutes with my legs round him I had to hug him after O Lord I wanted to shout out all sorts of things fuck or shit or anything at all . . . (754)

Joyce's unpunctuated stream of consciousness technique is well-suited to express the flow of Molly's dream-like fantasies, mixing memories of sex with different men, lingering on her post-coital pleasure, capturing her pleasure in a lubricious verbal orgy. Joyce also provides a contrast with Flaubert's milk imagery which conjured up kindness and purity. Once when Molly's breasts had become painfully filled with milk she had Leopold suck on them to relieve the pressure. As she recalled, "I had to get him to suck them they were so hard he said it was sweeter and thicker than cows then he wanted to milk me into the tea well hes beyond everything I declare" (754).

Molly's reverie contrasts further with the "erotic" dream of Jane Eyre. After she ran away from Rochester, while enduring the chilling courtship of ascetic St. John Rivers, she dreamed about Rochester. "I used to rush into strange dreams at night," she reported, "dreams many-coloured, agitated, full of the ideal, the stirring, the stormy—dreams where, amidst unusual scenes, charged with adventure, with agitating risk and romantic chance, I still again and again met Mr Rochester, always at some exciting crisis; and then the sense of being in his arms, hearing his voice, meeting his eye, touching his hand and cheek, loving him, being loved by him—the hope of passing a lifetime at his side, would be renewed, with all its first force and fire" (393). Like most unmarried young women at that time Jane was a virgin and her sexual fantasies were understandably vague and confused. Her dreams offer a rare glimpse into that vagueness and confusion. They were in color and agitated but "full of the ideal." Did dreams in 1847 actually idealize sex? Dream imagery materializes and eroticizes rather than idealizes or sublimates. Did "agitating risk" screen Jane's anxious anticipation? Was "romantic chance" a cover term for an accidental vision of the body or an unexpected opportunity for sex? Did "exciting crisis" refer to her own sexual arousal or orgasm? The most decipherable imagery in her dream was conventional, although it may have captured all she knew about sex—she saw herself in Rochester's arms, hearing his voice, seeing his eyes, and touching him cheek to cheek. Did erotic touching in Victorian dreams go no further than cheek to cheek? Did Brontë, who in 1847 was also a virgin, know more about sex than she lets Jane know? These questions remain unanswered. Jane's dreams are all Brontë revealed about erotic dreams. If these dreams are representative, they suggest that even when Victorians were free from the censorship of their own waking consciences, they limited, more than did the moderns, those parts of the body which they included in sexual fantasies.

II

In addition to the growing variety of meeting places for lovers, there were also more places to have sex. Middle-class Victorian sex, like the entire courtship ritual, was confined to a small number of appropriate places, usually in the bedroom and in bed.[1] In the twentieth century several new technologies helped diversify the locations for having sex. Bicycles enabled lovers to get away easily. In Maurice Leblanc's *Voici des ailes!* (1898) two couples become so liberated during a bicycle holiday that they switch partners *en route*. Intoxicated by the freedom of the open air and the speed of their movement, the women are inspired to cycle through the countryside bare-breasted by day and bed down with their new partners by night. Automobiles provided mobile seclusion. Rupert and Ursula made love in an automobile during their first night on the road. In a poem of 1913 Blaise Cendrars recalled a trip he had made on the Trans-Siberian Railway in 1904, which inspired a fantasy of sexual ubiquity: "All the days and all the women in the cafes and all the glasses / I should have liked to drink and break them."[2] The cinema suggested exotic locales for sex, such as Valentino's tent in the Arabian desert, the setting for *The Sheik* (1920). In *The Thibaults* Rachel and Antoine start making love in a private box at the cinema. The massive displacement of men and women during World War I created new places for sex, such as the Milan hospital bed described in *A Farewell to Arms*. The concentration in cities of different nationalities was another technic that diversified sexual mores with strange new ways. Among the urban experiences that Rilke's hero Malte Laurids Brigge thought necessary to prepare one to write poetry were "many nights of love, each one different from all the others" (20).

III

Victorians viewed any deviation from "normal" sex as morally suspect. One source for their overbearing moral-religious framework is Richard von Krafft-Ebing's textbook—*Psychopathia Sexualis* (1886)—which became an influential catalogue of deviations. Its medical nomenclature supplied protective cover for Victorians eager to learn about what their own limited experience and restrictive sexual morality had kept out of sight and mind. Adopting the posture of moral outrage they could indulge in this "medico-forensic" peep-show of sexual hyperaesthesia, parasthesia, aspermia, polyspermia, spermatorrhoea, sadism, masochism, fetishism, exhibitionism, psychic hermaphroditism, satyriasis, and nymphomania. For all the author's scholarly trappings and scientific credentials, traditional moralizing about female sexual desire prevailed. "The unfaithfulness of the wife, as compared with that of the husband," he argued, "is morally of much wider bearing, and should always meet with severer punishment." The cause of many of these pathologies, he warned, was childhood masturbation, which he characterized as a premature, pathogenic manifestation of the sexual instinct.[3]

Krafft-Ebing's view of masturbation accorded with the Victorian tracts that regarded it as a "solitary vice." In contrast some modern novelists treated masturbation as neither solitary nor a vice. In *The Thibaults* there is a vivid description of Jacques masturbating, and although he is secretive, he enjoys it: "He flung himself out of bed, pulled off his nightshirt and, standing before the glass, fell to kissing his arms, hugging himself with a sort of desperate frenzy" (213). In *Ulysses* masturbation is not solitary but a shared experience. Leopold regards his masturbation with the help of Gerty's self-exposure as "a kind of language between us." In the Circe episode we learn that Gerty somehow lost her virginity while displaying herself to Leopold, and although Molly's stream-of-consciousness summation of her past sex life is autoerotic, it also plays off Leopold, asleep at her side.[4]

Modern lovers indulge in even more extravagant sexual practices. Leopold Bloom indulges in coprophilia, masochism, voyeurism, and transsexualism as well as masturbation. In *Remembrance of Things Past*, during a heated exchange, Albertine says to Marcel: "I'd rather you left me free once in a while to go and get myself *(me faire casser)* . . ." (343). Later Marcel realizes that she stopped herself before saying the words *le pot*, which would have completed the slang expression for anal intercourse. In *Point Counter Point* Spandrell seduces innocent young girls into all sorts of unnamed perversions.

Lawrence criticized such perverse sex, but he was fascinated by one perversion which he believed had to be performed, if only once, to dispel the shame associated with the darkest sources of eroticism. In *Women in Love* Ursula learned that Rupert desired something "deeper than the phallic source." She was at first repelled by his "strange licentiousness," but she was also fascinated. She submitted to his desire and performed digital anal erotism. "With perfect fine finger-tips of reality she would touch the reality in him, the suave, pure, untranslatable reality of his loins of darkness." She "established a rich new circuit, a new current of passional electric en-

ergy, between the two of them, released from the darkest poles of the body"
(311, 306).

In *Lady Chatterley's Lover* Mellors went the final step and sodomized
Connie. The act had historical significance, because it involved "burning out
the shames, the deepest, oldest shames, in the most secret places." Although
Mellors took over the active role, the focus was on her response. Connie
submitted "like a slave," but still "the passion licked round her, consuming,
and when the sensual flame of it pressed through her bowels and breast, she
really thought she was dying: yet a poignant, marvelous death." This forbidden love-making cauterized the wound of shame that Lawrence believed was
killing sexual fulfillment in his time. "[Connie] would have thought a
woman would have died of shame. Instead of which, the shame died. Shame,
which is fear: the deep organic shame, the old, old physical fear which
crouches in the bodily roots of us, and can only be chased away by the sensual fire, at last it was roused up and routed by the phallic hunt of the man
. . . She felt, now, she had come to the real bed-rock of her nature, and was
essentially shameless" (231–232). Thus in two major novels Lawrence used
sexual love to conquer shame by having his lovers engage in what Victorians
had viewed as an unspeakable perversion.

Krafft-Ebing's codification of sexual perversions expanded the sexual
realm beyond the practices that Victorians believed constituted respectable
sex, although he persisted in viewing perversions as immoral and illegal.
Twenty years later Freud introduced his first developmental psychology
with an essay on "The Sexual Aberrations," which de-moralized and de-
criminalized sexual perversions, although Freud stigmatized them as pathological. Modern novelists avoided the moral model and had no use for the
medical model but instead relied on an aesthetic model, which treated new
sexual combinations as the subject matter of art.

IV

Sex was less satisfying for Victorians than it was for the moderns because
the Victorians had more to fear. Toward the end of the nineteenth century
discussion began, at first in medical circles, of the reasons for these fears and
for the sexual failures they caused. The more intense discussion concerned
women, but even the debate about men's problems focused on women's
changing experience. Pierre Garnier's tract *Impuissance physique et morale*
(1881) offers an early reaction to the apparent assault on male potency by

women who were becoming more sexually aware. In addition to justifying the man's right to initiate sex, remain the more active, and regulate the pace of pleasure, Garnier implied that women were taking a more active role. He charged that women's lack of response may cause a man's failure. Although he assumed that the man should still control, he revised the conventional strong-weak gender dichotomy by proposing that the woman's responsiveness was desirable, indeed essential, if only to prevent male dysfunction. The typical Victorian patriarch would not as easily have admitted that his performance or his pleasure were dependent on female responsiveness, which would have conjured up the very female sexual desire that his own presumed sexual preeminence could not allow. The increasing number of such studies from the 1890s to the 1910s does not indicate that men were experiencing impotence more frequently, but rather that they were learning to cope with it. Men are far more willing to discuss their impotence (or write a book about it) when it is a past episode than when it is a current problem.

Victorian women had difficulty enjoying sexual intercourse because they were afraid of it. The unmarried woman risked her reputation as well as her health and life, and even the Victorian wife was beset with fears. She had to worry about venereal disease from her husband, who knowingly or unknowingly could infect her. She also ran the risk of pregnancy, which was life-threatening, however much extolled. She had concerns about her husband's impatience and lack of experience, her own sexual ineptitude (a consequence of her highly prized innocence) or, if she had some experience, her husband's fear of her own desire and orgasm. There was also the stigma of her devaluation (implicit in the term "defloration" and explicit in the reigning sexual morality), the prospect of exhausting child-rearing (which was entirely her responsibility), the specter of the "fallen woman" (whose life was sustained by the vulgar monetary value of debased sex), and the abiding judgment of Christianity (which stigmatized even marital sex with a hint of sin).

The Victorian novel did not discuss the sex act, so we must rely on retrospective interpretations and critiques of Victorian sexual practices in modern novels. The first novel to treat a woman's *sexual* unhappiness was *Jude the Obscure*. Echoing St. Augustine's asceticism, Sue writes to Jude: "No poor woman has ever wished more than I that Eve had not fallen, so that (as the primitive Christians believed) some harmless mode of vegetation might have peopled paradise" (179). She leaves Phillotson to live with Jude but is unable to enjoy sex with him, especially after she learns that he has taken her to the same hotel where he had been with Arabella. In a heated exchange following that disclosure she reveals that Phillotson disgusted her so much that she jumped out of the window to get away. Several times she reminds Jude, "*I* jumped out of the window"—each time emphasizing the "*I*." When Jude later charges her with being an unusual "bodiless creature," she replies, "I am not so exceptional a woman as you think. Fewer women like marriage than you suppose, only they enter into it for the dignity it is assumed to confer, and the social advantages it gains them sometimes" (205).

Sue's dilemma is that she has a strained, convoluted desire for Jude but at the same time is sickened by sex and wants to substitute for her desire "some harmless mode of vegetation." In *Strait is the Gate* Gide dramatizes how fatal such conflict can be. In contrast, Colette, Proust, Wells, Hemingway, Fitzgerald, West, Joyce, Lawrence, Huxley, and Musil vividly show lovers enjoying sex more than did their Victorian predecessors. In *The Man Without Qualities* Musil concludes a gratifying moment between Ulrich and his mistress Bonadea with their frank post-coital discussion about the history of sexual relations. "The problem is," she tells Ulrich, "nowadays women have a new, different approach to the sex problem: a woman doesn't just want the man to act, what she wants is for him to act with proper understanding of feminine psychology!" Men are reluctant to understand women because they fear their own sexual inferiority: "a woman can be made love to even when she doesn't want to be," while "very often when a man wants to make love he can't." Men try to compensate for this deficiency by keeping women subordinate in sex and society. The proper solution is authentic sex. "If one wants to get a rapturous embrace out of one's sexual partner, one has to grant him or her equality of status, not merely regard him or her as a complement to oneself, without any will of his or her own" (III, 257–260). With Bonadea's demonstration Ulrich learns what most Victorian men were reluctant to admit—that a sexually active and gratified woman increases the man's pleasure.

Much scholarly debate has focused on the argument that Victorian sexuality was "repressed." Michel Foucault dubbed that argument "the repressive hypothesis" and rejected it as superficial. He argued that the Victorian medical threats, parental warnings, and moral condemnations were not merely sex-negative injunctions that codified sexual repression but were also, and more fundamentally, an affirmative "incitement to discourse" that valorized sex even while condemning it as a cause of disease, perversion, or sin. Foucault provided an important corrective to a pervasive but facile argument about nineteenth-century sexuality, but in dubbing that argument "the repressive hypothesis," he did a disservice to the clarity of future study.[5]

I did not attempt to compare levels of repression between the Victorians and the moderns, because repression is an unconscious mental process that is difficult to document. I have, however, compared levels of *suppression,* which is a conscious mental process that is far easier to document.[6] If a Victorian man or woman insisted that the lights be turned out so that sex could take place in darkness, how can we know that he or she was repressed? The Victorian rule was that a proper man or woman must not see one another's naked body. Such a man or woman may have been repressed, but that is something that cannot be known with as high a degree of certainty as the fact that he or she turned out the lights in deference to a public code of behavior. Victorians suppressed the visual sense not only by turning out the lights but by looking away. They also confined their sexual pleasure anatomically, restricted the locations where they had sex, and feared its many real and unreal dangers, which became far less threatening to twentieth-century lovers.

V

Another source of evidence for the increasing enjoyment of sex is the increasing sense of humor about it. While the Victorians who idealized the other-worldly perfection of sex were deadly serious about it, the moderns found humor in its earthy deficiencies. In *The Vagabond,* as Renée ponders whether to let herself go with her lover, she recalls affectionately how while making love he gave out a "little amorous grunt" (128). In *Point Counter Point,* as Walter puts his hand on Lucy's breast to begin some serious loving, her parrot startles him with a piercing squawk. Lucy explains that her parrot won't be quiet unless the cage is covered. Even after covering it, as the undaunted Walter resumes his caressing he is again interrupted by a chirpy "good-morning, Auntie" (176). In *Lady Chatterley's Lover* Connie affectionately views the humorous appearance of Mellors's lovemaking. "Yes," she thinks, "this was love, this ridiculous bouncing of the buttocks, and the wilting of the poor insignificant, moist little penis. This was the divine love!" (161).

Victorians were too afraid of sex to laugh about it. Victorian men took their penises very seriously and never described them. Joyce described Leopold's limp penis as a "languid floating flower." Lawrence described Mellors' post-coital penis as poor, insignificant, moist, and little. In *Tropic of Cancer* (1934) Henry Miller described his own penis with masculine bravado as well as good-natured ridicule. His descriptions of vaginas are similarly irreverent. One character, "cunt-struck" Van Norden, examines a prostitute's shaved genitals with a flashlight and confesses to Miller his disappointment. "When you look at it that way, sort of detached like, you get funny notions in your head. All that mystery about sex and then you discover that it's nothing—just a blank. Wouldn't it be funny if you found a harmonica inside . . . or a calendar?" (140). Miller's jocularity contrasts with the seriousness of Victorian men who would not have dared to look directly at, let alone inside, a vagina or acknowledge its humorous aspects.

While Lawrence wrote of playful sex and its ridiculous moments, he remained serious. Miller wrote of serious sex in the midst of grief that was nevertheless always full of laughter. His autobiographical *Tropic of Cancer* opens with images of hunger, vermin, and disease, but the book is essentially a story of his discovery of his vocation as an artist and is scored with laughter and song. He explains that to be an artist one must learn to sing, if a bit off key. To liberate writing from censorship one must write off key, which he will do by treating sex irreverently. "This is not a book," he proclaims, it is "libel, slander, defamation of character." Throughout all the bitterness and disillusionment he keeps his sense of humor. While working on the novel Miller listened to an African laughing record blaring from a Victrola.[7] His persistent amusement energizes the ideological heart of the novel—a riotous twelve-page peroration about writing, fucking, and the history of the universe, set off by an account of a whore who grabs his head between her legs, forcing him to stare into her crotch and causing images to stream out of his mind "like ants pouring out of a crack in the sidewalk." He sees "the great sprawling mothers of Picasso, their breasts covered with spiders . . . and Molly Bloom lying on a dirty mattress for eternity." The crack, he continues, seems to be "laughing at me too, laughing through the mossy whiskers." He would like to penetrate far enough into that crack to make her eyes "waggle," to hear once again the words of Dostoevski "with all the undertones of misery now lightly, humorously touched, now swelling like an organ note until the heart bursts and there is nothing left but a blinding, scorching light, the radiant light that carries off the fecundating seeds of the stars." Miller shifts from brutal realism to joyous surrealism, ransacking Western culture for images of creation and passion and laughter—anything that lives and flows—to counter the only real obscenities, which he believes are inertia and paralysis. But as bad as life gets, he is always able to let loose "wild, wild utterly uncontrollable laughter" (247–248).

Anaïs Nin's preface to the novel assesses its contribution. "Here is a book which, if such a thing were possible, might restore our appetite for the fundamental realities." One of those realities was humor, and, compared with the Victorians' solemnity, Miller's novel was indeed a restoration of a long tradition of sexual humor that went back as far as Aristophanes.

VI

In arguing that Victorian sex was abruptly over, I refer not to the time it took from start to finish but to the duration of and attention given to the post-coital interval. While the pleasures of sexual union tend toward the universal, post-coital repose draws lovers back to their individuality. In describing Emma's post-coital state as a time when "soft sweetness seemed to be seeping from the trees," Flaubert depersonalized the uniqueness of her return to herself. The sweetness is saccharine, and the image of trees is a cliché which the consummate stylist allowed himself to use with no intended irony—anything to avoid describing what really happened afterwards.

A change in what actually happens after sex is suggested by the contrast between a passage in a Victorian love letter and a scene from a modern novel. In 1865 Laura Lyman wrote to her husband Joseph, "How I long to see you—how I long to 'be all night in the hollow of my husband's shoulder' as Dr. Breen used so felicitously to express it in his sermons."[8] Perhaps Joseph had extraordinary vascular strength, but as anyone knows who has tried to cradle a sleeping lover all night, the result is temporary paralysis rather than nocturnal bliss. In *Chéri* Colette offered a more realistic account of what usually happens when one tries to cushion a lover's post-coital languor for any length of time. After some savage lovemaking, Léa and Chéri collapsed onto one another. They did not fall asleep, but some of their carelessly positioned body parts did. Although Chéri's neck became numb, in this sexual aftermath the woman endured the greater pain. Léa "bore almost the full weight of his unsparing body." The upper part of it lay across her thigh, crushing her knee. Her left arm, which was bent under her own body, became "cramped and pricking with pins and needles" (116). Her shoulder was on fire. While the Victorian wife etherealized sexual pleasure by fancying a night-long romantic tableau, the modern novelist counterposed the intensity of her heroine's sexual pleasure with a realistic account of its consequent pains.

The most disturbing post-coital scene I found was in *Anna Karenina*. It clarified the meaning of the novel's epigraph—"Vengeance is mine; I will repay"—making it clear that the vengeance was the lovers' own bad conscience, which erupted following their first sex. Tolstoy's brief account of "that" for which the couple longed (we learn only that it "had come to pass") contrasts with his lengthy account of their remorse.

> That which for nearly a year had been Vronsky's sole and exclusive desire, supplanting all his former desires: that which for Anna had been an impossible, dreadful, but all the more bewitching dream of happiness, had come to pass. Pale, with trembling lower jaw, he stood over her, entreating her to be calm, himself not knowing why or how.
>
> "Anna, Anna" he said in a trembling voice, "Anna, for God's sake! . . ."
>
> But the louder he spoke the lower she drooped her once proud, bright, but now shame-stricken head, and she writhed, slipping down from the sofa on which she sat to the floor at his feet. She could have fallen on the carpet if he had not held her.
>
> "My God! Forgive me!" she said, sobbing and pressing Vronsky's hand to her breast.
>
> . . . There was something frightful and revolting in the recollection of what had been paid for with this terrible price of shame. The shame she felt at her spiritual nakedness communicated itself to him. But in spite of the murderer's horror of the body of his victim, that body must be cut in pieces and hidden away, and he must make use of what he has obtained by the murder.   (135–136)

Adulterers in any period might feel remorse following the consummation of their forbidden lovemaking, but Anna's sudden helplessness and spiritual nakedness, Vronsky's disorientation and trembling panic (which Tolstoy suggests was like that of someone who has just murdered and hacked a body to pieces and must now either hide away or "make use of" the bloody remains) all belong to an age when sex itself was profoundly suspect.

In contrast, modernists used post-coital scenes to explore the deficiencies of sex as well as the new sexual freedom and sexual prowess of women. In

The Man Without Qualities, after vigorously making love, Ulrich observes "a few tiny hairs sprouting in his mistress's nostrils," while she feels "satiated and battered" (I, 263). In *The Counterfeiters* Gide mocks the genuineness of conventional post-coital etiquette. After Bernard disengages himself from a sleeping lover, Gide editorializes—"What! Without one more kiss? Without a lover's last look? Without a supreme embrace?" Gide insists on the falseness of the final kiss and the supreme embrace, the artificiality of denouements and epilogues, the counterfeit nature of "true love" as well as the novel form itself. He further interrogates the meaning of the farewell. "Is it through insensibility that he leaves her in this way? I cannot tell. He cannot tell himself. He tries not to think; it is a difficult task to incorporate this unprecedented night with all the preceding nights of this history. No; it is an appendix, an annex, which can find no place in the body of the book" (307).

The Victorian novel linked the logic of love with conventional narrative form and located the aftermath of sex in some appropriate part of a story. Gide tagged on to the end of stories their critically important moments, he located aftermaths at first meetings, and he lodged expectant hopes in hopeless farewells. Two years after publication of *The Counterfeiters* he published *Journal of "The Counterfeiters,"* in which he explained how in the novel he tried to avoid the artificiality of a plot and built the novel not forward in time to a conclusion but backwards—to even before the chapter originally conceived as first—and ended it not with conventional closure but rather had it "disperse, disintegrate" (409, 431, 449). He believed that sexual love was a mixture of alternating anticipations and recollections of precoital and post-coital feelings.

In *A Farewell to Arms* all sex seems post-coital. Frederic recalled the many "nights when the room whirled and you needed to look at the wall to make it stop, nights in bed, drunk, when you knew that that was all there was, and the strange excitement of waking and not knowing who it was with you, and the world all unreal in the dark and so exciting that you must resume again unknowing and not caring in the night, sure that this was all and all and all and not caring" (13). Hemingway thus found a metaphor for postwar disillusionment in post-coital depression.

Victorian women had tried to make themselves appealing by pushing their breasts up and out. Huxley's eroticized heroine Lucy Tantamount, in one of her most alluring moments after having had sex with Walter, clasps her hands behind her head, revealing her flat breasts lifted by the pull of the stretched muscles (207). Her exposed and seemingly vulnerable breasts in fact indicate sexual confidence, and her underlying stretched muscles imply physical strength. Rachel assumes a similar post-coital pose in *The Thibaults,* when, after making love with Antoine, she relaxes on the bed with her hands behind her head (419).[9] During post-coital interludes both Lucy and Rachel take control of their man by pulling his head down for an embrace. Annoyed with Walter's insistent questioning whether she loves him, Lucy snaps impatiently that love is rare and that one must do something in the interval. Then she pulls his head down by his forelock and says, "In the intervals, Walter darling, there's you" (207).

For Victorians the post-coital interlude was particularly embarrassing, because eyes opened, lights came on, and couples were obliged to look at one another or else away and begin to speak or else endure a nerve-wracking silence. In contrast Lawrence celebrates it as a moment for freely thinking and talking about sex and for looking at and exploring the beloved's still responsive body. He suggests the historical significance of *Lady Chatterley's Lover* by contrasting the harmonious sex between Connie and Mellors with the outdated, disjunctive sex that Connie had with Michaelis, who climaxed too quickly. "She had to go on after [Michaelis] had finished, in the wild tumult and heaving of her loins, while he heroically kept himself up, and present in her, with all his will and self-offering, till she brought about her own crisis, with weird little cries." Michaelis is humiliated by this routine, as he complains to her: "I have to hang on with my teeth till you bring yourself off with your own exertions" (51).

Although Connie's first sexual experience with Mellors is disappointing, subsequent ones improve. One time Connie literally holds on to the aftermath of lovemaking—she does not take a bath because "the sense of his flesh touching her, his very stickiness upon her, was dear to her, in a sense holy" (128). The post-coital moments following a later episode are sensuous and loving. Mellors gazes upon "the beautiful curving drop of her haunches," the "heavy roundness of her buttocks!" In addition to looking and caressing *after* he has had sex, Mellors speaks about her body. "Tha's got a real soft sloping bottom on thee, as a man loves in 'is guts. It's a bottom as could hold the world up, it is!" As he speaks his fingers brush the "two secret openings to her body," and he says, "Here tha shits an' here tha pisses: an' I lay my hand on 'em both an' like thee for it." They wind up this earthy moment, a shocking obscenity for many readers, by decorating one another's pubic hair with flowers. After weaving some forget-me-nots into Connie's, Mellors steps back to evaluate his handicraft and departs, expressing the hope that the flowers will deserve their name and remind her of precisely where he wants not to be forgotten—"That's where you won't forget me!" (207–208). Lawrence thus locates his own position in the history of sex where the Western world would not forget him—on Connie's body.

The historical significance of their post-coital expression of affection and playing with one another's pubic hair can be sharpened with a comparison to the deadly seriousness with which Robert Browning and Elizabeth Barrett fetishize a pre-coital exchange of locks of head hair. In 1845 Robert had written to Elizabeth: "Give me . . . so much of you—all precious that you are—as may be given in a lock of your hair—I will live and die with it." She replied that she had never given a lock to anyone except some relatives and female friends, adding that "it is just three weeks since I said last to an asker that I was 'too great a prude for such a thing'!"[10] In *Sonnets From the Portuguese* (1850) Elizabeth revealed her subsequent private act, daring for her time, of kissing a lock of Robert's hair and laying it on her naked breast.

> . . . from my poet's forehead to my heart . . .
> [I] lay the gift where nothing hindereth;
> Here on my heart, as on thy brow, to lack
> No natural heat till mine grows cold in
>   death.   (Sonnet 19)

Unlike Elizabeth Barrett, Lawrence did not have to use synecdoche to represent the entwining of bodies with the entwining of hair, he did not have to veil direct reference to the naked body with a doubly negative phrase such as "where nothing hindereth," and he did not have to cool off an image of feverish desire with the prospect of death.

Nineteenth-century artists rarely painted an explicit post-coital scene. Courbet's *Sleep* shows two naked women sleeping in one another's arms, but it was a notorious exception, produced for a private collector. For all Courbet's realism it glamorized the women's gracefully entwined forms and idealized the moment as one of complete satisfaction. Moreover the women are unconscious of whatever sexual pleasure they experienced. In contrast, some modern artists did what no non-pornographic painter of the nineteenth century could have done—painted and exhibited a post-coital man and woman (with at least one of them wide awake) cut off from identifiable surroundings and hence from any external excuses, conscious of and answerable for their feelings.

Two drawings by Schiele in 1913 are powerful images of post-coital isolation.[11] In both drawings the couple's thoughts appear to be elsewhere, while their relaxed bodies lie entwined like pretzels, a contrast that accentuates the emotional distance that separates them. In the first, the man is naked except for his socks which have fallen down his ankles that still casually clasp the woman's buttocks. The woman is on her knees, while her bent torso lies between the man's spread legs and over his chest. She seems distraught rather than discharged and clutches her head, positioned under his left armpit. The man stares into the distance. In the second drawing the same man has the same facial expression, and his reclining body lies between the woman's legs. Schiele accents the casualness of this post-coital moment by depicting the woman absentmindedly scratching her knee.

VII

Sexual intercourse for the moderns, as compared with the Victorians, included more of the body, took place in a greater variety of locations, was less constrained by a strict morality, was more satisfying, included more humor, and continued longer after climax. That it became more authentic is implied by these changes, for each identifies a new way of experiencing and understanding sex.

Another source of evidence for that understanding was the more forthright way moderns began to talk about sex. And there was lots of talk. In 1892 a group of artists and writers, including Munch and Strindberg, began to meet in a Berlin wine cellar (Zum schwarzen Ferkel) and participate in discussions led by Stanislaw Przybyszewski, who advocated restoration of primal sexual passion. In 1897 Alfred Schuler and Ludwig Klages organized the Cosmic Circle, a Munich discussion group that affirmed instinct and eroticism over reason and analysis and worked to restore the "blood-knowledge" that had been drained out of love in the modern world. Otto Gross and Frieda von Richthofen communicated the Cosmic Circle's ideas to Lawrence. Somewhat more earthy was the sex talk of the Bloomsbury group which in 1908 became noticeably risqué. During one meeting Lytton Strachey asked Virginia Woolf's sister Vanessa if a stain on her dress was from "semen" and in so doing triggered a riot of laughter and exuberant discussion of sex. "With that one word," Woolf recalled, "all barriers of reticence and reserve went down . . . Sex permeated our conversation. The word bugger was never far from our lips. We discussed copulation with the same excitement and openness that we had discussed the nature of the good." Around 1910 a group of Greenwich Village feminists schooled on Havelock Ellis, Edward Carpenter, Charlotte Gilman, and Freud began to campaign for birth control, sex education, and free love in addition to the vote. The British Society for the Study of Sex Psychology, founded in 1914, promoted sex reform with publications and discussion. In 1919 Magnus Hirschfeld opened the Institute for Sexual Science in Berlin, a center for research and discussion which offered counseling on how to improve sex.[12] In 1910 Freud founded the International Psychoanalytical Association, which did more than any other institution in history to develop language for talking about sex. One goal of psychoanalysis was to remove sexual inhibitions by a treatment which required that the patient learn to think about sex and talk about it freely, both to the therapist and to a beloved. For the man who invented the "talking cure," learning to talk about sex was crucial.

But just as excessive talk can screen genuine insight in a psychoanalysis, so can idle chatter screen the actuality of authentic sex. Several novelists criticized those who were so eager to achieve uninhibited sexual release that they replaced feeling with talking. In *This Side of Paradise* Eleanor boasts to Amory that she is "hipped on Freud." Amory is also well versed in current jargon, but he is worried that talking may interfere with sex. "We who consider ourselves the intellectuals cover [sex] up by pretending that it's another side of us, has nothing to do with our shining brains; we pretend that the fact that we realize it is really absolving us from being a prey to it" (238). *Point Counter Point* is full of sophisticated sex-talk. When Walter met Marjorie, "love was talk" (11). When Mark met Mary he was shocked at how she spoke about sex in "her calm matter-of-fact way" (116). Spandrell justifies his lasciviousness with historical precedents, and Lucy teases Walter with sexual repartee. "Romantic, romantic," she chides, "try to be a little more up-to-date" (209). In *The Man Without Qualities* Bonadea complains to Ulrich: "Good heavens, every single day I hear of nothing but sexual practice, embrace brought to a successful conclusion, erotic stimuli, glands, secretions, repressed urges, erotic training, and regulation of the sexual instinct!" (III, 261). Fitzgerald, Huxley, and Musil exposed the counterfeit nature of overly talkative sexuality to clarify the value of real coin.

The epigraph for this chapter could also be an epitaph for Lawrence himself. His purpose in writing was to help men and women understand the meaning of sexual love. Some of his characters also talked about it too much, but even they communicated a part, if only a passing exaggeration, of his abiding message. In *Women in Love* Lawrence ridicules Hermione's deliberate spontaneity and aggressive sexuality. She had a taste for perversity, but even that was intellectualized. "What you want is pornography," Rupert charges, "watching your animal actions in mirrors, so that you have it all in your consciousness" (36). When she defends herself, saying that she wants to enjoy sex completely unaware of herself, Rupert seems to shift his position in arguing that the desire to forget oneself in sex is precisely what is wrong with their age. People have sexual problems "not because they have too much mind, but too little." Confused, Hermione asks what is wrong with her knowledge, and Rupert seems to shift again in answering that it is too much in her head. Knowledge should be "in the blood" (34–36).

In *Lady Chatterley's Lover* sex talk, implied by Clifford's surname, again comes under fire. A group of people who believe in the life of the mind meet for regular chats at the Chatterley estate, much like the groups that were meeting in the cultural capitals of Europe and America. One discussant takes a position the novel will eventually refute—"that sex is just another form of talk, where you act the words instead of saying them" (32). Other members talk about the "resurrection of the body" and the "democracy of touch," but their words cannot become flesh; the women are frigid or sexually frustrated, and the men are impotent or have premature ejaculations. These sex intellectuals are an easy target for Lawrence, but he never entirely rejects the need for talking about sex. As one discussant reminds the group, "Real knowledge comes out of the whole corpus of the consciousness; out of your belly and your penis as much as out of your brain and mind" (35).

In "A Propos of *Lady Chatterley's Lover*" Lawrence explains how mankind lost such "real knowledge." Buddha, Plato, and Jesus separated mankind from the body by teaching that "the only happiness lay in abstracting oneself from life . . . and in living in the 'immutable' or eternal spirit." His own writing seeks to restore reverence for the cycle of seasons, the ritual of dawn and sunset, the rhythm of life and death, and the pulse of blood in sex. "In the blood, knowing and being, or feeling, are one and undivided: no serpent and no apple has caused a split." For Lawrence blood is more than a metaphor for sex. "The phallus is a column of blood that fills the valley of blood of a woman." Knowledge of sex is "blood knowledge," which is achieved only with the marriage between mind and body, word and deed.

Lawrence echoes the attacks of Fitzgerald, Huxley, and Musil on the substitution of sex talk for actual sex. He criticizes "the modern young jazzy
and high-brow person" and those lovers who "love 'talking' to one another." Their "nerve-sympathy" is no substitute for "blood-sympathy." But
no matter how deep his suspicion of words, they are essential even to his
sacred blood knowledge. Men and women must be able to talk about sex in
order to think about it "fully, completely, honestly, cleanly" (85–107). They
must be able to use words just like novelists to explore the possibilities of
sex. The substitution of words for deeds may dilute fulfillment, but, as in
writing, those deeds are incomplete without words, because only words enable us to communicate and understand. Without words and thought sex
loses its variety, its uniqueness, its responsiveness to the quirks and vicissitudes of particular relationships. A conspiracy of silence reduced Victorian
sexual intercourse to a mute and mindless routine. Modern lovers broke
that silence, sometimes with annoying exuberance, but their thinking
and talking enabled them to fashion ways of having sex that was more
their own.

17 Marriage

GOOD MARRIAGES do not make good reading. In my own research I found no major love story written before the twentieth century which focused on a fulfilling love between a married couple. Odysseus was happily married to Penelope, but *The Odyssey* is about his travels while away from her and ends when he returns. In troubadour poetry love was from afar or adulterous and by definition outside of marriage. Launcelot and Guinevere, Tristan and Isolde, Paolo and Francesca were archetypical adulterers. Dante hoped to join Beatrice in heaven, Petrarch's love for Laura was fueled by her unattainability, and Don Quixote's love for Dulcinea was a fantasy. In *Othello* jealousy destroys a marriage; in *Romeo and Juliet* two families prevent one; in *Antony and Cleopatra* a marriage destroys two nations and an epic love. *Clarissa* traces endless refusals to marry. The heroine in *Pamela* marries her kidnapper half-way through, at which point the novel flattens into a tale of domestic harmony and loses the interest that sustained it throughout the first half. In *Tom Jones* love triumphs over deceit, there is a happy wedding, and the novel ends. In both *The New Heloise* and *The Sorrows of Young Werther* a young man yearns eloquently but in vain for another man's wife.

In the Victorian novel couples who are either already married at the beginning or marry in the course of the story are invariably unhappy, in part because they understand little about their spouses. Thus the marriages of Edward Rochester, Edgar Linton, Heathcliff, Roger Chillingworth, Charles Bovary, M. Arnoux, Edward Casaubon, Tertius Lydgate, Alexey Karenin, Henleigh Grandcourt, Gilbert Osmond, Bartley Hubbard, Edmund Widdowson, Geert von Innstetten, Jude Fawley, Richard Phillotson, and Léonce Pontellier are miserable. Rochester marries Bertha before he discovers her "disgusting secret" that she is deranged. Edgar cannot make Cathy happy because he is a stranger compared with Heathcliff, while Heathcliff's own wife, Isabella, after six torturous weeks of matrimony, writes and asks a friend "to explain, if you can, what I have married" (173). Hawthorne's hazy sketch of the circumstances which led Hester into marriage recreate her own haziness at that time. M. and Mme. Arnoux are complete strangers. What Emma Bovary knows about marriage comes from romantic novels, and Charles knows less. In *Middlemarch* the marriage of Dorothea to Casaubon and that of Lydgate to Rosamond are grounded in ignorance. Dorothea, "with all her eagerness to know the truths of life, retained very childlike ideas about marriage" (4). She marries a myth and stumbles into the reality of marriage: "the large vistas and wide fresh air which she had dreamed of finding in her husband's mind were replaced by anterooms and winding passages which seemed to lead nowither" (136). Rosamond decides to marry Lydgate because he is not a Middlemarcher and hence an alluring mystery. Eliot cannot contain herself: "Poor Lydgate! or shall I say, Poor Rosamond! Each lived in a world of which the other knew nothing" (114). Karenin and Anna are shunted into marriage when, after a two-week courtship, he is threatened with social ostracism if he does not propose. Society takes charge before either has time to realize how little they care for one another. In *Daniel Deronda* Grandcourt has no idea of what he is getting into when he begins the outwardly grand courting of Gwendolen, and she knows nothing about his inwardly deficient feelings. In *The Portrait of a Lady* Isabel discovers that marriage is not an "infinite vista of multiplied life" but rather "a dark, narrow alley with a dead wall at the end" (424). The meager understanding that she and Gilbert eke out of their painful confrontations brings them no closer. These Victorian marriages were forged in mystery, sustained by secrecy, and buried in silence.

Other Victorian marriages promised happiness. There were the hopeful first marriages of Cathy II and Hareton, Ranthorpe and Isola, Margaret and Thornton, Cosette and Marius, Mirah and Daniel, Clara and Vernon; and there were the promising second marriages of Jane and Rochester, Estella and Pip, Bathsheba and Gabriel, Dorothea and Will; but these all begin at the end of novels and are more hope than actuality.

A painting by George Hicks illustrates one Victorian conception of marriage. At first glance *Woman's Mission: Companion to Manhood* (Figure 47, 1863) seems to show marital harmony at a moment of tragedy. The grieving husband clutches a black-bordered death announcement, while his wife cozies up to comfort him, her face radiating unqualified love; but in fact the

47. George Hicks, *Woman's Mission: Companion to Manhood*, 1863.

husband and wife are in different worlds. Hicks pictorially narrates the husband's melodramatic withdrawal—how he opened the letter, threw the en-
velope on the floor, stood up, tossed his napkin on the chair, turned away
from his wife, moved to the mantle for support, covered his eyes in grief,
and found no comfort in his wife's good housekeeping which is indicated by
the neat breakfast setting with tea pot, milk pitcher, sugar, butter, dishes,

48. George Grosz, *Man and Wife*, 1926.

newspaper, and carefully arranged morning mail. The painting intends to idealize the Victorian marriage, although it also reveals not so much sharing and a harmonious division of labor as isolation and the wife's subordination.

To illustrate changing images of marriage by contrasting this painting with George Grosz's *Man and Wife* (Figure 48, 1926) is a bit strained. The significance of the moments depicted are different, and the former is a cliché while the latter is an intentionally disturbing exposé by an enraged iconoclast. Nevertheless the former captures the Victorians' sentimental idealization of marriage, while the latter expresses the impatience with such idealization that was widespread during the 1920s. Grosz's portrait of his sister

Lotte and her husband is an emphatically unidealized moment in the routine of marriage. Husband and wife are in different worlds but far more intimate than Hicks's couple, who are posed to affect intimacy. The contrasting significance of eyes reveals two ways of relating in marriage. Hicks's husband covers his eyes in heroic self-sufficiency, while Grosz's husband leers at his wife's body through horned-rimmed glasses, his erotic dependency accented by the arrow-like form of the cigarette and collar which points to the source of his attachment. While Hicks's wife idolizes her husband, Grosz's wife admires herself. The former couple act out conventional roles, while the latter couple act on what they feel. Contrasting wifely roles are further implied by the still lifes on the tables: one is a neat arrangement of things for the husband's satisfaction, while the other is a disarray of beauty aids for the wife. The numerous petticoats under the Victorian wife's dress make a substantial base for her body which is positioned against her husband like a flying buttress, although her sartorial excess is useless because her husband leans on the mantle. In contrast the modern wife's transparent camisole does not create an illusion of substance or of support but highlights her sexual nonchalance. Hicks's idealized couple is fine-featured and well proportioned; Grosz's earthy couple is rough-featured and posed to exaggerate the disproportion of a large wife towering over her husband. Hicks's image of marital harmony suggests on close examination the couple's actual alienation, while Grosz's image of alienation brings out the couple's frank acceptance of their different interests. Hicks's sentimental idealism seems staged, while Grosz's brutal realism and *Sachlichkeit* (objectivity) rings true.

I see the history of marriage implied by this contrast as moving in the direction of authenticity, because in the first image posturing is offered as reality, while the second exposes the realities underneath such posing. Hicks closes off reflection on the meaning of being married, whereas Grosz investigates it. Into the twentieth century, novels about love in marriage also become more authentic in four respects. First, in comparison with Victorian novelists, modernists reflect more on the deficiencies of marriage as an institution. Second, modernists explore the positive aspects of love in marriage as the thematic focus of their novels and not just as a concluding hope. Third, one modernist novelist, D. H. Lawrence, deals with the meaning and possibilities of sex, both marital and extramarital. Fourth, modernists experiment more inventively with the function of marriage in the novel, specifically by varying the convention of using marriage to achieve closure. This latter formal change is part of a larger development in modern literature (and art) which, as I have emphasized, involved increasing reflection on the creative process.

I

While Victorian writers questioned the overbearing social forces that pressed the innocent and the ill-prepared into marriage, they emphasized the mismatch of specific husbands and wives. By the 1890s novelists were more inclined to question the institution of marriage itself. In *Jude the Obscure* Sue and Phillotson are clearly ill-suited, but Hardy accents the more fundamental deficiency of the bride's ignorance of the meaning of marriage itself. Before marrying Phillotson, she tells Jude, "I had never thought out fully what marriage meant" (171). Phillotson is similarly ignorant, as he tells a friend: "I had not the remotest idea—living apart from women as I have done for so many years—that merely taking a woman to church and putting a ring upon her finger could by any possibility involve one in such a daily, continuous tragedy as that now shared by her and me!" (184). Hardy's concluding indictment of marriage, far more sweeping than was typical of Victorian novelists, is put in the words of Phillotson's housekeeper, when she sees him carry Sue into his bedroom for a moribund consummation of their marriage and whispers ruefully to herself, "Weddings be funerals."

Wilde had a lighter touch. *The Importance of Being Earnest* questions the importance of being married, beginning with the opening exchange between Algernon and his manservant Lane.

> ALGERNON: Why is it that at a bachelor's establishment the servants invariably drink the champagne?
>
> LANE: I attribute it to the superior quality of the wine, sir. I have often observed that in married households the champagne is rarely of a first-rate brand.
>
> ALGERNON: Good heavens! Is marriage so demoralizing as that?
>
> LANE: I believe it *is* a very pleasant state, sir. I have had very little experience of it myself up to the present. I have only been married once. That was in consequence of a misunderstanding between myself and a young person.

Lane exposes the frivolousness of public sentiments about marriage by defending it frivolously. His apology for having had only one marriage on which to basis his evaluation mocks the value of fidelity. His scandalous reasoning from the quality of wine to the quality of marriage further trivializes that evaluation and implies that by a "very pleasant state" he means intoxication.

Allen and Gissing condemned the subjugation of women in contemporary marriage. The heroine of *The Woman Who Did* is in fact punished for what she did not do—marry her beloved. The "brave women" before her who lived with a man out of wedlock, she explains, did so because of some external circumstance such as his being already married. Mary Godwin finally married Shelley after his wife died, and George Eliot married after the death of Lewes, who was also married. These women did not refrain from marriage in principle "of their own free will from the very beginning" (44). Herminia intends for her historical act to be just that: her beloved Alan is unwed and wants to marry her, but she will refuse in principle to protest an institution which she regards as degrading to women.

In *The Odd Women* Rhoda makes a similar statement on behalf of freedom with the intention of "hastening in a new order." She counsels young women to postpone marrying until they can do so for the right reasons. "Let them marry later, if they must," she explains, but let them first understand that "marriage is an alliance of intellect—not a means of support, or something more ignoble still" (58). The novel centers on Rhoda's romance with Everard and comes to a climax with his proposal of marriage, which she finally rejects not because of antipathy, for she does love him, and not because of a tragic misunderstanding, as was the case with many a Victorian predecessor, but on principle. Gissing explains: "If it became known that she had taken a step such as few women would have dared to take—deliberately setting an example of new liberty—her position in the eyes of all who knew her [would remain] one of proud independence" (264). She remains unmarried to inspire other women to think before marrying and only proceed in liberty.

Into the twentieth century, novelists also searched for fresh metaphors and original arguments to clarify the deficiencies of marriage. In *The Golden Bowl* Charlotte explains that marriage makes her feel stuck like a pin "up to its head in a cushion" (199). Ann Veronica thinks of married people as "insects that have lost their wings" (74). In *Howards End* marriage makes Margaret think of a brood of lawyers "who creep out of their holes" (176). To Colette's vagabond, being married means "Tie my tie for me! . . . Get rid of the maid! . . . Cut my toe-nails! . . . Get up and make me some camomile!

. . . Prepare me an emetic!" (147). For the women of *Herland,* who have never seen a man, marriage is inconceivable. On the first page of *Women in Love* Ursula tells Gudrun that marriage must be "the end of experience," and later Rupert refers to it as "the most repulsive thing on earth" (34). In *The Age of Innocence* Archer describes it as "a dull association of material and social interests held together by ignorance on the one side and hypocrisy on the other" (44). Forster's Miss Quested envisions a similar marriage routine displaced to India: "She and Ronny would look into the club . . . every evening, then drive home to dress; they would see the Lesleys and the Callendars and the Turtons and the Burtons, and invite them and be invited by them, while the true India slid by unnoticed" (47). The idea of marriage makes Leopold Bloom think of parlor games: "dominos, halma, tiddledywinks, spillikins, cup and ball, nap, spoil five, bezique, twentyfive, beggar my neighbour, draughts, chess or backgammon" (686). The increasing interrogation of the institution of marriage during the 1890s along with the passionate and imaginative criticism of it in the twentieth century constituted the reflective background for the more authentic marriages depicted in the modern novel.

II

Modernists were also more inclined than Victorians to explore the creative possibilities of love and understanding in marriage, and these creative efforts, however tortuous and incomplete, make up the heart of the novels, not merely its concluding hope. These developments reflect new legislation which secured greater legal status to women and helped equalize the rights of husbands and wives. Although these laws changed at a different pace in different countries, the direction of the change was similar and can be indicated by a survey of what happened in England.[1]

In 1850 the English wife's legal existence was absorbed into that of her husband in a condition referred to as coverture: "the husband and wife are one person; that is, the very being, or legal existence, of a woman is suspended during marriage, or at least incorporated and consolidated into that of the husband, under whose wing, protection and cover she performs everything."[2] More specifically the law held that unless the wife's personal property had been secured to her prior to marriage in a Court of Equity, she did not retain ownership of that property or have control over any subsequent earnings. In marriage she was not responsible for her debts, had difficulty getting credit, and had no legal rights over her children. In a society that viewed a man's sense of himself as bound up with his ability to control his property and heirs, these laws deprived a married woman of every such tangible aspect of selfhood. A wife or a husband could retrieve legal independence by divorce, but it could only be granted by an Act of Parliament and was rare. And whereas the husband could divorce by proving his wife's adultery, she had to prove that her husband's adultery was "aggravated" by cruelty, bigamy, or incest.

A series of Parliamentary Acts gradually accorded legal selfhood to women and equalized the grounds for divorce. The Matrimonial Causes Act of 1857 made divorce less expensive and more widely available but retained the unequal grounds while adding desertion, rape, sodomy, and bestiality to the list of aggravations, at least one of which a wife was obliged to prove in addition to her husband's adultery. The Married Women's Property Act of 1870 gave a wife ownership of income from property and wages earned during her marriage. A Parliamentary Bill of 1882 gave a woman legal control over real property she owned at the time of her marriage or acquired afterwards. An Act of 1884 abrogated the husband's legal right to imprison his wife. An Act of 1923 gave a wife the power to obtain a divorce on the basis of adultery alone without additional aggravating grounds. In 1937 wives were given the right to sue for divorce on the ground of desertion, cruelty, or insanity alone, without also proving adultery.

The moral implied by these new laws—that a wife was entitled to the same legal status as her husband—was not shared by everyone. Many women resisted change, preferring to enjoy the privileges accorded to them under coverture. Most men and women were reluctant to tamper with an institution which they saw as the foundation for personal love, social cohesion, economic stability, and national strength; but the considerable change in the status of married women toward legal selfhood is unmistakable. Many adventurous women and men lined up to fight for these changes out of a conviction that married women must be accorded rights equal to man's over their property, earnings, children, bodies, and selves. The love relationships that resulted from these developments were the subject of several major novels.

The Golden Bowl, as I have argued, marks a shift toward more authentic modes of disclosure, jealousy, and selfhood; it also marks a shift toward a more authentic marriage, which James presents in a distinctively modern way. His novel focuses on marriage and emphasizes its tentative, piecemeal nature instead of its eternal vows or absolute commitments. His narrative recreates experience from the perspective of both lovers. As his Preface explains, Book One shows Maggie through her husband's vision of her and Book Two shows her husband "with at least an equal intensity" through Maggie's vision of him. James dates their marriage historically by contrasting it with the first marriage of Maggie's father, who "had supposed himself, above all he had supposed his wife, *as* married as anyone could be, and yet he wondered if their state had deserved the name" (126). The father's passing thought about the meaning of his Victorian marriage contrasts with the extensive inquiry that his daughter undertakes to understand her more modern marriage.

The opening discussion between Maggie and Amerigo reveals how little she knows about him. She knows something of his public self, but there is a private self about which, he tells her, "you've found out nothing" (33). She claims to look forward to discovering his other "particular self," but she has no idea what that will involve. His seductive charm veils his secret romance, and her charming innocence veils her naivete. With her growing suspicion that his affair with Charlotte preceded her wedding and resumed afterwards, Maggie begins to lose her innocence.

Her coming of age is an agonizingly slow unraveling of both Amerigo's deception and her self-deception. One pivotal exchange occurs when he unexpectedly enters a room just after Fanny has crashed the golden bowl to the floor and realizes that Maggie knows of his affair. The rest of the novel concerns who knows and, more important, who knows who knows. Knowledge is power, and, Maggie realizes, it places her husband in the position of needing her: "Hadn't she fairly got into his labyrinth with him?—wasn't she indeed in the very act of placing herself here, for him, at its centre and core, whence . . . she might securely guide him out of it?" (427). But she does not know the way out. It will take more than this traumatic confrontation for her to be able to speak her mind. Their talk centers so much on who knows what that he becomes irritated by her repeated use of the word "know." She concludes one exchange—"Find out for yourself!" (438). The novel continues to recount what she might have said to him but could not and how he crushed talk with hugs. She gradually realizes that his embraces are inhibitory, and she works to seize power without destroying the princely charm she loves. Tentatively, they grope together toward understanding.

The Golden Bowl embodies several aspects of authenticity in marriage: it deals with the deficiencies and creative possibilities of a loving marriage more forthrightly than did most Victorian novels, it focuses on such love more reflectively by making it the substance of the story, and it avoids the narrative strategy of using the prospect of a happy marriage to force an artificial tidy ending. Similar claims can be made for *Ulysses*.

Leopold first reflects on the deficiencies of his marriage while sitting on the toilet, straining with his chronic constipation. As he reads, his mind wanders to his marital problems, chiefly Molly's interest in Blazes. Like his bowels, his marriage is strained but operative. Joyce locates his married couple emphatically in the real world, beginning with Leopold in the morning and ending with Molly straddling a chamber pot before settling next to her husband in bed at night.

As an introduction to their mutual love, Leopold's first interior monologue includes a fantasy that he and Molly might co-author a story signed "By Mr and Mrs L. M. Bloom" (69). Throughout the day he repeatedly thinks about her. On the way to a funeral he recalls the death of their son Rudy and then remembers her craving for sex on the night the baby was conceived. While watching others eating in a restaurant he recalls the time she passed the chewed seedcake into his mouth during a kiss. After masturbating, stimulated by Gerty's exhibitionism, he compares Molly to other men's wives and thinks, "Molly can knock spots off them" (373). Even his jealousy universalizes his love into a reflection on the deficiency of all love. When he sees Blazes leave the bar to have sex with Molly he remains the "unconquered hero," a tag Joyce uses to suggest Leopold's resilient heroism in spite of his marital difficulties.

Molly's final stream of consciousness begins and ends with the word "yes"—both words an affirmation of her husband. While thinking about her premarital and extramarital loves she returns affectionately again and again to her overweight, quasi-potent husband who has sex by ejaculating on her "bottom." She remembers Blazes's erection, like a "thick crowbar," but prefers Leopold because he "has more spunk in him" (742). Comparing him to other husbands she realizes that she would "rather die 20 times over than marry another of their sex" (744). Appreciatively she thinks, "if I only could remember one half of the things and write a book out of it the works of Master Poldy" (754). Like Leopold she is able to transcend jealousy when she sees a letter sticking out of his pocket and assumes, incorrectly, that he is having an affair. As Robert Kiely concludes, she and Leopold "understand one another and share, like their marriage bed, an inviolable field of experience that extends through their daughter Milly into new life, through Rudy into death, and through their consciousness and memory into the continual narration, revision, and interpretation of their own story." [3] Compared with the typical Victorian marriage, that of Leopold and Molly is more reflective, more reciprocal, more sexually inventive, and better able to deal with its deficiencies.

Mrs. Dalloway is a meditation on what it means to be married. Unlike Clarissa Dalloway's eighteenth-century namesake Clarissa Harlowe, who says "no" to the very end, this Clarissa, long before the novel begins, has already said "yes," but after thirty years of marriage is still discovering the implications of her vows. Back then, rather than marry Peter, who had insisted that everything be "gone into," she decided to marry Richard, who had promised her more freedom. "In marriage," she now believes, there must be "a little independence . . . which Richard gave her, and she him" (10). But independence becomes isolation. She resents her husband's independence when he lunches privately with Lady Bruton, although she fights off her jealousy. Intimacy is another problem for Clarissa, who is frigid and sleeps in a narrow bed in her own room. But she loves from within her isolation. As she settles into bed alone she is overwhelmed with affection for Richard, whom she hears upstairs preparing to get into bed and swearing as he drops his hot-water bottle—"How she laughed" (47). Typical of Woolf's lovers, Richard cannot tell her that he loves her and instead brings flowers. In receiving them Clarissa thinks about the mutual respect that sustains their marriage: "There is a dignity in people; a solitude; even between husband and wife a gulf; and that one must respect . . . for one would not part with it oneself, or take it, against his will, from one's husband, without losing one's independence, one's self-respect—something, after all, priceless" (181). Woolf finds a priceless dignity and measure of fulfillment for a frigid wife and a distant husband.

To the Lighthouse is about a similarly strained but dignified and contemplative marital love. Mrs. Ramsay is often frustrated and insecure, while Mr. Ramsay is remote, tyrannical, even unjust. Their bickering over going to the lighthouse is the dramatic focus for their numerous incompatibilities, but in spite of them they have flashes of understanding and intimacy. One such moment is envisioned by Mrs. Ramsay's observer Lily Briscoe. After thinking how Mr. Ramsay neglected his wife, Lily suddenly looks up and sees how "what she called 'being in love' flooded them. They became part of that unreal but penetrating and exciting universe which is the world seen through the eyes of love. The sky stuck to them; the birds sang through them" (72–73). Lily is momentarily overwhelmed by the glory of married love which accents her own feeling of isolation and seems to substantiate Mrs. Ramsay's motto that "an unmarried woman has missed the best of life." But Lily's fulfillment will come from something else.

In the final section, ten years after the opening scene, Lily is still working on the canvas she had been struggling with the day the Ramsays argued about going to the lighthouse. She is thinking about Mrs. Ramsay's "mania" for marriage when she sees a link between marriage and art. Woolf establishes the link with a seemingly illogical stream of consciousness: "[Lily] had been looking at the table-cloth, and it had flashed upon her that she would move the tree to the middle [of her painting], and need never marry anybody, and she had felt an enormous exultation" (262). The logic of Lily's jump from discovering a place for the tree to realizing that she need not marry is startling: she need never marry anybody because she is free to place the tree where she wants, and she is free to do that because she is an artist. Woolf's juxtaposition of painting and marrying implies that both are potentially self-affirming activities which may yield "enormous exultation" if seriously pursued. The emphasis in Lily's realization that she "need never marry anybody" falls on "need," for once the necessity is eliminated, marriage can offer an exalted freedom similar to art. One must be freely centered in oneself whether in placing a tree on a canvas, marrying out of a free choice, or having an income of five hundred pounds a year and a room of one's own.

James, Joyce, and Woolf focused on the struggles of the already married to rethink and rework relationships which already exist at the outset of the story. Their novels imply that some joys of love are only possible in a marriage, but one which has been either tempered by knowledge from painful disclosures as in *The Golden Bowl,* leavened with toleration and mutual respect as in *Ulysses,* strengthened by granting a little independence to one another as in *Mrs. Dalloway,* or refined from the magical benefits of simply being married as in *To the Lighthouse.*

III

An authentic marriage also includes being able to think about the meaning of marital sex. Victorian novelists made no reference to marital sex except by inference from the (usually sudden) appearance of a child. They shared the protective sense that Hugo announced in *Les Misérables:* "At the door to every bridal chamber an angel stands, smiling, with a finger to his lips" (1139). Although most modern novelists also kept quiet about what happened in the marriage bed, a number of psychiatrists, sociologists, and moralists diagnosed the problems of marital sex and noisily called for improvement.

Already in the 1880s some of Freud's colleagues insisted that sexual problems were "always" behind their married patients' neuroses. Josef Breuer told him that "these things are always *secrets d'alcôve*," and by "alcove" he meant "marriage bed." Freud recalled another memorable incident, when Jean Charcot "suddenly broke in with great animation, '*Mais, dans des cas pareils c'est toujours la chose génitale, toujours . . . toujours . . . toujours*' [But in this sort of case it's always a question of the genitals—always, always, always]; and he crossed his arms over his stomach, hugging himself and jumping up and down on his toes several times." Rudolf Chrobak also shocked the young Freud with a prescription for the anxiety attacks of a wife whose husband was impotent: "R. Penis normalis—dosim repetatur!" [4] By the early twentieth century Freud had incorporated these observations into psychoanalysis and popularized the idea that sexual failures lay behind wrecked marriages.

Other researchers made similar observations. In 1906 the American sociologist Elsie Parsons scandalized her readers by recommending that couples be able to live together in a "trial marriage" which would allow them to discover if they were sexually compatible before legally marrying.[5] In 1911, like many a Victorian wife before her, Marie Stopes married without any clear understanding of what would be expected of her sexually. Her husband was impotent and the marriage remained unconsummated until, after six years of agonizing frustration, it was annulled. In 1918, to spare others the same trauma, she published an advice book with the title *Married Love*—a cover for its real subject, namely married sex. She described the physiology of sexual arousal and urged creativity by varying the setting, frequency, and techniques of coitus. She concluded with a call to authentic marital sex: "Each pair must, using the tenderest and most delicate touches, sound and test each other, learning the way about the intricacies of each other's hearts." [6] Aside from a few euphemisms such as "hearts" for sex organs, little remained of the reticence that had ruined her own marriage. In 1926 Theodore Van de Velde's *Ideal Marriage: Its Physiology and Technique* offered ways to improve marriage with better understanding of sexual techniques. The following year the American judge Ben Lindsey recommended a "companionate marriage" based on free discussion of sex, use of contraception, and, if necessary, provision for inexpensive divorce.[7] Further evidence of a growing awareness of the importance of sex in marriage is the change of emphasis in complaints made by wives during divorce proceedings in Los Angeles and New Jersey between 1880 and 1920. Although the major sexual complaint throughout this period remained the husband's unbridled lust, by 1920 the wife was more likely to mention also his inability to satisfy her sexually.[8] By the early 1930s "the sexual question" was old hat. In *The Man Without Qualities* Diotima complained about the spate of new books that approached sex like gymnastics. "In these books man and woman were referred to only as 'the sexual partner,' and the boredom between them, which was to be obviated by means of all sorts of mental and physical variations, was termed 'the sexual question'" (III, 255).

Modern novelists, for all their eagerness to dramatize the highs and lows of marriage, were reluctant to explore marital sex. James, Gide, Colette, Mann, Proust, Woolf, Hemingway, Fitzgerald, and Musil provide no explicit accounts. Joyce includes some vivid descriptions of past moments between Leopold and Molly, but their current sex is adulterous. Only with the later novels of Lawrence is there a beginning of the end of that traditional literary restraint. He first ventured into marital sex in *The Rainbow*, which was censored because of the scene in which Anna flaunts her erotic desire for God while dancing naked and pregnant in front of her husband. That scene is actually the high point of the couple's sexual estrangement, but it also breaks up their emotional deadlock and makes possible a resumption of more fulfilling marital sex. And although Lawrence sets their marriage in the late Victorian period, his rendering is modern. In *Women in Love* Ursula and Rupert's premarital "shameful" sex anticipates what will happen after they marry, and her thoughts following one night of marital sex reveal the meaning of her rite of passage through these aberrant sexualities. "She was bestial. How good it was to be really shameful! There would be no shameful thing she had not experienced. Yet she was unabashed, she was herself. Why not? She was free, when she knew everything, and no dark shameful things were denied her" (403). Lawrence believed that one cannot be oneself in loving so long as a part of oneself—the sexual part—is missing, and after centuries of asceticism that part could only be restored by some irreverent exorcism.

Lawrence reserved his boldest exorcism for *Lady Chatterley's Lover*. Although neither Connie nor Mellors is yet divorced, Lawrence presents their "wedding" in the woods as valid—a more reflective and meaningful joining than any conventional wedding. Their last lovemaking is at the cutting edge of history: it confronts and transcends some of their deepest sexual fears. I interpret it as a comment on marital sex, because they intend to marry as soon as they each can divorce, and because Connie is already pregnant with Mellors's child. The scene begins with Connie asking Mellors the meaning of his existence. When he replies that he does not know, she assures him that it must include the courageous "tenderness" which he shows when he runs his hand over her loin and tells her that she has a "pretty tail." That tenderness involves a special kind of awareness and sensuality, as he explains: "Ay! it's tenderness really; it's cunt-awareness. Sex is really only touch, the closest of all touch. And it's touch we're afraid of. We're only half-conscious, and half alive." Both lovers conceive new meanings for "tenderness" and "awareness." Connie associates tenderness with the way Mellors strokes her "pretty tail," and he pushes that association further to include "cunt-awareness" (259). Lawrence's modern couple thus tries to unify the traditional dichotomies of mind and body, tender and crude, while redefining their existence together as grounded in sex.

Their discussion leads to an ultimate sacrilege, because Connie insists on including her fetus in their sexual loving. She says, "Kiss my womb and say you're glad it's there." He hesitates and she insists again, "Be tender to it, and that will be its future already. Kiss it!" He repeats her words to himself and swells with love. Then, Lawrence narrates, "he kissed her belly and her mound of Venus, to kiss close to the womb and the fetus within the womb." Lawrence does not leave to metaphor this expression of sensuous loving across generations. "'Oh, you love me! You love me!' she said . . . and he went in to her softly, feeling the stream of tenderness flowing in release from his bowels to hers" (260–261). The moment sums up the most historically significant sexual themes of Lawrence's corpus. Instead of the lack of sex education, the conspiracy of silence, the double standard, the public oppression, and the sexual suppression that so paralyzed the Victorian woman, Lawrence presents the fulfillment of a woman who not only demands a genital kiss but does so when pregnant. Instead of the painful reserve, fear of pregnant women, and sexual inexperience of the Victorian man, Mellors is an expert in tender "cunt-awareness" and gets down on his knees to kiss "the fetus within the womb." Connie does not wait for him to say he loves her but cries out confidently at the moment of penetration, "You love me!"

Their climax includes the deepest excitation "flowing in release from his bowels to hers," scandalously close to the fruit of their love, their hope for the world. Lawrence explores the meaning of legal marriage by taking his unmarried lovers through the most intense intimacies of sexual conjunction he could imagine.

IV

Modern novelists also reworked the function of marriage in the novel's form. The traditional novel sequenced tales of love toward the goal of marriage in accord with dominant values affirming a tightly knit family and a hierarchically ordered society. The central role marriage would play in the novel throughout the nineteenth century was anticipated in the famous opening line of *Pride and Prejudice:* "It is a truth universally acknowledged, that a single man in possession of a good fortune, must be in want of a wife." The sweeping public aspect of Austen's confident generalization and the vigorous forward movement of her sentence underscored the ineluctability of the "truth" in her time: that there can be no desirable goal for love other than marriage. Tying the knot offered a simple way to conclude stories about the search for closure. Dickens tagged the climactic goal of that search with his title, *Great Expectations,* which ends with the fulfillment of Pip's great expectations in love with his marriage to Estella. Brontë proclaimed the classic coda to love in marriage with Jane Eyre's opening line of the novel's last chapter—"Reader, I married him." Jane then informs everyone she knows of the good news before coming back to her reader with a concluding report on ten years of marital happiness. Also in 1847, Lewes concluded *Ranthorpe* with a joyous wedding: "And now our hero's troubles are o'er. He is happy; his bride stands at the altar beside him" (347). After years of marriage, we learn in the epilogue, Ranthorpe is "exquisitely happy" because his two children "are playing round his knees, and twining their embraces round his heart." In the end of *Crime and Punishment* (1866) Raskolnikov and Sonya will have to wait until he serves his eight-year prison sentence for murder, but their eventual marriage is a certainty. "It was love that brought them back to life: the heart of one held inexhaustible sources of life for the heart of the other" (558).

Some Victorians such as Flaubert and Eliot questioned specific matches but not the institution itself. Although *Madame Bovary* ends with a wife's suicide, Charles reaffirms the value of marriage by having Emma buried in her wedding dress. The most fully explored marriages in *Middlemarch* and *Daniel Deronda* (Dorothea to Casaubon and Gwendolen to Grandcourt) are disasters, but the novels end upbeat with Dorothea's second marriage to Will and Daniel's first marriage to Mirah. In the finale to *Middlemarch* Eliot explains that marriage creates a satisfying end to a love story, because it is a "complete union which makes the advancing years a climax, and age the harvest of sweet memories in common" (573).

Later in the century Howells, Gissing, and Hardy question the institution of marriage but rely on traditional expectations about marriage to structure the form of their novels. *A Modern Instance* ends with a divorce, but the novel's momentum is sustained by the problems of courtship and marriage. In *The Odd Women* Rhoda wishes that "every novelist could be strangled and thrown into the sea" for misleading women with fictions that idealize marriage, and in the end she speaks out for some respected vocation for women other than marriage, but Gissing nevertheless sustains the suspense to the end with his heroine's courtship and the expectation of marriage as its goal (58). *Tess of the d'Urbervilles* assails many aspects of marriage but ultimately conforms to literary convention by ending with the prospect of a marriage. In anticipation of her execution, Tess asks Angel to marry her sister Liza-Lu. When the black flag is hoisted, indicating that Tess has been hanged, Angel and Liza-Lu observe it from a hilltop. The novel ends with a last line that promises their renascent marriage: "As soon as they had strength they arose, joined hands again, and went on." Even pessimistic Hardy, if only for formal purposes, bowed to the "universally acknowledged" truth of Austen's generalization.

Modern novelists refused to bow. James was scandalized by the "happy ending" of most conventional novels with their "distribution at the last of prizes, pensions, husbands, wives, babies, millions, appended paragraphs, and cheerful remarks." [9] The ending of *The Golden Bowl* did not distribute spouses but strained their marriage, with Maggie closing her eyes and burying her head on her husband's breast. Forster argued that "nearly all novels are feeble at the end" because they cannot continue to "open out" as life does, although he acknowledged, grudgingly, that "if it was not for death and marriage I do not know how the average novel would conclude." [10] *A Room with a View* ended with a happy marriage, but *Howards End* concluded inconclusively with a marital exchange of dubious sincerity, following Henry's confession that he "set aside" his first wife's will, which gave her home, Howards End, to Margaret. In response Margaret remained silent

and then "something shook her life in its inmost recesses, and she shivered."
He asked whether he did wrong, and she said "You didn't, darling. Nothing
has been done wrong." In spite of her reassurance, Forster leaves his reader
with a final impression that Margaret will continue to shake and shiver
while married to Henry. If *Howards End* is about the difficulty of connecting, *A Passage to India* questions its possibility. The marriage that prompted
Miss Quested to book a passage to India falls apart toward the end of the
novel, and Fielding, in consoling her, questions the institution altogether.
"Marriage is too absurd in any case. It begins and continues for such very
slight reasons. The social business props it up on one side, and the theologi-
cal business on the other . . . I've friends who can't remember why they married" (262).

   The Good Soldier offers an original interrogation of the meaning and possibility of marriage by ending with the narrator waiting for a marriage that
is impossible because his fiancée has gone insane and cannot comprehend its
meaning. "I should marry Nancy," he explains, "if her reason were ever
sufficiently restored to let her appreciate the meaning of the Anglican marriage service. But it is probable that her reason will never be sufficiently restored to let her appreciate the meaning of the Anglican marriage service.
Therefore I cannot marry her, according to the law of the land" (236). With
this, Ford also hints that perhaps no one knows the meaning of the marriage
service. As the novel draws to a close, the narrator loses his grasp on his
own story, including why Nancy went mad. "I don't know. I know nothing.
I am very tired," he confesses and then relinquishes all authorial responsibility to his reader—"I leave it to you" (245–246).

   Wharton sets up the ending of *The Age of Innocence* with the prospect of
Archer rejoining his beloved Ellen twenty-six years after he left her to marry
May. Now a widower, he goes to Paris with his son, who persuades him to
visit Ellen. His son goes up to her apartment while Archer waits outside for
a sign to come up. Soon Ellen's servant comes out on her balcony, draws up
the awning, and closes the shutters. Wharton concludes with a final narration: "At that, as if it had been the signal he waited for, Newland Archer got
up slowly and walked back alone to his hotel." If Ellen had narrated the last
chapter, Wharton might well have had her say, "Reader, I *didn't* marry
him." Wharton understood that love has meaning precisely because it can
succeed or fail. If the story is about a failure, as indeed Archer failed to love
Ellen, then the author must keep the meaning of the ending in accord with

the relationship and not suddenly change it merely to achieve closure or gratify readers, as did several Victorians.[11]

Novelists of the lost generation were especially reluctant to end with happy marriages. In *This Side of Paradise* Amory and Rosalind love one another but cannot marry because they do not have enough money. She tells him that their love must die if it is cooped up in a little flat. She wants to worry not about money but about whether her legs will get slick and brown when she swims in the summer. Victorians could still believe in the other side of paradise where unexpected financial windfalls, as in *Jane Eyre* or *Great Expectations,* made love possible, but on this side of paradise love is not miraculously saved by an inheritance. In the end money wins out and Rosalind marries the rich but dreary Dawson Ryder whom she does not love. In *The Sun Also Rises* Jake and Brett cannot marry because his penis was shot off in the war. Victorian soldiers like Sergeant Troy and Count Vronsky were not particularly reliable lovers, but their deficiencies were a source of their appeal. Hemingway explodes the ancient myth of Mars and Venus by having his soldier-hero retain his testicles so that he remains desirous of Brett but unable to satisfy himself or her. The novel ends with the frustrated couple talking about the impossibility of their love. "'Oh, Jake,' Brett said, 'we could have had such a damned good time together' . . . 'Yes.' I said. 'Isn't it pretty to think so?'" The war also blocks the marriage of Frederic and Catherine in *A Farewell to Arms,* although in the end it is not war but Cesarean delivery that causes her death. Hemingway offers no hope for a transcendent reunion in the hereafter, not even the prospect of a long cherished memory. For these modernists love does not transcend poverty, impotence, or death; marriage offers no resolution to deficient love; and novels end as tentatively as the loves they describe.

Lawrence ended *The Rainbow* with Ursula walking away from marriage to Skrebensky. She finally marries Rupert in *Women in Love,* but by the end they still are not entirely in step. Ursula enjoyed Rupert fully, Lawrence explains, "but they were never *quite* together at the same moment, one was always a little left out" (427). Rupert seeks in vain to compensate for this deficiency by including in their marriage his loving someone else. Scandalized, Ursula tells him that he will not get his wish because it is "false, impossible." The novel ends with his defiant reply, "I don't believe that." At the end of *Ulysses* Leopold and Molly lie in bed side by side but head to foot, a final image of their marital discord. Joyce fashioned *The Exiles* to accent the inconclusiveness of the marriage between husband and wife. As he explained in notes on the play: "The doubt which clouds the end of the play must be conveyed to the audience not only through Richard's questions to both but also from the dialogue between Robert and Bertha" (125). Mann ended *The Magic Mountain* with the disappearance of his hero in the front lines of World War I, while Musil left *The Man Without Qualities* unfinished.

The French modernists were equally reluctant to end with unprepared and undeserving happy marriages. *The Vagabond* ends with the heroine's letter of refusal; *Remembrance of Things Past* ends, like *To the Lighthouse*, with the discovery of the vocation of art as a substitute for the vocation of marriage, and *The Counterfeiters* ends with the introduction of a completely new character in accord with Gide's stated intention that the novel replicate life and be without closure.

The historical significance of this shift in the function of marriage in the ending of novels is enormous, because ultimately the meaning of marriage (and by implication, love) is determined by the way it ends. Throughout the entire period of my study, marriage remained the goal of love even among the most searching of modernists, but the period between the Victorians and the moderns saw a dynamic history of its literary function and ultimate meaning.

Many Victorians believed, or at least desperately wanted to believe, in an omniscient God, an afterlife, the triumph of good over evil, a hierarchically ordered society, a tightly knit family, and the transcendent power of love. The promise of marriage (not generally its reality) fulfilled all of these beliefs. The ideal union was witnessed by an omniscient god in the sacrament of marriage; it offered hope for immortality through legitimate offspring; it rewarded good people with loving spouses; it insured the social hierarchy by publicly sanctioning private love; it secured the family unit with stringent divorce laws; and it enabled the isolated self to transcend barriers of nation, class, and religion.

Victorians were aware of marital mishaps, to be sure, but they were not as willing as the moderns to question the institution itself, as is particularly evident in the way novels end. In tragic Victorian novels, troubled marriages end with the death of ill-suited spouses such as Bertha Rochester or Roger Chillingworth, with the death of inadequate spouses such as Casaubon or Catherine Linton, with the death of evil spouses such as Grandcourt or Lady Audley, or with the death of adulteresses such as Emma Bovary or Anna

Karenina. In comic Victorian novels the good are rewarded with the prospect of happy marriages. Endings support the logic of the Victorians' hierarchical ordering of heaven and earth, family and community, individual and society, good and evil.

Several historical developments began to challenge this world view. The rise of democracy challenged the legal and political privileges of aristocratic society; the economic and social dynamism of burgeoning capitalism further eroded class lines based on law and redefined class lines based on wealth; new feminist movements questioned gender roles; new marriage laws wiped out legal coverture. The modernist response to these developments included new ways of interpreting marriage.

Modernists were especially scornful of the ritualized institution of marriage they inherited from the Victorians. Ritual is inauthentic because it determines courses of action, even ways of feeling, without requiring the personal reflection about meaning essential for authentic loving. In defiance of the ritual of literary conventions modernists created endings that preserved the uncertainty and complexity they believed were essential to fulfilling love. They tried to end novels artfully without completely solving the riddle of love—without reaffirming the promise of heavenly reward or reunion in an afterlife, without poetic justice based on the morality of good and evil, and without a final distribution of marital prizes. They refused to force closure with marriage precisely because they had such a high regard for the artistic significance of endings and the existential significance of marriage. Their imaginative marriages move into an uncertain future tentatively as in *The Golden Bowl*, with a shiver of uncertainty as in *Howards End*, with a touch of insanity as in *The Good Soldier*, with a poignant disjunction as in *Ulysses*, with a defiant reply as in *Women in Love*, and with a chilling reminder of human finitude as in *To the Lighthouse*.

18 Ending

LOVE IS grounded in existential finitude. Whereas ending is a chronological category that locates an experience in the sweep of time, finitude is an ontological category that anchors the way we experience every moment of life, including the particular instance of ending. Finitude grounds our awareness that love is always in some ways deficient, even during the magic of a first meeting or a first love when life seems to overflow with the prospect of endless joy. But such moments are so intense precisely because we cannot escape the awareness that at one time our love did not yet exist, that at present it is fraught with deficiencies, and that at any future moment it may stop. We tend to avoid such awareness, as is evident in the exuberant expressions of love which deny its finitude—"We were destined to meet"; "I love you with all my heart"; "I'll love you forever." In *Tropic of Cancer* Miller offered an emphatically un-Victorian expression of such futile aspirations when he fantasized, "I am fucking you, Tania, so that you'll stay fucked" (6). Love cannot last forever any more than a woman can stay fucked. The hope for endless love is a natural but absurd denial of its finitude. Three major subthemes of the finitude of love are conflict, rejection, and death.

I

The phenomenologist who most emphasized a fundamental conflict between human beings was Sartre. In *Being and Nothingness* (1943) he argued that at the heart of human existence is an inescapable nothingness that cries out to be filled. We experience concrete aspects of that nothingness in absence, questioning, regret, dread, destruction, time's passage, and the constant "elsewhereness" of consciousness. One of many ways we try and fill that nothingness is with love, but it is also always somewhat elsewhere. Love cannot fill the nothingness, and that failure causes conflict. This is no mere reworking of the ancient idea of the battle of the sexes, for Sartre held that all human relations are necessarily grounded in conflict, not just those between men and women. Love is grounded in conflict because it is ultimately absurd. In a world without a transcendent and omniscient God there can be no infinite perspectives or eternal values to which I must, or can, conform. I am alone in a sea of possibilities. I am responsible for giving meaning to my existence and hence to my love. It is absurd to look to my beloved to return all the subjectivity that has been drained from me under the objectifying gaze of others, because no one can give to me what must be grounded in myself—my subjectivity. Sartre did not despair of trying to love; he merely tried to clarify love's inherent absurdity so that its possibilities might be experienced more authentically.

While the Victorians were acutely aware of conflict, they were less willing than the moderns to see it as intrinsic to love or as having a constitutive function. In art they displaced conflict onto fictitious characters, often onto *femmes fatales* in distant, ancient, or imaginary places. They painted Sirens luring sailors to their death, drunken Maenads attacking Orpheus, Circes transforming men into pigs, and Sphinxes throttling their victims. There were formidable Salomes, Delilahs, and Judiths, but they did not love the men for whose death they were responsible. Regnault's *Salome* (1870) contradicts the reputation of her namesake. She looks up from the sword and empty charger on her lap as if it were her knitting, and her sweet smile gives no hint of her talent for deadly dancing. Moreau's icy Salomes look like jeweled mannequins holding bloody severed heads, remote from the emotions that might lead to a beheading. Victorians used literary surrogates to project responsibility for conflict away from themselves and treat it anecdotally, avoiding its fundamental nature.

In Gérôme's *The Cock Fight* (Figure 49, 1847) conflict is projected back to antiquity and displaced onto the cocks. Although the cocks are in fact both male, their coloring suggests different sexes. The more reluctant cock has brown coloring that approximates the woman's blond hair, while the fiercely combative black cock is more like the dark-haired man. The cocks symbolize the man and woman whose conflict is therefore not their own. Nor is their identity or their sexuality. Their figures are idealized and their sexual organs are obscured with typical Victorian disguise—his genitals are posed out of view, while her frontally visible pubis shows nothing but smooth skin. The man has ulterior motives for staging the fight; the woman

49. Jean-Léon Gérôme, *The Cock Fight*, 1846.

recoils even though she stares in fascination and is obviously somewhat
aroused by the mortal combat. These young lovers do not do their own
fighting, do not assume responsibility for it, deny its erotic purpose, and
seem scarcely capable of reflecting on its significance.

Kokoschka's *The Tempest* (Figure 50, 1914) is an image of meditation on
conflict. It shows the artist holding in his arms a sleeping Alma Mahler at a
time when their love was disintegrating. In contrast to the way Gérôme projects conflict away from the present into a mythic past and localizes it in the
fighting cocks, Kokoschka dates the conflict in the present and locates it in
the couple, graphically accented by concentric spheres of mounting tension—the swirling force of the storm, the shell of the boat that holds them,
the disparity between the sleeping woman and the anxiously wide-awake
man, and at the center of this vortex the fidgety tension of the artist's fingers.
The painted discord was intended to be their own, as can be documented by
reference to the underlying conflict between the couple over the abortion of
their child, which Kokoschka opposed and which precipitated their break-
up shortly after his painting was completed. The couple's identity is not ob-

50. Oskar Kokoschka, *The Tempest*, 1914.

scured, for the artist portrayed his own face and that of his famous lover. Although the painting makes no explicit reference to sexual conflict, intimations of it appear in the title and the energy of the surrounding storm of wind and sea that spirals into the man's fingers and loins. The motive for the painting was explicitly sexual: it resulted from Alma's decision to abort her fetus. Regarding her decision Kokoschka wrote, "One must keep awake to the meaning of life and not be content to vegetate."[1] The painting shows his own vigilant reflection on Alma's independence, her abortion, and the meaning of their conflicted love, which he equates with "the meaning of life." The uniqueness of Kokoschka's painting stems from these biographical circumstances which were also, like the painting itself, distinctly twentieth-century.[2]

Similar personal and historical circumstances surround Schiele's *Maiden and Death* (Figure 51, 1915), which is about the ending of a relationship

51. Egon Schiele, *Maiden and Death*, 1915.

between the artist and his mistress-model Wally Neuzil. It also depicts the
death of both Christian faith and the sexually moribund message of Christianity, indicated by the title and the self-portrait of the troubled artist wearing a monk's habit. Tense conflict permeates everything. It rumbles out of
the barren rough-cut rocks, through the sheet into the woman's toes and
knees, up her flexed calves and thighs, across her back, into her head pressed
awkwardly against the man's chest, and into her index fingers which strain
to stay hooked together around his back. His bony fingers clutch her shoulder and fiery red hair, while he plants an open-lipped kiss on the top of her
head in a last gasp of love. The sense of conflict is intensified by the picture's
compressed space and the couple's posture. Their upper bodies are tenuously supported on awkwardly bent knees and separated by a gaping
space, which implies that sexual relations have stopped. They appear penitent and sexually depleted. Although Schiele implies that a Christian sense
of sin might be partly responsible for the failure of their love, he does not

project responsibility as literally as did Gérôme, because Christian conscience involves reflection on one's own responsibility. But unlike earlier images of penitent lovers, which were a reminder of the need to harken to Christian sexual morality, Schiele's offers an image of the breakdown of that morality itself along with the possibility of love. This couple's conflict is emphatically their own, even though it also symbolizes the cultural-historical event of a dying Christian sexual morality.[3]

My argument is not that the moderns experienced more conflict than did the Victorians, merely that they were more aware of it as intrinsic to loving, more willing to assume responsibility for it, and more willing to render it in their art as an integral part of love and not as some accidental occurrence or degenerative form. The breakdown of Schiele's and Kokoschka's loves inspired paintings that sought to capture their anxieties without narrating a story, without pointing a moral, and without projecting responsibility for their conflict onto an imaginative literary world.

II

While conflict may shape any phase of love, rejection is usually a specific moment. Its specificity in time provides a sharper focus for interpreting historical change, as is shown by contrasting Arthur Hughes's *Aurora Leigh's Dismissal of Romney* (Figure 52, 1860) and Munch's *Ashes* (Figure 53, 1894). While Hughes muted the actuality of rejection by compressing it into the "best" moment in a specific story, Munch captured the fuller actuality of rejection by using more exclusively artistic imagery.

Hughes illustrates the moment in Elizabeth Barrett Browning's poem "Aurora Leigh" when Aurora rejects Romney's proposal because he does not take her seriously as a poet and because he wants her to stop writing and assist him in his work. With a strong sense of self she explains, "You want a helpmate, not a mistress, sir. / A wife to help your ends—in her no end!" The substance of Aurora's reasons for rejecting Romney are modern in that they call for recognition of her selfhood. My focus, however, is on the form of her rejection. Her response is based on clear motives, it is justified, and it is communicated to Romney so that he cannot misunderstand. The different causes of rejection in Hughes and Munch are historically significant. Both rejections are in some sense caused by the red forms at the center—Aurora's book of poems and the undergarment of Munch's woman. In Hughes the cause is straightforward and literary—doubly so since it is a

52. Arthur Hughes, *Aurora Leigh's Dismissal of Romney,* 1860.

book which is itself part of a story. Hughes sacrifices ambiguity to achieve
intelligibility, while Munch does the opposite. In order to evoke the tormenting ambiguity and confusion of a rejection, he uses a symbol which has
several possible meanings. The visible section of the woman's undergarment
is shaped like her pubis and heart and is located between them. It is the color
of blood and fire which may imply sexual desire, sexual injury, prostitution,
a broken heart, or the ashes of despair. While Hughes uses a narrative detail
to bring to mind a specific story, Munch uses a simple colored form to evoke
an assortment of sexual anxieties.

In a letter to the woman who commissioned his painting, Hughes ex-

53. Edvard Munch, *Ashes,* 1894.

plained why he chose the moment when Romney turns away. "If I had not chosen that moment, the story as Romney's dismissal would I think have been confused—it would rather have seemed a quarrel of which we did not see the end nor know the cause."[4] In keeping with the requirements of narrative art, Hughes used the scorned book of poems to symbolize the cause of Aurora's rejection. In actual rejections, however, one does not generally see the end or know the cause. Munch came closer than Hughes to capturing the bewilderment of a rejection, the uncertainty of its cause.

The different settings also indicate different futures. Romney's future loneliness is symbolized by the dark forest into which he is about to walk, while Aurora's bright future is indicated by the brilliant white lilies in front of her and the sunny patch of forest behind, both of which await her after she rejects Romney. But in moments of despair there is no future, no prospect of happiness, no clear understanding. While Hughes's woman seems composed and confident, Munch's woman seems as despairing as the rejected man, implying that the two have rejected each other. While Romney looks to Aurora sadly but understandingly, Munch's man turns away in confusion and despair. In a brief description of his man's state of mind Munch wrote: "There was something in her expression that frightened him. He did not know what it was." [5] The man's bewilderment and dread permeate the painting, especially the setting. The leafless upright trees echo the woman's rigid posture and uncomforting arms, while the barren rocks frame the man's defeated passion. The ashes of love come out of the smoking log that burns near his elbow.

Instead of the emotional closure of Hughes's narrative painting, Munch offers aesthetic closure with a powerful composition of man and woman, horizontal and vertical, man and nature, rocks and trees, and log and fire that together make an icon of the dissolution of love. Munch's choice of aesthetic unity over narrative closure is a feature of the history of art which moves in the direction of authenticity. As art reflects on itself as an expressive form, it becomes increasingly able to exploit its distinctive expressive powers.

In the Victorian novel, as in Browning's poem, rejections bring about "poetic justice." They are made for reasons which are known to both parties and adequate to the loves that are ending. When Jane first rejects Rochester, she does so for the "good" reason of her discovering the existence of his living wife; when Maggie Tulliver lets down Philip, she is sensitive to his infirmity; when Daniel Deronda rejects Gwendolen he includes some morally uplifting advice; the three times Isabel Archer rejects Goodwood, she is respectful of his devotion. But in fact rejections are clumsy and insulting to one's intelligence and dignity, as twentieth-century novelists were more willing to acknowledge. In *The Colonel's Daughter* (1932), for example, Richard Aldington dramatizes the clumsiness of rejection and makes a mockery of poetic justice. Georgie has secretly loved her cousin Geoffrey during his visit to her home while he was on leave from military duty. Geoffrey's letter to Georgie, explaining his intention to marry another woman, concludes with the chilling postscript—"I find I left a pair of pajamas and a hair-brush in the hurry of packing. Would you mind very much sending them to me at the address I give? Thanks awfully. G." (344).

Even though Georgie never expressed her love for Geoffrey, this letter is a rejection; and it captures what modernist novelists and painters strove to express—how inept lovers are at understanding one another and expressing themselves. The Victorians were well aware that many women and men loved secretly and in vain, but most of them embellished those sufferings and defeats with the pathos of a high drama distinctive to their age. Modernists avoided such embellished endings, preferring everyday oddities that made their works ring true, such as a thoughtless request for pajamas and a hairbrush.

Images of the aftermath of rejection reveal a similar historical shift. Victorians show the rejected woman in conventional melodramatic poses—holding her broken heart, slumping in a chair, clutching a letter, lying in a crumpled heap, wasting away in despair, or contemplating suicide (generally by drowning). Less frequent images of the jilted man are equally melodramatic, although the man assumes different postures. Men hold their heads rather than their hearts, stand or sit stiffly rather than slump or collapse, drink themselves into oblivion rather than waste away, and kill themselves with ropes or guns rather than by drowning. Comparing Briton Riviere's *Jilted!* (Figure 54, 1887) to George Grosz's *Lovesick* (Figure 55, 1914) reveals two distinct moments in the history of this theme. In typical Victorian fashion Riviere shows the cause of the rejection, embellishes the heroism of the man's response, and implies some ennobling prospect. For Grosz there is no clear cause, no admirable response, and no hope.

Riviere shows a man who thinks he knows why he has been rejected, for he clutches the letter with the bad news. Grosz offers a picture of bewilderment but no letter of explanation. Rather his lovesick man is surrounded by objects that symbolize confusion: a bottle of alcohol, a cocktail glass, a syringe, a pipe, and, if all else fails, a gun surrealistically suspended under his decal heart.

Riviere glamorizes his stalwart man dressed in a stylish riding outfit. The man is hurting, but he will bounce back and rejoin the "hunt" like a good sport. His spurred boots splay out in defeat, but the rest of his pose indicates a will to deal with the situation. His strong jaw is set; his brow is knitted in concentration. He is a model of determination in the face of bitter disappointment. In contrast Grosz portrays a man of indeterminacy. He has pale skin, dark sunken eyes, painted lips, and an anchor tattoo (ironically, a symbol of hope) on his shaved head. He is about to do something not heroic but malevolent, perverse, or destructive—possibly commit suicide.[6] In Riviere's painting one of the man's hands holds on for balance, while the other firmly grasps the letter, indicating how he will take hold of himself. In the Grosz painting both hands are ineffectual. One delicate hand weakly fingers a thin

54. Briton Riviere, *Jilted!*, 1887.

cane, and the other dissolves into runny paint. Riviere's jilted man steadies himself to regain his strength, while Grosz's man is sunk in defeat with nothing to do but choose the means of his self-destruction. The fish skeleton under the potted plant suggests that a loss of love is like being stripped to the bone.

Hope in the Riviere is symbolized by the frisky dog which offers faithful companionship. He is indeed this man's best friend, with ears perked up as if to listen and understand, seemingly smart enough to put a comforting paw on the man's hand to take the pain away from the letter in it. In contrast Grosz evokes unbreachable loneliness. His man sits in a public restaurant, a setting that accentuates his isolation, and is surrounded by empty chairs set out for other lost souls. His only company is a dopey mutt, curled up into itself in the blueish-orange light, oblivious to the man's suffering, not even

55. George Grosz, *Lovesick,* 1914.

interested in the crossed bones in front of his muzzle—another symbol of death.

While Riviere portrays a rejected gentleman with recuperative potential, Grosz portrays a rejected roué with a hopeless obsession. Riviere narrates this moment of dubious authenticity with melodrama, while Grosz evokes the tone of a rejection with a variety of innovative artistic techniques. His distortion of perspective and confusion of inside and outside exaggerates the man's spatial dislocation. The light source is ambiguous, and its disturbing colors create an atmosphere appropriate to the man's disturbed state of mind. The tilting of the table toward the plane of the picture surface creates a sense of disequilibrium and makes it easy for the viewer to see the objects whose shapes are simplified to accentuate their purpose. The eerie light, the spatial ambiguity, the surreal gun, the fish skeleton, the anchor tattoo, the dissolving hand, the leafless tree, and the morbid dog capture the utter annihilation of a rejection.

The rendering of extreme emotions is one characteristic of modernism, as is evident in another pair of images showing a young woman and a much older man: William Orchardson's *Marriage of Convenience—Before* (Figure 56, 1884) and Otto Dix's *Mismatched Lovers* (Figure 57, 1925). These images of deficient love relate to all three subthemes of my final chapter—they capture a special kind of conflict, they forecast an inevitable rejection, and they portend death.

Compared with twentieth-century women, young Victorian women had fewer educational and professional opportunities and were therefore more susceptible to parental or social pressures to marry older men for the money and security that they could not provide for themselves. Victorian novels are full of such marriages. Rochester is 20 years older than Jane, Sergey is 19 years older than Masha, Casaubon is 26 years older than Dorothea, Levin is 14 years older than Kitty, Grandcourt is 15 years older than Gwendolen, Osmond is 11 years older than Isabel, Widdowson is 23 years older than Monica, Innstetten is 21 years older than Effie, Phillotson is 18 years older than Sue. The hero of Maupassant's *Bel-Ami* (1885) winds up marrying his mistress's daughter. By the end of *The Well-Beloved* (1892) Pierston is pursuing the granddaughter of his first beloved. Although some novelists such as Charlotte Brontë and Tolstoy were not troubled by such unions, most interpretations were negative, in accord with Chillingworth's confession to Hester: "I betrayed thy budding youth into a false and unnatural relation with my decay" (100). The average age difference in all the nineteenth-century novels I read is eleven years, whereas in the twentieth-century novels it is two years (see the Appendix). There are some big age gaps in the modern period—Darrow is 13 years older than Anna, Axel is 16 years older than Lena, Archer is 10 years older than May—but such gaps are not so large, so typical, or so important as they are in Victorian novels.

Orchardson's painting is frequently reproduced because it captures not only the corruption of such May-December unions but also their rationale in his time. It shows a moment when the meal is over, although there is still plenty of food on the table, implying that this husband and wife do not eat much, do not enjoy eating, and are never satisfied. The husband presses against the table, as he is unable to do against his wife, while she has pushed away from that same table as she has no doubt pushed away from him in bed many times before. He is being poured more wine, while her glass if full, indicating a more pervasive pattern of his wanting more and her wanting less. Power is divided between her ability to refuse human affection and his ability to purchase human services, personified by his faithful butler as well as his young wife. Her material compensation, represented by the expensive dinner dress, affords no pleasure. Its revealing neckline accentuates the absurdity of their union, for he stares at it impotently and pathetically, while she looks away in quiet resentment.

In addition to these details, typical of Victorian narrative art, Orchardson makes innovative uses of light and space to intensify his moralizing. The lamp illuminates the hostile space that separates this couple, while the mirror image of the lamp magnifies the emptiness of the surrounding space. Together these lights intensify the sense that this couple is isolated from the world as well as from one another while trapped in the empty space that they have made for themselves. The fringed lamp shines down on their combat zone like the center light of a boxing ring.

Although these creative uses of light and space suggest the breakdown of this unhappy marriage, much remains intact. The furniture is substantial and neatly arranged, the table is elegantly set, the dinner courses have followed a proper order, the butler knows his place, the couple is well-dressed, and, for all their mismatch, they dine in a formal manner. In sharp contrast is Dix's image of "mismatched" *(ungleich)* lovers. Although his pair is not married, he treats the same basic theme as does Orchardson—a woman's youth exchanged for a much older man's money. But Dix shows more of that mismatching by partially undressing his couple who are seated in a most informal manner. We see the man's bunions, varicose veins, and arthritic hands. He is stooped and barefoot, while the overpowering woman sits triumphant in his lap, wearing only stockings and high-heeled boots. In contrast to Orchardson's withdrawn wife, who remains lifeless in a deadly calm atmosphere, Dix's bulging-eyed female flares her nostrils to suck in the surrounding tempest that blows her wild hair. Orchardson implies sexual incompatibility by showing the woman withdrawn from the table and lost in thought, while Dix flaunts it by centering his painting on the old man's

56. William Orchardson, *Marriage of Convenience—Before*, 1884.

57. Otto Dix, *Mismatched Lovers*, 1925.

futile grasping of the quivering puckered buttocks and arched back of the aroused woman who is riding his emaciated thigh, no doubt in autoerotic pleasure. Their incompatibility is further accented by the woman's firm breast and pink nipple profiled against the man's ashen pate.

Orchardson treats the futility and corruption of a marriage of convenience but leaves his viewers to imagine its sordid details, whereas Dix leaves little to the imagination. He is the more daring and relentless in exposing the consequences of a loveless match and capturing aspects of it that Orchardson did not show. By using a moralistic title and depicting an easily identifiable bad marriage, Orchardson tames his subject further and makes it possible for viewers to console themselves that they might avoid trouble by not marrying for the wrong reason. Dix, on the other hand, offers no way out, no simple tag to enable his viewers to label and dismiss. He shows an extraordinary moment which is nevertheless about the deficiency of sex and the limits of human libido in general. More than Orchardson, he obliges his viewers to think about the extraordinary incongruities that at times compromise all their loves, whatever their age or marital status. Orchardson instructs, while Dix unnerves.

The sets of images interpreted in this chapter document two aspects of a historical movement in the direction of authenticity. More than Victorian artists, who projected away intensities of experience with mythological, literary, or historical subjects, the modernists captured those intensities with all their physical conflict, sexual clashing, emotional intensity, uncanniness, and panic. And the modernists focused more on the process of revealing the meaning of conflict and rejection with artistic uses of light, atmosphere, color, composition, and form. This latter distinction is not about the quality of art. I am not arguing that modern art is superior to Victorian art, or more moving, but simply that it is more authentic in the precise way that I have defined that distinction throughout this book.

III

Heidegger argued that authentic human existence includes awareness of what it means "to be going to die" *(Sein zum Tode)*. An authentic individual understands that death cannot be shared, because it is unalterably one's unique own. Death cannot be mediated, taken over, made easier, or rendered meaningful by anyone else. Death has no transcendent purpose: it is not a stage to some other or higher existence, because it is the end of existence. There is no heaven, and the dead do not meet others who have died before. Such an understanding of death does not involve a morbid preoccupation with death. Rather, Heidegger insisted, being aware of what it means *not to be* enhances our awareness of what it means actually *to be*.

Authentic love includes being aware of what it means for love to end in death. Inauthentic love flees such awareness. It believes that love will never end because lovers are united in death. It looks to others to mediate, share, take over, and interpret death. Although at the mid-century people questioned faith in the hereafter, the Victorians held to a fundamentally Christian hope that lovers are reunited in death. As Michael Wheeler concluded, "the idea of heaven as a blessed home or country in which friends and loved ones meet is the most characteristic of the age."[7]

In "How Do I Love Thee?" (1850) Elizabeth Barrett Browning wrote that "if God choose," she would love her beloved "better after death." That same year Rossetti's poem "The Blessed Damozel" reworked the story of Dante and Beatrice, with a Victorian Beatrice, after ten years in heaven, waiting on "the rampart of God's house" for her beloved. When he arrives, she hopes, they will bathe "in God's sight."

> There will I ask of Christ the Lord
>   Thus much for him and me:—
> Only to live as once on earth
>   With Love,—only to be,
> As then awhile, for ever now
>   Together, I and he.

Nine years later Wagner premiered the opera in which his Tristan and Isolde sing together their "ardently desired love in death!" *(sehnend verlangter Liebestod!)*.

The classic Victorian novel about love in death is so literal that it becomes its own parody. Cathy is seven months pregnant and dying when she sees Heathcliff for the last time. Their desperate exchange is full of concern about the fate of their love after she will have died. She is "wearying to escape into that glorious world" of the hereafter (196). She assures him that if any word of hers should distress him, "think I feel the same distress underground." After he leaves, around midnight, she delivers a child and dies.

The night she is buried Heathcliff digs up her grave. When he is about to open the coffin he hears a sigh, feels a warm breath on his face, and senses her presence. Her ghost remains with him as he refills the grave, and it plagues him night and day thereafter. Eighteen years later her husband Edgar dies. As the sexton is digging Edgar's grave, Heathcliff gets him to remove the earth from over Cathy's coffin, which is next to the grave. Heathcliff opens the lid and looks at her face, which has not changed, because, as he later explained to Nelly, "it is hers yet" (319). He then pries loose one side of her coffin and bribes the sexton to remove that side entirely and later, when he is eventually buried next to her, to remove one side of his own coffin so that he and Cathy will in effect be in a single coffin. Later Heathcliff tells Nelly about his hope of "dissolving" with Cathy in the grave. He was reassured, he explains, when he saw her face after eighteen years and discovered that she had not yet "dissolved into earth." "I expected such a transformation on raising the lid, but I'm better pleased that it should not commence till I share it" (320).

Less than a year later, as Heathcliff lies dying, Nelly urges him to repent, because he has lived a selfish, unchristian life and is unfit for heaven. He refuses: "I have nearly attained *my* heaven; and that of others is altogether unvalued, and uncoveted by me!" (363). He dies and is buried as he had arranged. There is a final attestation to the couple's love in death—a little boy's report of having seen the ghost of Heathcliff and a woman on the heath. Although Heathcliff defiantly rejects Christian last rites, he believes in *his* heaven; and Brontë's faith pervades the entire novel, as it is expressed by Nelly, who, in gazing upon Cathy's dead body, becomes convinced "of the endless and shadowless hereafter . . . where life is boundless in its duration, and love in its sympathy, and joy in its fullness" (202).

In *Les Misérables* Marius experiences a similar sentiment but without Heathcliff's fastidious preparations and brooding morbidity. In his first letter to Cosette, before he has spoken a word to her, Marius expresses his ultimate desire: "O, to lie side by side [with you] in the same tomb and now and then caress with a finger-tip in the shades, that will do for my eternity" (805). Such literal concerns about the actual mingling of dead bodies was on Hawthorne's mind when he specified at the end of *The Scarlet Letter* that Hester's grave was near to Dimmesdale's but separated by a space "as if the dust of the two sleepers had no right to mingle" (275). They had a single tombstone, however, as did Maggie and Tom Tulliver in *The Mill on the Floss,* one inscribed with their names and an epitaph: "In their death they were not divided." Some Victorians were not themselves united with a beloved in death but made a union of other lovers possible. The dying Jean

Valjean tells Cosette and Marius that in death he will not be far away: "I shall watch over you from where I am." In *A Tale of Two Cities* Sydney Carton sacrifices himself to the guillotine of revolutionary Paris so that Charles Darnay can escape beheading and marry Lucie. Carton's last thoughts, uttered miraculously as if from heaven after his death, include a vision of the distant future when Darnay and Lucie as an old couple still honor his memory. His last words have become a cliche for self-sacrifice and faith in the hereafter: "It is a far, far better thing that I do, than I have ever done; it is a far, far better rest that I go to than I have ever known."

Modern novelists refused to conclude love stories with deaths that were better than anything done in life or with deaths that united couples in the hereafter. They also refused to treat parental self-sacrifice heroically. Whereas Valjean's death blesses the love of his daughter, the suicides of two modern mothers (Herminia in *The Woman Who Did* and Marion in West's *The Judge*) are a curse. Herminia's daughter enters a corrupt marriage, and Marion's son winds up killing his brother.

Even deaths in childbirth are strikingly different. In *Wuthering Heights* Cathy dies in childbirth but her daughter lives on to try and realize the earthly love that her mother was unable to achieve. In death Cathy had an expression of "perfect peace." As Nelly observes, "No angel in heaven could be more beautiful than she appeared;[8] and I partook of the infinite calm in which she lay" (201). In *A Farewell to Arms* Catherine gives birth to a still-born baby, strangled on its umbilical cord. During the unsuccessful Cesarean delivery she hemorrhages and dies, never regaining consciousness to utter some pithy farewell. She is observed by Frederic, who narrates at the end. "She was unconscious all the time, and it did not take her very long to die." After he got the nurses out of the room he looked at her dead body and took his leave: "It was like saying good-by to a statue." Brontë's heroine dies slowly and dramatically and lives on in the flesh through her daughter, lives on as a ghost through Heathcliff's abiding love, and presumably lives on in heaven as Brontë would have her readers believe. Hemingway's heroine dies quickly in a bloody mess, and her child does not survive. She does not appear angelically beautiful or at peace. While Heathcliff continues to talk to the ghost of his beloved and search the countryside for her, Frederic says goodby to a statue-like corpse of his beloved and walks back to his hotel in the rain.

Victorians experienced the death of a beloved less authentically than did the moderns. Victorians looked to clergy to mediate, facilitate, and interpret death in accord with religious doctrine, thereby stripping death of its uniqueness. They believed that death could somehow be shared with the beloved, if not as morbidly as Heathcliff planned. Many believed that death was transcendent, a passage to an afterlife where lovers would be reunited eternally "in God's sight." In all these beliefs they denied that the awareness of what it means "to be going to die" was a lonely reflecting on the meaning of one's existence.

A poem by Hardy from the 1890s, "In Death Divided," marks a transitional moment in the depiction of love in death. It deconstructs the Romantic convention of symbolizing love in death with a shared tombstone or side-by-side tombstones, because the lovers are buried in different graveyards and have differently styled tombstones:

> The simply-cut memorial at my head
>   Perhaps may take
> A rustic form, and that above your bed
>   A stately make;
> No linking symbol show thereon for our tale's sake.[9]

Hardy looks ahead to the moderns by emphatically resisting the conventional "linking symbol" but looks back to the Victorians by valorizing the grave sites and tombstones themselves.

Modernists avoided the Victorian celebration and ritualization of death. Few lovers die in modern literature, and when they do, their deaths are lonely, sudden, absolute, unique, nonreligious, absurd. In *Heart of Darkness* Marlow lies to Kurtz's "Intended" in telling her that just before dying "the last word he pronounced was—your name." In fact Kurtz's last words were "The horror! The horror!" In "Death in Venice" Aschenbach is sitting in a beach chair when he suddenly dies from indeterminate causes—probably a combination of physical debilitation from cholera, the frustration of an impossible love, and the momentary pain of witnessing a bully humiliate his beloved Tadzio. In *The Magic Mountain* the hero dies, presumably alone, when he disappears into the smoke of no-man's-land in World War I. In *Howards End* Margaret views death "stripped of any false romance" (277), and Leonard dies when struck by a falling bookshelf. In *A Farewell to Arms* Catherine bleeds to death during a botched Cesarean. Proust's beloved Albertine is killed when thrown from a horse. The narrator of *The Good Soldier* almost forgets to inform his reader that Edward cut his own throat.

Most modernist authors were primarily intent on avoiding the evasions and denials of death. One especially realistic treatment of death in modern literature is that of Mrs. Ramsay in *To the Lighthouse*. In the midst of a lyrical description of how time passes and how the Ramsay house aged during a ten-year interval, Woolf stuns her reader with a sudden bracketed remark that announces the death of Mrs. Ramsay. "[Mr. Ramsay, stumbling along a passage one dark morning, stretched his arms out, but Mrs. Ramsay having died rather suddenly the night before, his arms, though stretched out, remained empty.]" (194). In this way the death of the heroine is indicated as an aside, halfway through the novel. Woolf focuses on the way Mr. Ramsay's arms missed his wife, as if they alone retained the essence of her memory. The bracketed interruption breaks into the flow of the sentence and the movement of the story, replicating the way death breaks so unexpectedly into the flow of life and the movement of love.

Woolf resumes interpreting the meaning of Mrs. Ramsay's death after ten years have elapsed, on a day when the Ramsay family is once again planning a trip to the lighthouse. She begins this final section of the novel with the fundamental question, "What does it mean then, what can it all mean?" (217). What follows is not a ritualized memorializing of death, typical of the Victorians, but a penetrating inquiry into the meaning of the death of a beloved that moves in and out of the minds of the two characters who are most affected by it.

At first Lily is confused about what she feels, having come back so many years after Mrs. Ramsay died. The house, the morning, the people seem aimless and chaotic. Even the death of Mrs. Ramsay seems to have little effect on her. Mr. Ramsay appears and Lily overhears him mutter to himself the word "Alone" and then the word "Perished." His words set in motion her reflection on the meaning of death. "If only she could put them together, she felt, write them out in some sentence, then she would have got at the truth of things." With this first "communication" between Lily and Mr. Ramsay begins a recovery of the meaning of a death and the life it ended.

Lily rephrases the fundamental question about meaning as a question about creation. "Going to the Lighthouse . . . Perished. Alone. The grey-green light on the wall opposite. The empty places. Such were some of the parts, but how bring them together? she asked" (220). Suddenly she recalls how ten years ago there had been a leaf pattern on the table cloth, how there had been a problem about the composition of her painting, and how she had decided to move the tree to the middle of it but had not. She resolves to

complete her picture, which becomes a symbol of the recapture of the meaning of Mrs. Ramsay's life.

But Mr. Ramsay interferes with her painting. He can only take, as he had
taken from Mrs. Ramsay, and Lily feels deprived of creative energy in his
presence which makes it impossible for her to see color, line, or mass. She
rationalizes that it is somehow Mrs. Ramsay's fault that she cannot paint—
Mrs. Ramsay, who gave and in giving died and left everyone behind incomplete and dependent on her. The equation of loving and creating sharpens as
Lily realizes that her art must substitute for the creative energy that Mrs.
Ramsay supplied and that her death shut off. But what the death of Mrs.
Ramsay took away, her life remembered begins to restore. In pondering the
big questions, Lily realizes that the answers are in "little daily miracles"
such as a breaking wave or Mrs. Ramsay's attempt to make things permanent, as when she suddenly ordered: "Life stand still here." Lily reflects that
"in the midst of chaos there was shape" (241).

Mr. Ramsay also realizes that he owes his well-being, the meaning of his
life, to his dead wife. His rational arguments remain unchallenged. He is
triumphant in that he knows such things as the directions of the compass,
which women in the hopeless "vagueness of their minds" cannot comprehend, but his arms are empty and he is alone. He suddenly bursts out, "we
perished," and then, "each alone." He begins to understand that the "vagueness" of Mrs. Ramsay's mind was part of her appeal, that he "had been
wrong to be angry with her," and that he misses her desperately.

As he and his children push off in a boat to go to the lighthouse, Lily
continues "tunnelling her way into her picture, into the past" (258). She
thinks about a young couple that Mrs. Ramsay brought together who are
having marital problems, and she realizes that Mrs. Ramsay is fading away
because being dead she knows nothing of those problems and because Lily
can "over-ride her wishes, improve away her limited, old-fashioned ideas"
(260). There is so much that Mrs. Ramsay can never know or affect. The
dead continue dying.

As Mr. Ramsay and his children get further from Lily, she sees more
clearly her creative vocation. She recalls how ten years earlier she was in
love with the place where she put her easel. She realizes the creative power
of love, for lovers are able to "choose out the elements of things and place
them together and so, giving them a wholeness not theirs in life, make of
some scene, or meeting of people (all now gone and separate), one of those
globed compacted things over which thought lingers, and love plays" (286).

Her meditation on love and death centers on her own art, which becomes a symbol of love. She becomes the resurrection and the life of her dead friend. She must find the meaning of the past, the possibility of love, and the composition of her painting on her own. "It was a miserable machine, an inefficient machine, she thought, the human apparatus for painting or for feeling; it always broke down at the critical moment; heroically, one must force it on" (287).

At the moment when Lily is certain that Mr. Ramsay has reached the lighthouse she blurts out "he has landed," adding, "It is finished." These, the last words uttered by Christ, refer also to the novel itself, the Ramsays' journey to the lighthouse, Lily's memorializing of the death of Mrs. Ramsay, and Lily's painting. She draws a line in the center, and, Woolf narrates, "It was done; it was finished." For that moment it fills the emptiness, completes the vision, and affirms the life of the woman who inspired it.

Woolf is careful, however, to avoid any implication of ultimate meaning. Even as she brings to completion Lily's painting which was ten years in the making, she takes away any implication of permanence or finality: the painting will hang not in public where all can see it but in attics where it will eventually be destroyed. There will be no marble or granite tombstone for Mrs. Ramsay. She will be remembered for a while and then fade from memory as her ideas and projects become increasingly irrelevant even to those who loved her most. Woolf refuses to idealize even the absoluteness of death, for her beloved dead heroine will continue to die long after her physical death, until her memory, like her artistic image, has also passed into oblivion.

In denying the absolute finality of death Woolf accepted the actuality of human finitude. Victorians lit candles in church and planted flowers by tombstones to pay tribute to an eternal life in the hereafter, a life that would continue in the memory of those who lived after as well in the mind of an omniscient God. The moderns believed that no omniscient God preserved the memory of the departed, let alone their spirit or their bodies. Moderns acknowledged that the dead continue to dissolve even in the memory of the living; and in refusing to memorialize the dead as if their death were something that itself does not change in time (which it does), they accepted an aspect of it that Victorians were unwilling to accept.

Moderns acknowledged the pervasiveness of conflict in love and were therefore better able to understand its constitutive function. They did not project the cause of rejection onto imaginary characters or displace it to distant places or historical periods, and therefore they were better able to capture its varieties and modes. The celebration of death in Victorian art and literature was a screen against the actuality of human finitude. Moderns were not as easily tempted to mediate, share, ritualize, or deny the reality of death and were therefore better able to accept the nature of finitude. The moderns' more authentic renderings of conflict, rejection, and death enabled them to capture a fuller sense of what it means for love to come to an end.

Conclusion

THROUGHOUT the research and writing of this book I was plagued by the thought that, for all the apparent change, love might be a universal. Especially unsettling was evidence of Victorians who seemed modern, moderns who seemed Victorian, and some modern writers who, at least momentarily, proclaimed love's transhistorical nature. But even among these examples there was abundant evidence for the historical nature of love that such passages seemed to question.

In *Jane Eyre*, for example, Rochester anticipates modern theorizing about the power of the gaze when he thinks about how Jane's look affects him: "Consider that eye: consider the resolute, wild, free thing looking out of it, defying me, with more than courage—with a stern triumph. Whatever I do with its cage, I cannot get at it—the savage, beautiful creature!" (344). This thought resembles Sartre's philosophy of the gaze, but as I have shown, the novel is full of distinctly Victorian ways of loving. In "A Woman Waits for Me," from *Leaves of Grass* (1855), Whitman includes a most un-Victorian survey of the aspects of sex.

> Sex contains all, bodies, souls,
> Meanings, proofs, purities, delicacies, results, promulgations,
> Songs, commands, health, pride, the maternal mystery, the seminal milk,
> All hopes, benefactions, bestowals, all the passions, loves, beauties, delights of the earth,
> All the governments, judges, gods, follow'd persons of the earth,
> These are contain'd in sex as parts of itself and justifications of itself.

Whitman was simply ahead of his time, and although this poem is addressed to a woman, he was bisexual, and his celebration of sex was energized by some exceptional difficulties he had with mid-century sexual morality.

Hardy was a transitional, late-Victorian figure who adopted a modern view of the pitfalls of romantic love. In *Far from the Madding Crowd* he held up as a goal the final relationship between Gabriel and Bathsheba. After they learned about the "rougher sides" of each other's character, their love could at last emerge out of "hard prosaic reality" and establish a genuine "camaraderie," but that, Hardy added, is rarely part of love, "because men and women associate, not in their labours, but in their pleasures merely" (458). Hardy's observation is historical in rejecting contemporary ways of loving and anticipating a future when camaraderie will not be so seldom an occurrence.

One of the characters from the modern period who seems Victorian is Cecil in *A Room with a View,* crushing his pince-nez against Lucy's face during a clumsy formal kiss. Forster's characterization of him as "medieval" is meaningful only against a history of change. Georgie's mother in Aldington's *The Colonel's Daughter,* in advising her daughter on sex, sounds like a typical Victorian prude: "If you're ever married, remember that unpleasant things happen. But pay no attention to them—I never did" (281). Far from compromising my periodization, Aldington's character documents it, since the mother sounds Victorian precisely because she is eighty years behind the times. Wharton and Lawrence create similar characters with Victorian attitudes who are all the more believable against the background of history. In *Sons and Lovers* Miriam's panic about sex harkens back to a dated morality that Lawrence tried to transform, and in *The Age of Innocence* the New York society of the 1870s that governs Archer's marriage to May and blocks his love for Ellen is an accurately crafted historical artifact.

Several modern writers implied doubt about change by creating characters who love across the centuries. Rilke's Malte Laurids Brigge is enamored of the twelfth-century love letters of Heloise and those of a seventeenth-century Portuguese nun as if they had been recently posted; Mann's Gustav von Aschenbach justifies his love for Tadzio with the model of homoerotic love in ancient Greece, and T. S. Eliot's Tiresias watches the crude coupling of a typist with a clerk and realizes that he has seen it all centuries before. Virginia Woolf pushes the universality of love back even farther. In *Mrs. Dalloway* Peter hears a beggar woman singing in the streets and reflects on the abuse that loving women have suffered at the hands of men since prehistoric times. "Through all ages—when the pavement was grass, when it was swamp, through the age of tusk and mammoth, through the age of silent sunset, the battered woman—for she wore a skirt—with her right hand exposed, her left clutching at her side, stood singing of love—love which has lasted a million years" (122). Although these passages may express momentary doubt about a history of love, the works from which they come testify to an overall historical movement.

Some works deny progress along with any historical logic. Kierkegaard writes that "no generation has learned from another to love, no generation begins at any other point than at the beginning, no generation has a shorter task assigned to it than had the preceding generation, and if here one is not willing like the previous generations to stop with love but would go further, this is but idle and foolish talk." [1] In *Tess of the d'Urbervilles* Hardy theorizes that "what are called advanced ideas are really in great part but the latest fashion in definition—a more accurate expression, by words [ending] in *logy* and *ism*, of sensations which men and women have vaguely grasped for centuries" (105). In a single sentence, Musil's man without qualities both rejects a history of love and calls for it to begin: "Once I know that women five thousand years ago wrote word for word the same letters to their lovers as women do now, I can't read another such letter without asking myself whether there ought not to be a change for once!" (I, 254). In *Journal of "The Counterfeiters"* Gide proposes that his next novel show how "those of a new generation, after having criticized and blamed the actions and attitudes (conjugal, for example) of their predecessors, find themselves gradually led to do almost the same things over again" (447). And Forster momentarily gives up on human relations altogether with the breakdown of love in *A Passage to India*. Mrs. Moore, despairing of the marriage between Ronny and Adela that she had journeyed to India to witness, concludes that after "centuries of carnal embracement . . . man is no nearer to understanding man" (135).

Despite such specific arguments against a history of love, these writers argue more generally on its behalf. Although Kierkegaard thundered against Hegel's sweeping historicism, he nevertheless believed in the logic of a history he held responsible for draining the spiritual vitality out of authentic Christian faith, and he wrote books to try and modify its direction. Hardy, although a fatalist, campaigned for improvement in the way men and women love. Musil's hero devoted his life to divesting himself of all the qualities he had inherited from history. Gide craved a historical change that would give him the freedom to express his sexual preference. In 1926, after years of suffering in secret, he achieved a breakthrough by making his homosexuality public. Forster also needed history to move forward so he could experience his homosexual love with less secrecy and deception. He completed *Maurice* in 1914 with the intention of keeping it out of print until the literary world was ready to accept a novel about homosexual love. These writers questioned the possibility of a history of love and scoffed at the notion that it was progressive because they were so frustrated by its slow pace.

There is thus a logic to the history of love. If that logic moves in the direction of authenticity, what value can we attach to that movement? Or, to put it simply, is authenticity good?

Every moment of consciousness creates values, which, as Sartre remarked, spring up all around us like partridges out of the grass. Our conscious existence is like that of an eye that is perpetually out of focus, straining to bring what is all around us into focus. We desire to see clearly, to understand what we see, to make what we see our own, even to become what we see. And if we desire something, it takes on value: we like it, we judge it to be good, and it becomes what we want to be. In trying to understand the history of love, which I have argued is a movement toward greater authenticity, I have found it impossible not to valorize the direction of that movement.

Among the evidence already presented, the example of vision provides a graphic instance of this historical development. Victorian love was blind—almost literally. Victorian art shows many lovers who choose not to look. In Solomon's *Doubtful Fortune* (Figure 2) the woman looks away from the cards that are supposed to reveal her future, whereas in Valadon's *The Future Unveiled* (Figure 3) the woman looks directly at the cards. In Frith's *The Sleeping Model* (Figure 15) the model is asleep, whereas in Dix's *Self-Portrait with Muse* (Figure 16) the large model challenges the diminutive artist with wide-open, all-seeing eyes. Victorian men and women often kiss with eyes closed, whereas the moderns experiment with new ways of seeing. Picasso (Figure 22) superimposes a wide-open eye on a man's genitalia which somehow also see, since they are located in his head. Magritte (Figure 23) accents the importance of seeing in love by shrouding his kissing lovers in unnerving, opaque veils. In Brancusi's series of sculptures of the kiss, wide-open eyes at first rival the sensuous intimacy of kissing lips and eventually displace the lips altogether as in his climactic *The Gate of the Kiss* (Figure 26). Picasso's androgynous *Head of a Woman* (Figure 29) takes on intelligence with the placement of an open eye on the cheek/buttock, which unifies upper and lower body, penis and vagina, art and love. The Victorian refusal to look is even apparent in the contrasting paintings that show males observing a sleeping naked female. In Etty's *Sleeping Nymph and Satyrs*

(Figure 36) the observing males are not men but mythological characters, far removed from the real world and hence from actual human vision, whereas Picasso's *Sleeping Nude* (Figure 37) shows an ordinary man standing over a woman, meditating about what he sees, perhaps even about the act of seeing.

One reason why Manet's *Luncheon on the Grass* created a scandal in 1863 was that the undressed woman was shown staring directly at the viewer with a disconcerting nonchalance. Victorian men and women were afraid to be seen or to see themselves as sexual beings. Peter Gay has argued that for the Victorian bourgeoisie modesty, prudishness, and hypocrisy about sex were "defensive tactics" that "kept sensuality alive but out of sight." But when such defensiveness and refusal to look are enforced by sex-negative moral codes, sensuality atrophies and mental health is imperiled.[2] Modesty and especially prudishness and hypocrisy are not just attitudes toward an intrusive public; their very meaning and possibility stem from attitudes toward one's own self as well as others, which persist after the door is closed and the shades are drawn. Victorians were not sexually anesthetized, but their constriction of the visual sense followed them and haunted them in private. Ruskin's marriage fell apart, indeed never really got started sexually, because on his wedding night, as his wife recalled, he became disgusted when he saw her naked body, for "he had imagined women were quite different from what he saw I was." Ruskin was an accomplished writer and, unlike most Victorian men, was good at talking about sex, but he was not so accomplished at seeing.

Beautiful eyes are the most striking feature of the Victorian heroines Emma Bovary, Lady Audley, and Elfride Swancourt, but their eyes are not beautiful as organs of vision or metaphors for insight but merely as decorative features for show. So too are the eyes of the Victorian heroine in *The Age of Innocence*, whose "bandaged" eyes "look out blankly at blankness" (83). They contrast with the eyes of the modern woman, Ellen: their beauty comes from their power of vision, which sharpens her love for Archer and enhances his understanding of the world.

Hugo warned that "every glance" at a virgin girl is a "profanation." Other Victorian novelists discreetly hid nakedness from view, just as their characters hid their nakedness from one another. Far different was Joyce's celebration of Leopold's ecstatic outburst—"Watch! Watch!"—as he glimpses a woman's legs, or later when he becomes aroused from seeing what Gerty shows him underneath her dress. In *Tropic of Cancer* Miller's

mock-hero Van Norden gets out a flashlight to look even closer; and to reveal how desire works beneath the skin, Mann invoked the x-ray, a modern
metaphor for the eager, penetrating vision of modern loving. In *The Thibaults* Antoine pries open the closed eyes of his lover to combat her momentary evasiveness. Two classics of modernism use images of impaired vision
to emphasize the importance of seeing. Dali and Buñuel celebrated the new
ability to see that is characteristic of modern cinematography with the
slashed eyeball that opens *An Andalusian Dog,* and Eliot explained in notes
to *The Waste Land* that the essence of his poem was what the blind Tiresias
sees, which is the history of love.

The powder that some extremely modest Victorian women put into their
bath water to cloud any view of their own naked bodies may caricature
Victorian prudishness, but its conception and occasional practice at that
time is but an exaggerated manifestation of a pervasive, if not quite so frantically restrictive, sexual morality. When Victorian women looked in mirrors
to make themselves beautiful, they generally did it to enhance a face for
someone else to look at. Modern women were not all as modern as Colette's
Renée, but her "dangerous, lucid hour," when she looked into the mirror as
an instrument for self-reflection, is distinctly modern if not typical. And Renée was dangerous precisely because she was lucid.

The Victorians' preference for having sex in the dark does not prove that
they were repressed, but it does indicate that they suppressed the sensory
richness of vision. They were in keeping with a romantic tradition going
back at least to Arthurian legend and the story of Tristan and Isolde, for
whom the light of day brought the end of love. For most Victorian lovers
being found out was not a matter of life and death as it was for Tristan and
Isolde, but the aura of secrecy and the stigma of shame compromised their
lovemaking even in marriage.

What the Victorians did not see they could not understand, and that was
a source of dread from which they turned away. James concludes *The
Golden Bowl* with a considered look at one such moment of dread. Maggie
has long since discovered Amerigo's numerous character flaws and his infidelity with Charlotte, and he has slowly, tortuously discovered that she
knows. In the end he moves toward Maggie to try and take what she offers.
"He tried, too clearly, to please her—to meet her in her own way; but with
the result only that, close to her, her face kept before him, his hands holding
her shoulders, his whole act enclosing her, he presently echoed: 'See? I see
nothing but *you.*'" Amerigo's remark is absurdly overstated. There follows

a description of her response which "so strangely lighted his eyes that, as for pity and dread of them, she buried her own in his breast." In contrast to this restrained and believable account of a husband and wife trying, and largely failing, to see and understand one another, there is Jane Eyre's boast that before her husband's eyesight returned she was "literally . . . the apple of his eye. He saw nature—he saw books through me; and never did I weary of gazing for his behalf." Their marriage, she concludes, was "perfect concord." At this moment Jane's claim is unbelievable. In the final moment of *The Golden Bowl* Maggie cannot bear to look her husband in the eye. James's lovers can scarcely see for themselves, let alone for anyone else, but at least what they can see is their own. More than the Victorians the moderns opened their eyes to see and understand more of the possibilities and impossibilities of love.

The ethical value of authenticity is more crudely obvious in another aspect of seeing. When one learns, for example, that Victorian obstetricians examined pregnant women without looking at their vaginas, there is no need to add that such examinations are wrong. One does not need a utilitarian, Kantian, Christian, Marxist, or feminist ethical standard to judge that such unsighted examinations are not only bad but dangerous. Today they would be subject to malpractice suits. My interpretation has been presented in the language of seeing versus not seeing rather than in overtly ethical language, because direct language best captures basic experience; but the Victorians also loved blind, and although the historical record may provide explanations, the historical conscience calls for ethical judgment.

That judgment must go against the Victorians. In comparison with the moderns, Victorian love was deficient. Often it was a disaster. Victorians had less time to court and were more rushed toward irreversible, now-or-never decisions about a one-and-only lover. They had a more restricted courting space, a smaller pool of lovers from which to draw, and greater anxiety about the judgment of society, family, and God. Courting was more regulated by chaperons and match-makers. Childbearing was more dangerous, gender roles more rigidly dichotomous, and power relations more a dominion of the physically stronger. Their language was more constrained by rhetorical formalities, clichés, and laws against obscenity. Men were under more pressure to propose marriage, and women to accept; formulaic weddings and ritualized marriages followed. Victorians understood less about their bodies and especially about their sexuality and were less able to understand and treat sexually transmitted diseases. Their sex was more suppressed, humorless, and guilty. During coitus they explored less of the body and in fewer locations and afterwards spent less time exploring the sexual possibilities of the post-coital interlude. Their deeper faith in love after death sapped the energy out of their love in life.

These final judgments will no doubt trouble those who revere the rich cultural legacy of the Victorian world, which is indeed the anvil on which I have pounded out this history. I hesitated before criticizing the historical circumstances reflected in Victorian culture, especially the novels of George Eliot, which are so brilliantly crafted, so sensitive to complexities and subtleties of the deepest stirrings of love. After studying what Jane Eyre was up against, I became increasingly moved by her struggle to love. Elizabeth Barrett and Robert Browning's love was painfully constricted by contemporary moral codes, but her love poetry took on special power when read in that historical context. Although my judgment is made with reservations, it must stand.

This judgment is not about the quality of art or literature. Aside from my argument that modern art and literature are more authentic than Victorian art and literature in that they are more explicitly reflective of the creative process, my concern is not with the quality of any novel or painting but with the loves that they depict. I am not arguing that modern literature and art were better. Such an argument would be groundless, futile, and absurd. Indeed, much of Victorian culture achieves its power from the troubled, blind, suppressed loving that it attempts to capture.

Our response to Victorian love as expressed in the love duet from Wagner's *Tristan and Isolde* is intensified by our understanding its historical meaning. Isolde's agonizing high-pitched shrieks of hope against Tristan's deep moaning are especially moving precisely because we know something about the formidable obstacles that blocked their love. Their struggle to love rings true with undiminished force more than a century after the opera's premiere. It indeed expresses a universal human feeling, but one shaped by medieval circumstances—interpreted through Victorian sensibility—that made their happiness impossible. By the twentieth century the historical conditions that made the reality of their love so difficult and the art of their love so exquisite were not as firmly in place. The moderns may have lost some of the Victorians' delicacy and poignancy, perhaps even some of their heroism, but in exchange became more reflective of what it means to be in love and hence better able to make that loving more their very own.

Appendix

Primary Works Cited

Notes

List of Illustrations

List of Fictional Characters

Index

Appendix. Ages of Fictional Characters

Some of the novels I used gave the age of only one lover or none at all. Forty-two gave both. I divided these into two lists: one of twenty-three titles up to 1898, another of the remaining nineteen titles up to 1933. Both record the age when these loves began, not when the couple met or married. Whenever the author contrasted two kinds of love (between two couples or between successive loves of an individual) I have included ages at the starting date of those other relationships in parenthesis. My numerical calculations are based on the primary relationship. Lack of any indication of age in the novels explains the omission of some major lovers, such as Heathcliff and Catherine, Hester and Dimmesdale, Anna and Vronsky, Jude and Sue, Hans and Clavdia, Marcel and Albertine.

AGES OF MEN AND WOMEN—NINETEENTH CENTURY

1847, *Wuthering Heights*	Hareton, 23	Cathy II, 18
1847, *Jane Eyre*	Rochester, 38	Jane, 18
1853, *Villette*	John, 26	Lucy, 23
1855, *North and South*	Thornton, c.30	Margaret, 18
1859, *Family Happiness*	Sergey, 36	Masha, 17
1859, *On the Eve*	Dimitri, 26	Elena 20
1860, *The Mill on the Floss*	Stephen, 25	Maggie, 19
1862, *Les Misérables*	Marius, 21	Cosette, 15
1872, *Middlemarch*	Will, 25	Dorothea, 21
	Casaubon (45 plus)	Dorothea (19)
	Tertius (27)	Rosamond (22)
1873, *A Pair of Blue Eyes*	Knight, 32	Elfride, 20
1873, *Anna Karenina*	Levin, 32	Kitty, 18
1874, *Far from the Madding Crowd*	Gabriel, 28	Bathsheba, 22
	Boldwood (38)	Bathsheba (22)
1876, *Daniel Deronda*	Grandcourt, 35	Gwendolen, 20
	Daniel (c.30)	Mirah (19)
1879, *The Egoist*	Willoughby, 32	Clara, 18

1881, *The Portrait of a Lady*	Osmond, 30 plus	Isabel, 19
	Warburton (35)	Isabel (19)
1882, *A Modern Instance*	Bartley, 26	Marcia, 20
1891, *Tess of the d'Urbervilles*	Angel, 26	Tess, 20
	Alec (24)	Tess (17)
1892, *The Well-Beloved*	Pierston, 20 (40) (60)	Avice, 17
1893, *The Odd Women*	Everard, c.33	Rhoda, 32
	Widdowson (c.44)	Monica (21)
1894, *Effi Briest*	Innstetten, 38	Effi, 17
	Von Crampas (42)	
1895, *The Woman Who Did*	Alan, 30 plus	Herminia, 22
1895, *The Importance of Being Earnest*	Jack, 29	Cecily, 18
1898, *Hellbeck of Bannisdale*	Alan, 37	Laura, 21
Mean	*29.4 years*	*19.7 years*

AGES OF MEN AND WOMEN—TWENTIETH CENTURY

1899, *The Awakening*	Robert, 26	Edna, 28
1909, *Ann Veronica*	Capes, 32	Ann, 21
	Hubert (35)	
1910, *The Vagabond*	Maxime, 33	Renée, 34
1910, *Howards End*	Henry, c.50	Margaret, 29
1912, *The Reef*	Darrow, 37	Anna, 24
1913, *Sons and Lovers*	Paul, 23	Clara, 30
	Paul (21)	Miriam (16)
1915, *The Rainbow*	Anton, 27	Ursula, 22
1915, *Victory*	Axel, 35 plus	Lena, 19
1920, *Women in Love*	Rupert, c.30	Ursula, 26
	Gerald (30)	Gudrun (25)
1920, *This Side of Paradise*	Amory, 19	Isabelle, 16
1920, *Chéri*	Chéri, 19	Léonie, 43
1920, *The Age of Innocence*	Archer, c.30	Ellen, c.30
	Archer	May (21)
1922, *The Judge*	Richard, 30	Ellen, 17
1922, *Les Thibaults*	Antoine, 29	Rachel, 26
1925, *Mrs. Dalloway*	Peter, 53	Clarissa, 52
1927, *To the Lighthouse*	Mr. Ramsay, 50 plus	Mrs. Ramsay, 50
1928, *Point Counter Point*	Walter, 24	Lucy, 29
1933, *The Man Without Qualities*	Ulrich, 32	Agatha, 27
1933, *Tender Is the Night*	Dick, 34	Nicole, c.24
Mean	*32.2 years*	*28.6 years*

Primary Works Cited

Original publication dates are in italics.

Aldington, Richard. *The Colonel's Daughter. 1932*. London: Hogarth, 1986.

Allen, Grant. *The Woman Who Did*. Boston: Roberts Bros., *1895*.

Bagnold, Enid. *The Happy Foreigner. 1920*. London: Virago, 1987.

Braddon, Mary Elizabeth. *Lady Audley's Secret. 1862*. Oxford: World's Classics, 1987.

Brittain, Vera. *Testament of Youth. 1933*. New York: Wideview, 1980.

Broch, Hermann. The Sleepwalkers. *1931*. Translated. New York: Grosset & Dunlap, 1964.

Brontë, Charlotte. *Jane Eyre. 1847*. New York: Penguin, 1966.

—— *Villette. 1853*. New York: Penguin, 1979.

Brontë, Emily. *Wuthering Heights. 1847*. New York: Penguin, 1965.

Cather, Willa. *One of Ours. 1922*. New York: Vintage, 1971.

Chopin, Kate. *The Awakening. 1899*. New York: Norton, 1976.

Colette, Sidonie. *Chéri. 1920. The Last of Chéri. 1926*. Translated. New York: Penguin, 1974.

—— *The Vagabond. 1910*. Translated. New York: Farrar, Straus, 1955.

Collins, Wilkie. *The Woman in White. 1860*. Oxford: Oxford University Press, 1986.

Conrad, Joseph. *Victory. 1915*. New York: Anchor, 1957.

Dostoevski, Feodor. *The Brothers Karamazov. 1880*. Translated. New York: Penguin, 1958.

—— Crime and Punishment. *1866*. Translated. New York: Penguin 1951.

Dickens, Charles. *Great Expectations. 1861*. New York: Penguin, 1965.

Du Gard, Roger Martin. *The Thibaults. 1922–1929*. Translated. New York: Viking, 1939.

Eliot, George. *Adam Bede. 1859*. New York: Penguin, 1985.

—— *Daniel Deronda. 1876*. New York: Penguin, 1986.

—— *Middlemarch. 1872*. New York: Norton, 1977.

—— *Mill on the Floss. 1860*. New York: Penguin, 1979.

Fitzgerald, F. Scott. *The Great Gatsby*. New York: Scribner's, *1925*.

———— *Tender is the Night*. New York: Scribner's, *1933*.

———— *This Side of Paradise*. 1920. New York: Scribner's, 1960.

Flaubert, Gustave. *Madame Bovary*. 1857. Translated. New York: Modern Library, 1957.

———— *Sentimental Education*. 1869. Translated. New York: Penguin, 1964.

———— "A Simple Heart." *1877*. Translated in *Three Tales*. New York: Penguin, 1978.

Fontane, Theodor. *Effi Briest*. *1894*. Translated. New York: Penguin, 1967.

Ford, Ford Madox. *The Good Soldier: A Tale of Passion*. *1915*. New York: Vintage, 1951.

Forster, E. M. *Aspects of the Novel*. New York: Harcourt, Brace, *1927*.

———— *Howards End*. New York: Vintage, *1921*.

———— *Maurice*. *1914* (completed but not published). Toronto: Macmillan, 1971.

———— *A Passage to India*. New York: Harcourt, Brace, *1924*.

———— *A Room with a View*. 1908. New York: Vintage, 1986.

Gaskell, Elizabeth. *North and South*. 1855. New York: Penguin, 1970.

Gissing, George. *The Odd Women*. 1893. New York: Norton, 1977.

Gide, André. *The Counterfeiters*, with *Journal of "The Counterfeiters."* 1925, 1927. Translated. New York: Vintage, 1973.

———— *Strait Is the Gate*. 1909. Translated. New York: Penguin, 1973.

Gilman, Charlotte Perkins. *Herland*. 1915. New York: Pantheon, 1979.

Goethe, Johann Wolfgang von. *The Sorrows of Young Werther*. *1774*. Translated. New York: Vintage, 1973.

Hall, Radclyffe. *The Well of Loneliness*. 1928. New York: Avon, 1981.

Hardy, Thomas. *Far from the Madding Crowd*. 1874. New York: Penguin, 1986.

———— *Jude the Obscure*. 1895. New York: Norton, 1978.

———— *A Pair of Blue Eyes*. 1873. New York: Penguin, 1986.

———— *The Return of the Native*. 1878. Oxford: Oxford University Press, 1990.

———— *Tess of the d'Urbervilles*. 1891. New York: Norton, 1979.

———— *The Well-Beloved*. 1892. Oxford: Oxford University Press, 1986.

Hawthorne, Nathaniel. *The Scarlet Letter*. 1850. New York: Penguin, 1970.

Heidegger, Martin. *Being and Time*. 1927. Translated. New York: Harper, 1962.

Hemingway, Ernest. *A Farewell to Arms*. New York: Scribner's, *1929*.

———— *The Sun Also Rises*. New York: Scribner's, *1926*.

Howells, William Dean. *A Modern Instance*. 1882. New York: Penguin, 1984.

Hugo, Victor. *Les Misérables*. *1862*. Translated. New York: Penguin, 1976.

Huxley, Aldous. *Point Counter Point*. 1928. New York: Perennial, 1965.

Ibsen, Henrik. "The Wild Duck." *1884*. In *Hedda Gabler and Three Other Plays*. Translated. New York: Anchor, 1961.

James, Henry. *The Golden Bowl*. 1904. New York: Penguin, 1966.

———— *The Portrait of a Lady*. 1881. New York: Penguin, 1963.

Jaspers, Karl. *Philosophy*. 1932. Three Volumes. Translated. Chicago: University of Chicago Press, 1970.

Joyce, James. *Exiles. 1918.* New York: Viking, 1961.

———— *Ulysses. 1922.* New York: Vintage, 1961.

Kafka, Franz. *The Trial. 1925.* Translated. New York: Schocken, 1984.

Lawrence, D. H. "A Propos of *Lady Chatterley's Lover.*" *1929.* Reprinted in Harry T. Moore, ed., *Sex, Literature, and Censorship.* New York: Viking, 1959.

———— *Lady Chatterley's Lover. 1928.* New York: Signet, 1962.

———— *The Rainbow. 1915.* New York: Viking, 1961.

———— *Sons and Lovers. 1913.* New York: Penguin, 1983.

———— *Women in Love. 1920.* New York: Penguin, 1976.

Leech, Margaret. *Tin Wedding. 1926.* New York: Norton, 1986.

Lewes, George Henry. *Ranthorpe. 1847.* Athens, Ohio: Ohio University Press, 1974.

Mann, Thomas. "Death in Venice." *1911.* Translated in *Death in Venice and Seven Other Stories.* New York: Knopf, 1930.

———— *The Magic Mountain. 1924.* Translated. New York: Knopf, 1966.

Meredith, George. *The Egoist. 1879.* New York: Penguin, 1968.

Mill, John Stuart. *On Liberty. 1859.* New York: Norton, 1975.

Miller, Henry. *Tropic of Cancer. 1934.* New York: Grove, 1961.

Musil, Robert. *The Man Without Qualities. 1930–1943.* Translated. London: Picador, 1979.

———— "The Perfecting of a Love," *1911.* Translated in *Five Women.* Boston: Nonpareil, 1986.

Nietzsche, Friedrich. *Thus Spoke Zarathustra. 1883–1885.* New York: Penguin, 1978.

Proust, Marcel. *Remembrance of Things Past. 1913–1927.* Translated. New York: Random House, 1981.

Rilke, Rainer Maria. *The Notebooks of Malte Laurids Brigge. 1910.* Translated. New York, Vintage, 1985.

Rostand, Edmond. *Cyrano de Bergerac. 1898.* Translated. New York: Bantam, 1982.

Stendhal [Henri Beyle]. *On Love. 1822.* Translated. New York: Universal Library, 1967.

Stoker, Bram. *Dracula. 1897.* New York: Signet, 1965.

Tolstoy, Leo. *Anna Karenina. 1873.* Translated. New York: Norton, 1970.

———— "Family Happiness." *1859.* Translated in *Great Short Works of Leo Tolstoy.* New York: Perennial, 1967.

Turgenev, Ivan. *On the Eve. 1859.* Translated. New York: Penguin, 1985.

Ward, Mrs. Humphrey. *Helbeck of Bannisdale. 1898.* New York: Penguin, 1983.

Wells, H. G. *Ann Veronica: A Modern Love Story. 1909.* New York: Modern Library, n.d.

West, Rebecca. "Indissoluble Matrimony." *1914.* Reprinted in Sandra M. Gilbert and Susan Gubar, eds., *The Norton Anthology of Literature by Women.* New York: Norton, 1985.

———— *The Judge. 1922.* New York: Dial, 1980.

———— *The Return of the Soldier. 1918.* New York: Dial, 1980.

Wharton, Edith. *The Age of Innocence*. *1920*. New York: Scribner's, 1968.
────── *The Reef*. *1912*. New York: Collier, 1987.
────── *Summer*. *1918*. New York: Perennial, 1980.
Wilde, Oscar. *The Importance of Being Earnest*. *1895*. In *Oscar Wilde Plays*. Baltimore: Penguin, 1954.
Woolf, Virginia. *Mrs. Dalloway*. *1925*. New York: Harcourt, Brace, 1953.
────── *Night and Day*. *1919*. New York: Harcourt, Brace, 1920.
────── *Orlando*. *1928*. Frogmore, St Albans, Herts: Panther, 1977.
────── *A Room of One's Own*. *1929*. Frogmore, St. Albans, Herts: Panther, 1977.
────── *To the Lighthouse*. *1927*. New York: Harcourt, Brace, 1955.
────── *The Voyage Out*. *1915*. New York: Harcourt, Brace, 1920.
────── *The Years*. New York: Harcourt, Brace, 1937.
Zola, Emile. *La Bête humaine*. 1890. Translated. London: Penguin, 1977.
────── *The Sin of Father Mouret*. *1875*. Translated. Lincoln, Neb.: Bison, 1969.

Notes

Introduction

1. Virginia Woolf, *A Room of One's Own* [1929] (London, 1977), 70.

2. In affirming the literary quality of the classics Nina Baym implies their evidentiary value. After examining 140 lesser-known Victorian novels by American women, she concludes, "although I found much to interest me in these books, I have not unearthed a forgotten Jane Austen or George Eliot, or hit upon even one novel that I would propose to set alongside *The Scarlet Letter.*" *Women's Fiction: A Guide to Novels by and about Women in America, 1820–1870* (Ithaca, 1978), 15.

3. Peter Gay, *The Bourgeois Experience: Victoria to Freud.* Vol. I, *Education of the Senses* and Vol. II, *The Tender Passion* (New York, 1984, 1986); Irving Singer, *The Nature of Love.* Vol. I, *Plato to Luther.* Vol. II, *Courtly and Romantic.* Vol. III, *The Modern World* (Chicago, 1984, 1984, 1987); Phyllis Rose, *Parallel Lives: Five Victorian Marriages* (New York, 1983).

4. Earlier metaphysics approached human existence as a thing with attributes. Heidegger investigates not what kind of a thing a human being is, but what it means to be human. The prefix *"Da,"* whether translated as "there" or "here," signifies that human existence is always located in the immediate environment. *"Sein"* refers to an activity and is best translated by "to be" rather than "being." Heidegger's use of *Dasein* implies that human existence is not an entity but a way of being or set of activities in the world. I translate *Dasein* as "human existence" but retain the German in direct quotations from his English translators, who left the word in German. For my understanding of this word and of Heidegger's philosophy in general I am indebted to Michael Gelven's *A Commentary on Heidegger's "Being and Time"* [1970] rev. ed. (Dekalb, Ill., 1989).

5. Hans-Georg Gadamer, *Philosophical Hermeneutics* (Berkeley, 1976), 141.

6. Among the many historians of modern art who have made this interpretation, Roger Lipsey highlights it in his title, *An Art of Our Own,* which is drawn from Brancusi's remark in 1926 that "it is time we had an art of our own." (Boston, 1988), 244. Lipsey also quotes from Kandinsky's *Reminiscences* (1913), which records his search for an authentic art. "For many . . . years . . . I was like a monkey in a net; the

organic laws of construction tangled me in my desires, and only with great pain, effort, and struggle did I break through these 'walls around art.' Thus did I finally enter the realm of art, which like that of nature, science, political forms, etc., is a realm unto itself, is governed by its own laws proper to it alone" (41).

1 Waiting

1. On this and other Valadon nudes see Patricia Mathews, "Returning the Gaze: Diverse Representations of the Nude in the Art of Suzanne Valadon," *The Art Bulletin* (September, 1991): 415–430.

2. Valadon entered the art world first as a model, and her art was based on that experience. In her own nude paintings, as Rosemary Betterton argued, "she is both subject and object, viewer and viewed . . . in a way which begins to redefine and reconstruct the relationship of artist and model and, in turn, of spectator and image. "How Do Women Look? The Female Nude in the Work of Suzanne Valadon," in Rosemary Betterton, ed., *Looking On: Images of Femininity in the Visual Arts and Media* (London, 1987), 226. In 1927 Valadon did several full-body nude drawings of a female artist painting with one outstretched hand and holding a palette in the other. See Paul Pétridès, *L'Œuvre complète de Suzanne Valadon* (Paris, 1971), drawings 264–267.

3. Bram Dijkstra reproduced dozens of images of late Victorian women in states of collapse, sleep, and death and interpreted them as images of powerlessness created by the predominantly male artists of the time, who were threatened by the prospect of female sexuality. I view these images of passivity and waiting as much a record of how little women were allowed to do as well as an exorcism of what they might do. See Dijkstra, *Idols of Perversity: Fantasies of Feminine Evil in Fin-de-Siècle Culture* (New York, 1986), 25–82. For more sleeping Victorian women in art see Kenneth Bendiner, *An Introduction to Victorian Painting* (New Haven, 1985), 121–143.

4. These works are reproduced in Jeremy Maas, *Victorian Painters* (New York, 1969), 154–159.

5. There are a few male sleepers. In *The Dream* (1857) Fitzgerald's sleeping artist dreams of gold coins cascading into his pocket from the hands of an elf as he paints a beautiful woman. Ferdinand Hodler's tense nude male with hands clutched and head thrown back is shown in the predella of *The Dream* (1903) under the object of his dreaming—a woman kneeling in contemplation of a red flower. But most sleepers are women.

6. This painting is reproduced in Susan Casteras, *Images of Victorian Womanhood* (Cranbury, 1987), 58. Elsewhere she writes that all such images share "the underlying assumption of a thornless garden, an exiled haven or insular retreat in which the woman is left, deserted, or hidden, perhaps preferring to wait in seclusion for her fate to unfold." See her "Down the Garden Path: Courtship Culture and Its Imagery in Victorian Painting" (Ph.D. diss., Yale University, 1977), 115.

7. See John Horsley, *The Soldier's Farewell* (1853), Dante Gabriel Rossetti, *Re-*

gina Cordium (1866), and Jean-Léon Gérôme, *The Rose* (1887) and *Almeh at the Window of Her Moucharabieh* (1887).

8. For paintings of needlework see Richard Redgrave, *The Sempstress* (1846) and Charles Cope, *Life Well Spent* (1862). Cope's *Home Dreams* (1869) shows three waiting themes: a young woman has fallen *asleep* by a *window,* with *needlework* in her hands.

9. See Dante Gabriel Rossetti, *The Bower Meadow* (1872). Frank Potter's *Girl Resting at a Piano* (1880s) shows a woman who has grown as tired of life as of her music and stares blankly into the foreground and her future.

10. Jean Wyatt's interpretation of the moment prior to Jane's first meeting with Rochester is true of the nineteenth-century waiting woman generally. "Building on a girl's daily experience of the excitement injected into domestic routine by the return of her father from the glamorous outside world, this sequence of life suspended followed by life intensified upon the entrance of the hero encourages female readers to think of their time alone as mere prelude, perhaps even a necessary prelude: if they wait long enough, the right man will enter so life can begin. This waiting robs women's time alone of meaning, save that of preparation and expectation." "A Patriarch of One's Own: *Jane Eyre* and Romantic Love," *Tulsa Studies in Women's Literature* 4 (Fall, 1985): 203–204.

11. Vera Brittain, *Testament of Youth* (New York, 1978), 41.

12. Elizabeth Gaskell, *The Life of Charlotte Brontë* [1857] (Middlesex, England, 1975), 379.

13. The model for Ursula was Else von Richthofen, who was a schoolmistress at seventeen, paid for her own university education, and in 1900 was one of the first fully matriculated female students at Heidelberg. There she took a doctorate in economics in 1901. At Max Weber's home she met leaders of the Women's Movement in Germany. Martin Green, *The von Richthofen Sisters: The Triumphant and the Tragic Modes of Love* (New York, 1974), 16–17. In an address of 1902, one member of the University of Chicago faculty complained that when "men and women share the same quadrangle, sit side by side in the class-room, jostle each other in the halls and on the walks, cultivate interest in the same sports, form as far as possible a solid community, each sex loses something." Rosalind Rosenberg reinterprets this experience as a gain for each sex and offers it as evidence of historical change in her *Beyond Separate Spheres: Intellectual Roots of Modern Feminism* (New Haven, 1982), 78.

14. Cited in Frederick Lewis Allen, *Only Yesterday: An Informal History of the 1920s* (New York, 1931), 65.

2 Meeting

1. Alfred de Foville, *La Transformation des moyens de transport* (1880), 47, quoted in Eugen Weber, *France, Fin de Siècle* (Cambridge, Mass., 1986), 177.

2. Sandra M. Gilbert and Susan Gubar wrote: "Images of enclosure and escape . . . metaphors of physical discomfort manifested in frozen landscapes and fiery in-

teriors—such patterns recurred throughout this tradition [of nineteenth-century literature], along with obsessive depictions of diseases like anorexia, agoraphobia, and claustrophobia . . . Both in life and art . . . the artists we studied were literally and figuratively confined." Their description of the archetypical trembling Victorian heroine "who can't quite figure out the mansion's floor plan," is compelling, if exaggerated. *The Madwoman in the Attic: The Woman Writer and the Nineteenth-Century Literary Imagination* (New Haven, 1979), xi, 337.

3. Henry Adams, *The Education of Henry Adams: An Autobiography* (Boston, 1918), 444.

4. Ellen K. Rothman, *Hands and Hearts: A History of Courtship in America* (New York, 1984), 23.

5. Peter Gay views the meeting of Otto Beneke and Mariette Banks in 1841, like that of Walter Bagehot and Eliza Wilson in 1857, in the woman's home, as typical examples of this practice. *The Bourgeois Experience.* Vol. I, *Education of the Senses* (New York, 1984), 5–6.

6. Leonard Woolf met Virginia Stephen at gatherings of Cambridge University's Society of Apostles. When he left England for Ceylon in 1904 the Society would not admit women, but upon his return it did. He elaborates: "People who were born too late to experience in boyhood and adolescence the intellectual and moral pressure of Victorianism have no idea of the . . . fetters which weighed one down . . . To have discussed some subjects or to have called a spade a spade in the presence of Miss Strachey or Miss Stephen seven years before would have been unimaginable." Leonard Woolf, *Beginning Again: An Autobiography of the Years 1911 to 1918* (New York, 1963), 34–35.

7. A number of scholars have cautioned against facile generalizations about the impact of war on gender roles, in particular the durability of change once peace was restored. Margaret R. Higonnet and Patrice L.-R. Higonnet argue that "in the long run . . . the dynamic of gender subordination remains as it was" (35). I find that the war had a considerable effect of accelerating and focusing changes that were under way before it broke out but that continued after the peace. See Margaret R. Higonnet et al., *Behind the Lines: Gender and the Two World Wars* (New Haven, 1987).

3 Encounter

1. Thomas Hobbes, *De cive* (1642), VIII, 1.

2. John Locke, *Second Treatise on Government* (1688), ¶27.

3. René Descartes, *Discourse on Method* (1637) and *Meditations* (1641), in *The Philosophical Works of Descartes,* ed. Elizabeth S. Haldane and G. R. T. Ross (Cambridge, England, 1972), I, 101, 155, 186–192.

4. John Stuart Mill, *On Liberty* [1859] (New York, 1975), 3, 56, 11.

5. Max Scheler, *Zur Phänomenologie und Theorie der Sympathiegefühlen und von Liebe und Haas.* A second edition appeared in 1923 as *Wesen und Formen der Sympathie.* I used the 1954 English translation of that edition, *The Nature of Sym-*

pathy (Hamden, Conn., 1970), 244–247. Heidegger did not argue on the basis of childhood experience, because that evinced the chronological priority instead of the ontological priority that he sought. Numerous phenomenologists nevertheless appealed to early childhood experience as a compelling example of the primacy of relatedness over individuality.

6. He introduced the concept of "Das Zwischenmenschliche" in 1906 in an article with that title, which was translated as "Elements of the Interhuman" in Martin Buber, *Between Man and Man* (London, 1947).

7. Martin Buber, *I and Thou* [1923], tr. by Walter Kaufmann (New York, 1970), 53–78. In the text Kaufmann translated "Du" as "You." I have substituted "Thou" in his translations, because "You" does not capture the sense of intimacy carried by the familiar German "Du." He retained "Thou" in his title.

8. Heidegger uses "care" in a technical sense, which I explain briefly in my introduction to Chapter 5.

9. Ian Watt, *The Rise of the Novel* (Berkeley, 1957), 15.

10. The phrase comes from Richard Martin, *The Love That Failed: Ideal and Reality in the Writings of E. M. Forster* (The Hague, 1974), which is more nuanced than his title suggests, for he views *Howards End* and the other novels as unfulfilled projects of love rather than complete failures.

11. Stephen Kern, *The Culture of Time and Space: 1880–1918* (Cambridge, Mass., 1983), 65–81.

12. In "Down the Garden Path: Courtship Culture and Its Imagery in Victorian Painting" (Ph.D. diss., Yale University, 1977), Susan Casteras interpreted these symbols and supplied the source of Hunt's remark in John Guille Millais, *The Life and Letters of Sir John Everett Millais* (London, 1900), I, 136.

13. From *The Magazine of Art* (1878), quoted in Casteras, ibid., 234.

14. For this interpretation of the connection of love and art see Trygve Nergaard, "Despair," in Robert Rosenblum, ed., *Edvard Munch: Symbols and Images* (National Gallery of Art, Washington D.C., 1978), 113–141.

15. Vivian Endicott Barnett has documented some possible sources for the embryonic interpretation of these biomorphic forms in "Kandinsky and Science: The Introduction of Biological Images in the Paris Period," in the Guggenheim catalogue, *Kandinsky in Paris 1934–1944* (New York, 1985), 66 *ff.*

16. Wassily Kandinsky, *Point and Line to Plane* (New York, 1979), 65, 86–92, 120–121.

17. Sigmund Freud, "Civilization and Its Discontents," *The Standard Edition of the Complete Psychological Works of Sigmund Freud* (London, 1957), XXI, 66–67.

4 Embodiment

1. Husserl and Heidegger had surprisingly little to say about embodiment. In *Ideas II,* Husserl distinguished between the physical object of scientific study, *Körper,* and the lived body as subject, *Leib.* That work was published posthumously. He

began to consider the lived body to a limited extent in his later writings on the *Lebenswelt*. Heidegger briefly mentions the existential *directionality* (referring to left and right) as an aspect of Dasein's spatiality but declines to elaborate: "This 'bodily nature' hides a whole problematic of its own, though we shall not treat it here" (143).

2. Gabriel Marcel, *Metaphysical Journal* [1927] (Chicago, 1952), 241–287. He began to meditate on the problem of the body in January 1914.

3. Maurice Merleau-Ponty, *Phenomenology of Perception* [1945] (London, 1962, rev. 1979), 137, 98.

4. See "Man and Adversity," in Merleau-Ponty, *Signs* (Evanston, 1964), 226–227.

5. The classic example of such reductionism is Emil du Bois-Reymond, who in 1842 wrote that only "chemical-physical forces inherent in matter, reducible to the force of attraction and repulsion" will be allowed to explain the human organism. Thomas Huxley's article "On the Physical Basis of Life" (1868) argued that "digestion, respiration, thought, imagination . . . in the machine [of the body] naturally proceed from the mere arrangements of its organs, neither more nor less than do movements of a clock." For these and other sources on nineteenth-century materialism see Stephen Kern, *Anatomy and Destiny: A Cultural History of the Human Body* (New York, 1975), 67–79.

6. In *Body and Mind* (1870) the pioneer of British psychosomatic psychology, Henry Maudsley, protested "against the unjust and most unscientific practice of declaring the body vile and despicable, of looking down upon the highest and most wonderful contrivance of creative skill as something of which man dare venture to feel ashamed" (73). In *Point Counter Point* Huxley gave such an outlook to Lord Edward, "a fossil mid-Victorian child," who loved his young wife "timidly and very apologetically; apologizing for his ardours, apologizing for his body, apologizing for hers. Not in so many words . . . but by a silent pretending that the bodies weren't really involved in the ardours, which anyhow didn't really exist" (23).

7. Jeanne Fahnestock explains the more frequent appearance of heroines with "irregular features" after the mid-century by novelists' need to supply a growing reading audience with more believable characters than the "perfect" heroines of the early nineteenth century. The rise of photography also helped physiognomists to systematize and reproduce correlations between features and character. "The Heroine of Irregular Features: Physiognomy and Conventions of Heroine Description," *Victorian Studies*, 24 (Spring 1981): 325–350.

8. Elizabeth Gaskell recalled: "She [Charlotte] once told her sisters that they were wrong—even morally wrong—in making their heroines beautiful as a matter of course. They replied that it was impossible to make a heroine interesting on any other terms. Her answer was, 'I will prove to you that you are wrong; I will show you a heroine as plain and as small as myself, who shall be as interesting as any of yours.'" *The Life of Charlotte Brontë* (Harmondsworth, England, 1975), 308. Who

was right or wrong is not as historically interesting as the terms of the disagreement, because what they did not dispute was the importance of their dispute.

9. Alexander Walker, *Physiognomy Founded on Physiology* (1834), quoted in Fahnestock, "The Heroine of Irregular Features," 342.

10. Elisabeth G. Gitter surveys the Victorian obsession with women's head hair and its associated symbols and meanings: power (crown), vitality, eroticism, saintliness (aureole), innocence (blond), passion (brunette), protection and comfort (the "hair tent"), language (weaving), wealth (gold), duplicity (false hair), entrapment (mermaid, spider, web), strangling (noose), biting (snakes), strangling (coils). While one can interpret those many meanings as evidence of the Victorian imagination (Gitter laments how the twentieth century "divested women's hair of its complex and potent meanings"), I view the Victorians' obsession as a response to the restrictions of sexual morality. Victorians were obliged to pack all that meaning into a part of the body that was visible and at furthest remove from other parts of the body which that morality put off limits. "The Power of Women's Hair in the Victorian Imagination," *PMLA*, 99 (October 1984): 936–954.

11. In frontal nude portraits of the nineteenth century, pubic hair is conspicuously absent.

12. In *The Flesh Made Word: Female Figures and Women's Bodies* (New York, 1987), Helena Michie offers a perceptive interpretation of the hand and heart as a synecdochal chain between the man's formal request for the hand and his ultimate "entrance into the female body" (98–99).

13. Frederick Marryat, *A Diary in America* (Philadelphia, 1839), II, 45.

14. Throughout the nineteenth century there had been May Day, festival, and tournament queens, but none appeared in bathing suits. The public display of women in bathing suits for the first Miss America Contest in 1921 was facilitated by the influence of the director Mack Sennett, whose films included women in bathing suits. One of his stars was the competitive swimmer Mabel Normand. Promoters of the contest also staged swimming exhibitions to legitimize the bathing-suit competition. The Australian swimmer Annette Kellerman used her athletic ability and appearance to enhance her career in vaudeville and movies. The one-piece bathing suit she designed to cut down on water friction also exposed more of her body and was worn by many early contestants. Lois W. Banner, *American Beauty* (New York, 1983), 249–270.

15. Other paintings in which only the woman's tippy toes touch the water include Courbet, *Bather Sleeping by a Brook* (1845), *The Bathers* (1853), *The Source* (1862), and *The Three Bathers* (1868); Ingres, *The Source* (1856); Manet, *Surprised Nymph* (1861); Millet, *Goose Girl* (1863). Even two of the nymphs struggling to seduce a satyr in Bouguereau's *Nymphs and a Satyr* (1873) have only their toes in the pool.

16. Bram Dijkstra has reproduced a number of such creatures depicted between 1890 and 1911; *Idols of Perversity* (New York, 1986), 258–271.

17. Beatrice Farwell argues that Manet's "female nude was rendered fatally unlike any previous example, whether modern or old master, by the contemporary clothing of the men and the recognizable portraiture of all the models." "Manet's Bathers," *Arts Magazine,* 54 (May 1980): 127.

18. "Because of extensive government control of brothels by the end of the century, prostitutes carefully attended to rules concerning health and cleanliness. It is likely that the women had tubs in their rooms and that they bathed in front of their clients." Eunice Lipton, "Degas' Bathers: The Case for Realism," *Arts Magazine,* 54 (May 1980): 95. See also Eldon N. Van Liere, "Solutions and Dissolutions: The Bather in Nineteenth-Century French Painting," ibid, 104–114.

19. Claire Freches-Thorny, "Brittany, 1886–1890," in Richard Brettell et al., *The Art of Paul Gauguin* (Washington, 1988), 147.

20. See Sharon Latchaw Hirsh, "Carlo Carrà's 'The Swimmers'," *Arts Magazine,* 53 (January 1979): 122–129. The Symbolist Charles Laval's *The Bathers* (1888) is a possible precedent. It shows three women bobbing in rough surf, but they are not suited, not swimming, and are called "bathers." The women in Klimt's *Moving Waters* (1898) are fully immersed but not suited and not swimming, as they are rather swept along by the fast current. Klimt's *Water Serpents II* (1904) do not use their arms or kick and in fact seem to be drowning.

21. Latchaw Hirsh, "Carlo Carrà's '*The Swimmers,*'" 122–129; Victor Koshkin-Youritzin, "Thomas Hart Benton: 'Bathers' Rediscovered," *Arts Magazine,* 54 (May 1980): 98–102.

22. From J.[acques] P. Maygrier, [1822] *Midwifery Illustrated* (tr. New York, 1834), Plate #29.

23. Charles D. Meigs, *Females and Their Diseases* (Philadelphia, 1848), 19.

24. For a discussion of this trial and full citations see Virginia G. Drachman, "The Loomis Trial: Social Mores and Obstetrics in the Mid-Nineteenth Century," in Judith Walzer Leavitt, ed., *Women and Health in America* (Madison, 1984). According to Drachman, White's demonstration was "the first time in the United States that medical students had been permitted to observe a delivery" (166).

25. Hemingway explained where he got the idea for Jake's infirmity. "When I was in the Italian army I had been nicked in the scrotum by a piece of shrapnel and had spent some time in the genito-urinary ward and saw all those poor bastards who had had everything blown off." But Jake did not lose everything, "and that was very important to the kind of man he was. His testicles were intact. That was all he had, but this made him capable of feeling everything a normal man feels but not able to do anything about it." A. E. Hotchner, *Papa Hemingway* (New York, 1979), 49, 50. See also Wolfgang E. H. Rudat, *A Rotten Way to Be Wounded: The Tragicomedy of the Sun Also Rises* (New York, 1991).

26. See John Golding, "Picasso and Surrealism," in Roland Penrose and John Golding, eds., *Picasso in Retrospect* (New York, 1973), 77–121.

27. Following Darwin, interest in animal forbears included their reproductive processes, which among the lowest animals involved rudimentary olfaction. The

idea that a primordial olfactory tropism might persist among higher living forms inspired a number of studies of smell in human sexuality. Victorians approached the connection between smell and sex with considerable reserve. At the turn of the century a more forthright approach was pioneered by the German researcher Iwan Bloch (under the pseudonym Albert Hagen) in *Die sexuelle Osphresiologie: Die Beziehung des Geruchssinnes und der Gerüche zur menschlichen Geschlechtstätigkeit* (Breslau, 1900). On the history of smell in the nineteenth century see Stephen Kern, "Olfactory Ontology and Scented Harmonies," *Journal of Popular Culture,* 7 (Spring 1974): 816–824.

5 Desire

1. Franz Brentano, *Psychology from an Empirical Standpoint* [1874] (London, 1973), 88–89.

2. In *King Cadules* (1859) the King is so proud of his beautiful wife that he arranges for his friend Gyges to hide in their bedroom and watch her undress. The painting depicts the moment when the disrobed queen discovers that she has been observed. *A Roman Slave Market* (c.1884) shows an exquisite female slave hiding her eyes with a bent elbow while standing disrobed before an audience of ogling slave owners.

3. Degas identified the reigning prudishness about desire when he commented that Gérôme made this into a "pornographic picture" by depicting Phryné as "a poor, embarrassed wench who covers herself," when in reality she "was one of the glories of her time because of the beauty of her body." Quoted in Gerald M. Ackerman, *The Life and Work of Jean-Léon Gérôme* (London, 1986), 54–55. See also Joachim Heusinger von Waldegg, "Jean-Léon Gérômes 'Phryné vor den Richtern'," *Jahrbuch der Hamburger Kunstsammlungen,* 17 (1972): 122–142.

4. Linda Williams, *Figures of Desire: A Theory and Analysis of Surrealist Film* (Urbana, 1981), 53–105. Dali wrote that he intended the film to "carry each member of the audience back to the secret depths of adolescence, to the sources of dreams, destiny, and the secret of life and death." Quoted by Dawn Ades, *Dali and Surrealism* (New York, 1982), 50.

5. Dali's sexual concerns also appear in *The Great Masturbator* (1929), *The Enigma of Desire* (1929), and *The Birth of Liquid Desires* (1932).

6. William Acton, *The Functions and Disorders of the Reproductive Organs* (London, 1857). W. R. Greg opined that in men "the sexual desire is inherent and spontaneous, and belongs to the condition of puberty. In the other sex, the desire is dormant, if not non-existent, till excited; always till excited by intercourse"; in "Prostitution," *The Westminster Review,* 53 (April-July 1850): 456. George Napheys theorized: "A vulgar opinion prevails that [women] are creatures of like passions with ourselves; that they experience desires as ardent, and often as ungovernable, as those which lead to so much evil in our sex ... Nothing is more utterly untrue. Only in very rare instances do women experience one tithe of the sexual

feeling which is familiar to most men. Many of them are entirely frigid, and not even in marriage do they ever perceive any real desire." *The Transmission of Life: Counsels on the Nature and Hygiene of the Masculine Function* (Philadelphia, 1875), 173. John S. Haller and Robin M. Haller argue that Victorian women sublimated their desire into religious fervor, the only justifiable cover for renouncing the goal of childbearing, which everyone took to be their destiny but which repeatedly endangered their lives and stifled self-development. *The Physician and Sexuality in Victorian America* (Chicago, 1974). Nancy Cott argues that "passionlessness" was a norm that Victorian women adopted to enhance their power and self-respect, liberate themselves from the burdens and dangers of pregnancy and childbearing, free themselves from the inconsiderate, if not brutal, sexual passions of men, and redefine the grounds of their existence. "Passionlessness: An Interpretation of Victorian Sexual Ideology, 1790–1850," in Nancy Cott, ed., *A Heritage of Her Own* (New York, 1979), 162–181.

7. Martin Greene, *The von Richthofen Sisters* (New York, 1974), 362.

8. Ingres's *Vénus Anadyomène* (1848) gently holds her hair, as does Bouguereau's *Venus* and Eugène-Emmanuel Amaury-Duval's *La Naissance de Vénus* (1862). T. J. Clark, *The Painting of Modern Life* (Princeton, 1984), 127–131.

9. *Saint Augustine: Confessions* (Baltimore, 1961), 43, 55, 102. In *Adam, Eve, and the Serpent* (New York, 1989), Elaine Pagels emphasizes two distinctive features of Augustine's theology that contributed to Western Christendom's emphasis on original sin: (1) that Adam's act did not signify the free will at the heart of all ethical choice but rather the enslavement to lust that plunged him into the Fall; and (2) that Adam's Fall was not transmitted culturally as a bad example but biologically as a seminal infection.

10. The following letter of May 15, 1840 to Elizabeth Gaskell reveals the tortuous suspicion with which Charlotte Brontë viewed passionate desire: "Do not be overpersuaded to marry a man you can never respect—I do not say *love;* because, I think, if you can respect a person before marriage, moderate love at least will come after; and as to intense *passion,* I am convinced that is no desirable feeling. In the first place, it seldom or never meets with a requital; and in the second place, if it did, the feeling would be only temporary; it would last the honeymoon, and then, perhaps, give place to disgust, or indifference worse, perhaps, than disgust. Certainly, this would be the case on the man's part; and on the woman's—God help her, if she is left to love passionately and alone."

11. Huxley recreated such varieties among the several pairs of lovers in *Point Counter Point* (1928) and in the same year published a collection of essays, *Do What You Will*, which formalized his views. The essay "Fashions in Love" speculated that "the new twentieth-century conception of love is realistic," because it knows that "there is no such thing as Love with a large L, and that what the Christian romantics of the last century regarded as the uniquely natural form of love is . . . only one of the indefinite number of possible amorous fashions." He suggested several causes of the distinctively twentieth-century acceptance of the "diversity of love"—the shock

of World War I, the increasing practice of birth control, the scientific study of sex, D. H. Lawrence's "new mythology of nature," and Freud's theory that practices previously regarded as perverse were "statistically normal." *Collected Essays* (New York, 1958), 73.

12. Bram Dijkstra, *Idols of Perversity* (New York, 1986), 307.

13. Picabia's title, *Edtaonisl*, reconstructs language, like a Cubist reconstruction of visual experience. It was made with alternate letters from the first part of each of the two French words for star dancer *(étoile danseuse)*.

14. John Berger, *Ways of Seeing* (New York, 1977), 45–64; Norman Bryson, *Tradition and Desire: From David to Delacroix* (Cambridge, 1984) 69–70 *ff;* Wendy Steiner, *Pictures of Romance: Form Against Context in Painting and Literature* (Chicago, 1988).

15. *Webster's International Dictionary* (unabridged) gives another intriguing definition of a lay figure as "a puppet; one who serves the will of others without independent volition; a person or fictitious character of no marked individuality."

16. The many meanings of the mirror in Picasso and the Surrealists include the unconscious, the woman, truth, self-discovery, and desire. On these see Lydia Gasman, "Mystery, Magic and Love in Picasso, 1925–1938: Picasso and the Surrealist Poets" (Ph.D. diss., Columbia University, 1981), 1079–1192. For the erotic tie between artist and model see also Leo Steinberg, "Drawing as if to Possess," *Other Criteria* (New York, 1972), 174–192, and John Berger, Chapter 9, no. 29 below.

6 Language

1. Allan Janik and Stephen Toulmin, *Wittgenstein's Vienna* (New York, 1973).

2. Martin Buber, *I and Thou* (New York, 1970), 70

3. Macquarrie and Robinson explain that their translation of this sentence obscures the links between the German "hören" (to hear), "Hörigkeit" (bondage), and "zugehörig," which they translate as "in thrall." In English the noun "thrall" means a bondman, although there is an archaic verb form that means "enthrall." Heidegger unearths archaic varieties of root words to probe root experiences, such as the one for hearing that involves thralldom or listening with slavish devotion.

4. Ernest J. Simmons explains: "Throughout the notes [for *Crime and Punishment*] Dostoevski continually warns himself not to allow any expression of love on their part, which he obviously considered to be an artistic and psychological fault in this particular situation. A note such as the following is repeated in various forms. 'N.B. There is not a word of love between them. This is a *sine qua non.*'" *Dostoevski: The Making of a Novelist* (Oxford, 1940), 174.

5. George Eliot expressed a similar historical view in *Middlemarch*: "However slight the terrestrial intercourse between Dante and Beatrice or Petrarch and Laura, time changes the proportion of things, and in later days it is preferable to have fewer sonnets and more conversation" (249). Eliot's theory from 1872 compromises my periodization, but it affirms the logic of my history. Forster incorporates that histor-

ical logic into *Howards End* as the modernist Margaret tells the romantic (and unsuccessful) lover Helen: "There is the widest gulf between my love-making and yours. Yours was romance; mine will be prose—I'm not running it down—a very good kind of prose, but well considered, well thought out" (174).

6. Richardson is quoted by Sandra M. Gilbert and Susan Gubar in *No Man's Land: The Place of the Woman Writer in the Twentieth Century, The War of the Words* (New Haven, 1988), 248.

7. The sociologist William I. Thomas explained the difference by the separation of the sexes: "Men and women still form two distinct classes and are not in free communication with each other. Not only are women unable and unwilling to be communicated with directly, conventionally and truly on many subjects, but men are unwilling to talk to them. I do not have in mind situations involving questions of propriety and delicacy alone, but a certain habit of restraint, originating doubtless in matters relating to sex, extend[ing] to all intercourse with women, with the result that they are not really admitted to the intellectual world of men; and there is not only a reluctance on the part of men to admit them, but a reluctance—or rather, a real inability—on their part to enter." From "The Mind of Woman and the Lower Races" (1907), quoted in Rosalind Rosenberg, *Beyond Separate Spheres: Intellectual Roots of Modern Feminism* (New Haven, 1982), 129.

8. Some pictorial examples of communication between lovers include Sara Setchel, *The Momentous Question* (1842); Dante Gabriel Rossetti, *Beatrice, Meeting Dante at a Marriage Feast, Denies Him Her Salutation* (1852); Arthur Hughes, *Aurora Leigh's Dismissal of Romney* (Figure 52, 1860); Ford Madox Brown, *Take Your Son, Sir* (1851); Jacques Tissot, *The Farewell* (1871) and *Bad News (The Parting)* (1872); William Orchardson, *Her Mother's Voice* (1888); Marcus Stone, *An Appeal for Mercy* (1876); Vladimir Makovskii, *The Explanation* (1891).

9. The concept "too late" expresses the overwhelming dominion of public timetables for the uncompromising irreversibility of Victorian courtships. In *The Mill on the Floss* Maggie is tormented by anticipation of the consequences of her night on the river with Stephen. "But surmounting everything was the . . . dread lest her conscience should be benumbed again and not rise to energy till it was too late.—Too late! It was too late now, not to have caused misery—too late for everything, perhaps, but to rush away from the last act of baseness—the tasting of joys that were wrung from crushed hearts" (598).

10. Quoted in Werner Haftmann, *Painting in the Twentieth Century* (New York, 1965), I, 179.

11. For interpretation of the grillework I am indebted to Jack Flam, *Matisse: The Man and His Art, 1869–1918* (Ithaca, 1986), 250.

12. Sigmund Freud and Joseph Breuer, "On the Psychical Mechanism of Hysterical Phenomena: Preliminary Communication" [1893], in *Standard Edition*, II, 6.

13. It is difficult to understand how Peter Gay, who describes his method as "history informed by psychoanalysis," could conclude, with reference to Victorian sex, that "it would be a gross misreading of this experience to think that nineteenth-

century bourgeois did not know, or did not practice, or did not enjoy, what they did not discuss." *The Bourgeois Experience*. Vol. I, *Education of the Senses* (New York, 1984), 8, 458. One purpose of my chapter is to show, in accord with basic psychoanalytic theory, how inextricably linked knowing about, practicing, and enjoying sex are linked with talking about it.

14. Freud, "On the Universal Tendency to Debasement in the Sphere of Love," [1912] *Standard Edition*, XI, 189.

15. Although the word remains unspoken in the 1961 version, a passage in the Hans Walter Gabler edition of 1986 spells it out: "Do you know what you are talking about? Love, yes. Word known to all men." For the controversy surrounding this addition see Charles Rossman, "The New 'Ulysses': The Hidden Controversy," *New York Review of Books* (December 8, 1988): 53–58. Richard Ellman argued that this passage contains the clue to the "ultimate meaning" of the novel, which is love. *Ulysses on the Liffey* (New York, 1972), 147.

16. Stuart Gilbert, ed., *Letters of James Joyce* (New York, 1957), I, 135.

7 Disclosure

1. Zola recorded a similar fantasy of his own: "My bride should come to me straight from the hands of God; I should like her white, pure, but not yet living, and I should awaken her! She would draw from me the breath of life, she would know no one but me." Quoted in Frederick Hemmings, *Emile Zola* (Oxford, 1953), 141.

2. Effie Ruskin's wording modified slightly from her letter as quoted in Mary Luytens, *Millais and the Ruskins* (New York, 1967), 155–156.

3. For other works on the woman with a past see Rudolph Binion, "The Present Past" in *After Christianity* (Durango, 1986), 41–42.

4. Wharton's own traumatic wedding night was a consequence of her innocence, which she recreated in May Welland. Other than "a vague sense of contamination," Wharton's mother told her nothing, and, she noted, "this was literally all I knew of the process of generation till I had been married for several weeks." From "Life and I," quoted in Peter Gay, *The Bourgeois Experience*. Vol. I, *Education of the Senses* (New York, 1984), 401.

5. Susan Casteras' interpretation of this painting is accompanied by other examples of devastating disclosures in Victorian art such as E. H. Corbould's, *The Unhappy Discovery* (1857) and Marcus Stone's, *The Letter: An Appeal for Mercy* (1876). "Down the Garden Path: Courtship Culture and its Imagery in Victorian Painting" (Ph.D. diss., Yale University, 1977), 401–420.

6. Quoted in Hemmings, *Emile Zola*, 28. In fact this notion of sexual transmission is not as outmoded as it may sound, because a woman does in fact manufacture antibodies against male sperm, whether or not impregnation occurs. These antibodies, however, do not affect her "entire" being.

7. O. S. Fowler, *Love and Parentage Applied to the Improvement of Offspring* (New York, 1846), 27, 28.

8. B. A. Morel, *Traité des dégénérescences physiques, intellectuelles et morales de l'espèce humaine* (Paris, 1857). Nordau argued that when an organism becomes debilitated, its successors form "a new sub-species which . . . possesses the capacity of transmitting to its offspring, in a continuously increasing degree, its peculiarities, these being morbid deviations from the normal form—gaps in development, malformations and infirmities." *Degeneration* (tr. New York, 1895), 16.

9. In fact some fetal blood does leak through the placenta, and pregnant women form antibodies against that blood. If a second child has a different Rh factor, those antibodies may attack its blood cells and kill it, but the woman's antibodies do not affect her genetic makeup or that of any subsequent child.

10. Eduard von Hartmann, "Die Gleichstellung der Geschlechter," in *Moderne Probleme* (Leipzig, 1886), 44–45.

8 Kissing

1. In the following art works both lovers have their eyes closed or posed out of view: Ingres, *Paolo and Francesca* (1819); Rossetti, *Paolo and Francesca de Rimini* (1855); Rodin, *The Kiss* (1887); and Ford M. Brown, *Romeo and Juliet* (1870).

2. Eugen Weber points out that the scarcity and expense of Victorian dentists and the consequent bad teeth and overcharged stomachs made it likely "that most heroes and heroines of nineteenth-century fiction had bad breath, like their real-life models." *France, Fin de Siècle* (Cambridge, Mass., 1986), 61.

3. Hardy was subjected to censorship pressures. In the serial edition of *Tess* in 1891 his publisher insisted that the scene in which Angel carries Tess and two girl friends in his arms across a flooded road was too sexually suggestive. Hardy changed the transportation to a wheelbarrow that Angel found improbably sitting beside the road.

4. The more prosaic "genital kiss" referred euphemistically to simple cunnilingus. The term was used by the Dutch gynecologist Theodore Van de Velde in his best-selling and widely translated *Ideal Marriage: Its Physiology and Technique* (1926). Although he condemned such "kissing" to bring a woman to orgasm, he recommended it as foreplay, especially to induce lubrication.

5. This image of veiled faces has autobiographical origins in his mother's suicide by drowning in 1912, when Magritte was thirteen years old. When they retrieved her body a nightgown was wrapped around her face. A number of Magritte's other paintings contain veiled female figures. This trauma itself does not, to be sure, entirely explain the original way he transformed it into art, his adaptation of it to the surrealist agenda, and its appeal to viewers, critics, and art historians ever since. On the impact of this trauma see Mary Mathews Gedo, "Meditations on Madness: The Art of René Magritte," in Dawn Ades, ed., *In the Mind's Eye* (New York, 1986), 62–80.

6. For this dating and historical background of Rodin's sculpture see Albert E. Elsen, *The Gates of Hell by Auguste Rodin* (Stanford, 1985).

7. I am indebted to Sidney Geist's *Brancusi/The Kiss* (New York, 1978) for his interpretation of contrasts between these works as a watershed between two artistic eras.

8. Similar to the experiences that inform the Picasso and the Magritte, a personal experience may account for Brancusi's artistic preoccupation with the kiss. In a Brancusi studio photograph of 1905 there is a small sculpture of a woman turning away from a man trying to kiss her, which Geist named *The Rebuff*. Geist further speculated that it represented a traumatic rejection "in the real or dream life of Brancusi" that he reworked in sculpture for thirty years with the opposite result—*the kiss consummated*—in increasing harmony and union. Ibid., 41 and *passim*.

9. For the conversation from which this quotation is taken, see ibid., 76.

9 Gender

1. Friedrich Nietzsche, *Thus Spoke Zarathustra* (New York, 1966), 189.

2. Quoted in Rosalind Rosenberg, *Beyond Separate Spheres: Intellectual Roots of Modern Feminism* (New Haven, 1982), 12.

3. In 1849 A. A. Berthold removed the testicles of a rooster and transplanted them under the skin, thereby severing the duct for external secretion, but the effect was not that of castration. The testicles continued to produce secretions that continued to regulate sexual characteristics. The term "internal secretion" was coined by the French researcher Brown-Séquard in 1855, but research proceeded slowly and did not influence popular thinking about gender character until around 1900. Louis Berman, *The Glands Regulating Personality* (New York, 1921), 32–33, 134.

4. Michel Foucault, ed., *Herculine Barbin: Being the Recently Discovered Memoirs of a Nineteenth-Century French Hermaphrodite* (New York, 1980).

5. Franz von Neugebauer, "Interessante Beobachtung aus dem Gebiete des Scheinzwittertumes," *Jahrbuch für sexuelle Zwischenstufen,* IV (1902). Neugebauer personally treated 33 cases of hermaphroditism. In "Zusammenstellung der Literatur über Hermaphroditismus beim Menschen," ibid. (1904): 471–670, he surveyed 2,072 publications on hermaphroditism from the perspectives of embryology, comparative anatomy, botany, anthropology, mythology, pathological anatomy, endocrinology, forensic medicine, psychiatry, art, literature, philosophy, and religion.

6. L. A. S. M. von Römer, "Ueber die androgynische Idee des Lebens," *Jahrbuch für sexuelle Zwischenstufen,* V (1903): 715.

7. Charles Darwin, *The Origin of Species and the Descent of Man* (New York, n.d.), 525.

8. Wilhelm Fliess, *Die Beziehungen zwischen Nase und weiblichen Geschlechtsorganen* (Leipzig, 1897), iv.

9. Otto Weininger, *Sex and Character* (New York, 1906), 5.

10. Rosa Mayreder, *Zur Kritik der Weiblichkeit* (Jena, 1905), 33.

11. Sigmund Freud, "Three Essays on the Theory of Sexuality," *Standard Edition,* VII, 141, 219.

12. Carl Jung, "The Relation Between the Ego and the Unconscious" [1928], in *Two Essays on Analytical Psychology* (Cleveland, 1956), 198–223.

13. Quoted in Rosenberg, *Beyond Separate Spheres,* 234.

14. On the macroscopic level, as Leo Steinberg has argued, between 1840 and 1910 the image of Christ in art becomes "increasingly cloying, effeminate, and effete" as a consequence of reducing the meaning of Christ to "the single specialized function of loving-kindness." "No earlier Christ conceived in the Christian universe had been so deficient, so disqualified in terms of values actually held. The American Christ image in 1900 is at the furthest remove from what in man is felt to be worthy. The he-man who admires himself for being rugged, self-reliant, self-made, red-blooded, two-fisted, etc., visualizes a Christ whom he rejects in his guts." Leo Steinberg, "Objectivity and the Shrinking Self," *Other Criteria* (New York, 1972), 317–318.

15. After the hero/heroine of Woolf's *Orlando,* who is a man for the first thirty years of his life, is suddenly transformed into a woman, she undergoes similar humiliations. "She remembered how, as a young man, she had insisted that women be obedient, chaste, scented, and exquisitely apparelled." Now she has to follow a tedious discipline to fake these dubious virtues—an hour at the hairdresser, another hour at her looking-glass, staying and lacing, washing and powdering, constant changing clothes, and remaining chaste (98).

16. There is a striking precedent for Musil's brother-sister approach to gender roles in Rilke's letter of 1903 to a young poet: "And perhaps the sexes are more related than we think, and the great renewal of the world will perhaps consist in this, that man and maid, freed from all false feelings and reluctances, will seek each other not as opposites, but rather as brother and sister, as neighbors, and will come together *as human beings,* in order simply, seriously and patiently to bear in common the difficult sex that has been laid upon them." Rainer Maria Rilke, *Letters to a Young Poet* (New York, 1954), 38–39.

17. George M. Beard, *Sexual Neurasthenia* (New York, 1884), 106.

18. "By 1900 . . . medicine began to specify and narrow the definition of the sexual and to distinguish and classify sexual deviations in ever more discrete categories, particularly in the case of men. While early investigators had maintained that male sexual inversion involved transvestism, effeminacy, and such unmasculine characteristics as the inability to whistle, as well as sexual desire for men instead of women, Havelock Ellis and other writers tried at the turn of the century to redefine male sexual inversion in narrowly sexual terms." George Chauncey, Jr., "From Sexual Inversion to Homosexuality: Medicine and the Changing Conceptualization of Female Deviance," *Salmagundi* (Fall 1982–Winter 1983): 122.

19. Freud, "Three Essays on the Theory of Sexuality," *Standard Edition,* VII, 136.

20. In "The Intermediate Sex" Edward Carpenter insisted that homosexuals were "superior to the normal men . . . in respect of their love-feeling, which is gentler, more sympathetic, more considerate . . . than that of ordinary men." In Donald Cory, ed., *Homosexuality: A Cross Cultural Approach* (New York, 1956), 203.

21. Revelations about actual hermaphrodites (with gonads containing ovarian and testicular tissue) rather accented the value of sexual difference. These misfits desperately turned to drugs and surgery to wipe out either their quasi-masculinity or quasi-femininity and reach the haven of normalcy with just one sex. Earl Lind's autobiography (written in 1899, published in 1918) recorded his misery that only abated when at the age of twenty-eight he was surgically "castrated" to allow the emergence of the "woman's soul" that he believed had been erroneously lodged in his male body. *Autobiography of an Androgyne* (New York, 1918).

22. See note 6 above.

23. A. J. L. Busst, "The Image of the Androgyne in the Nineteenth Century," in Ian Fletcher, ed., *Romantic Mythologies* (London, 1967), 23.

24. On the official *Salon de 1869* and Paul Casimir Perier's critique of it see Joseph C. Sloane, *French Painting Between the Past and the Present: Artists, Critics, and Traditions, from 1848 to 1870* (Princeton, 1951), 139 *ff.*

25. Busst, "Image of the Androgyne," 38–39.

26. Ibid., 45–46.

27. My commentary on the influence of Péladan on this painting is indebted to William R. Oleander's "Fernand Khnopff 'Art or the Caresses'," *Arts Magazine, 52* (January 1978): 95–105.

28. Quoted in ibid., 18.

29. John Berger concluded that Picasso's sculpture is of the "shared subjectivity" of the sex act and is "purer and simpler and more expressive than any comparable works in the history of European art." *The Success and Failure of Picasso* (New York, 1965), 162.

30. Gaile Ann Haessly has made some exact counts of the times the head appears to document her indispensable study of the importance of this image in "Picasso on Androgyny: From Symbolism Through Surrealism" (Ph.D. diss., Syracuse University, 1983).

10 Power

1. Maudemarie Clark makes a clear distinction between these two uses in *Nietzsche on Truth and Philosophy* (New York, 1990), 205–244.

2. If *"Macht"* had been translated as "might" instead of "power," the association with "made" would have been more apparent.

3. In *The Second Sex* Simone de Beauvoir challenged one classic Marxist explanation for the oppression of women: according to Frederick Engels, it had been a consequence of the invention of bronze tools. "If the human consciousness had not included the original category of the Other and an original aspiration to dominate the Other, the invention of the bronze tool could not have caused the oppression of woman." *The Second Sex* [1949] (New York, 1989), 58. This pinpoints her phenomenological approach to those "original" (fundamental) categories of human existence which are shared by men and women and make possible gender modes and

historical variants of categories such as patriarchal domination. Her explication of this fundamental "imperialism of the human consciousness" is based on Sartre's philosophy of human relations, itself influenced by Nietzsche's will to power.

4. The right of the husband to force his wife had rarely been enforced in years just prior to 1891, but its abrogation nevertheless marks a step toward woman's appropriation of power over her own body. W. Lyon Blease, *The Emancipation of English Women* (London, 1910), 121.

5. For these symbols and historical precedents see "Gustave Moreaus 'Ödipus'— ein Kind seiner Zeit," in Toni Stoss, *Gustave Moreau Symboliste* (Zurich, 1981), 71–102. Bram Dijkstra found a similar periodization for images of Salome which first minimized her power and then accented it. "The Salomes who, in paintings of the 1870s by Henry Regnault, Alfred Stevens, and Benjamin Constant, had still been shown waiting in anecdotal, Orientalist fashion, with or without chargers in their laps but certainly always without the saint's head, now [c. 1895] began to carry around the bloody trophy." *Idols of Perversity: Fantasies of Feminine Evil in Fin-de-Siècle Culture* (New York, 1986), 382.

6. For these personal and other artistic influences see Jaroslaw Leshko, "Oskar Kokoschka's 'Knight Errant'," *Arts Magazine* (January 1982): 126–133.

7. Mark Girouard, *The Return to Camelot: Chivalry and the English Gentleman* (New Haven, 1981), 289.

8. Sandra M. Gilbert, "Soldier's Heart: Literary Men, Literary Women, and the Great War," *Signs*, 8 (Spring 1983): 429.

9. Leo Steinberg, "Picasso's Sleepwatchers," *Other Criteria* (New York, 1972), 101. The idea of contrasting this tradition with Picasso came from this article.

10. On other women sleeping in Victorian art see Chapter 1, n. 2 above.

11. Nina Auerbach, *Woman and the Demon: The Life of a Victorian Myth* (Cambridge, Mass., 1982), 17. Auerbach's argument, however, is about the subtext of narratives that are synonymous with the subjugation of powerless women under the gaze of overpowering men. Moreover, these men do not love their female subjects but seek to regulate their considerable artistic, life-giving, or libidinal power.

11 Others

1. Gabriel Compayré, *The Intellectual and Moral Development of the Child* (New York, 1896), 258; Georgiana B. Kirby, *Transmission, or Variation of Character Through the Mother* (New York, 1877), 11; Paul Möbius, *Geschlecht und Kinderliebe* (Marburg, 1904).

2. Sigmund Freud, "Introductory Lectures on Psycho-Analysis," *Standard Edition*, XVI, 329.

3. His explanation of this technique began with a critique of conventional techniques and might be seen as a critique of paintings such as Hayllar's—"pictures that seem . . . to be congealed on their immobile surfaces." The "secret depth" of his transparencies enabled him to express his "inner intentions" and to "remain under

[his] picture and not on top of it." Quoted in Maria Lluïsa Borràs, *Picabia* (New York, 1985), 340.

4. In a letter to Wilhelm Fliess of August 1, 1899, Freud wrote that every sexual act is "a process in which four individuals are involved." Although the four referred to were the male-male, male-female, female-female, and female-male bisexual composites that Fliess believed made up all adult personalities and explained sexual attraction, the idea of two other persons being present conjured up Freud's own emphasis on the continuing influence of parental models on the child's sexual development. Jeffrey Masson, ed., *The Complete Letters of Sigmund Freud and Wilhelm Fliess 1887–1904* (Cambridge, Mass., 1985), 364.

5. Freud, "The Future of an Illusion," *Standard Edition*, XXI, 41.

6. Although Jane agonizes about this choice, this quotation documents a conviction of God's wisdom behind her choosing and contrasts with the modernists emphasis on the absolute personal responsibility and loneliness of authentic choosing. Kierkegaard's insistence on the personal responsibility and loneliness of true Christian faith was not typical of popular religion in his time or since.

7. The pervasive religiosity of love is evident even in the writings of David and Mable Loomis Todd (1878–1881). Her strange diary of sex with David (including what day they had sex, who climaxed, and in what sequence) Peter Gay cites as unusual but revealing evidence of bourgeois Victorians' "enthusiasm for sexuality." Mable referred to sex as "a little *Heaven*" and "a sweet *communion*" and thanked God for *"giving"* her such a passionate husband. When she was pregnant David called her "*sacred, holy* mother." Quoted in Peter Gay, *The Bourgeois Experience*. Vol. I, *Education of the Senses*, 89, 83, 99, 88 (italics added). These terms, I would argue, not only invoke a generous, merciful God but also conjure up antithetical meanings—*Hell, excommunication, taking, profane,* and *unholy.* As Freud theorized, such are the instincts and their vicissitudes.

8. "Then spake Jesus again unto them, saying, I am the light of the world: he that followeth me shall not walk in darkness, but shall have the light of life" (John 8:12).

9. On Hunt's two paintings see Susan Casteras, "Down the Garden Path: Courtship Culture and Its Imagery in Victorian Painting" (Ph.D. diss., Yale University, 1977), 421–471.

12 Jealousy

1. A distinctive feature of existential philosophy was a growing appreciation of the constitutive function of seeming negativities, privations, and deficiencies in human existence. Kierkegaard's search for Christian faith involved recognition of the despair which is "sickness unto death," an estrangement of the self from the self. Nietzsche grounded his philosophy on a criticism of Christian self-hatred and contemporary "will to nothingness." Heidegger identified "being-towards-death" as the existential which most fully revealed the meaning of existence. Sartre approached

the "nothingness" at the heart of human existence by examining its "concrete" aspects such as absence, vertigo, nausea, and boredom which sensuously reveal "being-for-itself" as indeterminate, fluid, contingent, and free.

2. Mary Wood-Allen, *What a Young Woman Ought to Know* (Philadelphia, 1898), 154.

3. In 1859 an American attorney made the first full invocation of the "unwritten law" to justify homicide perpetrated by a jealous husband. There were fewer than thirty more such cases until the end of the century, but the logic of the legal precedent was based on the presumption that jealousy was a form of mental illness. By 1900 the persuasiveness of this argument was diminishing. Peter N. Stearns, *Jealousy: The Evolution of an Emotion in American History* (New York, 1989), 28–30. The legitimacy of the duel and the "satisfaction" it was supposed to achieve were based on similar values and followed a synchronous historical decline. Beginning in the 1870s German army officers began to be disciplined for dueling; in 1902 anti-dueling societies were established in Germany and Austria; by 1905 dueling was "running to seed" in France; after 1918 it became illegal in the Weimar Republic. Linked as it had been with hereditary aristocracy and military codes of honor all across Europe, the duel was wiped out during the First World War. V. G. Kiernan, *The Duel in European History: Honour and the Reign of Aristocracy* (New York, 1988), 250, 281, 318. Fontane treated Innstetten's duel in *Effi Briest* as a senseless archaic heritage, and Mann concluded *The Magic Mountain,* just before the outbreak of war in 1914, with a burlesque duel between two Poles over an insult to a man's wife.

4. Munch wrote of the landscape as a symbol of his own life: "Down here by the beach, I feel that I find an image of myself—of life—of my life. The strange smell of seaweed reminds me of her . . . In the dark green water I see the color of her eyes . . . And life is like that silent surface [of the horizon] which reflects the light, clear colors of the air. And underneath, in the depths—it conceals the depths—with its slime—its crawling creatures—like death. We understand each other. It is as though no one understands me better than the ocean." Quoted in Trygve Nergaard, "Despair," in Robert Rosenblum, ed., *Edvard Munch Symbols & Images,* National Gallery of Art (Washington, D. C., 1978), 131.

5. Haynes King's *Jealousy and Flirtation* (1874) and Ferdinand Fagerlin's *Die Eifersüchtige* (1895) have similar compositions: a woman flirts shamelessly with a man in full view of another jealous woman.

6. Munch intended to use this image to represent a basic emotion, as indicated by one of his notes on the painting: "Jealousy—a long, barren seashore." Quoted in Rosenblum, ed., *Edvard Munch,* 80.

7. The jealous man in Figure 41 was Jappa Nilssen, a teenage journalist who had an affair with Oda Krohg in the summer of 1891. Reinhold Heller, *Munch: His Life and Work* (Chicago, 1984), 74.

8. This interpretation exceeds the emotional elasticity of Munch himself, who was in fact tormented by jealousy. He and other members of a bohemian circle in Kristiania were inspired by the free love philosophy of Hans Jaeger but unable to

handle the jealousy that was rampant in the love triangles designed to make it a reality. In a more desperate mood Munch subsequently painted *Jealousy* (1895), which shows a contemporary Adam and Eve standing under an apple tree. The woman has bright red hair and wears a blood-red robe open down the front, exposing her breasts and pubis. In the foreground the jealous man (in fact Hans Jaeger) stares despairingly out toward the viewer. Munch, like all the avant-garde, was transitional.

9. In "Notes by the Author," Joyce explained that Richard's cultivation of his own jealousy was intended "to achieve that union [of love] in the region of the difficult, the void, and the impossible." *Exiles*, 114.

13 Selfhood

1. After God took a rib out of Adam and with it made woman, Adam said: "This *is* now bone of my bones, and flesh of my flesh: she shall be called Woman, because she was taken out of Man" (Gen. 2:23–24).

2. Denis de Rougemont comments that in *Tristan and Isolde* "music alone . . . can harmonize the plaint of the two voices, and make of it a single plaint" and convey "the transcendental interaction, the wildly contradictory and contrapuntal character of the passion of Darkness." *Love in the Western World* [1940] (New York, 1974), 229–230.

3. Pseudo-scientific foundation for this apotheosis of fusion was offered by researchers who argued that women became hysterical because their wombs were not regularly bathed by semen and that men and women commingled their selves by having sex, kissing, breathing the same air, or possibly even by the very presence of another person through some "animal-magnetism." John S. Haller, Jr., and Robin M. Haller, *The Physician and Sexuality in Victorian America* (Urbana, 1974), 112–115.

4. Willoughby Patterne's name comes from willow-pattern ware (an English porcelain depicting a pair of lovers, from a Chinese legend, who meet by a willow tree) and suggests "pattern," which contrasts with the one-of-a-kind personality we would expect in a genuine egoist.

5. David McWhirter surveys the evidence for James's identity behind this character in *Desire and Love in Henry James: A Study of the Late Novels* (Cambridge, 1989), 158–161.

6. Jean E. Kennard interprets *Ann Veronica*, *The Egoist*, and *A Room with a View* as subverting the rhetoric of female maturity that fills their pages by having that maturity come from the heroine choosing the better of two suitors and compromising her selfhood by seeking to lose herself in his. Clara chooses Vernon over Willoughby, Lucy chooses George over Cecil, and Ann Veronica chooses Capes over Manning. See Chapter 6, "Her Transitory Self," *Victims of Convention* (Hamden, Connecticut, 1978), 136–157.

7. Some Victorian women were so ashamed at seeing themselves naked that

some wealthier among them used special powders to cloud their bath water so that they might not catch a morally corrupting reflection of themselves as they stepped in or a clear vision of their body once submerged. Anne Martin-Fugier, "Bourgeois Rituals" in Michelle Perrot, ed., *A History of Private Life: From the Fires of Revolution to the Great War* (Cambridge, Mass., 1990), 460.

8. Woolf was aware of at least one historical precedent for this arrangement— that of William Godwin and Mary Wollstonecraft, who agreed to remain unmarried and maintain separate residences. When Mary became pregnant, however, they married but retained separate working rooms and social lives. They, like Woolf, were ahead of their times, only more so. See Woolf's essay "Mary Wollstonecraft" in *The Common Reader: Second Series* (New York, 1932).

9. Martin Green suggests some biographical and cultural determinants for Ursula's rejection of Skrebensky. "In 'Authority and Autonomy in Marriage,' an essay written in 1909, Marianne [Weber] insists that women too now feel the need to work with men, to build together with them . . . This is the drive that sends Ursula Brangwen out into the 'Widening Circles' of *The Rainbow,* a drive felt by both Else and [Lawrence's future wife] Frieda von Richthofen." *The von Richthofen Sisters* (New York, 1974), 220.

14 Proposal

1. Susan Casteras lists ninety proposal scenes in art from 1810 to 1904 in "Down the Garden Path: Courtship Culture and Its Imagery in Victorian Painting" (Ph.D. diss., Yale University, 1977), Appendix XI.

2. Graham Reynolds in *Victorian Painting* (New York, 1966), first assigned the title of *The Proposal* to this painting. In a second edition of 1987 he retitled it *The Lovers' Seat*. The couple shown is Shelley and Mary Godwin. Reynolds, following a remark made by Frith himself, interprets the scene as a moment in their courtship, but the painting also suggests the culmination of a courtship in a typical proposal scene such as can be found in numerous art works from that time.

3. Even though Chagall did not title his painting (Blaise Cendrars did), he accepted the title, and I believe he associated the scene with his own unconventional views on courtship ritual.

4. See George Leslie's *Ten Minutes to Decide* (1867) in Casteras, "Down the Garden Path," 520. Some Victorian women took an exceedingly long time, as for example Clara or Bathsheba, but their swains Willoughby and Boldwood are humiliated precisely because in their time quick replies were expected.

5. In *Interiors II* (1911) Chagall showed a similar scene with a woman jumping across a table onto the man's chest, gripping his beard with her right hand, and inserting her index finger into his mouth. The force of her rush has also broken his lamp.

6. In one town, "when a boy and a girl want to show that they love each other, they spit into each other's mouths." In another town such an exchange of spit secures

an engagement. Paul Sébillot, *Coutumes populaires de la haute Bretagne* (Paris, 1886), 105, cited in Martine Segalen, *Love and Power in the Peasant Family* (Chicago, 1983), 16. Franz Meyer speculates, with regard to the painting *Dedicated to My Fiancée,* that "the spittle which, like the froth of overflowing vitality, is spewed from the woman's mouth onto her partner's face—'diabolical spittle,' Chagall calls it—symbolizes the incendiary essence of life." *Marc Chagall* (New York, n.d.), 135. It also conjures up the scandalous intimacy that Joyce evokes in *Ulysses* when during a passionate kiss Bloom takes into his mouth a piece of Molly's "seedcake warm and chewed."

7. The actual proposal of Leonard to Virginia Woolf was singularly modern. Leonard was a Colonial Administrator in Ceylon from 1904 to 1911. In July of 1911 he met Virginia back in London; by January 1912, in the midst of an intense courtship, he wrote her: "God, I see the risk in marrying anyone & certainly me. I am selfish, jealous, cruel, lustful, a liar & probably worse still . . . I felt I could never control these things with a woman who was inferior & would gradually infuriate me by her inferiority & submission. You may be vain, an egotist [and] untruthful as you say [but] we like the same kinds of things & people, we are both intelligent and above all it is realities which we understand & which are important to us." This is smug but modern. He scrupulously surveys his own faults *and hers;* he appreciates the perils of excessive submission, the importance of shared values, and the need for equal intelligence and an understanding of "reality." On April 29, four days after his resignation, Virginia expressed her doubts because he was ruining his career for her, because she refused to look upon marriage as a profession, and because she sometimes felt "that no one ever has or even can share—something." When she considers marrying him she wonders, "is it the sexual side of it that comes between us? As I told you brutally the other day, I feel no physical attraction in you. There are moments—when you kissed me the other day was one—when I feel no more than a rock." Clive Bell, *Virginia Woolf: A Biography* (New York, 1972), I, 181–185. On May 29, 1912, after almost a year of such conscientious negotiations, she agreed to marry.

8. According to the German philosopher Eduard von Hartmann, this climacticality was particularly true for the woman. "Only once can woman learn practically what love is . . . A second blossom may unfold from a maiden's heart if the first has withered, but its full flowering only occurs when the love first aroused within her runs its course undisturbed." "Die Gleichstellung der Geschlechter," *Moderne Probleme* (Leipzig, 1886), 46–47.

9. The pathos of her brief moment of power is vividly manifest in painting. Casteras refers to five paintings between 1845 and 1886 with the same title—*Yes or No?* Other titles reflecting the limits of woman's consent include S. A. Hart's *Hesitation: Yes or No?* (1866), E. Squire's *Hoping for the "Yes" Word* (1872), A. Weitsz's *"Will She or Won't She?"* (1872), and E. Harris's *Between Yes and No* (1893). See her "Down the Garden Path," pp. 582–584. That moment of decision was of great interest to the larger Victorian art world. Millais's *Yes or No?* (1871) triggered such a

a public outcry that in 1875 he painted an answer, titled *No!* He further capitulated to public disappointment over that negative answer by painting a happier one two years later. It was titled *Yes!*

10. One Victorian manners book codified the contrast between the gentleman's choosing and what the lady is permitted to do. "A lady's choice is only negative— that is to say, she may love, but she cannot declare her love; she must wait. It is hers, when the time comes, to consent or decline, but till the time comes she must be passive." The gentleman's rights are greater. "A man may, and he will learn his fate at once, openly declare his passion, and obtain his answer. In this he has great advantage over the lady." Richard A. Wells, *Manners, Culture and Dress of the Best American Society* (Springfield, Mass., 1891), 225–226.

15 Wedding

1. "Its base was a square of blue cardboard representing a temple with porticos and colonnades and adorned on all sides with stucco statuettes standing in niches spangled with gold-paper stars. The second tier was a medieval castle in *gâteau de Savoie,* surrounded by miniature fortifications of angelica, almonds, raisins, and orange sections. And finally, on the topmost layer—which was a green meadow, with rocks, jelly lakes, and boats of hazelnut shells—a little Cupid was swinging in a chocolate swing. The tips of the two uprights, the highest points of the whole, were two real rosebuds" (32).

2. Dora and Erwin Panofsky, *Pandora's Box: The Changing Aspects of a Mythical Symbol* (New York, 1956).

3. Robert Graves recalled his own resentment over his wedding in 1918 and that of his bride, the feminist Nancy Nicolson. "Nancy had read the marriage-service for the first time that morning and been so disgusted that she all but refused to go through with the wedding." During the ceremony Nancy "savagely" muttered her responses, while Graves shouted them out in a parade-ground voice. *Good-Bye to All That* [1929] (New York, 1957), 272.

4. *The Complete Letters of Vincent Van Gogh* (Greenwich, 1959), III, 26.

5. Other Cubist weddings, such as Chagall's *The Wedding* (1910) and Duchamp's *The Passage from Virgin to Bride* (1912), show a similar emphasis on harmonizing line, color, and form rather than on telling a story or judging the morality of a specific wedding.

6. Ellen K. Rothman, *Hands and Hearts: A History of Courtship in America* (New York, 1984), 175, 282–284.

7. Laurence Lerner, *Love and Marriage: Literature and Its Social Context* (London, 1979), 156. Frank Kermode wrote that in *The Rainbow* Lawrence offered "an account of the intoxication of early married love unmatched in fiction." *D. H. Lawrence* (New York, 1973), 44.

8. The major influence on such a change in awareness of the erotic nature of nursing was Freud. Although he did not exactly discover the sexual nature of the

nursing, whether the infant's *Wonnesaugen* (rapturous sucking) or the mother's own erotic satisfaction from her baby's sucking, he interpreted and popularized the larger significance of that reciprocal sexual pleasure in the development of the mother-child relationship, particularly in the genesis of the Oedipus complex. On this see my article "Freud and the Discovery of Child Sexuality," *History of Childhood Quarterly,* 1 (Summer 1973): 119–141.

16 Sex

1. Images of confined women pervade Victorian culture. In *A Doll's House* Ibsen characterized Nora as like "a squirrel in a cage." Coventry Patmore's ideal wife was an "angel in the house." The cramped *mise en scène* of Victorian sex is further implied in the numerous images that Susan Casteras found of Victorian women trapped in towers, framed in windows, enclosed in gardens, observing (themselves as) caged birds, or sitting indoors in "suffocating seclusion." Casteras interprets these images as related to courting, but they also imply the confinement of places where men and women could properly have sex once they got together. *Images of Victorian Womanhood,* (Rutherford, 1987), 53, 55, 86. See also Elaine Shefer, *Birds, Cages, and Women in Victorian and Pre-Raphaelite Art* (New York, 1991).

2. Walter Albert, ed., *Selected Writings of Blaise Cendrars* (New York, 1962), 69.

3. Richard von Krafft-Ebing, *Psychopathia Sexualis* (New York, 1922), 9, 36.

4. Richard Ellmann argued that in *Ulysses* "for the first time in literature masturbation becomes heroic. It is a way of joining ideal and real, and while simplistic or vulgar, it is not negligible. It brings Bloom back to goodwill and away from indifference." *Ulysses on the Liffey* (New York, 1972), 133.

5. Michel Foucault, *The History of Sexuality.* Vol. I, *An Introduction,* (New York, 1978).

6. Even Freud, who emphasized the distinctively unconscious level of repression *(Verdrängung),* used the term only twice in his influential critique of nineteenth-century sexual morality—"'Civilized' Sexual Morality and Modern Nervous Illness" (1908). There he focused rather on the many ways conscious suppression (*Unterdrückung*) of the sexual instinct caused neurosis, but he contributed to subsequent confusion by emphasizing the unconscious level of sexual etiology. Adding to the confusion, in all the nineteenth-century novels in which I found the word "repression," it referred to what was in fact conscious suppression. For these uses see *Jane Eyre* (393), *The Scarlet Letter* (246), *Madame Bovary* (183), *Mill on the Floss* (628), *A Pair of Blue Eyes* (373), *Far from the Madding Crowd* (263, 333), *Daniel Deronda* (245), *Tess of the d'Urbervilles* (106), and *The Odd Women* (196).

7. Jay Martin, *Always Merry and Bright: The Life of Henry Miller* (New York, 1978), 251. Martin's title and interpretation emphasize Miller's sense of humor.

8. Quoted by Peter Gay, *The Bourgeois Experience.* Vol. I, *The Education of the Senses* (New York, 1984), 126.

9. Du Gard's further description of Rachel's uninhibited nakedness with legs spread open to view conjures up Pierre Bonnard's slumbering nudes, especially *Indolence* (1899) and *Blue Nude* (1900).

10. Evan Kintner, ed., *The Letters of Robert Browning and Elizabeth Barrett Barrett 1845–1846* (Cambridge, Mass., 1969), I, 288–290.

11. The first drawing is reproduced in Simon Wilson, *Egon Schiele* (Ithaca, 1980), pl. 45; the second, in Rudolf Leopold, *Egon Schiele: Paintings Watercolors Drawings* (London, 1972), pl. 138. Other post-coital couples are Grosz's *Couple in Room* (1915); Julius Pascin's *After* (1926), and Otto Dix's *Melancholy* (1930).

12. Reinhold Heller, *Munch: His Life and Work* (Chicago, 1984), 104–109; Quentin Bell, *Virginia Woolf: A Biography* (New York, 1972), I, 124; June Sochen, *The New Woman: Feminism in Greenwich Village, 1910–1920* (New York, 1972); Jeffrey Weeks, *Sex, Politics and Society: The Regulation of Sexuality Since 1800* (London, 1981), 180–186.

17 Marriage

1. For legislation that gave French women property and maternity rights and in 1884 reintroduced divorce, see James F. McMillan, *Housewife or Harlot: The Place of Women in French Society 1870–1940* (New York, 1981), 26–28.

2. From Sir William Blackstone, *Commentaries on the Laws of England* (1765–69), cited in Joan Perkin, *Woman and Marriage in Nineteenth-Century England* (London, 1989), 1–2. My survey of English law is drawn from Perkin, 1–31, 292–310.

3. Robert Kiely, *Beyond Egotism: The Fiction of James Joyce, Virginia Woolf, and D. H. Lawrence* (Cambridge, Mass., 1980), 101–102.

4. Sigmund Freud, "On the History of the Psycho-Analytic Movement," *Standard Edition*, XIV, 13–15.

5. Elsie Clews Parsons, *The Family: An Ethnological and Historical Outline* (New York, 1906).

6. Marie Stopes, *Married Love* [1918] (New York, 1931), 144.

7. Judge Ben B. Lindsey and Wainwright Evans, *The Companionate Marriage* (New York, 1927).

8. Elaine May, *Great Expectations: Marriage and Divorce in Post-Victorian America* (Chicago, 1980), concludes that this new emphasis indicated that "a fundamental change in attitudes toward sex within marriage had occurred in American culture" (113).

9. "The Art of the Novel," in Leon Edel, ed., *Henry James: The Future of the Novel* (New York, 1956), 8.

10. E. M. Forster, *Aspects of the Novel* (New York, 1927), 142–145.

11. Dickens altered the ending of *Great Expectations* to have Pip marry a miraculously changed Estella; Thackeray in a reworking of the ending of *The Newcomes*

rescued Ethel Newcome from an unhappy marriage; and Eliot added an epilogue to *Adam Bede* in which Adam and Dinah could marry. On these see Margaret Mason Kenda, "Poetic Justice and the Ending Trick in the Victorian Novel," *Genre*, 8 (1975): 337. Even artists were under pressure to manufacture happy endings. For Millais's capitulation see Chapter 14, n.9, above.

18 Ending

1. From Oskar Kokoschka, *My Life*, quoted in Jaroslaw Leshko, "Oskar Kokoschka's 'The Tempest'," *Arts Magazine*, 52 (January 1978): 95–105.

2. In a sketch and a short play with the same title, *Murderer, Hope of Women* (1910), Kokoschka transformed the *Liebestod* (love-death) into a *Liebestöten* (love killing). The love (or raw passion) between this "Man" and "Woman" (as they are called in the play) has turned to murderous hate, but the symbolism of the works suggests a historical change in thinking about conflict. In the sketch a knife-brandishing man attacks a woman. His right hand grasps her face and one finger sticks into her teeth, while his right foot pins down her torso just under her naked breast. In the play and the sketch, Carl E. Schorske concluded, "Death is not something to which the lovers surrender in the tradition of Tristan and Isolde, but which they inflict upon each other in the bitterness of a passion that contains aggression and love as indistinguishable ingredients." *Fin-de-Siècle Vienna* (New York, 1980), 335.

3. Alessandra Comini argues that Schiele's and Kokoschka's paintings of the breakdown of their own loves were personally as well as historically significant. "Both 'allegories' are of the twentieth century in that they relate to and depict a specific biographical event, rather than presenting a vague, general alienation of the sexes as symbolized by the Salome, vampire, or femme fatale of Jugendstil association." *Egon Schiele's Portraits* (Berkeley, 1974), 139.

4. Letter of Arthur Hughes to Miss K. O. Heaton in 1860, quoted in Rosalie Mander, "'The Tryst' Unravelled," *Apollo* 79 (March 1964): 222.

5. Munch is quoted in Reinhold Heller, *Munch: His Life and Work* (Chicago, 1984), 142.

6. In a different composition by Grosz titled *Suicide* (1916), the same man has shot himself in front of an open window in which stands a prostitute stripped to the waist displaying her bulbous breasts to attract business. Even though the painting suggests a specific cause of the suicide, the man's despair over the prostitute remains an unfathomable mystery of his soul.

7. Michael Wheeler, *Death and the Future Life in Victorian Literature and Theology* (New York, 1990), 6.

8. Anna Karenina is also especially beautiful in death, even though she has been run over by a train.

9. The poem is quoted by Wheeler, *Death and the Future Life*, 68.

Conclusion

1. Søren Kierkegaard, *Fear and Trembling* [1843] (New York, 1954), 130.

2. Peter Gay, *The Bourgeois Experience*. Vol. I, *Education of the Senses* (New York, 1984), 458. A hysterical disturbance of vision was one of the symptoms of the Victorian woman (Anna O.), whose neurosis provided the challenge which Freud and Breuer tried to overcome in conceiving the method of psychoanalytic therapy. In psychoanalysis there is a veritable equation between seeing, knowing, and achieving mental health. Sigmund Freud and Joseph Breuer, "Studies on Hysteria," *Standard Edition*, II, 21–47.

List of Illustrations

List of Fictional Characters

These are alphabetized by the name most commonly used in the original source. When this is the first name, the last name is in brackets. When this is the last name, the first name or title follows.

Agatha: *The Man Without Qualities* (Robert Musil)

Albertine [Simonet]: *Remembrance of Things Past* (Marcel Proust)

Alec [D'Urberville]: *Tess of the D'Urbervilles* (Thomas Hardy)

Algernon [Moncrieff]: *The Importance of Being Earnest* (Oscar Wilde)

Alissa [Bucolin]: *Strait Is the Gate* (André Gide)

Antoine [Thibault]: *The Thibaults* (Roger Martin du Gard)

Amerigo, Prince: *The Golden Bowl* (Henry James)

Amory [Blaine]: *This Side of Paradise* (F. Scott Fitzgerald)

Angel [Clare]: *Tess of the D'Urbervilles* (Thomas Hardy)

Ann Veronica: *Ann Veronica* (H. G. Wells)

Anna [Karenina]: *Anna Karenina* (Leo Tolstoy)

Anna [Lensky]: *The Rainbow* (D. H. Lawrence)

Arabella [Donn]: *Jude the Obscure* (Thomas Hardy)

Archer, Newland: *The Age of Innocence* (Edith Wharton)

Arnoux, Madame: *Sentimental Education* (Gustave Flaubert)

Aschenbach, Gustav von: *Death in Venice* (Thomas Mann)

Aziz, Dr.: *A Passage to India* (E. M. Forster)

Bartley [Hubbard]: *A Modern Instance* (William Dean Howells)

Bathsheba [Everdene]: *Far from the Madding Crowd* (Thomas Hardy)

Bertha [Mason Rochester]: *Jane Eyre* (Charlotte Brontë)

Bertha [Rowan]: *The Exiles* (James Joyce)

Blanche [Ingram]: *Jane Eyre* (Charlotte Brontë)

Blazes [Boylan]: *Ulysses* (James Joyce)

Boldwood, Farmer: *Far from the Madding Crowd* (Thomas Hardy)

Brett [Ashley]: *The Sun Also Rises* (Ernest Hemingway)

Capes, Jonathan: *Ann Veronica* (H. G. Wells)

Casaubon, Edward: *Middlemarch* (George Eliot)

Catherine [Barkley]: *A Farewell to Arms* (Ernest Hemingway)

Hans [Castorp]: *The Magic Mountain* (Thomas Mann)

Heathcliff: *Wuthering Heights* (Emily Brontë)

Helbeck, Alan: *Helbeck of Bannisdale* (Mrs. Humphrey Ward)

Henry [Wilcox]: *Howards End* (E. M. Forster)

Herminia [Barton]: *The Woman Who Did* (Grant Allen)

Hester [Prynne]: *The Scarlet Letter* (Nathaniel Hawthorne)

Heyst, Axel: *Victory* (Joseph Conrad)

Innstetten, Geert von: *Effi Briest* (Theodor Fontane)

Isabel [Archer]: *The Portrait of a Lady* (Henry James)

Isabella [Linton]: *Wuthering Heights* (Emily Brontë)

Isabelle [Borgé]: *This Side of Paradise* (F. Scott Fitzgerald)

Isola [Churchill] *Ranthorpe* (George Henry Lewes)

Jacques [Thibault]: *The Thibaults* (Roger Martin du Gard)

Jake [Barnes]: *The Sun Also Rises* (Ernest Hemingway)

Jane [Eyre]: *Jane Eyre* (Charlotte Brontë)

Jenny [Fontanin]: *The Thibaults* (Roger Martin du Gard)

Jerome: *Strait Is the Gate* (André Gide)

Jude [Fawley]: *Jude the Obscure* (Thomas Hardy)

Karenin, Alexei: *Anna Karenina* (Leo Tolstoy)

Kitty [Levin]: *Anna Karenina* (Leo Tolstoy)

Knight, Harry: *A Pair of Blue Eyes* (Thomas Hardy)

Laura [Fountain]: *Helbeck of Bannisdale* (Mrs. Humphrey Ward)

Léa [Léonie Vallon]: *Chéri* (Colette)

Lena: *Victory* (Joseph Conrad)

Léon [Dupuis]: *Madame Bovary* (Gustave Flaubert)

Léonce [Pontellier]: *The Awakening* (Kate Chopin)

Leopold [Bloom]: *Ulysses* (James Joyce)

Levin, Konstantine: *Anna Karenina* (Leo Tolstoy)

Lily [Briscoe]: *To the Lighthouse* (Virginia Woolf)

Linton [Heathcliff]: *Wuthering Heights* (Emily Brontë)

Lucy [Honeychurch]: *A Room with a View* (E. M. Forster)

Lucy [Snowe]: *Villette* (Charlotte Brontë)

Lucy [Tantamount]: *Point Counter Point* (Aldous Huxley)

Lydgate, Tertius: *Middlemarch* (George Eliot)

Malte [Laurids Brigge]: *The Notebooks of Malte Laurids Brigge* (Rainer Maria Rilke)

Maggie [Tulliver]: *The Mill on the Floss* (George Eliot)

Maggie [Verver]: *The Golden Bowl* (Henry James)

Marcel: *Remembrance of Things Past* (Marcel Proust)

Marcia [Gaylord]: *A Modern Instance* (William Dean Howells)

Margaret [Hale]: *North and South* (Elizabeth Gaskell)

Margaret [Schlegel]: *Howards End* (E. M. Forster)

Marius [Pontmercy]: *Les Misérables* (Victor Hugo)

Mark [Rampion]: *Point Counter Point* (Aldous Huxley)

Mary [Llewellyn]: *The Well of Loneliness* (Radclyffe Hall)

Mary [Rampion]: *Point Counter Point* (Aldous Huxley)

May [Welland]: *The Age of Innocence* (Edith Wharton)

Maxime "Max" [Dufferein-Chautel]: *The Vagabond* (Colette)

Mellors, Oliver: *Lady Chatterley's Lover* (D. H. Lawrence)

Mirah [Lepidoth]: *Daniel Deronda* (George Eliot)

Miriam [Leivers]: *Sons and Lovers* (D. H. Lawrence)

Molly [Bloom]: *Ulysses* (James Joyce)

Nicole [Warren Diver]: *Tender Is the Night* (F. Scott Fitzgerald)

Odette [de Crécy]: *Remembrance of Things Past* (Marcel Proust)

Orlando: *Orlando* (Virginia Woolf)

Osmond, Gilbert: *The Portrait of a Lady* (Henry James)

Paul [Emanuel]: *Villette* (Charlotte Brontë)

Paul [Morel]: *Sons and Lovers* (D. H. Lawrence)

Peter [Walsh]: *Mrs. Dalloway* (Virginia Woolf)

Philip [Wakem]: *The Mill on the Floss* (George Eliot)

Phillotson, Richard: *Jude the Obscure* (Thomas Hardy)

Pierston, Jocelyn: *The Well-Beloved* (Thomas Hardy)

Quested, Adela: *A Passage to India* (E. M. Forster)

Rachel [Goepfert]: *The Thibaults* (Roger Martin du Gard)

Ramsay, Mr.: *To the Lighthouse* (Virginia Woolf)

Ramsay, Mrs.: *To the Lighthouse* (Virginia Woolf)

Ranthorpe, Percy: *Ranthorpe* (George Henry Lewes)

Renée [Néré]: *The Vagabond* (Colette)

Rhoda [Nunn]: *The Odd Women* (George Gissing)

Richard [Dalloway]: *Mrs. Dalloway* (Virginia Woolf)

Richard [Rowan]: *The Exiles* (James Joyce)

Richard [Yaverland]: *The Judge* (Rebecca West)

Rivers, St. John: *Jane Eyre* (Charlotte Brontë)

Robert [Hand]: *The Exiles* (James Joyce)

Robert [Lebrun]: *The Awakening* (Kate Chopin)

Rochester, Edward: *Jane Eyre* (Charlotte Brontë)

Rodolphe [Boulanger]: *Madame Bovary* (Gustave Flaubert)

Ronald [Heaslop]: *A Passage to India* (E. M. Forster)

Rosalind [Connage]: *This Side of Paradise* (F. Scott Fitzgerald)

Rosamond [Vincy Lydgate]: *Middlemarch* (George Eliot)

Rupert [Birkin]: *Women in Love* (D. H. Lawrence)

Shelmerdine, Marmaduke: *Orlando* (Virginia Woolf)

Skrebensky, Anton: *The Rainbow* (D. H. Lawrence)

Stephen [Gordon]: *The Well of Loneliness* (Radclyffe Hall)

Stephen [Guest]: *The Mill on the Floss* (George Eliot)

Stephen [Smith]: *A Pair of Blue Eyes* (Thomas Hardy)

Sue [Bridehead]: *Jude the Obscure* (Thomas Hardy)

Swann, Charles: *Remembrance of Things Past* (Marcel Proust)

Tadzio: *Death in Venice* (Thomas Mann)

Tess [Durbeyfield]: *Tess of the D'Urbervilles* (Thomas Hardy)

Thornton, John: *North and South* (Elizabeth Gaskell)

Tom [Brangwen]: *The Rainbow* (D. H. Lawrence)

Tom [Tulliver]: *The Mill on the Floss* (George Eliot)

Troy, Sergeant: *Far from the Madding Crowd* (Thomas Hardy)

Ulrich: *The Man Without Qualities* (Robert Musil)

Ursula [Brangwen]: *The Rainbow* and *Women in Love* (D. H. Lawrence)

Vernon [Whitford]: *The Egoist* (George Meredith)

Vronsky, Alexei: *Anna Karenina* (Leo Tolstoy)

Walter [Bidlake]: *Point Counter Point* (Aldous Huxley)

Will [Brangwen]: *The Rainbow* (D. H. Lawrence)

Will [Ladislaw]: *Middlemarch* (George Eliot)

Willoughby [Patterne]: *The Egoist* (George Meredith)

Worthing, John "Jack": *The Importance of Being Earnest* (Oscar Wilde)

Index